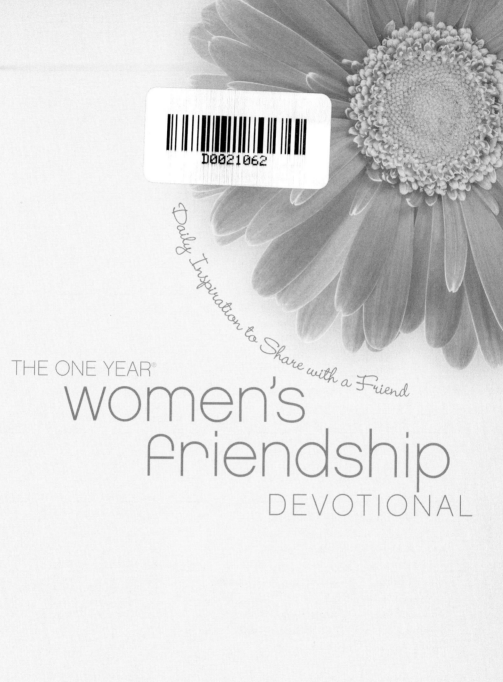

Daily Inspiration to Share with a Friend

THE ONE YEAR®
women's
friendship
DEVOTIONAL

Visit Tyndale's exciting Web site at www.tyndale.com

Visit Cheri Fuller's Web site at www.cherifuller.com

Visit Sandra Aldrich's Web site at www.sandraaldrich.com

TYNDALE and Tyndale's quill logo are registered trademarks of Tyndale House Publishers, Inc.

The One Year is a registered trademark of Tyndale House Publishers, Inc.

The One Year Women's Friendship Devotional

Designed by Jacqueline L. Nuñez

Edited by Susan Taylor

ISBN-13: 978-1-4143-1458-7

ISBN-10: 1-4143-1458-2

Printed in the United States of America

14 13 12 11 10 09
7   6   5   4   3   2

Introduction

Welcome to the devotional book written specifically to encourage friendships while deepening your connection and enjoyment of God and his Word.

As you read even a small portion of the Bible with a friend and discuss how that ancient, God-breathed wisdom applies to today, you will find your challenges more bearable. After all, Ecclesiastics 4:9-10 says, "Two people are better off than one, for they can help each other succeed. If one person falls, the other can reach out and help."

Although these verses speak specifically of the practical benefits that come from working together, the principles can be readily applied to the encouragement and fresh insight gained from discussing—and working through—the Word together.

In addition, if a particular day's devotional thought or verse touches a chord in your life or reminds you of a burden, we encourage you to lift this up to God together. It's as simple as asking each other, "What is your number one worry or concern right now?" and then praying for each other for a few moments. You'll be amazed at how this will decrease your stress, lift your concerns, and build your heart-to-heart connection, because friendship divides burdens and multiplies joys.

Each week in *The One Year Women's Friendship Devotional* focuses on a different topic that relates to a woman's life and experience. These topics include such themes as Facing Life's Fog, Hearing God above the Roar, Living with Hope, Caring for Our Bodies, Avoiding the Comparison Trap, A Joy-Filled Life, Handling Common Stress, Wading through Grief, and Making a Difference.

Each day's reading includes a Scripture verse or two, a devotional thought, a prayer, and an insightful quotation to help you reflect on what you've read that day.

As you incorporate this devotional book into your life, we encourage you to read the daily reading alone—in the morning or in the evening if that fits your schedule best—or with a friend. Then discuss the questions and your responses once or twice a week, perhaps in one of the following ways:

- Jot questions on an index card, and discuss them with a walking partner while you take a thirty-minute stroll together, giving a boost to three important parts of your life: your body, your spiritual growth, and your friendships.
- Talk about how God is speaking to you as you linger over coffee at a favorite community spot.
- Pick one or two questions from the list at the end of each week's devotionals and discuss them while you and your friend watch your children play at the park.

- Share your responses by e-mail or on the phone or via Webcam, and pray together if your friend is across the miles.
- Discuss a few of the questions for the week when you share a lunch break with a coworker who is also reading *The One Year Women's Friendship Devotional*.
- Use the book as a small-group resource at your church or a neighborhood women's gathering.

You may also find that journaling your responses to the questions can bring spiritual growth and fresh insights. If you get bogged down and miss a few days of readings, don't worry. It's not about performance but about *connecting*!

Our prayer is that through application of biblical principles, you will find your spiritual life energized and your friendships deepened. God bless!

—CHERI HEATH FULLER AND SANDRA P. ALDRICH

Stores don't sell, I must confess,
The joys of life that cheer and bless,
But friends and prayers are priceless treasures
Beyond all monetary measures.
—HELEN STEINER RICE

JANUARY 1

Faith That Pleases God

> It is impossible to please God without faith. Anyone who wants to come to him must believe that God exists and that he rewards those who sincerely seek him.   HEBREWS 11:6

From the Old Testament to the New, God encourages his people to walk by faith, pray in faith, and live lives of faith. What kind of faith is that? Faith that trusts the Lord in the dark as well as in the light, that believes his Word and follows it as the pathway of life. Faith that believes in the unseen reality of eternity and in God's existence so much that we seek him with all our hearts. Faith that trusts in the inspired Word of God more than in our feelings or the opinions of others. As today's verse from Hebrews expresses, God rewards faith, and it's *impossible* to please him without it.

God's Word gives us snapshots of the lives of biblical women who saw the invisible, believed the unbelievable, and received the impossible: Sarah, who because of her faith followed her husband and was able to become a mother in her old age. Esther, whom God brought into the palace of a king "for just such a time as this" to save the nation of Israel. Ruth, who though widowed at a young age, left her own country to live with Naomi, her mother-in-law, in a foreign land. Deborah, Rahab, Mary. They are all part of that huge cloud of witnesses who went before us.

Through the sacrifice of the Lord Jesus Christ on the cross we, too, have received a great inheritance of faith, not because of what *we* have done, but because of what *he* did for us. Since faith is a gift (see 2 Peter 1:1), what will we do with it? How can we grow in our faith and in our relationship with God? This week we will look at this vital part of the Christian life.   —CHERI

> Thank you, Father, for creating me to live in relationship with you, and for the cloud of witnesses of faithful women that surround me. Grant me grace to grow in faith in the Son of God, who loved me and gave himself for me.

Faith sees the invisible, believes the unbelievable, and receives the impossible. —CORRIE TEN BOOM (1892–1983), HOLOCAUST SURVIVOR, AUTHOR

JANUARY 2
The Faith of a Child

> "You don't have enough faith," Jesus told them. "I tell you the truth, if you had faith even as small as a mustard seed, you could say to this mountain, 'Move from here to there,' and it would move. Nothing would be impossible."   MATTHEW 17:20-21

The little half-European, half-Japanese girl looked out the window of the orphanage, distressed that the mountain blocked the view of her beloved Sea of Japan. Ill and bedridden, her greatest desire was to see the sea, but she couldn't walk and had no transportation to get over the mountain.

One day the minister read Matthew 17:20-21, and the little girl's faith was sparked. Believing God's Word, she asked the other girls to join her that night in praying that God would move the mountain so she could see the sea. The English missionary-houseparent heard the prayers and told her, "Don't get your hopes up, dear. This verse refers to God's removing spiritual obstacles, not real mountains."

But every evening the girl and her friends looked out the window and in faith asked, "Lord, please move the mountain and cast it into the sea!" The missionary left for a year of furlough, and when she returned, the little girls were huddled by the sick child's bed looking out the window with great joy. "Look! We can see the sea!" they called to her. Astounded, she went to the local authorities to ask what had happened. Due to erosion of the coast, bulldozers had gone up and down the mountain with great mounds of earth. They had actually moved the mountain and cast it into the sea. Before long, the little girl who loved the sea died, but the orphanage is still there, and because of her faith, generations of children have been able to look out the window at her beloved sea.

Jesus said this kind of faith—childlike faith—is necessary, or we will never get into the Kingdom of Heaven. Is your faith in God weak? Pray for the faith of a child that believes in a big God for whom nothing is impossible.   —CHERI

Lord, I believe. Help my unbelief. Restore my faith in you and your words so that your awesome ability and power might be manifested in my life and the world.

Faith goes up the stairs that love has built and looks out of the window which hope has opened.   —CHARLES HADDON SPURGEON (1834–1892), BRITISH PREACHER

JANUARY 3
The Process of Pruning

Jesus replied, "[My Father] cuts off every branch of mine that doesn't produce fruit, and he prunes the branches that do bear fruit so they will produce even more. You have already been pruned and purified by the message I have given you. Remain in me, and I will remain in you. For a branch cannot produce fruit if it is severed from the vine, and you cannot be fruitful unless you remain in me."
JOHN 15:2-4

I walked down the rural road near the house we rented in Maine. Everything was frozen. Bare trees stood stark against the white, snow-covered fields. The April sky was gray—again—and my soul felt as drained and gray as the sky. Would winter ever end?

Just then I noticed a rosebush that had been severely pruned, its branches covered with ice. That forlorn rosebush reminded me of our family. *We've been pruned, too,* I thought. *We've lost everything financially because of the crash in the building industry; we're two thousand miles from family and friends; we haven't found a church to be involved in, and I feel disconnected and useless.*

Then, into the midst of my thoughts, God seemed to whisper, *Like the rosebush, you will bloom again and be fruitful if you sink your roots deep into me. This rosebush wasn't cut back by accident. The gardener pruned it purposely so there would be abundant roses next summer. Trust me in this winter you're in.*

God did bring us through that long winter, and as we saw him provide again and again, our trust in him deepened. We grew a hardy endurance as Holmes worked an all-night job and I substituted at the high school by day and wrote magazine articles at night. By the next spring, although we still faced many difficulties, we were back home in Oklahoma. Eventually, my husband had construction projects again, and God opened new doors for me in ministry. Slowly, imperceptibly at first, the blooms began to appear. As surely as God had promised, spring did come again.

For all of us who belong to Christ, pruning is a part of growing in him and a means to greater fruitfulness. May we trust him in the times of pruning as well as when we bloom. —CHERI

Father, I choose to trust you in the times of pruning, knowing that your Word says pruning is an essential part of the growth process if I am to bear more fruit for you.

Growth is demanding and may seem dangerous, for there is loss as well as gain in growth. —MAY SARTON (1912–1995), AMERICAN POET AND NOVELIST

JANUARY 4

Growing in God's Word

All Scripture is inspired by God and is useful to teach us what is
true and to make us realize what is wrong in our lives. It corrects us
when we are wrong and teaches us to do what is right. God uses it
to prepare and equip his people to do every good work.

2 TIMOTHY 3:16-17

Dwight L. Moody said the Bible wasn't given for our *information* but for our *transformation*. In order for transformation to take place, the daily engraving of God's words on our hearts is imperative. And if we are to continue walking on the steep path through the narrow gate that leads to life, we need God's Word. There's nothing better for spiritual growth! A wood burner literally engraves or burns its mark down into the grain of the wood, leaving a permanent imprint. So should God's Word be imprinted in our hearts.

When we read and meditate on the Scriptures with teachable hearts, the Holy Spirit will engrave his truths into our lives so that those truths, too, leave a permanent imprint of God and his love for us. Today's verses from 2 Timothy tell us why we are not only to read the Bible from cover to cover but to ponder its words, study them, pray them, and believe them because the Scriptures are full of living power and are inspired by God. His Word teaches us what is true, prepares us in every way for what's ahead, and equips us for every good thing we're created to do during our time on earth.

The Bible is meant not only to instruct us but also to transform us into Christ's image. Although we veer at times from its counsel, the love and grace of the Father will lead us back to that Word which has been etched so deeply into our hearts.   —CHERI

Thank you, Lord, for your inspired Word, given so that I could
know what is true and be equipped for all you have planned for
me to do. Engrave your truths on my heart and mind and imprint
your love in my life so that I'll grow more and more like Christ.

The Spirit of God uses the Word of God to make us like the Son of God.
—RICK WARREN, PASTOR AND AUTHOR

JANUARY 5
The Psalms Prescription

> I will exalt you, my God and King, and praise your name forever
> and ever. I will praise you every day; yes, I will praise you forever.
> Great is the LORD! He is most worthy of praise!   PSALM 145:1-3

"God says he inhabits the praises of his people," the minister told the woman. "If God lives and dwells in the praises of his people, you invite his presence and power into your life and circumstances today through praising him."

"How do you expect me to praise God? I'm barely surviving. My husband has disappeared without a trace. We don't know whether he's dead or has just abandoned us and left a pile of debts. I have four children and I'm seven months pregnant. I have no hope inside me. I'm not in a praise mode."

"If your circumstances have obscured your view of God, I want you to read the last seven psalms and let them be your prayer. Think of this as a prescription to take every day. Pray the verses aloud to God, because as you declare that this is the truth, no matter what the circumstances are or how you feel, it will encourage your faith."

That sounded like harsh instructions for a woman so brokenhearted. But the next morning she gritted her teeth and read the last seven psalms aloud to God, first in a monotone: "Praise the LORD, who is my rock. . . . He is my loving ally and my fortress, my tower of safety, my rescuer" (Psalm 144:1-2). By the time she got to Psalm 145, tears flowed as she read, "The LORD helps the fallen and lifts those bent beneath their loads. . . . The LORD is close to all who call on him. . . . He hears their cries for help and rescues them" (Psalm 145:14, 18-19).

As she read these psalms aloud to God each morning as her sacrifice of praise—whether she felt like praising or not—she began to experience God lifting her up and, against all reason, giving her hope. While she faced the overwhelming responsibilities of single parenting in the years that followed, God never failed to care for her and her children.

I, too, have found the Psalms Prescription a sure antidote for discouragement or depression. Praising God through his own words will help you to focus on who God is, and the power of praise will grow a faith strong enough to sustain you through any storm.   —CHERI

> Lord, as I praise you, come and dwell within my worship and my heart. Thank you for your words of praise penned by the psalmists in the difficulties and trials of their lives.

In praying God's Word back to him, the Bible becomes a vast book of praise.
—CALVIN MILLER, POET, PREACHER, AUTHOR, AND TEACHER

Growing in Love

> Christ will make his home in your hearts as you trust in him. Your
> roots will grow down into God's love and keep you strong. And
> may you have the power to understand, as all God's people should,
> how wide, how long, how high, and how deep his love is. May you
> experience the love of Christ, though it is too great to understand
> fully.   EPHESIANS 3:17-19

One of the great messages of the Bible is that love is of supreme importance to
God. He wants us to grow in love toward him and others. Without love, Scripture
tells us, we are bankrupt, and all our good works are worth nothing (see 1 Corinthians 13:3). But how can we love unless we've deeply experienced the love of
Christ? This prayer from Ephesians 3 is not asking that we will simply have more
head knowledge *about* God's love but that we would *understand and comprehend
it*—that how very much he loves us would really sink in and go from head knowledge to heart knowledge. And most of all, that we would *experience* the love of
Christ for ourselves and be rooted in it. Knowledge isn't enough. Great speeches or
sermons won't suffice, nor will hearing what the Lord did in someone else's life. It
takes God's power imparted to each of us through his Spirit to fathom the depth
and length and width, the incomparable nature, of God's amazing love for us in
Christ Jesus.

Just as Paul prayed earnestly for the Ephesian Christians, we need to ask that
our roots would go down deep into the soil of God's marvelous love. And as we
continually pray this life-transforming prayer, we will drink deeply of love. When
we receive and experience the love of Christ in our own hearts, his love will grow
and will flow through us to others.   —CHERI

> Lord Jesus, I want to understand and experience your love in a
> deeper way than I ever have before. May your love be my anchor
> as your Spirit causes my roots to sink deeper in you. And may
> your love flow through me like a river to those around me.

We must daily come and drink at the fountain of divine love. Herein lies the purpose of all prayer.   —MARGARET THERKELSEN, AUTHOR AND SPEAKER

JANUARY 7

Growing in Service

[Jesus said,] "Whoever wants to be first among you must become your slave. For even the Son of Man came not to be served but to serve others and to give his life as a ransom for many."
MATTHEW 20:27-28

Flo Perkins was a woman who loved the Lord so much that every morning at 5:30, before feeding the family or going to work, she knelt at the east window of her home. She called that her "trysting place," an appointed meeting place for lovers, for Jesus was truly the Lover of her soul. As Flo launched her days from the trysting place, the little gray stucco house became a veritable lighthouse. She served the Lord through praise and prayer all day as she worked long, hard hours in the meat department and often cared for her grandchildren.

She finished only seventh grade before she had to go to work, but her study of the Bible bore good fruit. As she grew in Christ, she taught hundreds of people God's Word in Sunday school and Bible studies. Flo also ministered to generations of neighborhood kids during her fifty years in that home, feeding them wisdom along with cookies and Popsicles. With homemade quilts, sacks of groceries, and money, Flo gave needy people life-sustaining prayer, Bibles, and the greatest gift of all—Jesus. She wasn't in full-time ministry. She was an ordinary woman of small means with a family and a hard job at a local grocery store. But she served an extraordinary God and used all she had to serve others in his name.

Living a life of faith means being called to serve whether we are in college or our senior years, single or married, divorced or widowed, whatever color or background, whatever mistakes we've made. If you are a believer, God has given you talents and gifts, resources, and skills for the very purpose of serving him and others. I pray as you grow in service that the joy of the Lord will be your strength, just as it was my friend Flo's until she entered heaven and heard the Lover of her soul say, "Well done, my good and faithful servant!"   —CHERI

Lord, what can I do today to serve you? What have you given me that I could use for the good of others? Thank you for the way you do amazing things through ordinary people.

God is always calling on us to do the impossible. It helps me to remember that anything Jesus did during his life here on earth is something we should be able to do, too.   —MADELEINE L'ENGLE (1918–2007), AMERICAN WRITER, POET, AND ESSAYIST

To Ponder with a Friend

1. How can we grow in our faith and in our relationship with God?

2. There is something special about the faith of a child, and the story in the devotional for December 19 demonstrates that truth. Have you been touched by a child's faith and belief in God or a prayer a child has prayed for you? If so, write or share about this. What did you learn from that child?

3. Trusting God in the pruning times, in seasons of loss or grief, grows a hardy faith and causes our roots to go deeper into the soil of Christ's love. What experience has most caused your roots to sink deeper into God?

4. Would you take the next week to try the "Psalms Prescription"? Then jot down what happened in your heart, your emotions, and your faith walk.

JANUARY 8
Balancing Comfort, Adventure, and Caution

The LORD will guide you continually, giving you water when you are dry and restoring your strength. You will be like a well-watered garden, like an ever-flowing spring.   ISAIAH 58:11

Rachel agreed to go on her college group's mission tour—and hated every minute of it. She griped about the heat and dust. She complained that the local people stared at her clothing. She groaned when reminded that morning showers were limited to five minutes. She whined about the lumpy bed. And she complained about the national food. After listening to yet another complaint ending with "Why can't these people do it the right way?" the team leader took her aside.

"Rachel, these people aren't wrong; they're just *different*. How would you feel if they visited our town and complained that we were doing things wrong?"

His words hit their target, and for the rest of the trip Rachel limited her complaints to occasional sighs and silent vows that she would never again travel outside her borders. How sad that rather than enjoy this vast, exciting world, she demanded that everything fit *her* definition of "right."

I like my familiar comforts too. But like Rachel's youth leader, I learned a long time ago the difference between "wrong" and "just different." One thing that helped me to develop a less rigid attitude was the realization that Jesus didn't limit himself to only one "correct" way of healing. Sometimes he healed with a *touch*, as in Matthew 8:15 when he touched the hand of Peter's mother-in-law or in Mark 1:41 when he touched the leper.

Sometimes he *spoke*, as in Mark 3:5 when he commanded the man with the shriveled hand to stretch it out, or in Matthew 8:32 when he commanded demons to come out of men and go into a nearby herd of swine.

Sometimes he *sent* his healing ahead, as in the account in Matthew 8:13 when the centurion asked for healing for his servant at home.

And occasionally he even *spit*, as in John 9:6 when he spit into the dirt to make a mud paste for the blind man's eyes. I confess, I don't like that miracle. Not only do I find it disgusting, but it is outside my definition of how Jesus *should* heal. I have to wonder if I have refused his miracles in my own life because they didn't come in what I thought should be the correct package.   —SANDRA

> Lord, help me not to demand that others or you do things my way. And help me to rejoice in your miracles no matter how they are packaged.

Every time I reject Jesus' ability to handle any problem of my life, I am rejecting Him as the Lord of Life.   —CATHERINE MARSHALL (1914–1983), WRITER

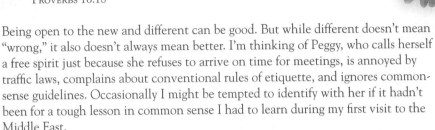

JANUARY 9
Proceed Carefully

> Pride goes before destruction, and haughtiness before a fall.
> PROVERBS 16:18

Being open to the new and different can be good. But while different doesn't mean "wrong," it also doesn't always mean better. I'm thinking of Peggy, who calls herself a free spirit just because she refuses to arrive on time for meetings, is annoyed by traffic laws, complains about conventional rules of etiquette, and ignores common-sense guidelines. Occasionally I might be tempted to identify with her if it hadn't been for a tough lesson in common sense I had to learn during my first visit to the Middle East.

A confident world traveler, I foolishly had decided to do a bit of exploring away from our group. Drawn by the intrigues of Old Jerusalem, I walked two miles beyond the usual tourist area and discovered I was almost out of water in an area where no one spoke English. I tried every foreign word I could remember for "water," beginning with the Spanish word *agua*. Of course, Spanish was just as useless as English in the heart of the Israeli town. Finally, I leaned against a low stone fence to ponder my situation. There, in my obvious American-tourist garb, I felt a pebble hit my back. Then another. And another. Knowing any displayed fear might incite the thrower to become even more aggressive, I slowly gathered the canvas bag holding the now empty water bottle.

Lord, I prayed inwardly, *I wasn't very smart to come into this non-English-speaking area by myself. But here I foolishly am, and I'm trusting you to lead me to safety.*

As I meandered back up the lane with what I hoped was a confident stride, I quoted Psalm 91:11 to myself: *"He will order his angels to protect you wherever you go."*

Lord, I know I was foolhardy to come here, I silently prayed again, *but I ask that your angels guard me right now. And if angels can choose any form they want, I'd like to request one who's about six feet eight, with longish brown hair held back by a don't-mess-with-me bandanna and can readily be seen by anyone whose heart is evil.*

Then, picturing my new, unseen companion by my side, I confidently walked the two miles back to the group, arriving not only thirsty but also wiser.
—SANDRA

Lord, often I am prone to jump into physical or emotional unknowns without listening to your warnings. Help me to remember to ask for your guidance and use the common sense you gave me. May I be aware of your presence moment by moment. And may I rejoice in it.

God cares for us. It is His business as a father to do so. All He asks of us is to let Him know when we need something and then leave the supplying of that need to Him. —HANNAH WHITALL SMITH (1832–1911), QUAKER LAY SPEAKER AND AUTHOR

Pleasing Everyone Is Impossible

Many people say, "Who will show us better times?" Let your face
smile on us, LORD.   PSALM 4:6

As we try to find balance between different and wrong, unconventional and foolhardy, we need to understand that while we can't *change* others, we can't *please* everyone, either. The ancient storyteller Aesop emphasized this point in one of his fables:

One fine spring morning, a father and his son were on their way to market
leading their donkey, which would carry their purchases home.

On the way, they met one of their neighbors, who said, "How silly of you
both to walk when you have such a fine donkey."

So the father set his son on the donkey, and they continued toward the market, still talking and enjoying the morning.

As they came to a bend in the road, they met another neighbor, who said to
the son, "How rude you are to ride while your old father must walk."

So the child slid down from the donkey's back, the father climbed on, and
they continued toward town.

As they topped a little hill, they were met by yet another neighbor, who
scowled at the father and said, "What a selfish father you are to make this dear
child walk while you, a grown man, ride."

So the father pulled his son up in front of him on the donkey's back. Of
course, it wasn't long until they met a fourth neighbor.

"How cruel you are," he said, "To make this poor donkey carry the two of you."

So they both slid off the donkey, and the strong father promptly picked up
the animal and put it across his shoulders.

As they walked along, still talking and still enjoying the day, they met
another neighbor, who doubled over with laughter. "That is the most stupid thing
I've ever seen! Donkeys are to be ridden, not carried!"

There's a fine line between what is right and what is mere local custom,
between what is wrong and what is only different, between what is wise action and
what is a pitiful attempt to please others. But as we seek God's direction, we will
find ourselves on a solid path even when moving outside our usual comfort zones.
We will also find excitement and challenge and a greater awareness of God's
creativity.   —SANDRA

Lord, I confess I want the approval of those around me. I listen to
their voices and accept their standards even though I know your
ways will bring peace rather than chaos, joy rather than regret.
Help me to ask for your guidance first and then to accept the
strength you offer to follow it.

Keep in mind when you come against irksome barriers, they are designed to build
character, not destroy it. The problem is, we tend to want our troublesome situations changed now.   —LEWIS B. SMEDES (1921–2002), ETHICIST AND THEOLOGIAN

JANUARY 11
Who Wants to Deflate Your Balloon?

No one will be able to stand against you as long as you live. For I will be with you as I was with Moses. I will not fail you or abandon you. JOSHUA 1:5

Deana felt like skipping as she left the church community room. The parts for the massive Easter pageant were posted, and she had been assigned the role of the mother of Jesus. When she first heard the announcement about the annual week-long production, she remembered the fun she'd had in her high school plays. Still, it had taken days for her to work up the courage to try out last weekend. And now she had a major part! She couldn't wait to tell her roommates. She hadn't told them she was trying out because she didn't want them to be disappointed for her if she didn't make it. Boy, would they be surprised!

Actually, Deana was the one who was surprised. When she burst through the door with her good news, her roommates reluctantly turned from the TV to stare at her. Finally one said, "But we never see you as it is."

The other one nodded and then added, "Now you'll start hanging out with your new artsy pals."

Deana started to apologize and reassure them she was still their best friend. But as she glanced at the TV, she realized she wanted her evenings to be filled with more than chocolate-covered ice cream and sitcoms. Smiling, she said, "Well, I'm excited about the part, and I hope you'll come. We open the week before Easter. Last year, more than six thousand people showed up to view the production. And a lot of them don't normally go to church. We'll have a live donkey, authentic costumes, a really sinister looking Satan, laser lights, the whole works. I can't wait."

Good for Deana! She refused to allow her roommates' attitudes and lack of encouragement to steal her excitement. Without meaning to (I hope), her roommates might have restricted Deana's activities and even her life to those patterns they were comfortable with. What about you? Do you have encouragement stealers in your life? Your own enthusiasm about your projects will lessen their power.
—SANDRA

Lord, why don't the people around me encourage me when I try something new? Why aren't they excited when I achieve a goal? Am I expecting too much of them? Am I looking to humans who are flawed, as I am, when I should be looking to you? Help me to care more about your calling and less about their restrictions. And help me to be gracious as I do so.

I've got an assignment from God, and I'm determined not to let jealousy and envy from others maim my efforts. —DEBRA WHITE SMITH, AUTHOR AND SPEAKER

JANUARY 12
Don't Expect Appreciation

> When you go through deep waters, I will be with you. When you
> go through rivers of difficulty, you will not drown. When you walk
> through the fire of oppression, you will not be burned up; the
> flames will not consume you. For I am the LORD, your God, the
> Holy One of Israel, your Savior.   ISAIAH 43:2-3

When Carolyn entered medical school, her uncle grumbled that women are more
suited to nursing because they were created to be helpers and not leaders. Instead
of arguing, Carolyn prayed and studied the Scriptures, looking for examples of
strong, godly women. Today, she has a busy inner-city medical practice and is
grateful she ran her long-ago decision through the Bible's filter.

Understanding that we can't expect appreciation, even from those closest to
us, can save us disappointment. I remember the summer I learned that lesson. My
husband, Don, and I drove to Kentucky to take my grandparents, Papa and Mama
Farley, and Aunt Adah to visit relatives. An eight-hour drive lay ahead, so my grandmother positioned a large lunch basket next to her on the front seat. On top she
placed a bunch of bananas, then settled her cane against her thigh, ready for the trip.

Back then, Interstate 75 hadn't been completed, and numerous detours
forced us over winding back roads. Topping one hill, we discovered that a rock
slide had covered the asphalt. Don got out of the car after hastily throwing the gear
of the still-running vehicle toward Park. Then, as he climbed onto the rocks to
survey the situation, the car stalled and began to roll backward.

I was in the backseat between Aunt Adah and Papa, but it was up to me to
reach the brake. Breathing a prayer for help, I threw myself over the seat, knocking
the lunch to the floor as I lunged toward the brake. When I got the car stopped, it
was several feet off the pavement. Beyond was a five-hundred-foot drop and no
guardrail.

With the car braked, I looked at Mama Farley. Surely she had some praise for
my quick action, which had saved us from severe injury if not death.

But she was busy picking up the lunch. "You smashed the bananas," was her
only comment.

So much for my need to have my efforts recognized. But Mama hadn't seen
the danger and therefore couldn't appreciate my action. Right then, I determined
to worry less about appreciation and more about important goals.   —SANDRA

> Lord, whether I am following your calling for my career or
> rescuing others from injury, may my goal be to please you. May I
> shut out the criticism of those who don't understand as I wait to
> hear your appreciative statement: "Well done, my child."

If the world seems cold to you, kindle fires to warm it.
—LUCY LARCOM (1824–1893), AMERICAN POET

JANUARY 13
Keeping a Proper Perspective

> Work willingly at whatever you do, as though you were working
> for the Lord rather than for people.   COLOSSIANS 3:23

We allow others to become encouragement stealers when we give them control over how we feel about ourselves. Former prisoners of war often report they were determined not to let their captors dictate their emotions. If the guard was in a bad mood, the prisoner forced himself to be cheerful. If the guard was jovial, the prisoner would be aloof.

We may say we understand the importance of not letting an enemy control our emotions even though that person controls our physical conditions, but often we do absorb the reactions we receive from others. I remember an account in which a famous pianist gave a performance before three thousand people. Afterward, the audience was on its feet, clapping and cheering. The pianist bowed, but his eyes were on the lone occupant of a box seat. That man remained seated. The pianist turned, strode offstage, and refused to return for an encore. Later, a friend who had witnessed the abrupt exit asked him about it.

"You had three thousand people on their feet shouting your praises," he said, "but you ignored them and looked only at that one man. Why?"

The pianist quietly replied, "That man was my teacher!"

How sad that he chose to look to the one he believed had power over him instead of the three thousand who were offering praise. But how often do we do the same thing? How would our days and our lives be different if we refused to be bound by perceived injustices? Recently I picked up a little gesture that really helps my attitude: Turning my palms down reminds me that whatever the latest irritation is, it certainly isn't worth my tension. It's my way of saying, "Let it go, Sandra. Let it go."

Then as I turn my palms up again, I'm saying to the Lord, "Fill my life with what you want me to have."

I confess I don't always turn my palms down in a gentle fashion. Sometimes I thrust them toward the floor so quickly it seems as if my hands will snap right off. But the gesture is a personal reminder to release an irritation. And isn't that better than continuing to carry it?   —SANDRA

Lord, often I ignore encouragement because it doesn't come from the one person from whom I long to hear it. I forget that person may be carrying a boatload of emotional pain and is incapable of offering what I think I need. Help me to let go of that dependence. Help me to hear what you want me to hear, including your voice and your encouragement.

Be sure to remember that nothing in your daily life is so insignificant and so inconsequential that the Lord will not help you.
—OLE HALLESBY (1879–1961), NORWEGIAN THEOLOGIAN AND TEACHER

JANUARY 14
Practical Actions

> Give all your worries and cares to God, for he cares about you.
> 1 PETER 5:7

Have you ever been weighed down by worry? Me, too. And if worry has us in its grip, we feel tired, unproductive, and ineffective. Our best option is to invite the Lord into the worry. When 1 Peter 5:7 says, "Give all your worries and cares to God," it offers a solution that works. But *how* do we give worry to him?

First, we need to understand he's inviting us to talk to him. When we show up for the ninety-seventh time with the same concern, he does not say, "Well, it's you, again?" He says, "Welcome. I'm glad you are talking to me about this." As we keep talking to him, we find calmness and, often, creative solutions.

Sometimes it helps to picture putting our concerns in an imaginary box. One woman pretended to place her worry in a big gift box. In her mind, she wrapped the box, put a big bow on it, and placed it on the closet shelf. Every time she'd find herself worrying about that particular problem, she'd force herself to go through the mental exercise of taking the box off the shelf, undoing the bow, unwrapping the box, and pulling out the worry. It was such a mental ordeal she finally decided the problem wasn't worth the effort of worrying about it.

If you don't like mental exercises, you can make a tangible God Bag. One of my friends writes "God Bag" on the outside of a brown lunch sack. Then every time she worries, she writes the concern on a scrap of paper and drops it into the bag. Once a month, she sorts through the paper slips and sees how God has solved many of them. Any still of concern to her are tossed back into the bag. She's found that as she places each worry in the God Bag, she's reminding the Lord and herself that she trusts him to answer in his time and in his way. What a difference her decision has made. "I can't control all the crises in life," she says. "But I can trust God to guide me through them." And isn't that wonderful peace during worrisome times? —SANDRA

Lord, giving you my worries is going to be a challenge since I'm prone to fret about the what-ifs and if-onlys. But I'm excited to try your way because my way hasn't worked. So right now I imagine putting my trembling hand into your strong one. Guide me in releasing my worries and cares to you.

It is always possible to be thankful for what is given rather than to complain about what is not given. One or the other becomes a habit of life.
—ELISABETH ELLIOT, MISSIONARY, AUTHOR, AND SPEAKER

To Ponder with a Friend

1. Describe a situation in which you allowed someone to determine your feelings.

2. Do you ever struggle because of the expectations of others? If so, in what areas?

3. Have you ever found yourself trying to please everyone? What was the result?

4. Over the years, what have you learned about worry?

JANUARY 15
The Reach of Your Heart

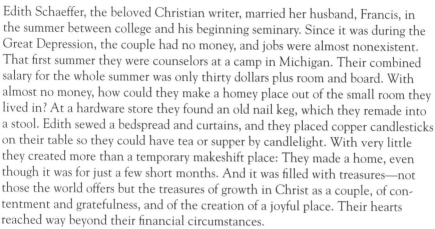

There is treasure in the house of the godly.   PROVERBS 15:6

Edith Schaeffer, the beloved Christian writer, married her husband, Francis, in the summer between college and his beginning seminary. Since it was during the Great Depression, the couple had no money, and jobs were almost nonexistent. That first summer they were counselors at a camp in Michigan. Their combined salary for the whole summer was only thirty dollars plus room and board. With almost no money, how could they make a homey place out of the small room they lived in? At a hardware store they found an old nail keg, which they remade into a stool. Edith sewed a bedspread and curtains, and they placed copper candlesticks on their table so they could have tea or supper by candlelight. With very little they created more than a temporary makeshift place: They made a home, even though it was for just a few short months. And it was filled with treasures—not those the world offers but the treasures of growth in Christ as a couple, of contentment and gratefulness, and of the creation of a joyful place. Their hearts reached way beyond their financial circumstances.

This became the pattern of their lives. In each place the Schaeffers lived, from a crowded little chalet in Switzerland when they began L'Abri ministry to the apartment near the Minnesota hospital where Francis received chemotherapy during his last months of life, they made a center of meaningful living and joyful enrichment wherever they were and invited others—hundreds of them over the years—to share what they had. In these days of fast-forward living and mobility, it's easy for the places we live to become stopovers where we microwave food and change clothes between activities. And if your living situation is "temporary," it's challenging to create a sense of home. But whether you are single or married, in a dorm room, duplex, apartment, or house, you can use your personality, uniqueness, and creativity to create a true home.   —CHERI

> Lord, in whatever place I'm living, give me a heart for my home, a desire to make it a place of beauty and refreshment, not only for me but for all who walk through the doors.

The size of one's home should never dictate the outreach of one's heart.
—LUCI SWINDOLL, SPEAKER AND AUTHOR

JANUARY 16
Our Apartment Adventure

Lord, through all the generations you have been our home!
Before the mountains were born, before you gave birth to the earth
and the world, from beginning to end, you are God.   PSALM 90:1-2

When my husband and I were in our late fifties, we moved to an apartment in
Dallas, where he was doing consulting work with a building company. We spent
weekends at our house four hours away in Oklahoma, but during the workweek,
our Dallas apartment was home. Suddenly we were living in 750 square feet of
space instead of 2,300 square feet. Instead of a yard, there was a small patio with
space for a few pots of flowers. At a time when most people our age were stable
and looking toward retirement, we were back and forth on Highway 35 in a very
new environment.

Surrounded by twenty- and thirty-somethings I met in the exercise room
and people from many cultures and backgrounds on pizza night, we never got
bored. When we were in Dallas, we welcomed overnight guests, who slept on our
blow-up bed covered with a fluffy down comforter, and offered simple meals prepared in the small kitchen. Mementos such as the hand-carved wooden giraffe and
elephant from our ministry trip to Africa and sunny colors and windows made it
feel like "home away from home," but what helped most of all was the lesson the
Lord taught me long ago: He—*not a physical house or a specific arrangement of
rooms—is our dwelling place*, so we can be content in whatever abode we find ourselves, small or large, temporary or long term. Actually, whether we own our homes
or rent, as we did this apartment, all the places we reside during our time on earth
are temporary because heaven is our real home and eternal destination. That
makes me even more grateful for the home God is making for us in heaven, for
there we'll never have to pack again!   —CHERI

I dedicate my home to you, Lord. Whether it's large or small, may
it be a place filled with joy and peace and welcome for others
and, most of all, for *you.*

Stop dreaming! Make the place where you live a place where you are expressing
your own taste right now. But also start collecting some things which will continue
to be used throughout life, and will be *your* familiar "things" that will give you
continuity.   —EDITH SCHAEFFER, AUTHOR AND SPEAKER

JANUARY 17
A Simple, Story-Filled Life

For the happy heart, life is a continual feast.
PROVERBS 15:15

After Caroline was widowed and her children became adults and moved into their own houses, she sold the roomy family home and took only meaningful things to her new tiny condo. One day an out-of-town friend was visiting. Vicky and her husband had moved into temporary housing and never unpacked because they thought they wouldn't be there long. As it turned out, they lived in that "temporary" housing for eleven years.

"How have you given such a sense of 'home' to this little place? You haven't even lived here a year," Vicky asked. Caroline began to tell her friend stories about the different pieces: the old brown tobacco basket that reminded her of the tobacco farm she'd grown up on in Kentucky, her great-grandfather's rocking chair. A lamp and table she and her deceased husband had found at an antique store in their first year of marriage. On the bed and the wall, the colorful, soft quilts made by her grandma. The condo wasn't cluttered with accessories she'd bought to impress people. It was the picture of simplicity—nothing fancy, but every piece full of heart, character, and memories. Instead of living in self-pity because she was alone, Caroline found life a continual feast and savored every moment. Vicky went home that day determined not to wait one more day to create a home right where she was.

Let me encourage you to do the same. Paint and fix up now, not later. When renting or buying a house, don't wait until you're putting it on the market to hang pictures and wallpaper and complete projects that would make it look more livable and comfortable. Think about what makes you feel at home. Is it a nook for your hobby? a throw to cuddle up in for an impromptu nap? a few green plants? a basket of books? Don't lose out on these precious moments by spending your time imagining that perfect house you may acquire in the future. Make a place *now* to share life with those you love.   —CHERI

> Blessed Father, thank you for the place you have provided for me to live and eat, sleep and enjoy during this season of my life, and thank you for the people you've provided to share it with. Help me not to put off enjoying it until I have a dream house but to be grateful for your gifts and make the most of them now.

We have this moment to hold in our hand,
    And to touch as it slips through our fingers like sand.
Yesterday's gone and tomorrow may never come.
    But we have this moment today.
—GLORIA GAITHER, SONGWRITER AND SINGER

JANUARY 18
Around the Table

> Do not let these memories escape from your mind as long as you live! And be sure to pass them on to your children and grandchildren. DEUTERONOMY 4:9

I remember my family sitting around the dinner table through my growing-up years and enjoying roast beef and mashed potatoes, chicken casseroles with bread-crumb topping, homemade banana pudding. Even when there wasn't an abundance in the pantry, Mom could put together a simple Sunday-night supper of goldenrod eggs served over toast for the six of us children and make it special. It was around that table I learned what was going on in my three big sisters' classrooms, picked up a bit of wisdom from our dad, and heard family stories and news from out-of-town relatives.

Today, families are pulled in lots of different directions, which can make it hard to meet at dinnertime. Yet for those who make it a priority, family meals can be a chance to connect, relax together, and bond. To pass on the stories of what God has done for us, and to transfer truth, as Deuteronomy tells us to. There's something about a shared meal that anchors a family, even on nights when kids are irritable. Research shows that children and teens who eat with their families are less likely to smoke, drink, do drugs, get depressed, or consider suicide. They tend to do better in school, delay having sex, and have better relationships with their parents.

Shared dinnertime is also important for a single woman living with roommates or a senior citizen who lives alone. These people may not have family available, but they can benefit from sharing a meal with a neighbor or friend. Jesus tells us to love one another, and that kind of loving begins with those who are closest to us, in our own homes and neighborhoods, as we create comfort, give the gift of conversation and good food, and pass on the love that God has so graciously given to us. —CHERI

Lord, our lives are moving so fast. Help us take time to share our lives over meals, to connect with one another, and to create comfort for those you bring into our circles at work, at school, and in our communities.

In a challenging world, family belonging provides a safe haven for parents and children alike. Family dinners not only satisfy our physical and emotional needs, but also offer a time and place to consciously teach our children the value of caring for others. —GAYLE PETERSON, PRENATAL AND CHILD DEVELOPMENT SPECIALIST

JANUARY 19
A Refuge in the Storm

All praise to God, the Father of our Lord Jesus Christ. God is our merciful Father and the source of all comfort. He comforts us in all our troubles so that we can comfort others. When they are troubled, we will be able to give them the same comfort God has given us. 2 CORINTHIANS 1:3-4

Once you have the walls painted and furniture arranged, it's easy to get so caught up in your job, grad school, or other pursuits that you neglect your home and have little left to give your family. Creating a home with a semblance of order, loveliness, warm hospitality, and cherished memories requires that you see the value of making a home in the first place. If your heart needs some warming toward this attitude, ask God for that desire. Ask him for whatever is lacking: a bigger picture of your influence, an understanding of the value of home as a refuge, or a mentor who can share practical tips and help you learn homemaking skills. The truth is, our homes are not just wallpapered, decorated, and fixed up to be pit stops where family members change clothes, grab a sandwich, and get some sleep in order to race off the next morning to the places where "real" life happens. No, home and family are meant to be places of refuge, places to be refreshed and renewed and to be understood by people who really care about us and want to share life together.

Home is also meant to be a refuge because the storms of life hit people of all ages and backgrounds—young and old, rich and poor, and everyone in between. Scripture says the rain falls on both the good and the evil people (see Matthew 5:45). There's no insurance policy that can guard us against having an accident that turns our lives upside down, being beset by severe depression, or having a long-term illness that makes us need care. All of us need comfort, and all of us— even the youngest among us—can give comfort in some way. Following Christ's teaching about caring for "the least of these" (see Matthew 25:40), feeding the hungry and caring for the sick *begin at home* and then ripple out into our communities and into the world. When we experience comfort at home, we understand and become prepared to give it to others.   —CHERI

Lord, help me to make time to care for others, starting with those in my own home and family. Give me a heart of compassion and service so that I do it in your name and for your sake.

The family and home are meant to be the environment where human beings can find shelter, warmth, protection, and safety in each other.
—EDITH SCHAEFFER, AUTHOR AND SPEAKER

JANUARY 20
A Welcoming Place

> Accept each other just as Christ has accepted you so that God
> will be given glory.   ROMANS 15:7

This verse from Romans is full of meaning and promise for those of us who
endeavor to make a home. In the original language, the word *accept* means "to
welcome." So this verse is saying to us, "Welcome one another, as Christ has welcomed you."

Actress Jane Seymour's mother was born in the Netherlands and had lived in
Dutch Indonesia. There she endured three and a half years in a Japanese concentration camp and vowed that if she and her friends survived, they and their future
children would always open their homes to one another. As a result, this remarkable woman has had a very open, warm home, and even as a widow in her nineties,
she still welcomes and cooks for a continuous stream of friends, family, and other
visitors. The ripples of her hospitality have gone further than she would ever have
imagined.

Everyone desires to be wanted and included, so opening our doors to others
meets a great need. The fact that most cities have an ample number of motels,
hotels, fast-food franchises, and other restaurants doesn't mean people don't need
home cooking! If you are a single woman, you may think a welcoming home
includes a family and children or at least a certain standard of housing, but it
doesn't have to. You can welcome people into a small apartment or a dorm room.
The single women I've known who have had the most interesting, fulfilling lives
are those who invite others to share whatever they have in whatever places they
live. They make room in their busy lives to practice hospitality wherever they are.
And as they do, they, too, are refreshed and filled.   —CHERI

Lord, give me your Spirit of welcome, acceptance, and love for
people. Help me to make room in my life to be sensitive to the
needs of others and to invite them into my home.

When there is room in the heart there is room in the house.
—DANISH PROVERB

JANUARY 21

Creating Comfort for a Stranger

> When God's people are in need, be ready to help them. Always
> be eager to practice hospitality.   ROMANS 12:13

In Romans 12, Paul describes what it means to give ourselves to God and to be a
vessel he can use: to be devoted to loving others, to serve God, to be faithful in
prayer, and to *practice hospitality*. The writer of the book of Hebrews encourages
Christians not to forget to entertain strangers, because some people have entertained angels without knowing it (see 13:2). In 1 Peter 4:9, we're told to "cheerfully share [our homes] with those who need a meal or a place to stay." In fact,
hospitality was a practice of God's people in both Old Testament and New Testament times.

In today's crazy-busy world, hospitality is in danger of becoming a lost art.
But when women open their hearts and homes to strangers, acquaintances, or
neighbors, the impact can be powerful. Years ago, with two boys under the age of
five and a three-week-old baby, we moved to Oklahoma City shortly before Christmas. With all three kids sick and no family or friends in town, cabin fever quickly
set in. I felt isolated and sad in the long days and nights while my husband worked.
If only I knew someone to call or a neighbor who had kids too.

Suddenly there was a knock at my door. A young woman with two little ones
in tow smiled and held out a handmade invitation to her neighborhood Christmas
coffee the following Saturday. "Bring your kids, too, and cookies," she said. "Join us
if you can!"

That time of coffee, comfort, and conversation in front of the fireplace was
the highlight of my winter, a real lifeline. My neighbor's open heart and home
meant the world to me and to other new people on the block. My weary soul was
refreshed and warmed by the fellowship. I met other women, and we started a
playgroup for our children. We got to know one another, and I saw my loneliness
dissipating over peanut butter sandwiches and outings to a nearby park. As
humans, we are created for relationship. We function best with someone to share
the joys, struggles, and burdens of our lives. To whom could you open your heart
and home this week?   —CHERI

> Jesus, grant me an open heart and home and a desire to
> practice hospitality for your sake, even—and especially—
> to those outside my circle of friends and family.

To create a meal and a memory for loved ones or friends is a gift; to create comfort
for a stranger is a blessing!   —NANCY DEWITTE

To Ponder with a Friend

1. What benefits would there be—not only for you but also for your family and others—of having an open heart and an open home?

2. What elements in an apartment, dorm room, or house—whether yours or someone else's—make you feel truly comfortable and at home?

3. What are two or three simple things you could do to make the place you live more of a refuge and a refreshing, warm environment?

4. In this week's devotionals, Cheri wrote about several women who inspired her to have an open home. Who has offered you hospitality or been an example of openhearted kindness to others in her home?

JANUARY 22
Rejoice and Be Glad

This is the day the LORD has made. We will rejoice and be glad in it.
PSALM 118:24

Molly enjoyed her job in the customer service department of a major publishing company, was active in her church, and loved her extended family of growing nieces and nephews. But even with her always-present smile, she was growing tired of hearing favorite aunts, coworkers, and even strangers ask, "You are such a lovely young woman. Why aren't you married?"

She was starting to wonder that herself. *Yes, what is wrong with me?* she thought as she tried not to watch couples holding hands, laughing over dinner, looking at furniture together. For long moments she stared into the mirror each morning and evening, pondering what she could change that might make her more attractive. Maybe if she lost weight. Or changed her hair color. Or worked more on the leg machine at the gym. Gradually her life goals were narrowed to this: *Get a man!* And that meant everything else was put on hold.

When three of the young women from her department invited her to join them for a long weekend at a popular tourist spot two hours away, Molly refused, claiming a busy schedule. Actually, she had heard so many good things about the resort that she was determined to save the experience to share with her future husband.

During a going-out-of-business sale at a nearby household store, she passed up incredible savings on her favorite china pattern, thinking, *I'll wait until I'm married so we can choose our pattern together.* Even her uncle's offer to re-cover Molly's comfortable but threadbare chair was met with refusal as she thought, *Once I'm married, I'll get it redone in my husband's favorite color.* And, of course, she would never consider building equity by purchasing her own town house, even though several in her complex became available at a lower-than-market price the week the landlord decided to move to Arizona.

Putting her life on hold meant that Molly was ignoring the invitation of Psalm 118:24: "This is the day the LORD has made. We will rejoice and be glad in it." While she supposedly planned for the future, she deliberately missed embracing today's joy. —SANDRA

> Lord, help me to embrace today's joy and not foolishly waste it
> by trying to deposit it in future happiness. May I be aware of your
> presence and your pleasure as I hug present moments with a
> thankful heart.

Morning prayer: Good morning, God. I love You! What are You up to today? I want to be part of it. —NORMAN GRUBB (1895–1993), MISSIONARY, WRITER, AND SPEAKER

JANUARY 23
Avoid Undue Pressure

Take delight in the LORD, and he will give you your heart's desires.
PSALM 37:4

Not only was Molly robbing herself by refusing to enjoy the present, but she was putting undue pressure on a future husband to fulfill her dream of the perfect marriage. In fact, each time she thought the word *husband*, she easily could have replaced it with the title *Mr. Wonderful.*

How much better it would have been if she could have embraced each new day and concentrated on *being* the right person instead of *looking for* the right person. Molly was obsessed with the hope that maybe today *he* would appear to secure her future. And at the end of yet one more day in which Mr. Wonderful hadn't shown up, Molly grew more and more despondent. Soon she began to panic, thinking, *What if I never get married?* And sadly, any new man who did cross her path would sense her desperation and run rather than give the relationship a chance.

If questioned closely by an understanding friend, Molly might have confessed she was hoping Mr. Wonderful would ring her doorbell, hand her a dozen roses, and say, "Hi, I'm from the Lord!"

It's too bad she didn't know Joanne, who lived on the other side of her town house complex. Joanne had jumped at the opportunity to purchase one of the suddenly available units and bought paint—peach for the bedroom, crème and blue for the kitchen—the same afternoon she ordered new drapes. She was looking forward to getting married someday too, but she wasn't about to lose today's opportunities by waiting for tomorrow. And if Molly had tried to explain why it was important to sacrifice present joy for future hope, Joanne would have been astonished. To her that would have been like not breathing today just because she wanted to be breathing tomorrow.   —SANDRA

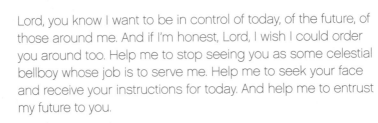

Lord, you know I want to be in control of today, of the future, of those around me. And if I'm honest, Lord, I wish I could order you around too. Help me to stop seeing you as some celestial bellboy whose job is to serve me. Help me to seek your face and receive your instructions for today. And help me to entrust my future to you.

Not getting what you want is not a tragedy. Getting what you want and realizing it wasn't worth the trouble is the tragedy.
—JEANETTE CLIFT GEORGE, FOUNDER AND ARTISTIC DIRECTOR OF A. D. PLAYERS, A PROFESSIONAL CHRISTIAN THEATER ORGANIZATION

JANUARY 24
Be Realistic

> Be careful how you live. Don't live like fools, but like those who
> are wise. EPHESIANS 5:15

Not only did Joanne understand the importance of rejoicing in *this* day, but she
had learned from her older sisters that even when Mr. Wonderful does show up,
it doesn't guarantee a perfect marriage. From those same sisters she had learned
the "Three Cs" guidelines for dating: Companionship, Common Interests, and
Commitment. Yes, dating provides someone to talk to, to share an evening with,
but often, desperate women jump from companionship to commitment and skip
the important consideration of common interests. Joanne had a couch-potato
cousin who had joined a Saturday hiking club just to snag a man. Two months after
the wedding, she discarded her hiking boots and settled into her old routine of
watching DVDs of 1950s movies. Her disappointed husband felt not only cheated
but lied to. That example was one Joanne was determined not to follow.

Joanne also learned no marriage exists in a vacuum. She wouldn't be marrying
just the individual but his entire family. One of Joanne's friends, Sandra, makes it a
habit before leaving for an extended-family gathering to pray, "Lord, help me to keep
my mouth shut." (She explains, "You never have to apologize for the ugly things you
don't say!") That reminder was helpful the Sunday afternoon Sandra's mother-in-law
sarcastically asked, "Well, what little wifey things did you do this week?"

Knowing she needed to prove she was capable of taking care of the woman's
son, Sandra thought of the chocolate chip cookies that had caused her groom to
exclaim, "Oh, these are my favorites!" So she answered, "I made his favorite cookies."

The mother-in-law nodded. "Oh, peanut butter."

Sandra looked bewildered. "No, chocolate chip."

The mother-in-law sat very straight. "I've been making cookies for him all
of his life. His favorite cookies are peanut butter!"

The new wife had the good sense not to argue, but she did ask her husband
for an explanation later. Always the diplomat, he answered, "Oh, my favorite ones
Mom makes are peanut butter, but my favorite you make are chocolate chip."

Obviously, Joanne has numerous examples to give her a reality check, but more
important, she has determined not to put off living and enjoying *today* just because
she's hoping to meet her future husband *tomorrow*. Her good attitude will likely bring
delightful surprises to her sooner than if she acted desperate. —SANDRA

Lord, help me to wait for you, who know best, to provide your
best. When it comes, help me to understand that it may come
with other people attached. Help me to know when to bite my
tongue and when to speak. And may I do both with love.

There are two kinds of people: those who say to God, "Thy will be done," and
those to whom God says, "All right, then, have it your way."
—C. S. LEWIS (1898–1963), IRISH WRITER AND LITERARY SCHOLAR

JANUARY 25
The Importance of a Good Attitude

Let the peace that comes from Christ rule in your hearts. For as
members of one body you are called to live in peace. And always be
thankful. COLOSSIANS 3:15

In any situation, a good attitude is a must. After all, a good attitude can brighten
not only our own day but the day of those around us. Whenever I mention the
word *attitude*, I always think of an experience my friend Lanson Ross had in his
adolescence.

Lanson said his mother was not the best cook in the world. As proof of that,
every morning she made the same thing for breakfast: oatmeal. She boiled the
water, threw in the oats, threw in the salt, and then *never* stirred it. So when
Lanson went downstairs to breakfast, he didn't know if he was going to get the top
part that was all raw, the side part that was all salt, or the bottom part that was all
burned. He just knew he was going to get a bowl of *bad* oatmeal.

One morning Lanson was particularly hungry and particularly irritated,
knowing what was waiting downstairs. And this was before the days of being able
to stop at the fast-food place on the corner and get a sausage biscuit. If you were a
growing boy and hungry, you ate what was waiting downstairs.

Lanson shared a room with his younger brother, who was one of those cheerful morning guys. You know the type: one who tap-dances and whistles while he's
buttoning his shirt. Normally Lanson ignored him, but on this particular morning,
he was hungry and irritated.

So he turned to his brother and snarled, "How can you be so cheerful every
morning? Don't you know we're going downstairs to the *same bad oatmeal?*"

His brother turned to him in surprise. "Oh, no, Lanson," he said. "It's never
the same. You don't know if you're going to get the raw part or the salty part or the
burned part. But it's never the same."

The same situation, but two different responses. At one time or another, life
will hand all of us repeated bowls of bad oatmeal. And our attitude will make a big
difference in how we face those situations. It may even make a difference in the
outcome. —SANDRA

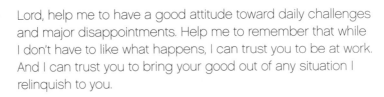

Lord, help me to have a good attitude toward daily challenges
and major disappointments. Help me to remember that while
I don't have to like what happens, I can trust you to be at work.
And I can trust you to bring your good out of any situation I
relinquish to you.

Sometimes relinquishment means giving up a cherished dream, a plan, an illusion.
Life is often a series of adjustments fitting our dreams to reality.
—RUTH SENTER, BIBLE TEACHER, CONFERENCE SPEAKER, AND AUTHOR

JANUARY 26
The Attitude of Gratitude

Always be full of joy in the Lord. I say it again—rejoice!
PHILIPPIANS 4:4

For years I misunderstood Philippians 4:4. I thought the command was to keep a constant smile in place. But it says, "Always be full of joy *in the Lord.*" Not in people, not in circumstances, but in the Lord. What a difference.

Those of us who were adults in 1981 remember media accounts of the kidnapping of Chet Bitterman Jr., a missionary in Bogotá, Colombia. What most of the reports were not telling, however, was his father's reaction. When the news first reached Chet Sr., he furiously paced his Pennsylvania home, wondering how he could rescue his son. Suddenly he heard within his spirit, *Give thanks.*

To give thanks was the last thing Chet Sr. wanted to do. But as he struggled with the Spirit's direction, he realized the command was to *give* thanks, not *feel* thanks. As he wondered what he could possibly be thankful *for*, he remembered that his son had memorized hundreds of Scripture verses. *Surely those verses are encouraging him right now,* he thought, and he immediately gave thanks for the courage the Word of God was giving Chet Jr. at that very moment.

Upon further reflection, Chet Sr. added thankfulness for his son's physical strength and emotional stability. The list grew. When young Chet's body was found in an abandoned bus forty-eight days later, the seeds of thankfulness already sown helped his father open his heart to the comfort the Lord wanted to give.

If Chet Sr. could find something to be thankful for in the midst of his great emotional pain, surely we can too. A thankful attitude allows us to live life with joy and to rejoin life after we are handed a tough blow. Without thankfulness, we can become bitter and a drag on ourselves and everyone around us.

We've seen the bumper sticker saying "Develop an attitude of gratitude." But it doesn't tell us *how.* Several years ago, at a New York chapel, writer/editor Elizabeth Sherrill offered three suggestions guaranteed to make every day one of thanksgiving:

1. Every day, surprise someone with a sincere thank-you.
2. Every day, thank God for something you have never thanked him for.
3. Every day, thank God for something about which you are not now happy.

I know this third one is tough. But if we can't thank God for the situation, we *can* thank him for being with us in it. That makes a world of difference.   —SANDRA

> Lord, thank you for your presence in tough times. Thank you for not giving up on me even when I want to give up on myself or others. Thank you that I do not pray to air but to the God who hears.

I have been driven many times upon my knees by the overwhelming conviction I had nowhere else to go.
—ABRAHAM LINCOLN (1809–1865), SIXTEENTH PRESIDENT OF THE UNITED STATES

JANUARY 27
Make a List

You will show me the way of life, granting me the joy of your
presence and the pleasures of living with you forever.
PSALM 16:11

Often we can't embrace today's beauty because we are convinced we don't measure
up to those around us. What if we refused to entertain those damaging comparisons
and instead began to appreciate our own abilities? What if we made an actual list
of all the things we can do right? Is that too difficult an assignment? Then pretend
you are an agent listing good qualities about your client to a potential talent scout.
And this time that client is you! Try it. Describe your abilities, achievements,
curiosity about the world, and considerate treatment of others.

Too often we have a tendency to disregard our own gifts and want the gifts
others have. When I list my abilities, I'm disappointed I can't play the piano. After
all, real Christian women are musical, right? But as I concentrate on the things I
can do instead of those I can't, I get to list public speaking. I can stand in front of
five thousand people, and my heart won't skip a beat.

Judy, too, struggled with listing what she could do. Finally she wrote, "I can
understand complicated dress patterns." Understand? I'll say! She can construct an
outfit that rivals any designer creation. (When I wear things in public I've sewn,
women always smile graciously and say, "Oh, did you make that?")

If Alice were to show us her list, she'd lament it took her forever to name
even one thing because she was so busy thinking of the things she can't do. When
she finally talked herself into thinking of the things she can do, she listed, "Give a
great whistle."

Having freed herself from listing "proper" activities, she had fun writing
down such things as changing her own oil, making Southern spoon bread that
calms her husband when he's upset, cutting fancy paper dolls freehand for their
daughters, and hanging wallpaper without getting impatient. That simple little list
started her grinning, and from that point on, she began feeling better about herself.

How encouraging we could be to ourselves if we would honestly appreciate
our own skills and then offer gratitude to the Creator of the universe, who placed
those skills within us. That's a marvelous way to embrace each new day.
—SANDRA

Lord, too often I want the talents of others instead of thanking
you for mine. When I look in the mirror, I complain about my size,
my nose, my hair, the lines at my eyes. Help me to be grateful for
my skills and appreciative of my health. May I joyfully anticipate
your presence in each new day rather than grumble about my
inadequacies.

Jesus does not give all of the gifts of the Spirit to one individual.
—CATHERINE MARSHALL (1914–1983), WRITER

JANUARY 28
A Merry Heart

A cheerful heart is good medicine, but a broken spirit saps a person's strength.   PROVERBS 17:22

When my children and I lived in New York, we ventured down to watch the Macy's Thanksgiving Day Parade with friends—and countless thousands of others. It was an incredible day, seeing the displays that had long been part of our holiday traditions but, until then, only on TV. The best part of the day for me, though, was meeting a subway-elevator operator.

He spends long hours each day trapped in a box under the streets of New York City, breathing air thick with dirt and fumes. I wouldn't have blamed him if he'd been grumpy and complained about being stuck underground. But he greeted us cheerfully and asked where we were from.

When he had delivered us to our requested level, he wished us well, asked us to come back again, and added a cheerful "I luv ya."

Later, as we were waiting for the subway train, we could hear him singing as he strolled in front of the elevator, waiting for his next batch of passengers. Rather than allow himself to become embittered or discouraged by his lot in life, he chose to bring freshness and joy to those who shared his day, even for those few moments.

Since that long-ago day, I've often thought about him when I'm tempted to whine about my latest crisis. Here's a thought: What if I didn't fret aloud but became like that subway singer and gave others reason to smile at our common memory?   —SANDRA

Lord, I want my surroundings to be pleasant, my days to be calm, my blessings to be abundant. But too often, stress is my companion, chaos fills my schedule, and grumpiness defines my attitude. Help me to concentrate on the good things in my life. And help me to pass that attitude and that example on to others who need a dose of encouragement.

If you see someone without a smile, give her one of yours.
—UNKNOWN

To Ponder with a Friend

1. Have you ever encountered a situation that caused you to doubt yourself? If so, describe it.

2. As you ponder your gratitude list, what new items can you add?

3. Make a list of your good qualities or abilities. Which ones make you most thankful?

4. Have you ever been impressed by the good attitude of another? How about by a bad attitude?

JANUARY 29
God's Presence

> Do not be afraid or discouraged. For the LORD your God is with you
> wherever you go. JOSHUA 1:9

Many years ago when my husband and I were living in Tulsa, Oklahoma, we experienced a spiritual awakening. Overwhelmed by such a great gift of salvation and grace, we gave our lives to God and told him, "We'll do anything you want us to do and go anywhere you have in mind!" We didn't know that would mean moving to Oklahoma City (an hour and a half away) and later to South Africa, Zambia, Switzerland, Singapore, Thailand, and Brazil (all much more than an hour and a half away). For us, the journey had begun.

Don't be afraid, I sensed God saying when he led me to quit my teaching job and begin writing a book for parents. *Don't be discouraged*, he encouraged my husband, Holmes, when he gave up a secure salary to go in a totally different direction in business and later to build houses. Our priorities changed. Our careers changed as we discovered that God had a very different plan for us than we'd had for ourselves. But the biggest change of all was that we found life to be a day-by-day adventure, not merely something to endure or survive.

I don't believe God brings us out of darkness into his marvelous light in order for us to stay in our comfort zones. Instead, I think he wants to move us beyond ourselves to a passionate pursuit of his purpose for our lives. Following Jesus isn't always comfortable; change and uncertainty can be scary, and difficulties and trials may lie ahead on our journey. New challenges may be daunting and always stretch us. But if we start living life as the great adventure God means it to be, then every difficulty, every obstacle, can be a door to greater purpose, life, and growth. In this week's devotionals, you'll discover some of the key principles we learned along the way that have helped us to continue the journey and to live life as a great adventure. —CHERI

> Lord, it's so tempting to retreat to my comfort zone. Help me to
> resist that temptation. As you call me forth to do your will, may
> I remember and believe that you are with me wherever I go and
> that your light and truth will lead me on the great adventure
> of life.

The initial call to discipleship was a call to adventure. The early disciples were called to leave . . . the comfort and security of familiar ways and places, to go they knew not where and to do they knew not what. Day by day they discovered that life was a great adventure, and that every hardship and every setback was a doorway to new service and maturity. —J. KEITH MILLER, AUTHOR AND SPEAKER

Show Up for Service

> The eyes of the LORD search the whole earth in order to
> strengthen those whose hearts are fully committed to him.
>
> 2 CHRONICLES 16:9

When you give yourself to God's plans instead of your own, in a sense you are "showing up for service." When you do, be ready for the adventure to accelerate, because as this verse tells us, God is looking for those "whose hearts are fully committed to him" in order to strengthen and support them. "Showing up for service" is a daily response; it means connecting with God to receive your marching orders. Before the crush of e-mails and phone calls, laundry, errands, and other tasks sets in, you surrender anew to God with an attitude that says, "Here is my life, my hands, my emotions and will, my intellect—all that I am. Use me today in whatever way you want, no matter how small the task." The specific words you use don't matter as much as the act of turning to God in whatever way helps you to give yourself and your day to him. As you undertake this kind of "reckless abandon," as Oswald Chambers termed it, you'll begin to find the purpose or mission you were created for in this particular season of your life.

God's Word says you are his masterpiece, created anew in Christ Jesus, *so that you can do the good things he planned for you long ago*, ahead of time, before you ever thought of them (see Ephesians 2:10). You may need some training or preparation to do those things. But whether it is painting pictures, planting a church in a foreign land, starting a ministry or business, teaching children, inventing something, singing, composing music, teaching and mentoring younger women, or any of the countless other "good things," you can be assured that the Lord has gifted and equipped you to fulfill the purpose for which he created you.   —CHERI

Lord, here I am, showing up for service. I give you my day and my life, for whatever you have planned for me. Thank you for creating me to have a purpose!

When praying, don't give God instructions; just report for duty.
—UNKNOWN

JANUARY 31
Walking One Step at a Time

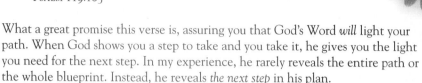

> Your word is a lamp to guide my feet and a light for my path.
> PSALM 119:105

What a great promise this verse is, assuring you that God's Word *will* light your path. When God shows you a step to take and you take it, he gives you the light you need for the next step. In my experience, he rarely reveals the entire path or the whole blueprint. Instead, he reveals *the next step* in his plan.

What are your interests and gifts? What are you passionate about? To what do you sense God calling you? As you discover these things, you can begin following the guidance he gives you *one step at a time*. What *are* those things God has planned for you and for me to do? I believe there are songs God wants someone to write, stories he wants told, missionary projects he has in mind, inner-city programs for tutoring at-risk kids. There are children crying in orphanages here and abroad, and he wants loving families to adopt them. He wants someone to share the gospel with unreached people groups. He has rescue operations already planned in heaven and is looking for willing vessels to carry them out on earth. But just like a miner who wears a hat that casts a beam six feet ahead to give just enough light to illuminate his next steps, until we walk those six feet, we won't be able to see more of the path God has for us.

Taking those steps often involves risk. In fact, someone once said that the word *faith* is really spelled R-I-S-K. Taking those steps may lead you to a country across the world, as it did my friend Paula, who served in Thailand for more than twenty years. Following God's direction may lead you to a little school in Florida to teach migrant workers' children, to a publishing company in a big city, or to any of a myriad of other destinies. It doesn't matter what age you are or at what stage of life. If you follow God's light, amazing things will happen on the adventure, and you'll never be bored.   —CHERI

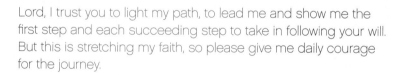

> Lord, I trust you to light my path, to lead me and show me the
> first step and each succeeding step to take in following your will.
> But this is stretching my faith, so please give me daily courage
> for the journey.

Life is a great adventure, or it is nothing. There is no such thing as security. Animals never experience it and children seldom do.
—HELEN KELLER (1880–1968), BLIND AND DEAF AMERICAN LECTURER

FEBRUARY 1

Keep Moving Forward

The LORD says, "I will guide you along the best pathway for your life. I will advise you and watch over you." PSALM 32:8

Once you have begun taking those first steps toward finding God's path for your life, don't be surprised if you encounter obstacles. It's kind of like sailing a boat. When you begin to say yes to God and seek the direction and purpose he has for you, you're putting your boat in the water. In taking the first action steps, you're moving away from the dock so the wind can fill your sails. But when you are really under way and obstacles come, don't get stuck on the sandbar of discouragement. Keep moving forward.

The old saying is true: You can't pilot a moored ship, especially one stuck in the dock (or on a sandbar). If God gives you an idea or a dream, keep your sailboat in the water and keep going forward, asking the Holy Spirit to move your rudder and to blow his wind on your sails.

When I started writing, I never had an editor appear on my doorstep with a check and ask me to write a book. I had to study how to write a nonfiction book, then create a proposal and send it out. In essence, I was putting my boat in the water as I worked and prepared. I was doing what I knew to do to keep my boat moving, doing my part and trusting God to do his. When I found a rejection letter in my mailbox, I saw that rejection as *redirection* and kept going, learning from it and persevering in writing the book.

I found that one of the ways God directs us is by opening or closing doors. Although the closed door of rejection hurt, the Spirit nudged me to keep getting up and putting that boat in the water. A year later, I met an editor at a writer's conference, and within two weeks I was sent a contract for my first book. Becoming a writer was a step-by-step process, but God has been immensely faithful and has led me these twenty years of writing the books and articles he's given me ideas for. He will do the same for you in your area of calling.   —CHERI

Father, I don't want to miss the adventure you've planned for me. I want to say yes to you and to what you choose for my life. Show me the way, and I will follow!

God often puts us in situations that are too much for us so that we will learn that no situation is too much for him.
—ERWIN LUTZER, AUTHOR AND PREACHER

FEBRUARY 2

Pilgrims on the Journey

Two people are better off than one, for they can help each other succeed. If one person falls, the other can reach out and help. But someone who falls alone is in real trouble. Likewise, two people lying close together can keep each other warm. But how can one be warm alone? A person standing alone can be attacked and defeated, but two can stand back-to-back and conquer.

ECCLESIASTES 4:9-12

When you and I set out on the adventure of following God's will and purpose for our lives, we aren't meant to be Lone Rangers. Today's verses from Ecclesiastes tell us why: When we're alone, we are more vulnerable to attack and defeat by the enemy and his forces around us. If we're alone and we tumble or fail, we're in deep trouble. But if we fall and have someone alongside us, our friend can reach out and help us. Moreover, two can accomplish *more* than twice as much as one can alone.

Today's passage is often read at weddings, but it also applies to our need for others when we're endeavoring to serve God. If we're open and teachable, he will send people to share our lives with, to encourage us, to speak truth to us, and to be "Jesus with skin on." People with strengths we lack will shore up our areas of weakness.

The Bible says, "Just as our bodies have many parts and each part has a special function, so it is with Christ's body" (Romans 12:4-5). We may be doing different tasks, but we are meant to work together, *not all alone.* Just as we need our own eyes, feet, and arms, we need the other people in the body of Christ, and they need us. Nobody is strong in every area, or we wouldn't need one another. God planned it this way! Accountability, prayer support, and the counsel of trusted people are crucial on the trail.

Even those who have gone before us in the journey of faith can inspire us. In addition to women in the Bible, there are Christian women throughout history whose lives and writings can encourage us: Amy Carmichael, Corrie ten Boom, Gladys Aylward, Elisabeth Elliot. They are all part of that "huge cloud of witnesses" (Hebrews 12:1) that cheer us on in this adventure of faith. Read their stories, and as you pursue what God has for you to do, remember that you are not alone.   —CHERI

Jesus, I'm thankful that I am part of your body and that there are many members. Please bring my path near to those you want me to support, and provide those who will bring strength where I'm weak. Thank you for glorifying yourself when we work together as members of your body on this earth.

Be united with other Christians. A wall with loose bricks is not good. The bricks must be cemented together.
—CORRIE TEN BOOM (1892–1983), HOLOCAUST SURVIVOR, AUTHOR

FEBRUARY 3
Knocked Down but Not Knocked Out

> We are pressed on every side by troubles, but we are not crushed.
> We are perplexed, but not driven to despair. . . . We get knocked
> down, but we are not destroyed. 2 CORINTHIANS 4:8-9

Have you ever felt thwarted by failure when you were sincerely committed to following God's will? If so, you have plenty of company. On the adventure, being hurt
by our own or another person's bad choices is inevitable. But God has a wonderful
way of making bitter experiences sweet. He can redeem our failures and weave
them into a pattern of his good purpose for our lives. Just look at the life of Joseph.
His brothers betrayed him and sold him into slavery. Potiphar's wife accused him
falsely and got him thrown into jail. Joseph was pressed by troubles. God had given
him a dream of serving in leadership, which must have been perplexing as he lan-
guished for months and years in prison. But even in the land of Joseph's suffering,
God made him fruitful. He used what was meant for evil in Joseph's life and turned
it to good. Nothing could thwart God's plans for Joseph.

Sometimes all we can see across our lives is a jumble of jagged lines or a
fragmented mess. But just as an artist can redeem a seemingly ruined painting
with careful brushstrokes, God's redeeming love and power can make beauty out
of our blunders, bring strength out of our weaknesses, and change our failures
into success. As today's verses say, we may be pressed with troubles, perplexed,
and knocked down, but we are never destroyed: "Our bodies continue to share
in the death of Jesus so that the life of Jesus may also be seen in our bodies"
(2 Corinthians 4:10). —CHERI

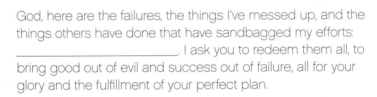

God, here are the failures, the things I've messed up, and the
things others have done that have sandbagged my efforts:
_____. I ask you to redeem them all, to
bring good out of evil and success out of failure, all for your
glory and the fulfillment of your perfect plan.

God would never permit evil if he could not bring good out of evil.
—THOMAS WATSON (1620–1686), PURITAN THEOLOGIAN

FEBRUARY 4
It's All about Perspective

> I am confident I will see the LORD's goodness while I am here in the land of the living.   PSALM 27:13

On any adventure or journey, we will almost always encounter trouble or difficulty, but that doesn't mean we've missed God's will. In the Chinese language, two characters make up the word *crisis*. One character means "danger," and the other means "opportunity." During the time when our dream or goal is delayed or maybe even looks impossible to accomplish, our perspective is all-important. We can choose to focus on the difficulties or on the opportunity those difficulties set before us.

As a woman on a plane buckled her seat belt, she noticed a strange thing: On one side of the airplane a sunset filled the entire sky with brilliant color. But out of the window next to her seat, all she could see was a dark, threatening sky. As the plane began to taxi down the runway, the woman heard a gentle voice within her: *You have noticed the windows. Your life, too, will contain some happy, beautiful times but also some dark shadows. Here's a lesson that will save you much heartache and allow you to abide in me with continual peace and joy: It doesn't matter which window you look through; this plane is still going to California. So it is in your life. You have a choice. You can dwell on the gloomy picture, or you can focus on the bright things and leave the dark, ominous situations to me. I alone can handle them, anyway.*

If we learn this life lesson, we will be free to live life as the great adventure it is. No matter what happens, we will be able to remain hopeful and confident in the One who is leading us on this great journey of following Christ and his plan for our lives.   —CHERI

> Jesus, when I am overwhelmed, lead me to the Rock that is higher than I. Grant me an eternal perspective so that I won't dwell on the darkness or the difficulties.

Never be afraid to trust an unknown future to a known God.
—CORRIE TEN BOOM (1892–1983), HOLOCAUST SURVIVOR, AUTHOR

To Ponder with a Friend

1. What are you passionate about? What are the gifts God has given you that are clues to how he may want to use you in his plan?

2. Think of a time when you took a step of faith or followed God's light on your path. What was the result? How did God meet you?

3. Share about a time when you faced an obstacle and the problem became an opportunity, or when God turned what looked like a failure into something beautiful that was useful for his purpose.

4. From this week's devotionals, what do you sense God wants you to embrace and apply to your life and journey with him?

FEBRUARY 5
Modern Battles

[The Lord] will conceal me . . . when troubles come; he will hide me in his sanctuary. He will place me out of reach on a high rock.
PSALM 27:5

Cassie prided herself on having come from a long line of strong, independent women, starting with her great-grandmother, who had kept her family of five fed and clothed during the Depression of the 1930s. When Cassie's history professor had talked about the development of the B-17 bomber, which allowed the United States to win World War II, she thought of her grandmother's twelve-hour shifts of riveting metal in the noses of planes at the Willow Run plant in Michigan. Cassie's own mother had been part of the first Peace Corps team that went into West Africa during an epidemic in the 1960s.

Now Cassie was carrying on that same strong tradition: She could balance her own checkbook, change the oil in her car, and figure her own taxes, all while running the computer software company that had grown from three employees to more than a hundred in the first five years of its existence. Cassie demanded a lot from her employees, but she was hardest on herself. She lived by one philosophy: If you want something done right, do it yourself. And she acted out that philosophy by double-checking everything her secretary sent out, calling her department managers several times a day, and asking for detailed reports on each step of a new project.

Cassie's favorite historical figure was Molly Ludwig Hayes, the young wife who followed her husband to the Revolutionary War and courageously carried water to the wounded and dying. The soldiers called her "Molly Pitcher." During one particularly fierce attack, Molly saw her husband fall beside the cannon he was firing. She ran to his side, not to cradle him in her arms but to take his place and fire the cannon herself. That's the type of woman Cassie wanted to be, and every day brought a new corporate battle in which she could fire figurative cannons. Whenever she was finished with a major project, she was exhausted, and so was everyone around her. —SANDRA

Lord, thank you for the examples of strong women in Scripture, in history, in my life. But help me to remember that although they were strong in a few areas, they were not strong in everything. Help me to listen to you as I concentrate on the responsibilities you have given me. Help me to enjoy the process as well as the finished product. And help me not to exhaust either myself or those around me.

Work doesn't make you who you are.
—JANIS LONG HARRIS, AUTHOR

FEBRUARY 6
Find Guidance in Scripture

Two people are better off than one, for they can help each other succeed. If one person falls, the other can reach out and help. But someone who falls alone is in real trouble. ECCLESIASTES 4:9-10

To the outside world, Cassie had it all together—the right clothes, the right car, the right job. But her doctor knew she had something else: a stress-related ulcer.

It's too bad she hadn't heard the statement from Helen Keller, the renowned American lecturer who was deaf and blind: "It's amazing what can be done when one person invites others to be part of the plan."

After the latest bout of severe stomach pain and extensive medical tests, her doctor dropped the report onto Cassie's hospital bed.

"I've known you for a long time," he said. "So I'm not going to beat around the bush. Whether or not you get well is in *your* hands, not mine. You have a choice: You can slow down and learn to share responsibilities with your staff, or your body will force you to slow down through collapse. What will it be?" He waited for Cassie's answer.

Finally she stammered, "But I'm the president *and* CEO of my company."

He remained unimpressed. By now he was scribbling on his prescription pad.

"It's up to you," he said, as he handed her a slip of paper. "But it's tough to run a company from a hospital bed."

As he left, Cassie glanced at his "prescription," which stated only, "Read the book of Nehemiah. Don't try to build the wall alone."

Cassie gave an exasperated huff, then opened her ever-present briefcase, filled with books for those moments when she was stuck in traffic or when service was slow in a restaurant. On the bottom of the stack was her Bible. She turned to the book of Nehemiah and began reading, but soon she was sorting through her briefcase again, this time in search of a notepad and a pen.   —SANDRA

Lord, help me to discern which activities are to be completed alone and which ones are to be shared. Point out the areas where I allow pride to cause me to take more onto my weary shoulders than I should. Help me to remember that a burden or a job or a responsibility is lighter when I allow others to help carry it. Then show me the individuals who are part of your plan to help me.

Yes, work should be meaningful, but nowhere in the Bible does God say work should overtake our life.   —RAMONA CRAMER TUCKER, AUTHOR

FEBRUARY 7

Applying Scripture

Your word is a lamp to guide my feet and a light for my path.
PSALM 119:105

Cassie plopped the notebook next to her open Bible on the tray table and then fluffed the hospital pillow. She was ready.

Gather information, she wrote, after reading of Nehemiah's questions to visitors about the Jews who had escaped exile and had remained in Jerusalem (see Nehemiah 1:2). Nothing new there. She never went into a new product line uninformed.

Pray. She paused as she read of Nehemiah's asking for God's direction (see 1:4). She knew she often jumped into a project without asking anybody's opinion, let alone God's.

Check feasibility of plan, she wrote next, as she read of Nehemiah's plan in chapter 2 to request a leave of absence from his employer, the king (see 2:5-8).

Invite others to help. Suddenly she forgot about her list as she got caught up in the account of Nehemiah's selecting those to accompany him to Jerusalem, where he methodically studied the ruins of the once-majestic wall. And always, he acted only after he had prayed. Soon the drama on the page was so real it was as if Cassie were watching it on a stage. She listened as Nehemiah invited the leaders and other citizens to be part of what God had directed him to do: "I said to them, 'You know very well what trouble we are in. Jerusalem lies in ruins, and its gates have been destroyed by fire. Let us rebuild the wall of Jerusalem and end this disgrace!'" (2:17).

"Let us rebuild," she read again. Then she felt a wash of relief. Maybe, just maybe, she could let the others in her business help too.

Cassie was released from the hospital the next morning, armed with pills to tone down the stomach acid and with her own determination to find other Scripture passages that would help her run the business.   —SANDRA

Lord, I'm so quick to run ahead of you, armed with my own knowledge and my own sense of the right way to do things. But when I trust my own understanding, I fail time after time. Help me to seek your wisdom through prayer, through your Word, and through the counsel of your people. And may I remember that anything in conflict with your Word is not of you. Thank you for not being the God of confusion. Thank you for guiding me once I ask.

The thinking woman doesn't allow others to do her thinking for her. While she graciously listens to the counsel of others, ultimately she bases her choices on what she knows is God-pleasing and what she senses He is saying to her.
—HELEN K. HOSIER, WRITER AND SPEAKER

FEBRUARY 8
Numerous Reminders

All Scripture is inspired by God and is useful to teach us what is
true and to make us realize what is wrong in our lives. It corrects
us when we are wrong and teaches us to do what is right. God uses
it to prepare and equip his people to do every good work.

2 TIMOTHY 3:16-17

In the days following her hospital stay, Cassie looked for Scripture to apply to her
circumstances. Soon she had written Matthew 11:28 in her notebook: "Come to
me, all of you who are weary and carry heavy burdens, and I will give you rest."

She noticed that in addition to the invitation to rest, the Lord reminded his
followers of their dependence on one another: Love one another (see John 13:34);
encourage one another (see Romans 15:2); pray for one another (see James 5:16).

Cassie was beginning to understand that humans have been created to be
*inter*dependent rather than *in*dependent. But even as she inwardly agreed, she
remembered a long-ago afternoon when she had called an uncle to ask advice
about a supplier. Instead of helping, he had scolded her and said if she was going
to run a business, she'd have to figure out things herself. After she hung up, she
determined never to ask for advice again. Now she realized that maybe she'd
caught her uncle on a bad day or maybe he didn't want to share what had taken
him years to learn.

Into her mind popped the saying "Pray as if everything depends on God, and
work as if everything depends on you."

She leaned back and spoke aloud: "Okay, Lord. Please help me to work on
this area. Show me ways I can be independent but still ask for help when I need it.
I need your help in this and in every decision I face."

Boy, this is new stuff, she thought. *What if I make a mistake? Oh well, mistakes
are nothing new. I won't always get it right, but as long as I pray first and work hard and
start inviting fresh ideas from others, I'll have less chance to fail.*

With that thought, Cassie smiled. If she could put these new ideas and truths
into action, she knew her world was bound to be better for her—and for everyone
around her.   —SANDRA

Lord, like a toddler clamoring to dress herself, I shout, "I do it
myself!"—even to you. Help me to welcome your guidance. Show
me how to humbly accept your help and that of others.

Remind yourself daily to slow down. Commit a short, motivating verse to memory,
like "Be still, and know that I am God" (Psalm 46:10), and repeat it to yourself
each time you feel tension building.

—MARY WHELCHEL, FOUNDER AND PRESIDENT OF THE CHRISTIAN WORKING WOMAN

FEBRUARY 9
Choosing the Right Mental Tapes

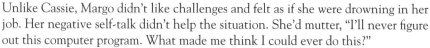

I am certain that God, who began the good work within you,
will continue his work until it is finally finished on the day when
Christ Jesus returns.   PHILIPPIANS 1:6

Unlike Cassie, Margo didn't like challenges and felt as if she were drowning in her job. Her negative self-talk didn't help the situation. She'd mutter, "I'll never figure out this computer program. What made me think I could ever do this?"

She played those mental tapes so much she finally convinced herself she had no option other than to quit.

We may think, *How sad*. Maybe we even wonder why she didn't talk to her supervisor about more training or why she didn't take a computer class at the community college. From the perspective of observers, of course, that seems logical. But don't we tend to play similar mental tapes when we're facing an emotional mountain? Perhaps we're still replaying memories of a drunken parent's lament over having produced us, or perhaps we're recalling a former teacher's critical assessment of our skills.

It's hard to erase those old tapes, even though we know they paralyze us emotionally and cripple us with defeatist attitudes. But what if we were to replace those old negative messages with encouraging thoughts? Consider these examples:

- This, too, shall pass.
- God didn't bring me this far to leave me alone.
- With God's help, I can do this.

A little mental encouragement might make a big difference.
—SANDRA

> Lord, help me to hear your loving, encouraging voice as I face new challenges. Help me to stop berating my lack of ability and be open—even excited—about learning new things.

Every time we beat ourselves up, we're helping the Enemy.
—SANDRA P. ALDRICH

God in the Darkness

> The faithful love of the LORD never ends! His mercies never cease.
> Great is his faithfulness; his mercies begin afresh each morning.
> LAMENTATIONS 3:22-23

Cassie nodded as she listened to a new editor in town tell of the tension her cross-country move had caused. The editor, who was a widow, and her family had been in Colorado Springs only a few months, but already things were not going well. The sale of their East Coast condo fell through after they already had purchased a new home. The latest storm had damaged the roof, the car's engine developed a short circuit, and an unexpected bill arrived.

Discouraged, she read the Scriptures she thought had directed their move west. She replayed every event that seemed to point to the rightness of their decision. Still, nothing removed the knot from her chest.

Then one Saturday at four in the morning, she dropped her son off at his high school to catch the bus for a regional event. But instead of going home, she drove to a nearby park noted for its majestic red rock formations. She needed to connect with God and be reassured she hadn't missed his voice in this move. And she thought she could do that best in his world instead of hers.

As she entered the blackness of the park, she pulled off the narrow road and got out to study the heavens, hoping the beauty of the star-filled sky would offer some encouragement. Suddenly, a bright green meteor shot across the full length of the sky, its brilliance a breathtaking contrast to the darkness around her. Stunned, she said aloud, "Oh! Thank you!" as she watched the glowing trail. As the vivid color faded into the horizon, her problems didn't seem as heavy as before. Oh, they were far from being solved, and she still had to deal with challenges around her, but she knew the memory of that scene would remain with her in the days ahead.

She also knew she would not have seen the Creator's glory in the meteor without the darkness. As she started the car and headed home, she felt peace wrapping itself around her—God's peace.

As the editor finished telling her story, Cassie smiled. She was beginning to understand that same peace.   —SANDRA

Lord, thank you for the reminders of your presence. Sometimes they are quiet whispers. Sometimes they are brilliant "shouts" that flash across the night sky. But always they carry the message that you have not forgotten us. May we be aware of your voice, no matter our circumstances. And may we face each challenge unafraid.

While you're suffering, you can't see the why. It's only after the fact that you see God makes true his promises [that] he works all things together for his good.
—JAN DRAVECKY, AUTHOR, SPEAKER, AND COFOUNDER OF OUTREACH OF HOPE

FEBRUARY 11
He Wants Us to Ask

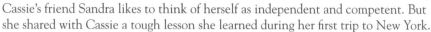

> Teach me how to live, O LORD. Lead me along the right path.
> PSALM 27:11

Cassie's friend Sandra likes to think of herself as independent and competent. But she shared with Cassie a tough lesson she learned during her first trip to New York.

She lived in Michigan and had been invited to a writers' meeting an hour north of New York City. She was both elated and nervous. New York was the end of the world to her back then, and she wondered how she would fly to LaGuardia Airport, rent a car, and even with a map, drive on those mysterious East Coast parkways.

Throughout the flight, she ran troublesome scenarios through her head. By the time the plane landed and she picked up the rental car, her nervousness had escalated. Before she put the key in the ignition, she leaned against the steering wheel and prayed: *Lord, you know I have a horrible sense of direction, so please help.* Then with a great sigh, she started out.

At each stoplight, she reexamined the map, often whispering, "Which way, Lord?" Amazingly, even at unmarked corners, she turned correctly.

She enjoyed an incredible meeting and a calm drive back to the airport.

That evening her plane landed on time. It was a mere twenty-five-minute drive home, a route she had driven dozens of times. As she located her car in the parking lot, she didn't say it, but her attitude was *Thanks, God. I'll take it from here.*

An hour later, her frustration growing, she was still trying to get onto the proper highway. It wasn't until she prayed, again asking for help, that she finally got on the correct road.

Since that long-ago evening, she has often had to turn her self-reliance over to the Lord and say, "Please don't let me take it from here!"

As Cassie pondered her friend's statement, she whispered, "I'm tired of being in charge, Lord. I give this part of my life to you."

And as soon as the words were out of her mouth, she knew her healing had begun.   —SANDRA

> Lord, even when my words don't say it, my attitude announces
> that circumstances, events, and even life itself are in my control.
> Help me to ask for your guidance. Then help me to follow it.

We work, we pull, we struggle, and we plan until we're utterly exhausted, but we have forgotten to plug in to the source of power. And that source of power is prayer.   —EVELYN CHRISTENSON, AUTHOR AND SPEAKER

To Ponder with a Friend

1. Do you identify with Cassie and her desire to be in control? If so, in what way? If not, what advice can you offer others?

2. What family members or historical characters do you most admire? Why?

3. Has God ever encouraged you during a depressing time? If so, how did you react?

4. Have you, like Sandra, ever been determined to "take it from here"? If so, what happened?

FEBRUARY 12
The Shelter of a Friend

A real friend sticks closer than a [sister].   PROVERBS 18:24

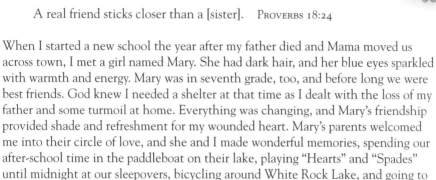

When I started a new school the year after my father died and Mama moved us across town, I met a girl named Mary. She had dark hair, and her blue eyes sparkled with warmth and energy. Mary was in seventh grade, too, and before long we were best friends. God knew I needed a shelter at that time as I dealt with the loss of my father and some turmoil at home. Everything was changing, and Mary's friendship provided shade and refreshment for my wounded heart. Mary's parents welcomed me into their circle of love, and she and I made wonderful memories, spending our after-school time in the paddleboat on their lake, playing "Hearts" and "Spades" until midnight at our sleepovers, bicycling around White Rock Lake, and going to ballroom dancing classes together.

That was the only year we went to the same school. In the decades since, we've never lived in the same city, but our friendship has held fast as we've exchanged countless letters, shared photos and celebrated the milestones of our kids, and sent birthday and Christmas gifts to each other. I've learned that the song that says, "Make new friends, but keep the old; one is silver, and the other is gold," isn't just something sung in childhood Brownie troops. The words are just as true in our adult years. We need treasured "old" friendships that we can enjoy, cultivate, and appreciate, and we need to keep our hearts open to new ones.
—CHERI

> Lord, thank you for the friends you have placed in my life. What a gift they are to me! Help me to treasure my friendships and to be a treasured friend to others.

A loyal friend is like a safe shelter; find one and you have found a treasure.
—UNKNOWN

A Friendship Centered on Christ

[Mary] entered the house and greeted Elizabeth. At the sound of Mary's greeting, Elizabeth's child leaped within her, and Elizabeth was filled with the Holy Spirit. Elizabeth gave a glad cry and exclaimed to Mary, "God has blessed you above all women, and your child is blessed. Why am I so honored, that the mother of my Lord should visit me? . . . You are blessed because you believed that the Lord would do what he said." LUKE 1:40-45

We all need a few friends with whom we can be real and transparent, friends who will keep what we share in confidence and respond with love in times of need or joy. Even research shows the benefits: When women get stressed, talking things through with a girlfriend releases the hormone oxytocin, which is profoundly calming, a balm for mind and body. No wonder we feel better after talking to a gal pal!

Elizabeth was that kind of friend to Mary. In the midst of the storm of a pregnancy that could shake Mary's whole world, Elizabeth's home was an oasis for her cousin. Elizabeth listened and shared her wisdom and her strong faith. But their friendship was not selfishly motivated: It was inspired by and centered on Christ from the outset.

Christian author Eugenia Price found that she needed that kind of friend in times of crisis, someone who understood her and provided companionship in some of her darkest days. During a difficult year when Eugenia's father was critically ill, Rosalind Rinker was that kind of friend. She prayed with Eugenia and with Eugenia's mother. She prepared meals for them. When Eugenia had spent long hours at the hospital and was too upset to sleep, Rosalind let her talk. Rosalind was *there*. And if Eugenia had ever needed a friend, she needed one during those endless weeks while her beloved dad lay dying.

Although the friendship between Rosalind and Eugenia was secure, it wasn't centered on just themselves. It was centered in Jesus Christ, who was the source of their security. They knew that in their humanness they could fail each other but that he would never fail or forsake them. When our friendships are centered in Christ in this way, we not only enjoy one another in the best of times and support one another in the worst of times; we look outward and fulfill God's purposes as well. —CHERI

Lord Jesus, help me to be the kind of friend who is present in times of difficulty, who keeps confidences and can be trusted. Most of all, may my friendships be centered in you.

Many people will walk in and out of your life. But only true friends will leave footprints in your heart. —ANONYMOUS

FEBRUARY 14

An Unlikely Friend

> When God's people are in need, be ready to help them. Always
> be eager to practice hospitality. ROMANS 12:13

When Cathy and Robert moved from New York to Oklahoma as college students,
the transition was difficult. But God used one unlikely woman to change Cathy's
views on how to be a friend. Sonia, a nurse who lived in their apartment complex,
wore strange clothes and had long, black, greasy hair. She had been abused as a
child and kept to herself. At first Cathy and Robert found it difficult to get to
know her, but over time Sonia slowly warmed up to the couple. She began knocking on their door to hand them plates of delicious food, saying simply, "I couldn't
eat it all myself."

Robert and Cathy didn't have much money or food. Sometimes they planned
to eat beans until the next paycheck came in. Then Sonia would appear at the
door with a platter of roast chicken and wild rice. When Robert and Cathy had
completed their studies and were preparing to move to Massachusetts, Cathy and
Sonia spent a day together at an arts festival. Near the end of the day Cathy said,
"Sonia, you give and give, and I don't have much to give you. But I'd like to pay
you back in some way for all the kindness you've shown us. What do I have that
you'd like?"

Sonia smiled at Cathy. "You can pay me back by being a friend to your new
neighbors in Massachusetts."

When the couple arrived in Boston, God often brought Sonia's request to
Cathy's mind. When she saw a new single mom in the apartment complex, he
would whisper, *There's someone who needs a friend*, and nudged Cathy to provide a
meal. She did laundry for a sick neighbor and invited a young couple and their
child to share a meal. Instead of being lonely in their new city, Cathy felt warmed
by friendship, for she had learned the secret of going out of herself to love others
at their point of need.   —CHERI

Lord, make me the kind of friend who sees and responds to the
needs of people around me and loves them with your love.

Our neighbor is the next person who needs our help.   —ANONYMOUS

FEBRUARY 15
The Prayer of a Friend

Pray for each other. . . . The earnest prayer of a righteous person
has great power and produces wonderful results.   JAMES 5:16

"I just start to feel like I'm 'all prayed up,'" a young woman shared with me, "and
then Sunday night a friend asks me to pray for her mom, who's in cancer treatment. Another woman needs prayer because her teenage son is driving her crazy.
Someone else e-mails me three prayer requests. As the needs pile up, I feel guilty
when I forget to pray."

When we're busy, it's easy to lose the sticky note on which we wrote a
friend's prayer request or simply to forget because there's so much to do. One of the
best gifts we can give our friends is to pray with them the moment they express a
need or prayer request. Five little words—"Could I pray for you?"—may make a big
difference in a friend's life. They did in mine.

A few weeks after my mother died, life had returned to "normal." The kids
had gone back to school, Holmes had returned to work, and I had resumed my
part-time teaching. But I couldn't get rid of the painful memories of how cancer
had devastated my mom's body. Those sad images weren't the way I wanted to
remember Mom, but they flooded in whenever I thought of her. I hadn't been able
to explain this to anybody, but God knew.

One day I got out of the car as my friend Patty was coming out of her
natural-food store. This busy woman came over and put an arm around me.

"Cheri, how are you doing?"

She must have seen the tears welling up as I tried to explain how bogged
down I was feeling.

"Could I pray for you?" she asked gently. Then Patty asked God to do something simple yet profound—to wrap his love around my memories of my mom. He
did just that, bringing a healing touch as my friend Patty prayed for me in the
parking lot. People all around us are longing for someone who cares enough about
them to ask, to listen, and to pray for them right then. Will you stop and do that
for someone today?   —CHERI

Lord, help me to be sensitive to the needs of others and to stop
and pray on the spot when that would be a blessing to a friend.

The best thing one woman can give another is a prayer from the heart and a warm
hand of understanding.   —CHERI FULLER

FEBRUARY 16
Bridging the Changing Circumstances of Life

> A friend is always loyal, and a [sister] is born to help in time of need.   PROVERBS 17:17

After Bethany got married, she no longer met her single girlfriends for dinner at a local restaurant. When they called, she was too busy to return the calls. Preoccupied with married life, her husband, and other couples, she didn't have time for her old friends. As the months went on, however, she and her husband went through a stressful time when the company he worked for was sold and his position was eliminated. Bethany grew lonely and realized that she missed women with whom she could be herself, women with whom she had history and with whom she could laugh or cry without feeling uncomfortable.

Just as friendship must extend across the miles, it must also bridge the changing circumstances of life. As you pack your boxes to move to a different company or plan the wedding you have longed for, be careful not to mentally dispose of your deep friendships with those you're leaving behind. Don't leave your girlfriends— including your single ones—in the dust. It's easy to get so wrapped up in excitement over the guy you've long dreamed of that you exclude old friends from your life. Instead, meet for lunch. Plan a girls' movie night. And whether you change your last name or just your address, avoid leaving a string of broken or neglected friendships behind.

God doesn't give us scores of close friends throughout our lives. That's why we should treat those relationships with such care. It costs something to be a friend: It takes time, patience, affection, strength, and love. But the blessing of a lasting friendship is more than worth the effort it takes, and the friendship gives back to us far more than we can imagine.   —CHERI

Change is such a way of life today. I'm thankful, Lord, that I don't have to leave my friends behind when the circumstances of my life change. What a great gift you have given me in my girlfriends! Please continue to knit our hearts together in love no matter where we go.

To have a friend is to have one of the sweetest gifts that life can bring: to be a friend is to have a solemn and tender education of soul from day to day. A friend gives us confidence for life. A friend remembers us when we have forgotten ourselves, or neglected ourselves.
—ANNA ROBERTSON BROWN LINDSAY (1864–1948), THEOLOGIAN AND AUTHOR

FEBRUARY 17
A Letter from a Friend

Gentle words are a tree of life.   PROVERBS 15:4

There's nothing that makes my day more than seeing a flower-bordered
envelope with my friend's handwriting in my mailbox. Letters mingle souls and
connect hearts even across the miles. It's not exactly like chatting over lunch
together, but sometimes those gentle words have arrived at just the right time to
lift me out of worry or cheer my heavy heart. E-mail is quick and makes it easy to
stay in touch, but keep those snail-mail letters and notes going, for they are some
of the delights of a long-distance friendship. These written reminders of love and
care can be tucked away in your journal and brought out on gray or anxious days
when you need some encouraging words. A letter can be read and reread. It calms
and soothes the sometimes turbulent waters of friendship.

Outside of our actual presence, a letter is the best physical proof we can offer
of our friendship, our care and concern for another person. Lifestyle philosopher
Alexandra Stoddard offers some lovely advice: "Sit by a crackling fire and read
some of your favorite letters. While sitting there soaking up all the love and support, think of one person you love and write a beautiful, loving letter to that person. Let the flame in your hearth warm your heart. One letter in a lifetime to a
mother, a daughter, or a special friend could make a greater difference than you
dare to believe."   —CHERI

Lord, help me to be the kind of friend who takes time to give the
gift of a letter, of gentle words or words of thanks written down.

Life is too fast-paced, too commercial, too technical. A true gift is one that touches
life's chords, is a true gift of oneself. How simple that a letter can be a gift of time
tucked away, saved, cherished, and passed on.   —ANNIE MORTON

FEBRUARY 18
A Gift from a Friend

It is more blessed to give than to receive.   ACTS 20:35

The week I arrived home exhausted and sad after my sister's death, I was met that first evening by my friend Susan, who brought a delicious hot meal of chicken and noodles, salad, cake, and fresh strawberries. A few days later, Corrie arrived at my door with a lovely vase of roses that brightened my heart all that week. Knowing I was alone, Cynthia, my friend a few doors away, invited me to her home for dinner one evening. These friends' gifts of kindness nourished my body and cheered my soul, helped me get through a difficult time of loss, and nurtured our relationships.

The kindness of a friend will stay with you forever. Remembering your friends in some thoughtful way when they've suffered a loss, are ill, or are just down in the dumps is a lovely way of saying, "I'm thinking about you. I care." These gestures of kindness and care don't have to be expensive or even store-bought. A spontaneous, unexpected gift from the heart is perhaps best of all: a bunch of flowers from your garden, homemade brownies, or a book you've enjoyed. Knitting or crocheting a "prayer blanket" and praying for your friend throughout the project warms both the body and the soul of the recipient. Whether the gift is thoughtfully chosen at a shop or comes from your garden or your kitchen, gifts given to friends in a spirit of love deliver buckets of kindness. The time and care expended to give a gracious, personal gift speak volumes and give pleasure both to the giver and to the receiver. To whom can you give an act of kindness and love today? Remember, although the gift may be small, love is all.   —CHERI

Father, you are the great Giver, and every good and perfect gift comes from you. Grant me a giving heart, and make me a woman who is sensitive to the needs of my friends and who finds joy in spontaneous acts of kindness.

There are good ships and wood ships,
    Ships that sail the sea,
But the best ships are friendships,
    And may they always be.
—IRISH SAYING

To Ponder with a Friend

1. What's your favorite way to connect with your girlfriend(s)? Share or journal about an experience when spending time with a dear friend lifted you out of a slump or a place of discouragement.

2. What are some ways you could bless a friend who is going through a rough time?

3. Sometimes a friendship hits a bump or you have a misunderstanding. How have you sorted things out with a friend when your relationship became strained or distant?

4. Research shows that strong connections with other women decrease stress and even boost our health. Yet our fast-paced, crazy-busy culture hinders deep friendships and contributes to disconnection and loneliness. What can you do to cultivate deeper, more lasting connections with women (e.g., carving out time in your schedule for a weekly lunch with friends, purposing to be more honest and transparent in your relationships, scheduling a regular walking time with a friend, etc.)?

FEBRUARY 19
Discard Checkbook Agony

> Better to have little, with fear for the LORD, than to have great treasure and inner turmoil. A bowl of vegetables with someone you love is better than steak with someone you hate.
> PROVERBS 15:16-17

Some time ago I ran into Debby, a young friend who had been hired right out of college by a prominent business in the Midwest. As we chatted over mango tea, she sighed as she recited a long list of credit-card debts caused by her attempts to maintain the image she thought her job called for: expensive clothes, a sporty car, and an upscale town house. She also confessed she wanted to be liked by the office decision makers, so she often picked up the tab for expensive lunches even though she was not reimbursed through an expense account. Now it seemed as if her coworkers *expected* her to bankroll their fancy culinary tastes. Further, her checking account was so horribly muddled she had been forced to change banks for the third time and open new accounts.

Even as I wondered how she, a bright woman of the new millennium, could have gotten herself into such a mess, I could sympathize with her checkbook agony. After all, I've gotten a lot of mileage out of my joke that the first time a friend asked if I had reconciled my checkbook after my husband died, I retorted, "Why do I have to reconcile myself to it? I'm not angry at it!"

But financial ignorance is not funny, and financial disaster can result from a woman's decision not to manage wisely whatever amount she has. Debby ended our mango-tea discussion with a promise to accept the invitation from one of the bank officers to take the company's financial planning class. As we parted, I felt confident she would regain not only financial control but her emotional freedom as well.   —SANDRA

Lord, how did I allow *things* to become so important? I thought I knew that shiny items won't bring happiness. I thought I was above trying to impress others. But I'm surrounded by "stuff" that has not made me content, nor has it gained me the deeper friendships for which I long. In fact, it has done nothing but push me into debt. I ask for your help in getting out of this mess. Help me to learn from this tough time. And may I invite you into each future financial decision.

The Lord holds us accountable for what we do with His provision.
—FLORENCE LITTAUER, SPEAKER AND AUTHOR

FEBRUARY 20
Early Training

Don't worry about anything; instead, pray about everything.
Tell God what you need, and thank him for all he has done.
PHILIPPIANS 4:6

Jennifer, a local CPA, often meets with women from her church who either find themselves in financial trouble or are making financial decisions alone for the first time. She always begins the session with an account of the afternoon she received her first allowance. As she describes staring in delight at the two shiny quarters her mother had placed in her eight-year-old palm, the attendees can almost see the sprinkling of freckles across the nose of the little girl. But along with that childhood delight came her thrifty parent's tough lessons about how not to "waste" her allowance.

Jennifer caught on quickly to the concept that 10 percent of the total should go to God in one form or another, either in the church offering plate or to missionaries of her choosing, not as a biblical command but as a way to say thank you to God for his many blessings.

But Jennifer had trouble with the concept of saving another 10 percent for a "rainy day." She had a long list of things she just had to have *right now*. Today, looking back, she understands how it must have hurt her mother to say *no* when Jennifer asked for additional money for an outing with friends after she had blown her weekly allowance on the latest fad.

As her session attendees nod in understanding, Jennifer adds, "But if my mother had bailed me out each time I wasted my money, she would have taught me I didn't have to be responsible and that good old Mom would rescue me whenever I had any financial problems."

Then Jennifer always manages to grab her listeners' attention with this comment: "Just as I learned to make financial decisions from *my* mother, *your* daughters will learn from you, for good or for bad." By then, the women in her audience, whether it's one woman or twenty, are ready to address the issues that may have contributed to their financial situations. After all, once we understand how we got into a mess, we can more readily learn how to get out.   —SANDRA

Lord, financial details weary me to the point where I actually identify with the old joke that says, "My bank account can't be overdrawn—I still have checks left." But not paying attention to the details of my income and my spending gets me into a real mess. Help me to take a deep breath and take an honest look at my checkbook. Then help me to develop a more mature attitude toward money.

God often allows us to be in situations that are too much for us so we will learn no situation is too much for Him.   —ERWIN W. LUTZER, PASTOR AND AUTHOR

FEBRUARY 21
A Wise Investment

> If you need wisdom, ask our generous God, and he will give it to you. He will not rebuke you for asking.   JAMES 1:5

Here's an interesting challenge: What if before we made a purchase, we asked God, "Should I buy this?" After all, bad financial decisions often start with making an impulsive purchase or giving in to the latest fad. We will also make wiser choices if we understand that fashion changes quickly and what is "in" today may look outdated tomorrow. (If you don't believe me, just ask your Aunt Jean about the avocado green and bright orange shag carpet she displayed throughout her house in the mid-1970s.)

It may take a while to learn to resist the compulsion to spend, especially if we don't accept the truth of Colossians 2:10: We are "complete" because of our union with Christ. While this Scripture verse is talking about spiritual completeness or fullness, we can readily apply it to material completeness, too. If we are aware of all we already have in Christ, we won't be as prone to strive to fill our lives and hearts with more things. And that's really what compulsive spending is trying to do—fill an emotional hole in the heart. One way to test whether you're trying to fill such an invisible hole is to think of the times you've gone shopping and returned home empty-handed. Did you feel a little empty inside, too? If so, you may be trying to meet an emotional need that will never be satisfied with just *things*. The story is told of a reporter who asked the richest man in the world how much money would be enough. "Just a little more," was the sad reply.

So if having more money than anyone else isn't enough if our hearts are empty, shouldn't we try to be content with what we do have? Our real security comes from the Lord, not from even the wisest of earthly investments. And if we do manage to accumulate great wealth, we are still only temporary stewards of God's property.   —SANDRA

> Lord, although breathing a prayer to ask whether I should buy something sounds a little goofy, I'll try it if that will help me to break impulsive buying habits. When I'm facing the temptation to buy, though, I need you to help me to remember to slow down long enough to ask.

We belong to a Redeemer God, and it is never too late for Him to redeem any part of our lives.   —EUGENIA PRICE (1916–1996), AMERICAN AUTHOR

FEBRUARY 22
Money's Hidden Meaning

> The love of money is the root of all kinds of evil. And some people, craving money, have wandered from the true faith and pierced themselves with many sorrows. 1 TIMOTHY 6:10

Occasionally I encounter people who believe it is worldly to be concerned about financial matters. They may even say money is evil. But the first part of 1 Timothy 6:10 says it's "the *love* of money" that causes problems, not money itself. Money is inanimate; it's how money is used that matters. But even though it is inanimate, it ranks as one of the most frequent reasons for arguments in married couples, especially if one spouse feels the other is trying to be the controller when it comes to financial matters.

Jim and Nikki were such a couple. She fretted over each purchase he made, whether it was a new radio or a newer car. Often her fretting turned into hand-wringing, tearful tirades. While their three children watched with fear-filled eyes, Jim would quickly respond with shouts and accusations that Nikki was nagging. Finally, to save their marriage, the couple agreed to see a counselor, whose first question was, "What does money mean to you?"

Initially, Jim and Nikki just wanted to accuse each other of either foolish spending or constant nagging, but the counselor continued to repeat his question. Gradually, as Jim was forced to ponder money's meaning, he realized that to him, money meant power. Having a fancy car, a membership at the country club, and the latest gadgets was his way of showing the world (and a former girlfriend, who had rejected him) he was someone of importance.

Nikki, on the other hand, saw money as security. She wasn't interested in proving anything; she just wanted to save money for that proverbial rainy day, even at great sacrifice. Once Jim and Nikki understood their arguments were about insecurity and fear rather than about the actual dollars, they were able to begin to look at money realistically and to work at restoring mutual respect within their marriage. —SANDRA

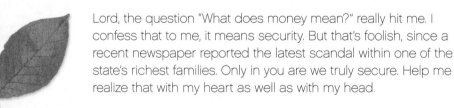

Lord, the question "What does money mean?" really hit me. I confess that to me, it means security. But that's foolish, since a recent newspaper reported the latest scandal within one of the state's richest families. Only in you are we truly secure. Help me realize that with my heart as well as with my head.

The love of money brings only grief. Contentment is a more logical approach to life and brings great blessing.
—HAROLD L. WILLMINGTON, AUTHOR, EDUCATOR, AND BIBLE LECTURER

FEBRUARY 23

God's Provision

Don't worry about these things, saying, "What will we eat? What will we drink? What will we wear?" These things dominate the thoughts of unbelievers, but your heavenly Father already knows all your needs. Seek the Kingdom of God above all else, and live righteously, and he will give you everything you need.   MATTHEW 6:31-33

I believe God provides for his children. However, I also believe the old saying, "God gives every bird its food, but he doesn't throw it into the nest!" So, while we are praying for God's provision, we can do our part to gain solid financial footing. Often that starts by following the four rules most debt counselors offer:

- Use no credit cards.
- Reduce existing debt.
- Balance the checkbook each month.
- Identify and conquer your biggest personal financial problem—whether it's overspending or impulse buying.

To that list I would add one more item: Ponder creative ways to make extra money. One of my single-parent friends, Christine, budgeted carefully to care for her three children. But one month it seemed as if every appliance needed repairs. Then, just as she paid to have the belt on the washing machine replaced, an unexpected bill for the house escrow shortage arrived—one hundred and seventeen dollars, due on receipt. Christine's paycheck wasn't due until the end of the month, and she wondered how she was going to pay the bill.

That night at the dinner table, she included this latest need in her prayer. After the *amen*, Christine's twelve-year-old daughter said, "Let's have a garage sale this Saturday." Even though it was too late to put an ad in the paper and they had only two days to prepare, Christine and her children cleaned closets, the shed, and the garage, searching for items they could sell. They also prayed God would send lots of buyers.

On Saturday morning, the first customer bought three dollars' worth of pink throw pillows. The next customer purchased two patio chairs that needed new webbing. By the end of the day, most of the items had been sold—for exactly one hundred and seventeen dollars. What an answer to Christine's need! And what a wonderful faith builder for her children.   —SANDRA

Lord, I now understand that you have promised to supply our *needs*, not our *wants*. I confess I want to be rescued instead of having to put in the extra effort needed to get out of debt. But I thank you for not abandoning me, and I thank you in advance for the creative ideas you will bring.

Charge cards are financial stranglers. After all, being in debt is one way to have less than nothing.   —SANDRA P. ALDRICH

FEBRUARY 24
Pay God First

> Trust in your money and down you go! But the godly flourish like
> leaves in spring.   PROVERBS 11:28

Even though tithing, or giving a tenth of one's income, is based on Old Testament practice rather than on New Testament command, I'm convinced supporting God's work is both a responsibility and a privilege. For years I've helped support three missionary families in addition to giving to my local church. I can't go to faraway places to present the gospel, but I can help others go. How exciting to be part of our heavenly Father's work, even through the writing of a check! And even though it was not my motivation for giving, I've been amazed and grateful as I've watched God stretch the remaining dollars in my budget when I take care of the tithe first.

Some pastors teach that we are to support our church with the full tithe and then support missionaries with gifts beyond the tithe. I remember, for instance, a Detroit minister who said, "Support where you worship. You don't dine at one restaurant and then go next door and pay the bill at another."

That's a good point. But talk over your giving with the Lord, and ask him what he wants you to do with your tithe. If you're convinced you can't give a full monetary tithe right now, consider tithing your time or talent by teaching a Sunday school class or painting a mural for the church nursery. The important thing is that you give back to the Lord a portion of what he has given you.

A word of caution, though: However we decide to pay our tithe, we should do so out of a spirit of thankfulness rather than out of the expectation that God will pay us back "ten times over" or "a hundredfold," as some people insist. We can never outgive God, of course, but neither does he *owe* us anything.

—SANDRA

Lord, what a privilege it is to share in your work. Help me to think of the tithe as a way of thanking you for your blessings rather than as a duty.

Riches are useless if we do not put them to work in a needy, hurting world.
—J. STEPHEN LANG, AUTHOR

FEBRUARY 25

Financial Reality

I am certain that God, who began the good work within you, will continue his work until it is finally finished on the day when Christ Jesus returns.   PHILIPPIANS 1:6

I wish I had a dollar for every time I heard one of my kids say, "But I *need* a new pair of jeans!"

When my children lived at home, my modest income prevented me from providing the wardrobes I would have liked to provide for them. But rather than constantly say, "We can't afford that," I involved both teens in the bill-paying sessions. They would watch in amazement as the salary deposit decreased with each check I wrote for the town house, utilities, car maintenance, and other household expenses.

A friend used a dramatic visual aid. She cashed her paycheck into one-dollar bills, which she stacked in the middle of the table. She didn't comment when her youngsters exclaimed, "Wow, we're rich!" Instead, she opened the stack of bills and asked the children to take turns counting out the amount needed. Finally, they had nine dollars left but three unpaid bills on the table. "What shall we do now?" she asked. She had made her point and didn't have to use the visual aid again.

When we struggled with a longing for *things*, I'd pull rank (mothers *are* allowed to do that) and plan a day trip to New York City.

We would catch the Saturday morning train out of the Chappaqua station and ride fifty-five minutes south. At Grand Central Station my son, Jay, and I marveled at the people representing all social levels, from Wall Street brokers to folks panhandling for change. But my daughter, Holly, felt as if I'd sentenced her to an unbearable day of dirt and noise.

One Saturday, a woman in a fur coat got on the train with us at Chappaqua and spent most of the trip chirping to her daughter about their anticipated shopping at several expensive shops.

As our train pulled into the 125th Street station—the stop just before Grand Central in the heart of one of New York City's most tired areas—the woman looked out the window at the weathered apartment buildings and exclaimed, "Ugh! Why don't they move out of here?"

Holly turned to me, stunned at the woman's insensitivity.

I nodded my head ever so slightly in acknowledgment, but the woman had made my point about materialism far better than I could have. That was the last time Holly complained about the journey being distasteful. On future trips, my young teen displayed appreciation for one of the world's grandest cities—and for our modest home.   —SANDRA

Lord, when I'm tempted to complain about not having more, open my eyes. Show me, in a new way, all of my blessings.

The fellow who has no money is poor. The fellow who has nothing but money is poorer still.   —BILLY SUNDAY (1862–1935), AMERICAN EVANGELIST

To Ponder with a Friend

1. What's your greatest financial challenge?

2. What does money mean to you? Why?

3. How do you feel about the practice of giving a tenth of your income to God's work?

4. What advice do you have for others who are struggling financially?

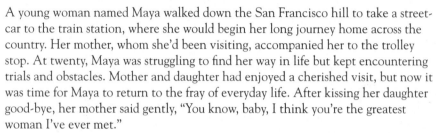

FEBRUARY 26

Encouraging Words Give Confidence

Gentle words are a tree of life.   PROVERBS 15:4

A young woman named Maya walked down the San Francisco hill to take a street-car to the train station, where she would begin her long journey home across the country. Her mother, whom she'd been visiting, accompanied her to the trolley stop. At twenty, Maya was struggling to find her way in life but kept encountering trials and obstacles. Mother and daughter had enjoyed a cherished visit, but now it was time for Maya to return to the fray of everyday life. After kissing her daughter good-bye, her mother said gently, "You know, baby, I think you're the greatest woman I've ever met."

Her mom turned and slowly made her way up the hill. Maya waited alone for the streetcar. *Suppose Mom is right,* she thought. *Suppose I really am somebody.* That was a turning point, one of those incredible moments when the heavens seem to roll back and the earth seems to be holding its breath. It filled her heart with confidence and hope.

Maya Angelou became a best-selling poet, novelist, and eventually, poet laureate of the United States.

With her creative words and talents, she has inspired countless people to achieve their potential. But the turning point came when her mother offered those encouraging words that brought life to her daughter.

Just as in Maya Angelou's life, encouraging words are like a stone tossed into the water. Their effect has ripples far greater than we can imagine. What ripples can you cause to touch those around you? There are people everywhere who desperately need a gentle word of encouragement: weary single moms, lonely senior citizens, stressed-out teens, and folks in our neighborhoods, schools, churches, and workplaces. Jot down the names of a few people you could encourage this week. You'll never know the ripple effect your words can have.   —CHERI

> Father, I want to be an encourager. Show me those who need a word to lift their spirits. May my words bring hope and confidence.

Drop a stone into the water—
    In a moment it's gone.
But there are a hundred ripples
    Circling on and on and on.
Say a word of cheer and splendor—
    In a moment it is gone.
But there are a hundred ripples
    Circling on and on.
—ANONYMOUS

FEBRUARY 27
Encouraging Words Bring Out the Best

If your gift is to encourage others, be encouraging. Romans 12:8

She was a shy, quiet girl with long, stringy, ash-blond hair. I didn't even know which child she was out of the fifty noisy fifth graders I'd been working with for nine weeks in the artist-in-residence program. Although most of the kids vied for attention and recognition, this child sat at the back, her nose in a book.

I called her name and asked, "Brandy, would you come up and read your marvelous poem entitled 'My Hand'? Students, listen carefully, because you're going to love the imagery and word choice in this poem." Slowly she walked up to the author's chair in our makeshift reader's theater and read her poem aloud to a warm, enthusiastic response.

"I didn't know you were such a good writer!" one girl said.

"Share some of your other poems," other kids suggested. Slowly, Brandy began to blossom as the class poet.

A few days later I realized how much my few words of encouragement had meant to her when I received this note of thanks: "Dear Mrs. Fuller. These few weeks have been the BEST days of my whole life! YOU brought out the person, the writer inside, that I didn't realize I had. I'll always remember you and cherish you for what you did for me. Your enthusiastic student, Brandy."

There are children like Brandy all around you and me who are desperate for an encouraging word. Kids have so much to learn and are so often criticized instead of built up by the adults around them. Our words of encouragement can bring out the best in them. When we catch them doing something kind, helpful, or creative and comment on it, they get a snapshot of what they are becoming. When we recognize kids' gifts or talents, we motivate them to be all that God meant them to be. Is there a young person you could encourage today?
—Cheri

Father, forgive me for so often pointing out what is wrong instead of telling kids what they are doing right. Help me to speak encouraging words today, and may they bear fruit tomorrow and in the days to come.

Take with you words, strong words of courage: Words that have wings! . . . Tall words, words that reach up, and growing words, with deep life within them.
—Jo Petty, inspirational writer

FEBRUARY 28

Encouraging Words Give a Blessing

Let everything you say be good and helpful, so that your words
will be an encouragement to those who hear them.   EPHESIANS 4:29

Billy Graham said that his mother was one of his greatest encouragers. She always
told him to "preach the gospel and keep it simple." Two weeks before she went to
heaven, she admonished Billy with these same words, and he responded, "Mother,
I'm going to preach his birth, death, and resurrection. I'll preach it till Jesus
comes."

His mother squeezed his hand and said, "I believe it!"

Having a mother who believed in him, blessed him, and encouraged him
meant the world to this man whose life has influenced millions, including presidents and leaders of other nations. What a treasure it is for parents to believe in
their children and to bless them as Mrs. Graham did, with words that inspired
hope and communicated love. But to do this, we must see with the heart the
potential that lies within rather than just the outward appearance of sports success,
high grades, or strong improvement. As the fox said in *The Little Prince*, "Here is
my secret, a very simple secret: It is only with the heart that one can see rightly;
what is essential is invisible to the eye. . . . Men have forgotten this truth. But you
must not forget it."

May we see with the heart, and if we are lacking in this ability, let us ask
God for his eyesight to see those we live and work with and teach day by day.
Then we can bless them with our words instead of discourage them. May we
become, like Billy Graham's mother, their greatest encouragers.   —CHERI

> Lord, let everything I say be helpful and good. May I see
> children, coworkers, and loved ones with your eyes, love them
> with your love, and bless them with words of encouragement
> and life.

If you want to keep your kids out of prison, *bless them*. The blessing always
involves a hug and a kiss. Not the kiss of abuse but of blessing. There's a vast
difference! "I love you, I bless you, I think you're terrific, and I'm so glad
you're mine." It's got to be said out loud. It's got to be stated. The blessing is
unconditional and it's continuous in order to be a real blessing—in order to
be real love.

—BILL GLASS, MINISTER AND FORMER NFL DEFENSIVE TACKLE

MARCH 1
Encouraging Words Lift the Heart

Worry weighs a person down; an encouraging word cheers
a person up.   PROVERBS 12:25

After former president Richard Nixon resigned from the presidency in shame and
humiliation, he had to undergo major surgery. Overwhelmed with his own failures,
disappointment, and physical pain from the surgery, Nixon became severely
depressed. No doubt he was anxious about the future, knowing that his political
career was over. Lying in the hospital bed day after day, he told his wife, Pat, that
he wanted to die. But at his very lowest moment, a nurse came into the room,
opened the curtains, and pointed to a small plane flying back and forth in front of
his window. The plane pulled a sign with bold letters that read: "GOD LOVES
YOU, AND SO DO WE!"

Seeing that letter written across the sky and sensing the love and prayers
behind it gave Nixon the courage to recover. Later, he found out that Ruth Bell
Graham had personally arranged for the plane to fly around the hospital. The former president not only survived but went on to serve both his family and his country, to orchestrate important negotiations between the United States and China,
and to make valuable contributions for several years until his death. What strength
can come from positive words of encouragement to one who is in the blackest pit
of life! Those words—whether spoken or written across the sky—not only cheer
the failing heart but are lifesavers to those who receive them.   —CHERI

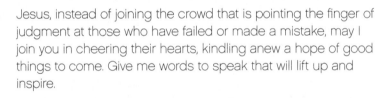

Jesus, instead of joining the crowd that is pointing the finger of
judgment at those who have failed or made a mistake, may I
join you in cheering their hearts, kindling anew a hope of good
things to come. Give me words to speak that will lift up and
inspire.

Encouragement after censure is as the sun after a shower.
—JOHANN WOLFGANG VON GOETHE (1749–1832), GERMAN WRITER

MARCH 2
An Act of Encouragement

Your kindness will reward you, but your cruelty will destroy you.
PROVERBS 11:17

As Dee was taking boxes into the moving van in Akron, Ohio, her husband called up the stairs, "Dee, you have a visitor!"

She was surprised to find Phyllis, a woman from her Bible study, perched quietly on a big box in the living room. Phyllis had never been to her home before. They'd never had coffee or gone to lunch. In fact, she was the quietest member of all the women in the Bible study Dee taught. Dee's surprise grew as Phyllis silently and gently held out a beautiful afghan throw. For months she had been spending evenings crocheting this wonderful expression of love. Spontaneously Dee hugged her. At first Phyllis's arms hung limply at her sides, but then she returned the embrace. Unwiped tears ran down their cheeks, and Dee's heart was encouraged for yet another move.

Sometimes even more than words, an act of kindness or an unexpected and thoughtful gift from the heart can make the difference. It can bring sunshine into the life of someone who needs it. My father often said that actions speak louder than words. Who could you encourage this week with an act of kindness? How could you spread the fragrance of Christ by sharing something you have with someone, making a meal for a new mother just home from the hospital, or asking God how you might be a blessing even in small, practical ways to those you meet on your daily path? This is a question the Lord loves to answer. And as this verse says, as you extend kindness to others, your own soul will be rewarded.
—CHERI

Jesus, make me a blessing to people I know and meet. Give me your eyesight to see the needs of others and a giving heart that delights in extending a hand of kindness. Thank you for giving yourself that we might love others.

One of the deep secrets of life is that all that is really worth doing is what we do for others.
—LEWIS CARROLL (PSEUDONYM FOR THE REVEREND CHARLES LUTWIDGE DODGSON, 1832–1898), ENGLISH AUTHOR, CLERGYMAN, AND PHOTOGRAPHER

MARCH 3

Barnabas, an Encourager

> When Saul arrived in Jerusalem, he tried to meet with the believers, but they were all afraid of him. . . . Then Barnabas brought him to the apostles and told them how Saul had seen the Lord on the way to Damascus and how the Lord had spoken to Saul. He also told them that Saul had preached boldly in the name of Jesus in Damascus. ACTS 9:26-27

Barnabas was such an effective encourager because he had the God-given ability to see and understand what the Lord was doing around him. He saw people not with critical eyes but the way God did. Just as Joshua and Caleb saw the potential in the land God had promised his people (see Numbers 14:6-8), Barnabas saw with spiritual eyes something of God's potential in everyone, even in the believers' former enemy, Saul. The other Christians feared Saul (later known as Paul) and rejected his ministry even though he had been transformed from the hateful and proud persecutor to the loving and humble servant of Christ. But Barnabas spoke up for him and declared what God had deposited in him. Barnabas continued to be a peacemaker and a bridge between Paul and the other apostles, and Paul was embraced and welcomed into the fellowship of believers.

Later, when John Mark failed on a missionary journey and Paul would no longer take him along with him, Barnabas took John Mark under his wing, believed in him, and encouraged him in a dark hour (see Acts 15:36-39). Thus John Mark was restored and encouraged to keep serving God. Are you a Barnabas? If you are willing, you could be just the person God uses to help someone who is in trouble. You could be the bridge of divine grace in another's spiritual journey.
—CHERI

> Lord, I want to be like Barnabas, an encourager. Use me to come alongside people who are in trouble and be an instrument of divine grace for them.

Every time we encourage someone, we give them a transfusion of courage.
—CHARLES SWINDOLL, PASTOR, AUTHOR, EDUCATOR, AND RADIO PREACHER

MARCH 4

God, Your Greatest Encourager

May our Lord Jesus Christ himself and God our Father, who loved
us and by his grace gave us eternal comfort and a wonderful hope,
comfort you and strengthen you in every good thing you do and
say.   2 THESSALONIANS 2:16-17

This week we've looked at the great value of encouragement and how you can
grow to be more and more an encourager to those around you. But what if your
own heart is discouraged? What if people in your home or at work aren't being
encouraging to you, and your "emotional tank" is empty? In times like these, look
to the Lord, for he is your greatest encourager. God's Word, his love letter to you,
is full of encouraging truth and precious promises that will infuse you with courage and hope: that he loves you with an everlasting, unconditional love and that
he chose you before you even existed (see Ephesians 1:11). He promises to be your
strength, to help you, to uphold you, and to guide you continually (see Isaiah 40;
58:11). He will hide you in times of trouble (see Psalm 27:5), and his plan for you
has always been filled with hope (see Jeremiah 29:11). When you pray, your
Father hears you (see Psalm 120:1) and is attentive to your voice. When you call
on him in even the greatest distress, he will answer you and set you in a large
place. He is for you, not against you, and he is on your side (see Psalm 118:5-6).

How encouraging to remember that the Lord knows every moment of our
lives and is always with us and for us. When we meditate on the endless encouragement in Scripture, the light of God's truth refills our hearts with confidence. I am
so thankful that God doesn't leave us to our own devices to muster up this confidence. Instead, he stands ready to fill us with hope, encouragement, and confidence whenever we ask and seek him in his Word.   —CHERI

Lord, when I'm discouraged or disheartened, let me look to you
as my greatest encourager. Thank you for the Bible, which has
encouragement for me in every situation.

God has in himself all power to defend you, all wisdom to direct you, all mercy
to pardon you, all grace to enrich you.
—THOMAS BENTON BROOKS (1836–1900), GEOLOGIST

To Ponder with a Friend

1. Looking back at this week's devotionals, what are four things that may happen in a person when she is encouraged?

2. Discouragement is epidemic in people today, both within and outside the church. Share some of the encouraging words you have spoken or written to someone who was discouraged. What was the result? If you have time, share how someone's words of encouragement were life giving to you.

3. Read aloud Hebrews 10:24-25. With this principle in mind, write down the name of a person who is in a difficult place and how you plan to encourage her this week.

4. In Bill Glass's quote on February 28, he shares about the desperate need that kids and teens have for our words and actions to communicate unconditional, loving blessing. Were you blessed to have received encouraging, life-giving words from a teacher or other adult? What ways have you found to bless and uplift your children or others in the way the quotation describes?

5. Here are some ways to encourage someone with the gift of words: Write a poem, dedicate an entry in your blog to show them and the world you care, make a homemade card, or write and record your own song lyrics to a popular tune. Try one of these ways of sending a word gift to someone this week. Then share next week how it affected that person.

MARCH 5
Painful Regrets

> Dear brothers and sisters, I plead with you to give your bodies to God because of all he has done for you. Let them be a living and holy sacrifice—the kind he will find acceptable. This is truly the way to worship him. Don't copy the behavior and customs of this world, but let God transform you into a new person by changing the way you think. Then you will learn to know God's will for you, which is good and pleasing and perfect. ROMANS 12:1-2

Kerri merely glanced at her reflection in the bathroom mirror as she splashed water on her face. She had thought going to bed with her new boyfriend would make her happy; she had thought she'd wake up glowing and smiling the way the young career women in the movie scenes do. She had been the last of her group to keep her virginity, and her friends were always kidding her about it, insisting she lived a sheltered life and needed to loosen up and live life the way it was supposed to be lived. So last night, knowing her roommate would be out of town for the rest of the week with *her* boyfriend, Kerri had planned a romantic dinner, complete with candlelight and soft music. After the raspberry torte, she had led her boyfriend to her bedroom, where he stayed until after midnight.

Now, instead of smiling, she was trying not to look at herself in the mirror. She hadn't counted on this empty, lost feeling in the pit of her stomach and her sense of dread at the thought of running into *him* in the coffee room. This wasn't the way it was supposed to be at all. She buried her face in the towel and sobbed, "I can't believe I made the wrong choice. Oh, I want to go back to the way I was!"
—SANDRA

Lord, when I was a child, we could call, "Do over!" during our games, thereby erasing the mistake and starting the activity again. I wish I could subject my bad decisions as an adult to the same "Do over" rule. Instead, I must face the consequences and the regrets of my impulsive, selfish, or wrong choices. Help me to lean on you. Give me the wisdom I need to make better choices in the future.

We must not fall into the confusion of mistaking normal aloneness, which is intended to draw us to God, with loneliness.
—EUGENIA PRICE (1916–1996), AMERICAN AUTHOR

MARCH 6
A Lovely Rose

You must be holy in everything you do, just as God who chose you is holy. For the Scriptures say, "You must be holy because I am holy." 1 PETER 1:15-16

On the other side of Kerri's community, another young woman, Linda, was dressing for her day as well and smiling as she thought about meeting her old roommate for lunch. Linda was looking forward to catching up on personal news, but she sighed as she thought about her former roomie's usual inquiry about the guy in the shipping department: "So, have you slept with him yet?"

Linda's coworkers didn't help matters with their Monday-morning accounts of their latest "conquests" or of weekend trips with their boyfriends. But she'd seen the wistfulness in some of their faces when she said she was saving herself for her future husband. Often she even quoted to them the first part of Psalm 37:7: "Be still in the presence of the LORD, and wait patiently for him to act." Then within her mind, she would quote the rest of the verse: "Don't worry about evil people who prosper." Linda always substituted the words *when coworkers succeed in their ways*.

Linda understands God wasn't being a killjoy when he set his guidelines; rather, he wants to offer something better than immediate and temporary solutions. Besides, he knows the human heart and understands the agony behind the sad words *if only* and *I wish*. In those moments when Linda is tempted to trade tomorrow's peace for today's gratification, she remembers the visual aid her ninth-grade Sunday school teacher offered before the big freshman dance. He had called all the boys to the front row, then handed the one closest to him an exquisite red rose with the instruction, "Pull one petal and pass it on."

Bewildered, each boy plucked a beautiful petal and then passed the flower to his classmate. When the last petal was taken and only the stem remained, the teacher had looked at the lad holding the barren rose and said, "Congratulations. That's your wife." Several of the students, boys as well as girls, gasped.

Even many years later, Linda was determined not to be that type of rose.

—SANDRA

Lord, the rose illustration is too dramatic for my tastes. But if it caused Linda and her classmates to think instead of being pulled into wrong decisions, then it was effective. So, help me to make decisions that will not cause pain to me or to others. Help me to seek your direction before I act.

There's nothing wrong with being tempted. It's what we do with the temptation that matters. —LEONARD E. LESOURD, PUBLISHER AND AUTHOR

MARCH 7
A Strong Weapon

Since [Jesus] himself has gone through suffering and testing,
he is able to help us when we are being tested.   HEBREWS 2:18

Linda has another weapon in her fight against temptation: She understands being
tempted is not the issue; how she chooses to respond to the temptation is. *After all,*
she reminds herself, *even the Lord himself was tempted.* And since he understands
her struggles, Linda has decided the best thing she can do is talk to him about
them. Daily she asks for continued strength, godliness, and faith that the Lord will
bring the right spouse into her life at the right time. In the meantime, she has
learned five important things about prayer:

- Prayer is our recognition of our dependence on God.
- Prayer restores our relationship to God.
- Prayer releases God's power.
- Prayer gives us God's peace.
- Prayer allows God either to change the situation or to change us.

Linda has chosen wisely. By inviting the Lord into every struggle, even the sexual
ones, she has a better chance to make good choices. And that's a wise choice for
all of us. From struggle and conflict we can gain a spiritual discipline that will
greatly strengthen our faith and establish our spiritual character.
—SANDRA

> Lord, I'm prone to try to fight my battles against temptation alone
> and to forget the greatest weapon I possess is prayer. Help me
> to remember to ask for your help when I'm tempted rather than
> ask you to bail me out of trouble later.

Temptation is necessary to settle and confirm us in the spiritual life.
—MRS. CHARLES E. COWMAN (1870–1960), MISSIONARY TO CHINA AND JAPAN AND AUTHOR

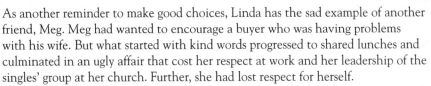

MARCH 8
Avoiding Trouble

If we confess our sins to him, he is faithful and just to forgive us our sins and to cleanse us from all wickedness. 1 JOHN 1:9

As another reminder to make good choices, Linda has the sad example of another friend, Meg. Meg had wanted to encourage a buyer who was having problems with his wife. But what started with kind words progressed to shared lunches and culminated in an ugly affair that cost her respect at work and her leadership of the singles' group at her church. Further, she had lost respect for herself.

One evening over dinner, Linda gave a depressed Meg the embroidered wall hanging Meg had often admired. The delicately fashioned words read:

Lord, I have a problem; it's me.
Child, I have an answer; it's me.

Stunned by the lovely gift, Meg burst into tears. Linda handed over a tissue, then patiently waited as her friend dried her tears.

After yet another sniff, Meg asked, "So what now? I'm such a loser."

Linda handed her another tissue. "This is where 1 John 1:9 comes in. It says, 'If we confess our sins to him, he is faithful and just to forgive our sins and to cleanse us from all wickedness.' And it says *all* wickedness. Not some. *All.*"

Meg blew her nose again. "Yeah, but I'm damaged goods now."

"You are *not* bound by past decisions. Starting today, you can make good choices and a commitment to get back to a virtuous lifestyle."

For the next several minutes Linda talked quietly about redirecting sexual energy into work, sports, creative productivity, or other wholesome activities. Then, further stressing the possibility of living a fulfilled life without a present physical relationship, she offered Meg practical advice:

- Plan ahead to avoid inappropriate dating situations.
- Avoid movies that will stir up longings.
- Avoid reading sensuous books or magazines.
- Stay out of the "Adult" corner of the video store.
- Work hard and go to bed tired.

Linda motioned toward the wall hanging. "God is the answer to our biggest problem. This is a new beginning. Better days *are* ahead for you."

Meg was beginning to believe it was true. —SANDRA

Lord, thank you for the reminder that while I am often my biggest problem, you are greater than anything I allow into my life. Help me to make decisions that will reap good results now and in the future.

There are no two ways around it: Women must have more dimension in their lives than "loooove!" —DR. LAURA SCHLESSINGER, SOCIAL AND CONSERVATIVE COMMENTATOR

MARCH 9
Other Opportunities

Because of the weakness of your human nature, I am using the illustration of slavery to help you understand all this. Previously, you let yourselves be slaves to impurity and lawlessness, which led ever deeper into sin. Now you must give yourselves to be slaves to righteous living so that you will become holy.   ROMANS 6:19

One of Linda's suggestions to help Meg reclaim a righteous lifestyle was to plan ahead to avoid inappropriate dating situations. In my high school home economics class, we had a unit on dating, to get us to think *before* the date. What if we applied some of that think-ahead mentality to our present relationships? If you're thinking about dating, perhaps my list of what *not* to look for in a man will help you compile your own list:

- Never date a man who isn't serious about the Lord.
- If you are a single mother, never date a man who doesn't like children, especially yours.
- Never date a man who makes fun of your cultural background, Southern or otherwise.
- Never date a man who is always borrowing money from you.
- Never date a man who says his boss or mother or first wife didn't understand him.
- Never date a man who says you'll never be as good a cook as his mama was.
- Never date a man who calls you by his dog's name.
- Never date a man who drinks—especially if he says he can "handle" his liquor.
- Never date a man who is rude to salespeople or restaurant workers.
- Never date a man who brags about cutting corners on his taxes.

And my favorite: Never date a man who wears a belt buckle embossed with "Hello, Darlin'."   —SANDRA

Lord, I chuckle as I read this silly list. But it does make me think about the specific qualities I want in a date and future husband. I don't want to desperately accept just anyone who meanders by, so help me to make my own list. And help me to talk over each point with you.

Whether it concerns her own life or the lives of others, the thinking Christian woman knows her thoughts, words and actions have eternal consequences. It is that knowledge that motivates her to evaluate all areas of her life in light of God's eternal values rather than the temporal ones of this world.   —HELEN K. HOSIER

MARCH 10
Other Challenges

> You will show me the way of life, granting me the joy of your
> presence and the pleasures of living with you forever.
> PSALM 16:11

I'm saddened by women who stay in bad relationships, the entire time telling
themselves things will get better. They seldom do.

I learned that not from a relationship but from an autumn walk. I had driven
my two children to school and decided to walk home, leaving the car for my return
walk. I looked across the field to my right and decided to take the shortcut. Soon
my shoes and socks were wet from the dew. The grass was deeper than I had
thought, but it surely wouldn't get any deeper. I'd keep going.

After a few feet, the field sloped. The grass that had looked only ankle deep
from the parking lot was now up to my knees.

I paused, looking at the grass ahead. *My shoes, socks, and slacks are already
soaked,* I thought. *It can't get any worse.* In less than a dozen steps, however, the
grass was over my head! I slogged ahead, feeling as if I were fighting through the
jungle in some B movie.

I'd gone too far now to go back. The worst was over. A few more steps, and
I'd be across the field. Sure enough, as I plunged ahead, the grass got shorter. It was
at my waist, then my knees, and finally just over my shoes. I was free!

My rejoicing was short-lived. Ahead was a deep, mud-filled gully. I studied
the muddy slopes that would be impossible to conquer. In a moment of wild Tarzan
fantasy, I surveyed the large tree nearby, looking for a vine on which I could swing
over. Nothing.

I looked back at the grassy field. I didn't want to claw my way through that
again. *Surely I can climb this tree someway and—no, they'll never find my body before
spring.*

I could do nothing but go back through that scary, wet grass. I drove home
then, but in much worse shape than if I'd taken the long way in the first place.

Some good did come out of that experience: Now when I'm tempted to take
what looks like the easy way out, I give the situation another look. And that second look has saved me from numerous difficulties.   —SANDRA

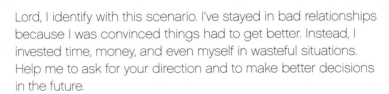

Lord, I identify with this scenario. I've stayed in bad relationships
because I was convinced things had to get better. Instead, I
invested time, money, and even myself in wasteful situations.
Help me to ask for your direction and to make better decisions
in the future.

In our relationship with God, the problem isn't that he doesn't speak; it's that we
are often unwilling to listen.
—SANDRA D. WILSON, RETIRED FAMILY THERAPIST, SEMINARY PROFESSOR, AND AUTHOR

MARCH 11
Deliberate Thoughts

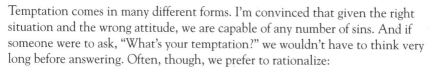

[Jesus said,] "The hearts of these people are hardened, and their ears cannot hear, and they have closed their eyes—so their eyes cannot see, and their ears cannot hear, and their hearts cannot understand, and they cannot turn to me and let me heal them."
MATTHEW 13:15

Temptation comes in many different forms. I'm convinced that given the right situation and the wrong attitude, we are capable of any number of sins. And if someone were to ask, "What's your temptation?" we wouldn't have to think very long before answering. Often, though, we prefer to rationalize:

- The gambler thinks the next bet will make up for all of her previous losses.
- The alcoholic says he can "hold his liquor" or can stop whenever he wants to.
- The addict viewing Internet porn tells himself that at least he's not visiting prostitutes.
- The gossip whispers about her neighbors and says she's offering warnings or sharing "prayer requests."
- The shoplifter convinces herself the item she took was overpriced anyway.
- The secretary pockets office supplies to balance her low salary.
- The taxpayer cheats the government and says everybody does it.
- The event planner ridicules fresh ideas because it's "never been done that way."
- The traveler watches X-rated movies in the hotel room because no one knows.

The list goes on and on. What if we stopped trying to rationalize our sins? What if our first prayer of the morning began, "Lord, this day is yours. I am yours. Help me to live in the light of that truth." What if we actually lived what we say we believe? What a difference that would make in this sad world—and in our own lives.
—SANDRA

Lord, why do I make living the Christian life so difficult? If I thought about my actions and my words instead of giving in to impulses, life would be calmer. So, help me to think before I act. Help me to bite my tongue instead of mouthing off. And may I invite you into every situation.

Every thought we think, in every hour we live, must be not necessarily about Christ, but it must be the thought Christ would think were He placed in our circumstances and subject to our conditions. This is what it means really to feed on Him and be nourished by the true Bread of Life that cometh down from heaven.
—HANNAH WHITALL SMITH (1832–1911), QUAKER LAY SPEAKER AND AUTHOR

To Ponder with a Friend

1. If you could rewind the tape of a particular day, what different decision would you make now?

2. Which situations do you feel you have handled well?

3. Which situations present a continuing struggle?

4. What advice do you have for family or friends who may be struggling with how not to give in to impulses?

MARCH 12
Don't Put Off Joy

> This is the day the LORD has made. We will rejoice and be glad in it. PSALM 118:24

My neighbor Sally had high expectations about how her life was to proceed. She had four active kids, a husband who worked long hours, and twenty postpregnancy pounds she couldn't get rid of. "When I lose this weight, then I'll be happy," she'd tell me. "And when these kids grow up and stop being so messy, I'll get new carpeting and keep the house cleaner!"

Unfortunately, as long as I knew Sally, things never got good enough, and she kept putting off joy until some far-off day. If, like Sally, you think joy will come when you lose weight or land that great job you want, when your kids shape up or your marriage improves, that day may never arrive. There's nothing wrong with these goals, but if you stake your joy on having those things happen, you may find yourself perpetually frustrated and may miss out on the very blessings God has for you in *this season* and *this day*. We can't control our circumstances or change the past, but we *can* choose our attitude. We can see the life we have today as a gift, no matter what challenges we are facing, and choose to live it to the fullest.

Anyone can sing when the sun is shining and the living is easy. But you and I have reason to sing in the dark when the clouds of trials descend on us, for we belong to Christ and he is with us in those trials. That's why we can choose joy in the midst of uncertainty and in situations that aren't ideal. A good place to start is to rehearse today's verse each morning: "This is the day the LORD has made. [I] will rejoice and be glad in it." Then ask for the grace to do just that.   —CHERI

> My Lord and my God, this truly is the day you have made. You have not promised me tomorrow upon tomorrow in which I can experience joy. You have given me the gift of the moment, the gift of today. May I rejoice in that gift and in you.

We're like a child standing in a beautiful park with his eyes shut tight. We don't need to imagine trees, flowers, deer, birds, and sky; we merely need to open our eyes and realize what is already here, who we really are.   —UNKNOWN

MARCH 13
Celebrate the Gift of Today

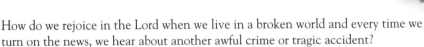

I am overwhelmed with joy in the LORD my God!
ISAIAH 61:10

How do we rejoice in the Lord when we live in a broken world and every time we turn on the news, we hear about another awful crime or tragic accident?

On my refrigerator is a card that says, "Celebrate today! I came that you might have life abundantly!" It's a reminder to me that in the darkest of times I can find something to celebrate. If it's rainy, I can celebrate the fact that I don't have to water the garden on a scorching Oklahoma day. I can celebrate a phone call from a friend or the richness of God's Word as I read it before I go to sleep. Each day is a gift, and although on some days it may take some thought, there is always something to rejoice about.

One of my favorite poems by William Wordsworth begins,

> My heart leaps up when I behold
> A rainbow in the sky:
> So it was when my life began,
> So is it now I am a man,
> So be it when I shall grow old
> Or let me die!

What makes your heart leap? What makes you want to jump for joy? Whatever it is, go do it. If it's flying a kite, then head for the park on a windy day. As you let the string out, you can consciously release your worries and burdens to God. If it's classic art, stroll through an art museum and let yourself be transported to another time or place. If it's service that touches your joy button, volunteer in your community, and you'll find your smile coming back.

When we look for the miraculous in every day—a sunrise heralding a fresh day filled with God's mercies (see Lamentations 3:23), the miracle of salvation and forgiveness, a child's giggle, even an angelic visitation—our hearts will leap up, wonder will fill our minds, and joy *will* flood our souls.   —CHERI

Jesus, help me to look for the miraculous in this day and season. Open my eyes to the reasons for joy so that I can celebrate life in all its fullness. Thank you for the life abundant you have graciously given us.

Every day brings a chance for you to draw in a breath, kick off your shoes, and dance.   —OPRAH WINFREY, TALK-SHOW HOST

MARCH 14

Radiant Joyfulness

Those who look to [the LORD] for help will be radiant with joy; no shadow of shame will darken their faces. . . . Oh, the joys of those who take refuge in him! PSALM 34:5, 8

Twice in these two verses we see the word *joy* connected to the act of trusting. This kind of joy indwells and encompasses a woman and leads her to exclaim, "Oh, the joy!" even in the midst of suffering, frustration, or uncertainty. Throughout the Bible, God promises his people joy—not happiness, which is based on circumstances—but the ability to rejoice in his very nature and presence no matter what the circumstances are. In Psalm 16:11, for example, he says he will grant us the joy of his presence, which is a foretaste of the pleasure we will experience when we live with him forever. In today's verses God offers not just a momentary lightness but radiant joy.

Perhaps, like me, you've met people who seem to have a special radiance about them, whether it's evident in their words, in their actions, or simply in their very presence. After spending time with them, we walk away with not only curiosity about how they live in such shining, luminous joy but a desire to know and experience it for ourselves.

How can we radiate this kind of joy in the Lord? By looking for signs of God's hand throughout the day, by seeking to know more of him, and by meditating on the wonder of his works instead of on the hassles and trials of this life. Once our perspective has shifted, we look with expectancy for ways he shows himself trustworthy, and when we see them, we find our fulfillment in him and are filled with joy.   —CHERI

Dear Lord, help me to look to you and trust in you today, and may my own life be radiant with your joy. Thank you for the joy we experience on earth as a taste of the wild joy yet to come.

Joy has something within itself that is beyond happiness and sorrow. This something is called blessedness. . . . It makes the joy of life possible in pleasure and pain, in happiness and unhappiness, in ecstasy and sorrow. Where there is joy, there is fulfillment. And where there is fulfillment, there is joy.
—PAUL TILLICH (1886–1965), GERMAN AMERICAN THEOLOGIAN AND PHILOSOPHER

MARCH 15
Finding Joy in Small Things

Fix your thoughts on what is true, and honorable, and right, and pure, and lovely, and admirable. Think about things that are excellent and worthy of praise.   PHILIPPIANS 4:8

I once stayed at a small house near the beach for a week. I had imagined myself walking along a lovely stretch of sand and soaking in the beautiful sights, sounds, and smells of the ocean. What I found was entirely different: Miles of black, stinky seaweed lined the beach. I couldn't think about the blessings and excellent things in God's creation because my focus was on that seaweed. In fact, on the first day, I shortened my beach walk because I just couldn't take any more of the smell. The second day, I was so frustrated because the beach crew hadn't cleaned up the seaweed that I didn't even notice the clear blue sky and the warmth of the sun. The next morning I went out and was annoyed that the odorous stuff was *still* lying on the beach for as far as I could see.

Then, a few hundred yards away I saw a father and son making a terrific sand castle, surrounded, of course, by the seaweed. But it didn't seem to dampen their creativity and fun. I realized in that moment that I had a choice. I could let my joy be diminished by the seaweed, or I could lift my gaze in another direction. As I did, I noticed fish jumping up out of the glittering water. The sun warmed my face. My steps lightened as a cool breeze of thankfulness blew through me. The seaweed was still there. It just wasn't taking my full attention because my focus was somewhere else.

Maybe you have some "seaweed" in your life right now: an unexpected sickness, a job loss, a difficult person or some other conflict. God wants you to look up and beyond what is obvious and to think about the things he's put around you that are lovely, excellent, and worthy of praise, things he has given you to lighten your steps: a hummingbird outside your window, good health, a dazzling sunset, your salvation and freedom in Christ. Fix your gaze on those good things, and you'll find renewed joy and your day redeemed, even if the "stinky seaweed" doesn't go away.
—CHERI

Lord, grant me eyes to see the beautiful, the excellent, the things all around me that are worthy of my notice and my gratitude to you.

The heart that finds joy in small things, in all things each day is a wonderful gift.
—UNKNOWN

MARCH 16
His Joy Is Our Strength

The people had all been weeping as they listened to the words
of the Law. And Nehemiah continued, "Go and celebrate with
a feast of rich foods and sweet drinks, and share gifts of food with
people who have nothing prepared. This is a sacred day before our
Lord. Don't be dejected and sad, for the joy of the Lord is your
strength!" NEHEMIAH 8:9-10

Nehemiah wasn't exactly home free when he instructed God's people to dry their
tears and go celebrate with a great feast. Although they had just completed the
work of rebuilding Jerusalem's walls, against fierce odds, Nehemiah still faced
enormous challenges as he endeavored to reorder the people's social, spiritual,
and economic lives. They had been through a tumultuous time and still faced
fierce enemies and many struggles. Having just heard the reading of God's law,
they wept bitter tears of repentance, aware of their great sin.

God knew that Nehemiah and his people would need *strength* for the struggles ahead and that strength was to be found as they learned to experience the
Lord's joy in the midst of their reality. Someone once said that if Satan can steal
your joy, he will get your strength, your hope, and everything else. But if you refuse
to let him rob you of joy, if you keep rejoicing in God, praising him, and looking to
him, then you can't be defeated.

The enemy intends to remove the joy from our lives and uses negative circumstances and thoughts, other people, and frightening news on television. That's
why Jesus told us that in this world full of tribulation and trouble, we can be of
good cheer. He knew that although we might lose a few battles, he has already won
the war. He has overcome the world (see John 16:33). In affliction or suffering, in
good times or bad, the joy of the Lord is our strength, and his promise is our greatest source of joy: "I have told you these things so that you will be filled with my joy.
Yes, your joy will overflow!" (John 15:11). Hallelujah!   —CHERI

> Father, forgive me for the times when I have let circumstances
> get me down and allowed the enemy to steal my joy. As I put my
> focus on you and obeying your Word, I ask you to restore my joy
> in you and let it strengthen me this day.

It is the consciousness of the threefold joy of the Lord, His joy in ransoming
us, His joy in dwelling within us as our Saviour and Power for fruitbearing, and
His joy in possessing us, as His Bride and His delight; it is the consciousness
of this joy which is our real strength. Our joy in Him may be a fluctuating thing:
His joy in us knows no change.
—J. HUDSON TAYLOR (1832–1905), BRITISH MISSIONARY TO CHINA AND FOUNDER OF THE
CHINA INLAND MISSION

The Joy of Following God

You will show me the way of life, granting me the joy of your presence and the pleasures of living with you forever.
PSALM 16:11

What does this psalm say you get when you follow God? *Joy!* There is delight in doing what God wants because only then are we doing what we were created to do. We are accomplishing our purpose. We are operating from the gifts he put within us. We are following the counsel of an all-knowing God and experiencing the countless benefits that come with that. We're not harming others and being eaten alive with guilt. We're not continually embarrassing ourselves (and those who love us) with our behavior.

But how in the world can we do what the Lord wants? By surrendering to him and immersing ourselves in his Word. When we do, we will begin to delight in doing what God has planned. Thinking about his law and his ways brings true joy, not only to *our* hearts but to *God's* heart as well. And that joy is contagious, for when those around us see God's joy in us, we won't be able to keep *them* away from *him.* —CHERI

More than anything in this world, Lord, I want to make you happy. I want to do and be all that you planned when you created me. It's your counsel I want to follow, your side I want to be on, and your heart I ask you to shape in mine. Help me to continually think of you and the words you wrote, that I might experience your joy. May I be a source of joy to your heart.

Joy is the most infallible sign of the presence of God.
—LEON HENRI MARIE BLOY (1846–1917), FRENCH NOVELIST, ESSAYIST, AND POET

MARCH 18
The Joy of Serving Others

You have been called to live in freedom, my brothers and sisters.
But don't use your freedom to satisfy your sinful nature. Instead, use
your freedom to serve one another in love.   GALATIANS 5:13

Some time ago I met a woman who lives with a contagious attitude of celebration,
joy, and generosity of spirit. Although she is a busy mother of three and a nurse
who works with critically ill patients, she has made time in the last few years for
three medical mission trips to the poorest parts of Mexico and the Amazon River
in South America. Whenever there is a tornado or other crisis, she sets up first-aid
stations in the affected community. In her spare time, she teaches classes in life-
saving CPR for the American Red Cross.

You might think this woman would at least take a break in the summer! But
for ten years she's served as a camp nurse for two hundred children and also
launched a clown ministry with the youth group she leads. In her forties, she has
tackled rock climbing and embarked on mountain-climbing adventures with the
Sierra Club. What is Peggy's secret to living a joyful, adventurous life?

"The size of your world is the size of your heart" is her motto. Peggy has
discovered that her heart is happiest when she's reaching out, not being self-
absorbed. She finds joy in *giving her life away, not in keeping it*: by bringing medical
care to "the least of these" who could never afford to pay her or the team back, by
serving people in her community, by cheering chronically ill kids at camp. Jesus
said something important about this: When we are willing to lose our lives for his
sake, we really find life (see Matthew 10:39; 16:25; Mark 8:35; Luke 9:24). Then
the joy that we give to others is the joy that comes back to us. Where would God
want you and me to give our lives away? Who around us needs a cup of cold water
or the benefit of the skills or resources that God has entrusted to us?
—CHERI

Lord Jesus, I can get so absorbed with "me, myself, and I" that
I forget there is a world of hurt out there and scores of people
who are needy. Forgive me for trying to "keep" my life instead of
being willing to share it. You said the fields are white for harvest
and the laborers are few. Show me the fields in which you want
me to serve. And may I experience your joy as I serve others in
your name.

I think we can do something which will cause the shortness of life to work in our
behalf, rather than against us. We can give our lives away! As the commercial
suggests, we can "reach out and touch someone." Instead of holing up in our own
four-square world, we can strive to be characterized by generosity.
—LUCI SWINDOLL, SPEAKER AND AUTHOR

To Ponder with a Friend

1. How do you define—and experience—real joy? Share an experience you've had that has produced sheer joy in your heart.

2. What hinders you from celebrating the gift of life *today*? What one or two things have you been hoping will change or get better so that you'll be happier?

3. Some of the biggest joy busters and happiness drainers are worry and anxiety. Identify and, if you feel comfortable doing so, share a "care" (burden, worry) you could give up to God today, lightening your load and thus increasing your capacity for joy. (See 1 Peter 5:7.)

4. What could you do to experience the joy of giving your life away by reaching out to meet someone else's need, as Luci Swindoll suggests in the devotional for March 18?

MARCH 19
Choosing Right Actions

A gentle answer deflects anger, but harsh words make tempers flare.
PROVERBS 15:1

Susan was everyone's friend and rescuer. If a friend needed someone to look after his dog while he was out of town, he called her. If a coworker needed to practice her Monday-morning office presentation, she called Susan. If a nephew needed a tutor for Spanish class, he called Susan. In fact, the people around Susan were so used to having her meet their every need, they resented her interest in a young assistant pastor who had asked her to dinner after they met while visiting a hospitalized mutual friend.

As time went on, though, the people who had grown to depend on Susan began to work out their own problems when they realized she was no longer in the rescue business. What made the difference? Susan's quiet apologies, presented without explanation when she wasn't available.

Amy, another young woman, also was drawn into every "crisis" her extended family experienced, whether it was the birth of new kittens or the breakup of yet another relationship. Each time the phone rang with another plea for help, Amy found herself getting more and more angry as she wondered, *Why do they insist that their crises have to become mine?* That anger boiled over during a tense moment at the rehearsal for her niece's wedding. When Amy's older sister snapped at her for having forgotten extra batteries for the video camera, Amy retorted she was tired of being responsible for the details of their lives. As she stormed out, she demanded none of them *ever* call her again. Obviously, she created more problems for herself than she solved.

These two young women responded to the demands of others in different ways and with different results.

Knowing when to say yes and when to say no can be tough. After all, we can't carry every responsibility. Sometimes we will need to gently nudge those who are too dependent on us to seek greater maturity. Other times, life will hand us moments when the only decent decision we can make is to drop everything and help another person. But whatever our decision, often the greatest help will come from our soft answer.   —SANDRA

> Yes, Lord, I get it. There's been only one Messiah—you—and I'm not a second one. So give me your wisdom when the people around me demand rescue. May I hear your direction and not their accusations. And no matter what my answer is, may I present it gently and with love.

A true friend will not always agree with you, but will be true to your best interests.
—NICOLE BEALE, AUTHOR

MARCH 20
A Welcoming Glance

> O LORD, do not stay far away! You are my strength; come quickly
> to my aid! PSALM 22:19

The story is told of the third president of the United States, Thomas Jefferson, who was traveling on horseback with his entourage. Rain had fallen for several days, so they were looking for a place to cross a swollen river. At last they came to a narrow place that looked safe between the two muddy banks.

As the group approached the water, a man stood up from under the tree where he was huddled. With rain dripping into his eyes, he looked into the face of each man. President Jefferson was near the end of the line, and it was to him the man directed this question: "Please, sir, may I ride across the river behind you?"

The president nodded and then held out his arm so the man could swing up onto his sturdy horse. As the party crossed safely to the other side, the man slid off the animal and graciously thanked his benefactor.

As the man started to walk away, one of President Jefferson's companions called to him. "Tell me, how is it you *dared* to ask to ride across the river behind the President of the United States?"

The man looked stricken. "Oh, sir, forgive me." Then he turned to his accuser. "I didn't know he is the president. But as all of you approached, I looked at each one. I saw *no* in your faces, but I saw *yes* in his."

What do people see in *our* faces? Indeed, there will be times when we need to drop everything to take a panicked mother into our car so we can follow the ambulance to the emergency room. We may need to welcome the children of the young woman who is taking her husband for chemotherapy.

But there will be other times we will need to say to a fretting friend, "I'm sorry, but I can't pick out new shoes with you."

Often, the only way to find the balance between what we truly need to do and what we feel compelled to do is to ask for the Lord's help each day. As we listen, his quiet instructions may arrive through a fresh insight, a creative thought, or the reminder that our gentle expression and gracious words can soften a necessary rejection. —SANDRA

> Lord, thank you for the reminder that your divine nature often
> is seen in our human faces. Even when I can't be or do what
> others expect, may they still feel loved.

The thread of our life would be dark, Heaven knows, if it were not with friendship and love intertwined. —THOMAS MOORE (1779–1852), IRISH POET

Martha's Example

> [Martha's] sister, Mary, sat at the Lord's feet, listening to what he taught. But Martha was distracted by the big dinner she was preparing. She came to Jesus and said, "Lord, doesn't it seem unfair to you that my sister just sits here while I do all the work? Tell her to come and help me." LUKE 10:39-40

Do you groan as you make your daily to-do list? I do. But what if we stopped complaining about that long list and instead saw it as a signal to cut a few projects? Better yet, what if we saw it as an invitation to lighten up?

We've heard sermons from Luke 10 about Martha's grumbling because the food preparation was left to her while her sister, Mary, calmly listened to Jesus' stories. I can imagine Martha storming into the scene with shoulders twitching and head jerking as she demanded that the Lord send Mary to the kitchen to help. Instead, he answered, "My dear Martha, you are worried and upset over all these details!" (Luke 10:41).

As a Southern woman who grew up with the cooking philosophy of "Honey, I'd rather have a bushel too much as a teaspoon not enough," I understand Martha's fussing. Surely she was originally from *southern* Jerusalem and was preparing three meats, nine vegetables, and at least two breads, one of which had to be Middle Eastern *cornbread*. Was she, like many of us, trying to impress him with all of her hard work on his behalf? Yes, Jesus needed a meal, but it didn't have to be as elaborate and nerve racking as the one Martha undoubtedly was preparing.

When it comes down to it, Martha's problem was not in her *serving* the meal but in her *attitude* toward serving. We know this is true because we see her serving again in John 12:2, after her brother, Lazarus, was raised from the dead, and this time the Lord did not reprimand her. Apparently she had taken to heart his earlier words. Or perhaps losing her brother to death for even those four days put life into the proper perspective. Either way, she no longer was stomping around the kitchen, complaining about the work.

That's a good reminder for all of us. —SANDRA

> Lord, I happen to like Martha. In fact, I'm convinced no home, business, or church can function well without at least one such person. But her perfectionism and need to control caused her to be unpleasant, even overbearing. Help me to understand that listening to you is a wonderful privilege. And help me to complete necessary tasks to your realistic standards rather than to my own without being demanding and critical.

The higher and truer knowledge we have of the goodness and unselfishness of God, the less anxiety, and fuss, and wrestling, and agonizing, will there be in one's worship. —HANNAH WHITALL SMITH (1832–1911), QUAKER LAY SPEAKER AND AUTHOR

MARCH 22
An Important Question

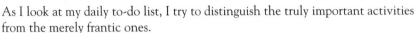

> When Jesus saw [the sick man] and knew he had been ill for
> a long time, he asked him, "Would you like to get well?"
> JOHN 5:6

As I look at my daily to-do list, I try to distinguish the truly important activities
from the merely frantic ones.

To do that, I remind myself of what I call the John 5 Principle. It was the
account of the healing at the pool near Jerusalem's Sheep Gate, sometimes called
"the pool of five porches," that helped me get over my own worried-Martha hostess
style. Around this pool gathered numerous people who believed the stirring of the
water signaled healing. Into this scene strode Jesus, who went to *one* man to heal
him. That means he walked past all those other people with legitimate needs to go
to only one person. Let women like Martha and me loose in a scene like that, and
we would feel as if we had failed unless every person had been healed.

When Jesus approached the man who had been an invalid for thirty-eight
years, he asked him an important question: "Would you like to get well?" I find it
fascinating the man didn't answer yes and he didn't answer no. Instead he said, in
effect, "It's not my fault," as he replied, "I have no one to put me into the pool
when the water bubbles up. Someone else always gets there ahead of me" (John
5:7).

Isn't it interesting that Jesus didn't argue with the paralyzed man? He wins
people, not arguments. But in verse 8 he told the man to take action: "Stand up,
pick up your mat, and walk!"

Yes, sometimes Jesus invites us to sit at his feet and listen to his quiet teach-
ings. Other times he gives us specific instructions for action. As we learn to listen
to him, we will know what action or nonaction to take.   —SANDRA

> Lord, how easy it is for me to blame others for all of my
> problems. I remember their bad decisions, their harsh words,
> their disapproving looks. But as I concentrate on all of those
> things, I become an emotional invalid. So, help me to make the
> decision to carry my own mat of responsibility. Help me to walk
> toward the hope-filled future you have for me.

We cannot please God without a faith that helps us to walk with God, an active
faith.   —MATTHEW HENRY (1662–1714), ENGLISH CLERGYMAN

MARCH 23
Holding the Course

I don't mean to say that I have already achieved these things or that I have already reached perfection. But I press on to possess that perfection for which Christ Jesus first possessed me.
PHILIPPIANS 3:12

Have you ever signed on for something and then in the middle of it decided the assignment was tedious, difficult, a mistake? Join the club.

What should we do when we hit those tough times? First, we should pray, asking for direction and insight. The most profound prayer we can ever offer is just one word: "Help!"

As we ponder what brought us to this tough place, if we discover it was rebellion or sin, it's time to confess that to the Lord and then get out of there.

If we're in the place where we need to be but we're in over our heads, we may have to ask a supervisor for clarification or seek extra training.

But if we're merely disappointed because things aren't going the way we hoped, thought, and prayed they would, it's time to analyze what we need to do. Sometimes we need to work longer hours. Sometimes we need a fresh reminder of our calling. Sometimes we just need to get over ourselves.

I remember times when I thought, *This isn't the way I thought it would be.* In fact, at one job I kept two yellow sticky notes in my top desk drawer and read them every morning. The first note held a quotation by nineteenth-century evangelist Dwight L. Moody: "Don't doubt in the dark what God has shown you in the light." The other simply said, "It's always too soon to quit." Both were good reminders to take a deep breath and tackle the task at hand.   —SANDRA

Lord, sometimes assignments, relationships, tasks, and even life itself are just too difficult. Lately, I feel like a child trying to climb an ice mountain. Just about the time I think I have solid footing, I slip into some scary crevasse. So here I am again, asking for your direction. Help me to recognize the situations I need to leave. And for those responsibilities that have come directly from you, give me the strength to see them through.

It is folly to believe God liberates us from all discomfort and affliction. What He does do is give us the will and determination to go on, even in the face of tough times. He works within us to give us peace and strength and courage; those things necessary to get through life. We can be sure that our trials will not come to an end, but the love of God will see that we get through anything that comes our way.
—DAN R. DICK, AUTHOR

MARCH 24
A Better Response

Fix your thoughts on what is true, and honorable, and right, and pure, and lovely, and admirable. Think about things that are excellent and worthy of praise. PHILIPPIANS 4:8

Emma and Clara are twins. Both are nurses at the local emergency room, Emma on the night shift and Clara on the day shift. Both are tall, have bright red hair and perfect teeth, and are generously built. But that's where the similarities end.

If faced with the proverbial eight-ounce glass holding four ounces of water, Emma would flash her gorgeous smile and say, "Why, anybody can see the glass is half full."

Clara, on the other hand, would say, "Look, I've got better things to do than answer silly questions about half-empty smeared glasses. I hope you aren't planning to drink out of that."

On their hospital shifts, Emma's most common statement is a soothing "Now, don't you worry. We're going to take good care of you." Clara's comment is more apt to be "Well, you've really done it this time, haven't you?"

Which nurse would you rather meet if you needed medical help?

These young women were raised in the same household by parents who emphasized the harshness of the world into which they were born. Both made early choices to go into nursing to help ease some of that harshness. But it was Emma who turned to the Bible for help during their tough RN training. As she read the command in Philippians 4:8 to think on "excellent and praiseworthy" things, she found her response to be life changing. And with that change came opportunities to encourage those around her.

I wonder, *How would our lives and the lives of those around us change if we made the same decision?* —SANDRA

Lord, you know I'm more of a glass-half-empty person. How can I not be when I see all the problems? The constant threat of terrorism, repercussions from global warming, starvation in developing countries, and hunger and abuse in my own city make me want to give up. But that's not a good solution. So help me to do what I can do to make this a better world and to brighten the world of those around me. Maybe, just maybe, if enough of us decide to make a little difference, we'll find we've made a big difference.

It is not because things are good, but because He is good that we are to thank the Lord. —HANNAH WHITALL SMITH (1832–1911), QUAKER LAY SPEAKER AND AUTHOR

MARCH 25
Facing Tough Times

I have fought the good fight, I have finished the race, and I have remained faithful.   2 TIMOTHY 4:7

When I know I'm on the right path but I'm discouraged with how things are going, I remind myself of this story: A worker wanted to know the secret of success, so she went to the remote home of an expert in her field. She knew he was known for terse answers, so she quickly expressed her longing and asked, "Where do I find success?"

He didn't speak but pointed to his right. She hurried toward that area only to be met with a mud hole. *Splat*—in she fell!

She pulled herself up, limped back to the expert, and said, "I must have misunderstood. Let me ask again: Where is the success I seek?"

Again he merely pointed toward the right. This time the mud hole was bigger. *Splat!* She tried to stand up. *Splat! Splat!*

Now she dragged one foot as she went back to the great professional. With tears running down her face, she said, "Please talk to me. Twice I've asked you where I can find success. Twice you've sent me off that way. And twice I've met nothing but *splat*. I must know. *Where* is the success I seek?"

This time the expert looked at her for a long moment, then said, "All you seek is just beyond splat."

So remember: If we are in the right place, what we seek is often just beyond the tough assignment.   —SANDRA

Lord, this is a story to which I can relate because I know that mud hole all too well. Help me to move past the "splat" areas of my life and into your victories. Help me to realize the setbacks are temporary. Encourage me to keep going when I'd rather just whimper and quit.

Every moment of our lives we are faced with spiritual hazards, and at the same time with spiritual opportunities.   —ELISABETH ELLIOT, MISSIONARY, AUTHOR, AND SPEAKER

To Ponder with a Friend

1. Do you ever feel pulled in too many directions? Why or why not?

2. Do you ever feel as if family and friends expect too much of you? If so, how do you handle that pressure?

3. In what areas of your life do you need to apply the lesson of John 5 as discussed on March 22?

4. Have you ever felt you were in the wrong place? If so, what did you do?

MARCH 26
Prayer: A Means of Grace

> Let us come boldly to the throne of our gracious God. There we
> will receive his mercy, and we will find grace to help us when we
> need it most. HEBREWS 4:16

This verse helps us catch a vision for the gift of prayer, for it is a grand and matchless invitation to come to the throne of our loving, gracious God to receive his mercy and grace in time of need. This is not a throne that dispenses condemnation or criticism. It is a throne that dispenses unlimited *grace*. To think that God has stored up and made available all the resources you and I need—not only for today but for every challenge and problem in the future—can cause us to breathe a sigh of relief and deep thanks.

This supply of grace and blessing—provision, wisdom, perseverance in times of trial; strength when we're weak; and resources to live lives that honor God—has *our names* on it. All that is necessary is for us to *come*, to not try to do life all by ourselves by managing people or situations, but to embrace and believe the truth of Hebrews 4:16 and open the doors of our hearts to Jesus through prayer. And how are we to come? This verse says *boldly*, as beloved daughters of the King, adopted and accepted in Christ. Just as presidents have invited their young children into the Oval Office to climb up on their laps, we are to come to God's throne through the way he has provided—this wonderful means of grace called prayer. The door is open! God gave his only Son and moved heaven and earth to provide access to his presence. If we catch a vision for what an incredible gift prayer is, we will have a fresh-brewed prayer life and spiritual life. Will you accept the invitation to come into God's presence? A great storehouse of blessing is waiting for you. —CHERI

> Dear Father, thank you for making your throne of grace
> accessible to me. What a great gift! What a loving invitation! I put
> my trust in you and come for the mercy and grace and help you
> have for me today.

In the morning, prayer is the key that opens to us the treasures of God's mercies and blessings; in the evening, it is the key that shuts us up under his protection and safeguard. —UNKNOWN

MARCH 27
The Value of Private Prayer

[Jesus said,] "When you pray, don't be like the hypocrites who love to pray publicly on street corners and in the synagogues where everyone can see them. I tell you the truth, that is all the reward they will ever get. But when you pray, go away by yourself, shut the door behind you, and pray to your Father in private. Then your Father, who sees everything, will reward you." MATTHEW 6:5-6

Jesus is our pattern for prayer, not only in giving us the Lord's Prayer, but in his prayer practices. The Son of God had a great mission and many people to heal and teach, but he often left the multitudes and his disciples and went apart to pray with his Father. He didn't just flash an eloquent prayer heavenward to impress his followers; he spent solitary, extended times talking and listening to God. In today's verses he exhorts us to do the same: not to pray like the Pharisees, who did it to impress others with their petitions, but to get alone with God and "shut the door" behind us. That means setting aside our tasks, separating ourselves from other family members and even our prayer partners for times of intimate conversation with our Father in heaven. If morning is the best time with the fewest distractions, meet with God then. If you're busy caring for the needs of others in the morning, come into God's presence after everyone else is asleep, and know that the Lord never sleeps and loves to communicate with you then.

One woman I know had such a big family that her place to get alone with God was in the bathroom or in her car in the garage. Another woman awoke very early before she left to teach high school and prayer-walked the streets of her town alone. Be assured that God, who sees and knows all secrets and the innermost parts of our hearts, promises to reward you. —CHERI

Lord, I long to connect with you and hear your voice, just as Jesus did. Help me to draw away from this frantic and busy world to be alone with you. Show me a window of time each day when I can do this.

From three to four each morning, that is my hour. Then I am free from interruption and from the fear of interruption. Each morning I wake at three and live an hour with God. It gives me strength for everything. Without it I would be utterly helpless. —TOYOHIKO KAGAWA (1888–1960), JAPANESE SOCIAL REFORMER

MARCH 28
Too Busy to Pray?

> The Lord said to her, "My dear Martha, you are worried and upset over all these details! There is only one thing worth being concerned about. Mary has discovered it, and it will not be taken away from her." LUKE 10:41-42

Have you ever found yourself praying, "Lord, help me to relax about insignificant details" or "Lord, help me to *slowdownandnotrushthroughwhatIdo!*" as you scan twenty-five e-mails that appeared in your in-box while you were in meetings, pick up a prescription on the way home, hurry through the grocery store, and rustle up something for the family's dinner before you collapse in front of the television? Our many responsibilities push our tendency to be like Martha, our counterpart in the New Testament, who was busy and distracted doing many things—so many, in fact, that she didn't have time for Jesus. Like Martha, I've often had many things to accomplish: laundry, dishes, cooking, caring for and spending time with our children when they were young, cleaning, juggling a teaching job and helping my husband in his business. Prayer time at Jesus' feet? How would I manage the time for that?

But what Jesus spoke to Martha, he also meant for you and me: "My dear . . . you are worried and upset over all these details! There is *only one thing* worth being concerned about. Mary has discovered it, and it will not be taken away from her" (Luke 10:41-42, italics added). That "one thing" is connecting and spending time with God our Savior. Sharing our longings and dreams with him and listening for his voice. Asking for marching orders so we'll spend our days doing what he created us for. Gaining the wisdom he gives to those who ask and praying blessings for our loved ones. Ask yourself today: *What* really *matters in time and eternity?* Then, like Mary, discover the one thing really worth being concerned about. —CHERI

> Jesus, help me not to be so busy and distracted doing so many things that I miss the most important thing—time with you. Give me an eternal perspective, and teach me today what really matters.

We are too busy to pray, and so we are too busy to have power. We have a great deal of activity, but we accomplish little; many services but few conversions; much machinery but few results.
—R. A. TORREY (1856–1928), AMERICAN EVANGELIST, PASTOR, EDUCATOR, AND WRITER

MARCH 29
Conversations with God

Keep on praying. ROMANS 12:12

My husband calls me when I'm out of town, and we share what has happened during our day. I call my adult children and their spouses to check in, and I save my grandkids' sweet messages on my cell phone. My sisters and I call each other to make plans for lunch or to empathize if we have a problem. No one has to tell me it's my duty to call these precious ones, and no one has to remind them to call me. We connect because we love and care about each other.

It's the same way with us and God. Prayer is all about relationship; it's how we know God instead of just know about him and what others think about him. God's aim is for us to have fellowship with him, a person who truly exists. Prayer is the language of his realm (just as French is the language of France and Chinese is the language of China). He invites us personally to call on him; we don't have to e-mail our prayers to the Wailing Wall in Jerusalem. We don't need a hotline through an intermediary person. Through the life, death, and resurrection of Jesus Christ, the Father has made a way for us to connect directly with him, and he promises to hear and answer us twenty-four hours a day, seven days a week, throughout all the years of our journeys on earth. When we think of prayer in terms of a love relationship—our love for God and his love for us—prayer becomes less of a duty and more a privilege. It becomes something we look forward to, not something we're obligated to squeeze into our already packed schedules.

Would you join me in thanking God for drawing us to himself and for inviting us to have fellowship with him through prayer?   —CHERI

Dear Father, what a great gift you have given us in prayer. May we love you more each day and be in conversation with you so much that it becomes as natural as breathing.

The Spirit of prayer makes us so intimate with God that we scarcely pass through an experience before we speak to Him about it, either in supplication, in sighing, in pouring out our woes before him, in fervent requests, or in thanksgiving and adoration.   —OLE HALLESBY (1879–1961), NORWEGIAN THEOLOGIAN AND TEACHER

MARCH 30
Confidence in Prayer

You faithfully answer our prayers with awesome deeds, O God our savior. You are the hope of everyone on earth, even those who sail on distant seas. You formed the mountains by your power and armed yourself with mighty strength.   PSALM 65:5-6

When we pray, we aren't talking to a God who is uninvolved or unable to intervene, as our culture may suggest. No, we are talking to the all-powerful God who created the earth by the power of his word, whose wonders fill the earth, and who faithfully answers our prayers with awesome deeds. God chooses, often in response to our prayers, to release his mighty power on the earth, in our lives, and in the lives of those who desperately need his help. It's like the huge generator one of the children in my prayer group drew to show what he had learned about prayer. We were preparing to pray for people whose homes and lives had been devastated by F5 tornadoes in our city.

"That's God," Grant said, pointing to the generator. "He's got all this power." Then he drew a long diagonal line from the generator to some stick figures representing a family. "That's who needs help. All the moms and dads and kids who were hurt by the tornado. And the power flows along the cord as we pray!"

How right he is! When we bring others to the throne of grace by intercession, we connect them with the God who can help them. And whether we are young or old, realizing God's awesome power changes the way we pray and the way we live. His power is available for every situation and need so that we can do everything through Christ, who strengthens us (see Philippians 4:13). This is a God we can trust to pray through us by his Spirit, even when the ones for whom we intercede are across the ocean (see Romans 8:26). This is the all-powerful God in whom we can have confidence when we pray.   —CHERI

Father, we praise you for your power. We believe, but help our unbelief, and fill us with fresh faith through the power of your Word. Enlarge our circle of prayer so that we pray not just for our needs and our own families but also for those who are hurting, oppressed, and lost around us. O God our Savior, you faithfully answer our prayers with awesome deeds. You are our hope and the hope of everyone on the earth!

An intercessor means one who is in such vital contact with God and with his fellowmen that she is like a live wire closing the gap between the saving power of God and the sinful men who have been cut off from that power.
—HANNAH HURNARD (1905–1990), MISSIONARY AND AUTHOR

MARCH 31
Prayers That Outlive Your Life

> The four living beings and the twenty-four elders fell down before
> the Lamb. Each one had a harp, and they held gold bowls filled
> with incense, which are the prayers of God's people.
> REVELATION 5:8

I have prayed many prayers for my husband, our two sons and our daughter, and their spouses. I've uttered many petitions for my six grandchildren, my nieces and nephews, my sisters and sisters-in-law, my brother, and my friends and acquaintances. For salvation, provision, healing, restoration of relationships, and help in time of need. Some of these prayers have been marvelously answered, and for some I am still awaiting answers.

At times I have been discouraged about what may look like "unanswered" prayers. Maybe you have too. But the fact that prayers aren't answered today or next week or in two months doesn't mean they don't have an impact. When I realized that truth, it transformed my prayer life. Today's verse tells us our prayers are held in golden bowls beside the throne of grace. They are set before God, and he doesn't ignore them. Even when my home address changes from earth to heaven, prayers will keep on being answered in the lives of people I prayed for.

The best word picture I know was given to us by Ole Hallesby, a Norwegian theologian. He said that those of us who pray have answers that gently shower our lives. When we pass out from beneath the shower of answered prayer, our dear ones will step into it. Every prayer and sigh you've uttered for their future welfare will, in God's time, descend on them as a gentle rain of answered prayers. This bigger picture of prayer can renew and transform your attitude and spiritual life if you catch it. The legacy of prayer is a legacy worth investing in, and it's the best thing we can leave to those who come after us.   —CHERI

Thank you, Father, that prayer is not just a gift for me but a gift
for all those for whom I intercede. And I thank you for the power
of this gift, which is so great that it outlives my earthly life and will
continue to bless those I pray for even after my heart stops and
I see you face-to-face.

God shapes the world by prayer. Prayers are deathless. The lips that uttered them may be closed in death, the heart that felt them may have ceased to beat, but the prayers live before God. . . . Prayers outlive the lives of those who uttered them; they outlive a generation, outlive an age, outlive a world.
—E. M. BOUNDS (1835–1913), METHODIST MINISTER AND AUTHOR

APRIL 1
Unceasing Prayer

Never stop praying.

1 Thessalonians 5:17

Women have asked me, "How can I keep on praying (or pray without ceasing, as some versions translate it) when my life is so hectic and I have so many commitments?" I have found that it is possible, because when we get up from our "tuning in" devotional time, we don't leave God behind, and he doesn't leave us. Just as we have an ongoing stream of thoughts moving through our minds while we work, we can have ongoing dialogue with God and continue to enjoy his presence.

Just as we wouldn't want a loved one to speak to us only once a day or only on holidays, the Lord doesn't want us merely to check in before going to work and then not communicate with him again until the next day (or next Sunday or Easter). We can weave prayer into every part of our lives. Our computer desk can become a prayer nook. The dining table can become a family altar as we thank God together and pray about the challenges each person faces at work or at school. Our kitchens can be holy ground as we bless the food and those for whom we're preparing it. During our drive to work, we can make space for God and request his guidance in our day. When we drive by our children's school (or any school, even if we don't have children there), we can stand in the gap for teachers and students.

Right where we are is a good place to pray, to pour out our disappointments and hurts, to express thankfulness and praise, and to listen to what God has to say to us. As we put our energy into these brief moments with God, we will find that living in an attitude of continual prayer brings countless blessings.   —Cheri

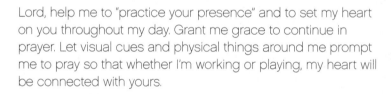

Lord, help me to "practice your presence" and to set my heart on you throughout my day. Grant me grace to continue in prayer. Let visual cues and physical things around me prompt me to pray so that whether I'm working or playing, my heart will be connected with yours.

We need not constantly be formulating verbal petitions, but we may enjoy the Lord like the psalmist who said that he keeps the Lord always before him (Psalm 16:8). We may leave the room where we pray, but we do not have to leave the inner sanctuary deep inside our being.

—Dr. John White, author, missionary, professor of psychiatry, and speaker

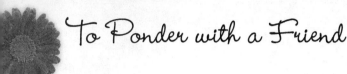

To Ponder with a Friend

1. As we have read in this week's devotionals, prayer can be a great source of grace and blessing in our lives. Yet sometimes we approach prayer as an obligation, just one more thing to squeeze into our busy, crowded lives. What are your frustrations or hindrances related to your prayer life?

2. When have you seen or experienced a big answer to prayer in your family? Share about it, and give thanks with a friend or a family member.

3. Do you know anyone who is no longer living who has prayed for you (perhaps a grandma, a mom, or a dear friend) and whose prayers have outlived that person's life and have had an impact on yours? Let me encourage you to take some moments to thank God for those people by name.

4. How would our lives be different if we didn't have access to God or if he hadn't given us the gift of prayer?

5. What do you sense the Holy Spirit is saying to you through the Scripture passages, prayers, and devotional thoughts from this week? How can you apply this in a practical way?

APRIL 2

A Simple Gesture

Keep on loving each other as brothers and sisters. Don't forget to show hospitality to strangers, for some who have done this have entertained angels without realizing it!   HEBREWS 13:1-2

Many people might consider my grandmother Mama Farley just a simple mountain woman like countless others who raised a family during the early part of the twentieth century. But stories of her faith in the Lord and her compassion toward those she called "pitiful souls" have affected several generations.

During the Great Depression of the 1930s, when men roamed the countryside looking for jobs but settling for handouts, Mama often fed strangers at her table. As she heaped the bounty of her hillside garden onto the plates of despondent men, she knew they needed her encouragement that the Lord had not forgotten them as much as they needed the food.

One afternoon Mama Farley stepped into her garden just as a traveler hungrily bit into a plump tomato he had pulled from the vine.

As Mama watched the juice run down the man's chin, she quietly said, "You come on to the house. That'll taste better with the chicken and dumplings left over from noon dinner."

The man gratefully followed.

Today, we don't have strangers appearing at our doors asking for food, and unfortunately, with the modern crime rate we'd worry if we did, but we still have numerous opportunities to display God's love to those who are hurting.

Where should we begin? With the next person we see.   —SANDRA

Lord, the world's overwhelming number of pain-filled situations depresses me. How can I possibly make a difference when there are so many needs? Isn't it like drawing an eyedropper of water out of the ocean's vastness? But then I go back to Mama Farley's example. She couldn't solve the problems resulting from the Depression, but she could offer food and encouragement in the midst of them. She made a great difference by offering the little she had. Help me to do the same.

Decisions must be made in the integrity of the heart before God with an unselfish attention to our brother's good and the glory of God.
—ELISABETH ELLIOT, MISSIONARY, AUTHOR, AND SPEAKER

APRIL 3
When Mistakes Happen

> Be kind to each other, tenderhearted, forgiving one another,
> just as God through Christ has forgiven you. EPHESIANS 4:32

I remember a tour years ago of Henry Ford's Greenfield Village in Dearborn, Michigan. At Thomas Edison's laboratory, one of the sites transplanted from the East Coast, the guide showed us where the famous inventor had worked for thousands of hours to develop the incandescent lightbulb.

Finally the moment had come when Edison could present to the world the crystal containing the filament that could be heated by electric current and would in turn produce the light to push aside darkness. As his staff assembled with joyful anticipation, their boss handed the bulb to his assistant, who would attach it to the connecting stand.

Then the delighted, nervous assistant dropped it!

The rest of the staff gasped as they saw the crystal shatter. The assistant clutched his hands to his chest in horror. But Edison merely patted him on the shoulder and ordered the fashioning of another bulb.

When that one was ready, the staff gathered a second time. The embarrassed assistant stood against the wall, far outside the gathering. But Edison glanced around, called him forward, and then handed him the *second* bulb.

What incredible encouragement that gesture provided for the young man. And what an incredible example Edison's compassion became for the rest of the staff.

Perhaps we won't choose inventing as a career, but life will still provide numerous opportunities to hand a "second bulb" to those who dropped it the first time. What if we planned *now* how we would like to react if a friend spills grape juice on our great-grandmother's tablecloth or a child impulsively plucks the frosting roses off the cake we've decorated for the church bake sale? Those moments *will* come.

And long after the tablecloth has been repaired and the frosting roses rebuilt, our reaction is what will be remembered. —SANDRA

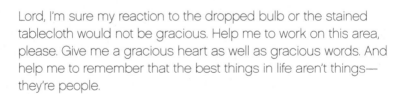

Lord, I'm sure my reaction to the dropped bulb or the stained tablecloth would not be gracious. Help me to work on this area, please. Give me a gracious heart as well as gracious words. And help me to remember that the best things in life aren't things— they're people.

Encouraging and equipping is not the same as pampering and indulging.
—SUSAN HUNT, WOMEN'S MINISTRY CONSULTANT AND AUTHOR

APRIL 4
A Kind Word

Timely advice is lovely, like golden apples in a silver basket.
PROVERBS 25:11

While it is important to show love and kindness to those around us, we don't have to limit caring expressions to people we know. I remember a church trip I took with my preteen son and daughter two summers after my husband died. The trip was supposed to be a gentle respite in the midst of my new status as a single parent, but frustration after frustration stormed into each hour.

At the end of that first stress-filled day, I stood with my children in the restaurant washroom line, close to tears. *How am I going to do this single-parent thing, Lord?* I inwardly prayed. *I can't handle even a goofy trip. This is hopeless. I'm hopeless.*

Just then one of the grandmothers from the Spanish-speaking group on our bus walked past us. All day she had watched as I looked around frantically for my son, who was prone to wander away, and stumbled over my daughter, who was so frightened by all the strange sights she clung to my side. As the grandmother passed me, she patted my arm and said in halting English, "You *good* mama."

Just three words: "You good mama." But it was just as if God had spoken and said, "You are not hopeless. I'm here with you, and you will do just fine."

Suddenly, I wasn't quite so exhausted, and my fears had been replaced with the hope that maybe, just maybe, I could pull off this single-parenting thing after all.

Even though that scene occurred years ago, those three words provided a raft for me as I navigated single-parenting's rough waters. —SANDRA

Lord, I do want to say the right thing to someone who needs encouragement. But I'm prone to think my sentences need to be long and my words eloquent. Since I don't speak like that, I tend not to say anything. Help me to remember that even the simplest words can carry great power when spoken with your love.

A pleasant word is a bright ray of sunshine on a saddened heart. Therefore, give others the sunshine, and tell Jesus the rest.
—MRS. CHARLES E. COWMAN (1870–1960), MISSIONARY TO CHINA AND JAPAN AND AUTHOR

APRIL 5
Welcoming New Friends

Show me the right path, O Lord; point out the road for me to follow. Lead me by your truth and teach me, for you are the God who saves me. All day long I put my hope in you.   PSALM 25:4-5

Making a difference in another person's life doesn't have to be dramatic. In fact, the greatest encouragement and the greatest statement of God's love often come in our simplest gestures.

Betsy and Pete were introduced by mutual friends a year after Pete's first wife had died in an auto accident. Eventually, they married and began attending Pete's boyhood church, the same one at which his first wife had been the choir soloist for the holiday cantatas.

The first Sunday after Pete and Betsy returned from their honeymoon, one of Pete's friends slipped and called Betsy by the first wife's name.

Then, when he tried to apologize, he made the situation worse by saying, "I'm sorry. It's just that I'm used to saying 'Pete and Patty.' Those names kind of go together, don't you think?"

Betsy nodded and tried to smile, but the implication hung in the air: "Pete and Patty" matched; "Pete and Betsy" did not.

At that moment, the friend's wife stepped forward and hugged Betsy. "You need to know we love you already, just because you love Pete," she said. "We're looking forward to getting to know you so we can love you for yourself. We're going to make lots of mistakes along the way, but we hope you'll forgive us."

In that moment, an emotional bridge was built, and Betsy knew she had a new friend who understood the special challenges she faced.   —SANDRA

Lord, it's so easy to say the wrong thing without meaning to. So, help me to be sensitive to the situations of others. And help me to guard my mouth while I'm opening my heart.

Be generous and understanding. Let no one come to you without feeling better and happier when they leave. Be the living expression of God's kindness: with kindness on your face . . . in your eyes . . . in your smile . . . in your warm greeting.
—MOTHER TERESA (1910–1997), FOUNDER OF MISSIONARIES OF CHARITY IN CALCUTTA, INDIA

APRIL 6
An Incredible Offer

> They even did more than we had hoped, for their first action
> was to give themselves to the Lord and to us, just as God wanted
> them to do.   2 CORINTHIANS 8:5

One of the many losses for me as a single mom has been the lack of a sounding board when I'm facing a tough decision. When I was first thrust into widowhood, one of the married business instructors with whom I taught suggestively invited me to dinner after I'd asked his advice about my new responsibility of balancing the checkbook. Startled at his invitation, I muttered, "I don't think that's a good idea" and returned quickly to my empty classroom, where I sobbed as I thought of the new, scary world in which I found myself.

In the days that followed, I suddenly felt awkward talking to men I had worked with for years. And suddenly their wives seemed to be standing closer to them at social events, as if to say, "I just want to remind you he is mine."

Often I wanted to say, "I just want to remind you that you don't have to worry."

My paranoia followed me into a new career, where it came face-to-face with the graciousness of Muriel Sandbo, a North Carolina woman. Her husband, Bob, was a member of the board for the New York organization at which I worked. She called me one day and said the Lord had placed me on her heart. Even though we hadn't met, she was praying for me because she knew I was in the process of planning a cross-country move. Then she said the most remarkable thing: "I know it must be difficult for a single mom not to have someone to run ideas by, so if you need a man's thinking on this, I hope you'll talk to Bob. He's very wise, so feel free to talk to him about the decisions you're facing."

I was astonished and most grateful. Even though I didn't take advantage of the offer, it was an incredible gift. Her security in her husband's love and her concern for someone who had once been a beloved wife came together in an encouraging gesture.   —SANDRA

Lord, when I was married, I know I wouldn't have made the same gracious offer Muriel did. Help me to get past my own insecurities and to encourage others in practical ways. And may your great love shine through even my little actions.

We cannot tell the precise moment when friendship is formed. As in filling a vessel drop by drop there is at last a drop which makes it run over, so in a series of kindnesses there is at last one which makes the heart run over.
—SAMUEL JOHNSON (1709–1784), ENGLISH ESSAYIST, BIOGRAPHER, AND CRITIC

APRIL 7

Simple Gestures, Great Love

> The King will say, "I tell you the truth, when you did it to one of
> the least of these my brothers and sisters, you were doing it to me!"
> MATTHEW 25:40

My parents cared for my elderly Aunt Adah, who for years lay paralyzed and rigid until the Lord lovingly released her to be with him. Her hospital bed was in my parents' living room so she could be in the center of daily life rather than shut off in a back bedroom.

Numerous relatives and most of her church friends forgot about her, but her minister, Pastor Ron Clark, and two church members, Billie Schneider and Patricia Marsden, often stopped in to say hello. Aunt Adah could no longer talk, and her facial muscles were locked, so visitors couldn't receive even a grateful smile from the one who once had been highly active.

Pastor Clark read the Scriptures and then gave Aunt Adah Communion, breaking the soft bread morsel into tiny crumbs she could swallow. Sometimes he also read a simple book with an encouraging theme.

Billie hadn't forgotten how much Aunt Adah loved to hear her sing on Sunday mornings, so she continued that ministry, giving a miniconcert for a bedridden audience of one.

Patricia stayed with Aunt Adah when Mother and Dad had a rare social function they wanted to attend together.

These folks came to minister to Aunt Adah, but their loving gestures provided glimpses of the Lord for the rest of the family as well. Often the simplest gesture can show the greatest love.   —SANDRA

Lord, help me to show your reality by reaching out to others. Remind me that providing an occasional meal or offering to stay with a bedridden family member so the rest can attend church together are forms of ministry too. I want to see beyond my little world so others can see you.

The things we do today, sowing seeds or sharing simple truths of Christ, people will someday refer to as the first things that prompted them to think of Him.
—GEORGE MATHESON (1842–1906), SCOTTISH THEOLOGIAN AND PREACHER

Loving God When No One Is Watching

A good person produces good things from the treasury of a good heart, and an evil person produces evil things from the treasury of an evil heart. What you say flows from what is in your heart.
LUKE 6:45

I visited my grandmother Mama Farley just after I earned my master's degree, a monumental accomplishment for me, as the oldest child in a large family.

The first morning, I awoke to sounds from the kitchen and hurriedly dressed. Mama's hearing had gotten worse, so she didn't notice me standing in the kitchen archway. As I watched her, I remembered long-ago scenes when she rolled out gingerbread cookies or snapped beans as she told stories. Occasionally she'd lament she had been kept home from school to plow, which resulted in her never learning to read or write. Predictably, she would insist I get all the education I could.

As I watched Mama, I noticed her back was more stooped and her hair whiter. But everything else was the same—even the wood-burning stove. The modern range her adult children had purchased sat in the corner, used only to warm leftovers. Mama insisted she couldn't regulate the heat in the new oven.

As I watched, she pulled a skillet of beautiful biscuits from her trusty old stove. I was determined to learn to make biscuits like that. Thinking of the compliments I would receive, I watched her scrutinize the golden crusts. I would have placed them on the serving plate with a self-satisfied sigh. But Mama set them in the center of the table and whispered, "Thank you, Lord."

Her gentle words hit me like a sharp rebuke. I backed into the hallway, tears filling my eyes. I had achieved an education Mama could never dream of, but it had not occurred to me to thank God for it. Right there in the hallway, I whispered my gratitude before hurrying into the kitchen to give Mama a hug.

Today her habit of thanking God for even the little things has become a part of my life too. Now, whether paying bills, planting spring flowers, or pulling a pan of golden biscuits out of my own oven, I think of Mama as I whisper my own "Thank you, Lord."

All of us behave differently when we think we're being watched. Usually, we are on our best behavior when we know someone else is around. The funny thing is, somebody *is* always with us: God. Is he pleased when he sees the way we act when we're alone?   —SANDRA

Ouch, Lord. Help me to remember to try to please you with my actions rather than try to impress onlookers.

God will help us be the people we are meant to be, if only we will ask. No one is more deserving of our best behavior than God.
—HANNAH WHITALL SMITH (1832–1911), QUAKER LAY SPEAKER AND AUTHOR

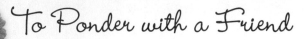

To Ponder with a Friend

1. What loving-kindness have you received at a low moment in your life? Who gave it?

2. What encouragement do you try to offer others?

3. When is it most difficult to show love?

4. Have you ever learned a lesson from someone who didn't know you were watching?

APRIL 9
Gifts from Our Gardens

> For everything there is a season, a time for every activity under
> heaven. A time to be born and a time to die. A time to plant and a
> time to harvest.   ECCLESIASTES 3:1-2

Every season I learn something from my garden and enjoy new gifts from it as well,
things such as there are times to plant and times when a peony bush dies despite
my best efforts. I've learned to be teachable and ask more experienced gardeners
their secrets to growing beautiful flowers. I've also learned that nothing is a total
failure. If a rosebush I plant in one place in the backyard doesn't do well, I experi-
ment with moving it to a front garden plot so it will get more sun. I've also learned
hope: In the spring when I plant yellow chrysanthemums, I enjoy their bright
blooms until their first blooming cycle ends. Then I look forward to seeing the
mums bloom a second time in the fall instead of pulling the plant up when it looks
ugly. When I plant daffodil and tulip bulbs in the fall, I wait all through the winter
when the ground is covered with ice or snow, hoping that in March, a glorious plot
of blooms under my oak tree will cheer up an otherwise overcast, rainy month.

Whether you have pots of flowers or lacy ferns on an apartment balcony, a
small patio garden behind your town house where you grow herbs, or an acre to
plant with flowers and vegetables, gardening will reward you with many gifts: a
perfect pink rose, purple verbena that comes up "volunteer" the next season when
you least expect it, or fragrant, fresh basil and rosemary to season your food.

Your garden also holds priceless lessons for life and spiritual growth, lessons
that we will explore this week. There's an old saying: "As the garden grows, so does
the gardener." Come, grow with me in the garden.   —CHERI

> Creator of all lovely things that grow, thank you for the gardens
> I've enjoyed at the neighborhood park, in my backyard, and in
> Grandma's garden when I was growing up. They are gifts that
> lighten my daily load and have much to teach me.

One is nearer God's heart in a garden than anywhere else on earth.
—DOROTHY FRANCES GURNEY (1858–1932), ENGLISH DEVOTIONAL WRITER AND POET

APRIL 10
Mama's Garden

When you produce much fruit, you are my true disciples. This
brings great glory to my Father.   JOHN 15:8

Some of my greatest inspirations for learning how to grow flowers were the gardens
my mother had throughout her fifty-nine years of life. I didn't start out with a
green thumb, but I'd seen Mom grow blue and purple morning glories and other
flowers on the fences wherever we lived (the first one I remember was on Morning-
side Lane—no kidding!), and I figured I could do it too. The gardens of my childhood held red and yellow roses and gardenia bushes because Mama took time to
plant and nurture them so we'd all enjoy the fragrant smell as we walked into the
house. Old fashioned irises always rimmed the edge of the yard where we played.

Mama's life bore much fruit in the five daughters and one son she mothered
marvelously, even though she was widowed at age thirty-six. She lived a life of
prayer, which will bear fruit for eternity, and her gardens bore fruit and flowers that
blessed many. When she realized her dream and was able to buy a little ranch in
East Texas, she grew vegetables, fig trees, and pear trees and was immensely proud
of the crisp pears from which she made pies to give away to neighbors and family.
Violets grew wild around the oak trees. Climbing rosebushes and zinnias thrived in
the sandy soil of her East Texas garden.

Mama's flowers gave me a small taste of the joys of heaven, where she is
enjoying seeing Jesus face-to-face today. Though she's been gone for more than
twenty-five years, I, too, have planted morning glories, roses, and zinnias in my
garden. In the backyard beneath a tree is one of the violets from Mama's ranch,
and it blooms like crazy every spring. Whenever I water or plant or see the blooms,
I think of my mother and her legacy of beautifying every place she lived with a
colorful riot of flowers, no matter how busy she was caring for six children and
running a household. And I ask God to bring forth a fruitful legacy from my life
as well.   —CHERI

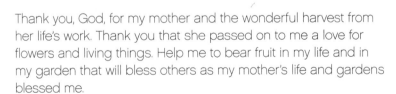

Thank you, God, for my mother and the wonderful harvest from
her life's work. Thank you that she passed on to me a love for
flowers and living things. Help me to bear fruit in my life and in
my garden that will bless others as my mother's life and gardens
blessed me.

There is a garden in every childhood, an enchanted place where colors are
brighter, the air softer, and the morning more fragrant than ever again.
—ELIZABETH LAURENCE, ACTOR

APRIL 11
Cultivating Patience

Each of us did the work the Lord gave us. I planted the seed in your hearts, and Apollos watered it, but it was God who made it grow. It's not important who does the planting, or who does the watering. What's important is that God makes the seed grow. 1 CORINTHIANS 3:5-7

I was not born with a great supply of patience, and I'm not alone. Patience isn't a virtue often seen in our world today. Nobody likes waiting in traffic or in grocery-store lines. People want what they want without delay. There are countless instant meals and a demand for rapid results from diets and self-help books. As an old saying goes, "Lord, give me patience, and I need it *now!*"

Since I have needed to grow in patience, gardening has given me some of the best lessons. Before planting bulbs in the fall, I prepare the soil, add manure to enrich the hard, red Oklahoma clay, and till the ground by hand to break up old roots. Then I dig holes to plant new bulbs of daffodils and tulips. Red, yellow, bright pink, the packages say. But it will be months after the hard work of planting fifty bulbs before I see the fruit of my labor. When I garden, seed, and weed, I do my part, but I can't *force* the plants to grow. The bulbs and other flowers and shrubs in my garden will grow on nature's timetable, not on mine.

And so in the watering and waiting period, I am reminded that patience learned in the garden can carry over to how we relate to our friends, our husbands, and our kids. Into their lives we plant the seeds of love, learning, good character, and faith. We water the seeds with our prayers and sometimes our tears. But it is *God* who brings the growth. We can't force growth. Our part is to accept our dear ones as they are—works in progress. They are God's field, not ours, and he is a faithful Gardener. As we wait with hope and grow in patience, we can trust that growth happens every day, even when we can't see it. I have learned in my garden, as I think you will too, that the harvest will be worth the wait. —CHERI

Grant me patience, Lord, as I garden and as I nurture the relationships you have given me.

A garden is a grand teacher. It teaches patience and careful watchfulness; it teaches industry and thrift; above all it teaches trust.
—GERTRUDE JEKYLL (1843–1932), BRITISH GARDEN DESIGNER, WRITER, AND ARTIST

Abiding in the Vine

> [Jesus said,] "I am the vine; you are the branches. Those who remain in me, and I in them, will produce much fruit. For apart from me you can do nothing." JOHN 15:5

My friends had old grapevines growing deep in their backyard near the woods that in the winter was full of dead, ugly, brown twigs. The previous owner of the property had once cultivated the grapevines and produced lovely green grapes. But as he and his wife grew older and infirm, they weren't able to care for the vines, which seemed to die out. Fortunately, they didn't pull out the vines, which remained in the ground but didn't produce any fruit for several years. When my friends saw the grapevines, they envisioned what they could become with much pruning, cultivating, and watering. So they worked and they worked. By the next spring, the vines were beginning to come to life, and by summertime the branches were filled with little green grapes.

Looking at those vines reminds me that when I feel most ungreen and unproductive, when things aren't going well, if I stay connected to Jesus, the true Vine, as today's verse says, he will bring forth not just *some* fruit but much fruit. Fruit that will honor and please him and fill me with joy, just as the new owners of those grapevines were filled with joy at their harvest.

This verse also reminds us of the truth that apart from Christ we can do nothing. No self-effort, no striving will produce good fruit if we're disconnected from his life. Remaining in Jesus is the key, but how marvelous that God takes the initiative to tend us and cultivate us as we remain in him.   —CHERI

> Thank you, Lord, for your precious promise that as I draw near and remain connected to you, I will draw strength from you, as a branch that drinks life from the Vine. Cause me to bear fruit that will remain.

If Christ, the heavenly Vine, has taken the believer as a branch, then He has pledged Himself, in the very nature of things, to supply the sap and spirit and nourishment to make it bring forth fruit. . . . The soul need but have one care— to abide closely, fully, wholly. He will give the fruit. He works all that is needed to make the believer a blessing.
—ANDREW MURRAY (1828–1917), SOUTH AFRICAN WRITER AND PASTOR

Roots Going Deep

[Those who delight in the law of the Lord] are like trees planted along the riverbank, bearing fruit each season. Their leaves never wither, and they prosper in all they do.   PSALM 1:3

Blessed are those who trust in the LORD and have made the LORD their hope and confidence. They are like trees planted along a riverbank, with roots that reach deep into the water.   JEREMIAH 17:7-8

One of the lessons I learn from gardening is the importance of a good root system. If I sow my flower seeds around the intricate roots of the large tree in the front yard, they can't develop their own roots and therefore don't grow properly. If I plant a tree in the ground three days before a cold snap or an ice storm, its roots haven't had a chance to grow so the little tree can't withstand the cold and promptly dies.

Throughout the Bible God gives us pictures of the importance of having our roots deep in him. In Psalm 1 we learn that those who delight in doing everything the Lord wants and meditate on his Word day and night are like trees planted along a riverbank: "Their leaves never wither, and they prosper in all they do" (1:3). In Jeremiah, we find that those who trust in God (in contrast to those who trust in human beings and have turned away from God) are like trees whose "roots . . . reach deep into the water." Even in long months of drought and stressful conditions, their leaves stay green, and they go right on producing delicious fruit even into old age (see Jeremiah 17:5-8). This means that though our bodies may decline or grow more fragile with advancing age, when we're grounded in the soil of God's love and truth, his Spirit will renew our inner strength day by day. As we are rooted in Christ's inexhaustible supply, we will continue to be productive and bring glory to God as long as we live. What amazing grace!   —CHERI

Father, you are my hope and my confidence. Let me never turn from you, but in each experience of life let my roots go deeper into you. May I stay in continual communion with you through prayer so that your life will flow through me and make my soul prosperous even into old age.

A person without prayer is like a tree without roots.   —PIUS XII (1876–1958), POPE

APRIL 14

Nothing Is Wasted

My dear brothers and sisters, be strong and immovable. Always work enthusiastically for the Lord, for you know that nothing you do for the Lord is ever useless.   1 CORINTHIANS 15:58

Some time ago my friend Katherine told me about her new gardening method called "lasagna gardening." This bed gets its name because preparing it is similar to how we prepare lasagna: We alternate a layer of long lasagna noodles, then a layer of meat, then cheeses, seasonings, then Italian sauce, and then the layers are repeated. In the same way, Katherine layers the garden refuse in the bed. She used to fill several dumpsters with blackberry clippings; dried up runners from cucumber, bean, and squash plants; and dead stalks from pepper plants. Now instead of pulling out and throwing away all the lifeless stems and leaves from the raised beds of her vegetable garden, she lays them down and begins to layer organic material on top of the bed.

She keeps a gallon ice-cream carton with a lid under the kitchen sink to collect potato peels, eggshells, coffee grounds, apple cores, etc. Every other day she dumps the contents of the carton on the garden bed. Layer after layer, week after week, all through the fall and winter, the lasagna garden bed grows rich in nutrients. Scores of earthworms do their part to aerate, dig, and enrich the soil. In the spring when it's time for Katherine to plant her new vegetables, all the nutrients are already in the bed, and she doesn't have to add chemical fertilizers. Nothing is wasted! Nothing is useless, even those things that look dry and dead. The soil produced by layering organic material is rich; as during the next season Katherine plants and waters, that soil produces the best vegetable gardens she's ever had.

Whenever Katherine or her kids take another carton and dump it on the lasagna garden bed, she is reminded that in the Lord's economy also, *nothing* in our lives is wasted. God takes things that look like throwaway material to us and makes something fruitful out of them when we give them to him.   —CHERI

Thank you, Father, for tending my soul, feeding my mind, and bringing to life dreams that have died. With you, nothing is wasted, for you make something wonderful out of what looks lifeless or ugly.

God's fingers can touch nothing but to mold it into loveliness.
—GEORGE MACDONALD (1824–1905), SCOTTISH NOVELIST AND POET

APRIL 15
A Well-Watered Garden

The LORD will guide you continually, giving you water when you are dry and restoring your strength. You will be like a well-watered garden, like an ever-flowing spring.   ISAIAH 58:11

After Corrie ten Boom's family was arrested for giving refuge to Jewish people, and before the Nazis sent her to a concentration camp, Corrie was alone in a jail cell for four months. She later described those months as a hard time of "plowing." She thought there would be nothing left of her after the cruelties of being incarcerated. Though she was desperate, she suddenly began to see God's side of things: that she was like a field being plowed and weeded. In the darkness of solitary confinement, Corrie remembered pastor Charles Spurgeon's words: "What a privilege it is to know that I am a field under heavenly cultivation, not a wilderness, but a garden of the Lord, walled by grace, planted according to a divine plan, worked by love, weeded by heavenly discipline, and constantly protected by divine power. A soul so privileged is prepared to bring forth fruit to the glory of God."

As Corrie meditated on those truths, she saw how heavenly discipline was cultivating her by pulling out the weeds of sin and how God had planted her where she was according to his divine pattern. She wouldn't be in jail a moment longer than God thought was necessary. In yielding to the Lord as the field does to the farmer, letting him shape and prepare her for what was ahead, she adapted to her lonely time of God's plowing and cultivation and was prepared to be with Christ in life and in death.   —CHERI

> Lord, how I thank you that I am a well-watered garden, walled by grace, planted according to a divine pattern, tilled by love, weeded by heavenly discipline, and protected by your divine omnipotence and power.

What are you? A wilderness or a garden for the Lord? If you are a wilderness, come to Jesus; He will not reject you. He has changed many wildernesses into gardens full of flowers and fruit.

—CORRIE TEN BOOM (1892–1983), HOLOCAUST SURVIVOR, AUTHOR

To Ponder with a Friend

1. Just as we work to care for our outdoor gardens—whether that means three pots of summer flowers or a large bed of roses—God is working within our inner gardens and lovingly tending us. Philippians 2:13 says, "God is working in you, giving you the desire and the power to do what pleases him." In what way is God working in the inner garden of your heart and life in this season?

2. In Matthew 6:26, Jesus says, "Look at the birds. They don't plant or harvest or store food in barns, for your heavenly Father feeds them. And aren't you far more valuable to him than they are?" What does this verse tell you about your value to God? How can *believing* that truth make a difference in your life?

3. Part of the great Gardener's work in our lives involves pruning and uprooting so we'll not just survive but thrive in a way that brings glory to him. Has God been doing any pruning or uprooting in your life recently? If so, what things has he been weeding out of you? What needs to be uprooted—an attitude, a destructive relationship, a negative habit?

4. I shared some things I've learned from gardening, such as patience. What have you learned from watching the seasons in a garden as they cycle from buds to leaves to blooms, to falling leaves, bare branches, and back to buds?

5. What "scraps, dead stalks, or cuttings" has God transformed or made something productive from in your life? Thank him for the marvelous knowledge that with God, nothing is wasted!

APRIL 16
A Child's Heart

Let the godly rejoice. Let them be glad in God's presence. Let them be filled with joy. PSALM 68:3

Renee leaned forward to better hear the psychology professor at the front of the lecture hall.

"Children learn early what the world thinks about them," he was saying, "and in turn, the world's opinion shapes their opinion about themselves. Believe me, there is no greater joy as a psychology clinician than to have a child smile as you ask her to say, 'I am a wonderful person.' Sadly, many children can't say that, and they grow into adults who feel as if they have no worth whatsoever."

Renee sat stunned, thinking, *How can anyone say, "I am a wonderful person," especially a child?*

The professor glanced at his watch and then assigned chapter 6 for Monday's class before striding out. Renee slowly gathered her notes, wishing he had offered a solution, some "magic wand" counseling formula that would allow children—and her—to say, "I am a worthwhile person."

As she walked to the library, she pondered the childhood events that had shaped her opinion of herself. She had grown up knowing she was an "accident" who had altered her mother's education plans. Once, her mother had even snapped, "It's a good thing abortion wasn't readily available back then!" How terrible to know your own mother would have killed you before birth if she'd had the chance. Oh, Renee knew about little kids not being able to say, "I am a wonderful person"!   —SANDRA

> Lord, even as an adult I'm prone to replay those old childhood mental tapes that tell me I'll never measure up to someone's expectations. Help me to refuse to listen to those old put-downs. Instead, let me listen to and follow only your strengthening and encouraging voice.

God cannot give us a happiness and peace apart from Himself, because it is not there. There is no such thing.
—C. S. LEWIS (1898–1963), IRISH WRITER AND LITERARY SCHOLAR

APRIL 17

New Encouragement

I am certain that God, who began the good work within you,
will continue his work until it is finally finished on the day when
Christ Jesus returns.   PHILIPPIANS 1:6

Renee had hoped the afternoon's bone-jarring aerobics session would shake the old memories from her mind. But even the strenuous activity and her understanding that "hurting people hurt people" couldn't lessen her struggle against those emotional ropes tying her to an awful past.

Two days later, on Sunday morning, she idly flipped past radio stations, searching for something soothing. She stopped just as the deep voice of a local pastor said, "The family you came from is important, but not as important as the family you will leave behind."

Stunned, Renee barely heard the rest of his sermon. She certainly didn't want to pass on to any future children the baggage she had carried throughout her own youth. After continuing to ponder that thought for the next two days, she finally called the church. Soon she was sitting in the pastor's office and stammering out her reason for being there.

"I'm tired of carrying all this junk around," she said. "I'm tired of feeling worthless. I'm tired of not getting anywhere in life. I'm tired of not feeling really loved." Then she shrugged and added, "But, hey, I don't like myself, so how can I blame anybody else for not liking me?"

The pastor nodded. "Are you familiar with the Alcoholics Anonymous phrase 'sick and tired of being sick and tired'? That's just what you've described. And that's good, because it means you're ready for a change."

Renee nodded. "'Sick and tired of being sick and tired'? That's me, all right. So what do I do?"

"Begin by asking God to help you to have a positive approach to life rather than a negative one."   —SANDRA

Lord, I have so much for which I can and should be thankful.
Help me to concentrate on those things instead of on my
failures and disappointments. Like Renee, I'm "sick and tired of
being sick and tired." Often I feel as if I have no one but you to
lean on. So please show me how to move past this gloomy self-
absorption into your bright future.

Many refuse to develop a positive attitude. The reason is simple: They plan to fail.
—ERWIN W. LUTZER, PASTOR AND AUTHOR

APRIL 18
Facing Truth

God showed his great love for us by sending Christ to die for us while we were still sinners. ROMANS 5:8

The pastor held his Bible toward Renee. "Listen to Romans 5:8: 'God showed his great love for us by sending Christ to die for us while we were still sinners.' See? When we realize we're tired of what we've done, Christ is waiting for us. Right here, it says we already are loved."

Renee shook her head. "But I've made stupid choices," she said.

The pastor leaned forward. "When we concentrate on our failings instead of on the Lord's power and grace to free us from guilt, we're helping Satan. Because as long as we're beating ourselves up, he doesn't have to!" He picked up a pen and drew three interlocking circles with a stick figure in the center.

"I'm not much of an artist," he said, "but the trapped figure is you, me, the whole human race. And these circles represent the different types of guilt: true, false, and misplaced. True guilt is what we feel when we've done something wrong. The only way to get rid of that nagging dread is to confess to God what we've done and accept his forgiveness. Sometimes that means we have to say, 'I'm sorry, will you forgive me?' to somebody else, first."

Tears sprang into Renee's eyes as she thought of the argument she'd had with her grandfather over the new lawn mower he wanted and could afford but had refused to buy. She had called him a stupid old man, and he had retorted that her entire generation was a bunch of ungrateful spendthrifts. Renee had never contacted him again. Four months later, her mother called, sobbing, to say he had died of a sudden heart attack. Instead of going to the funeral home, Renee had gone partying with classmates.

Now, in the pastor's office, she whispered, "Yeah, but what if you can't say you're sorry. What if they're dead?"

The pastor's expression softened. "Some counselors suggest writing a letter you don't mail or talking to an empty chair where you pretend the person is sitting. But when I've needed to ask forgiveness when it's too late, I just pray—usually crying—and ask the Lord to tell them I'm sorry."

He paused, then said, "Would you like to do that now?"

Renee shook her head. "No, but I'll think about it." —SANDRA

Lord, too many times I've failed family members, friends, myself, you. The memories of those failures shout at me even now. I hold out empty hands to you, asking for your forgiveness and your help.

From the body of one guilty deed,
A thousand ghostly fears and haunting thoughts proceed.
—WILLIAM WORDSWORTH (1770–1850), ENGLISH POET

APRIL 19
More Information

> If we confess our sins to him, he is faithful and just to forgive us our sins and to cleanse us from all wickedness.   1 JOHN 1:9

Renee gestured toward the pastor's drawing of the three types of guilt.

"Tell me about the other two kinds of guilt," she said.

The pastor tapped the paper. "After true guilt, the other two types, false and misplaced, are mean. When we are dealing with false guilt, we are convinced everything bad is our fault, and we use the words *I should have* a lot when we talk about the situation. We may even blame ourselves for a friend's accident because he or she stayed to watch a long video with us. But we didn't cause the wreck; the drunk driver who ran a stop sign did."

Renee stared at the false-guilt circle, trying to fit the pastor's words into the load of guilt she had carried over her mother's decision to leave college those many years before.

The pastor gestured toward the paper again. "The third circle represents misplaced guilt. Here, something happens that normally would be insignificant, but this time it causes a deep problem. It can be something as simple as thinking it's your fault a friend didn't do well in a game because you, the designated laundry doer, threw her 'lucky socks' in the wash."

"So where do I start?" Renee asked.

The pastor smiled. "You already have. In fact, I'm convinced you are closer to your goal than you think."   —SANDRA

Lord, I didn't know guilt came in so many forms. Help me to sort the true guilt from the false or misplaced guilt. Help me to ask forgiveness where I need to and to stop beating myself up over the rest. You offer peace and hope and forgiveness. Help me to accept those good gifts from your hand.

Hope is an adventure, a going forward, a confident search for a rewarding life.
—KARL MENNINGER (1893–1990), AMERICAN PSYCHIATRIST

APRIL 20
Positive Steps

> God loved the world so much that he gave his one and only Son, so that everyone who believes in him will not perish but have eternal life.   JOHN 3:16

Renee gave a frustrated huff. "I'd love it if you had a magic wand attached to your drawings."

The pastor shook his head. "I don't have a magic wand, but the teacher in me does have several assignments. First, I want you to ponder how much God loves you. He loves you so much that, as it says in John 3:16, he sent his own Son to die for our sins, yours and mine. For the whole world's, in fact. Emotional freedom starts with accepting his completed work and letting him guide you."

Renee frowned. "That's a lot to think about."

The pastor continued. "Next, start coming to church. We have a large college and career class, and you need to hang around kids your own age who are willing to talk about these issues. They've been where you are.

"Next, I want you to find ways to add more laughter to your life. Proverbs 17:22 says, 'A cheerful heart is good medicine, but a broken spirit saps a person's strength.' Laughter will help open your crushed spirit to God's healing. If you don't know where to start, rent movies from the classic comedies section at the video store. My favorites are the Marx Brothers. And finally, find a way to serve others. I guarantee as you make a difference in the life of another person, you'll find greater joy in your own. Fair enough?"

Renee nodded. "Fair enough," she said. Then she thought, *I'm on my way to being a worthwhile person after all.* And suddenly, she smiled.   —SANDRA

Lord, what the pastor said makes sense, but taking those first steps can be hard. Help me to be excited about what awaits rather than worried over imaginary details. Help me to seek your face and stop looking for magic wands. Show me who you are and who I am in you.

The ultimate stupidity is withholding from yourself the respect you deserve.
—DR. LAURA SCHLESSINGER, SOCIAL AND CONSERVATIVE COMMENTATOR

APRIL 21
Asking for Forgiveness

The Holy Spirit helps us in our weakness. For example, we don't
know what God wants us to pray for. But the Holy Spirit prays for
us with groanings that cannot be expressed in words.
ROMANS 8:26

One of my friends, whom I'll call Joy, understands what the pastor means about
praying and asking God to forward your request for forgiveness from someone who
has died. An elderly widower in her church, Mr. Smith, began calling Joy a few
days after his wife's funeral. He'd comment on the weather and the newspaper
headlines, ask about her day, inquire about the children's homework—all subjects
Joy didn't want to discuss while she was trying to prepare dinner for her husband
and growing family. Finally, one afternoon she asked if he would mind calling later
in the evening. He never called again.

Engaged in her busy routine, Joy forgot about Mr. Smith—until he died
unexpectedly. At the funeral home, his out-of-state daughter greeted her with
a hug.

"Thank you for being so kind to Dad," she said. "He told me how much it
helped him to talk to you. After Mother died, the dinner hour was awful for him
since they used to cook together and talk and laugh. You helped him so much."

Joy gulped down surprise and guilt as she accepted another hug. The next
several days were rough as she mentally replayed those phone calls with new
understanding. And as she remembered asking Mr. Smith to call later, her guilt
deepened. She gave herself pep talks about how busy her family kept her and how
inconsiderate Mr. Smith had been to call during her busiest time of the day. But
the guilt remained.

Finally one evening, she knelt by her bed and said through tears, "Lord,
please tell Mr. Smith I'm sorry. I didn't realize what those calls meant to him. If
I could do it over again, I'd handle everything differently."

Finally peace arrived, along with a new sensitivity to the grieving people
around her. —SANDRA

Lord, this account makes me sad because often I haven't
gotten the full story until it's too late. Help me to be sensitive
to your leading as I respond to others. Help me to see I can
make a difference in the lives of hurting people just by taking a
moment to listen and let them know I care. I realize I can't solve
everyone's problems, but I can remind those around me you
have not forgotten them.

Virtue is not secure until its practice has become habitual.
—BENJAMIN FRANKLIN (1706–1790), AMERICAN STATESMAN AND PHILOSOPHER

APRIL 22
Take Off the Mask

Show me the right path, O LORD; point out the road for me to follow. Lead me by your truth and teach me, for you are the God who saves me. All day long I put my hope in you.   PSALM 25:4-5

Have you, like the guilt-ridden Renee, ever struggled with showing who you really are? Well, welcome to the human race.

I remember preparing to speak at a women's retreat and praying, "Lord, help me to show these women how to remove their masks." Then, stung by the self-righteousness of that request, I amended my prayer: "No, Lord. Help me to remove *my* mask."

God, with his sense of humor, surely said, "Okay!" and I forgot to pack my makeup! The retreat was in the Rocky Mountains, so I couldn't just run out and buy what I needed. And I wasn't about to borrow someone else's makeup.

As I fretted about what to do, I recognized this predicament as the answer to my prayer. So, faceless, I stood before the group and explained my prayer as the reason for their not being able to see my eyes. Then I began to talk about some of the masks we hide behind at one time or another: control, happiness, self-righteousness, and perfectionism.

Later, one of the committee leaders wrote me a note about the effect my presentation had on her:

> In an instant I was stripped to the bone, and I was sobbing on the inside as you said, "Let's take off the masks." My husband and I have leadership positions within the church, but everything I do has to be "perfect," or I'm miserable for weeks and miserable to live with. I can't let people know who I really am since I am afraid they won't like me. But I don't think they like me very much now. Your getting up in front of all those women without your makeup really got my attention, especially as I realized I would have pled illness before I would have done that. Now I'm asking God to show me how to take off my mask, but I hope He's gentler with me than He was with you.

I chuckled at her last sentence and was sorry she hadn't signed her name. How I would love to know how the Lord answered her prayer! But I do know her freedom and mine began with the realization we don't have to be "perfect" for the Lord to use us.   —SANDRA

Lord, I'd like to think I'm a what-you-see-is-what-you-get person. But I know better. Help me to take off my mask and show your reality to the people around me. May they be encouraged and strengthened by my quiet honesty.

Proud people breed sad sorrows for themselves.
—EMILY BRONTË (1818–1848), ENGLISH WRITER

To Ponder with a Friend

1. Can you say, "I am a worthwhile person"? Why or why not?

2. Have you experienced any of the three types of guilt the pastor outlined for Renee?

3. Have you ever sent or needed to send a "please forgive me" request through prayer?

4. What are the masks you are prone to hide behind?

APRIL 23

God's Gifts to You

He chose to give birth to us by giving us his true word. And we, out
of all creation, became his prized possession.
JAMES 1:18

Did you know that your voice is as unique as your fingerprint and there is no voice
exactly like yours? God has carefully designed each of us. There is nothing happen-
stance or random about how he has created each person, including you! The Lord
had something special in mind when he gave some people visual, artistic talent
and others perfect pitch and the ability to compose music. Every good gift is from
God, the first chapter of James says. One gift is not better than another. He gives
some people melodious voices and others the ability to teach. He gives leadership
talent or gifts of mercy and compassion to still others.

God had something special in mind when he made you—your body, your
soul, your personality, your talents, and your brain. Everything about each of us was
carefully thought out and designed. He had songs he wanted sung, organizations he
wanted started and managed. There were messages he wanted hands on earth to
write. He wanted stained-glass windows created to provide a glimpse of glory as the
sun shines through, marvelous paintings and colorful gardens to fill the world with
beauty and reflect his love and creativity. So God gave gifts to men and women to
accomplish these and many other purposes. What we do with those gifts and our
lives is our gift to the Creator.   —CHERI

> What more can I say to you for your gifts than thank you, my
> God and Savior! Thank you for making me, for choosing me to
> be your child, and for having a purpose for my life. Help me to
> be aware of your plans and to make my life a gift to you.

What you are is God's gift to you. What you make of yourself is your gift to God.
—ANONYMOUS

APRIL 24

God's Marvelous Workmanship

> Thank you for making me so wonderfully complex! Your workmanship is marvelous—how well I know it.
> PSALM 139:14

I was reminded of God's unique design of each individual when I worked in a summer arts camp for gifted junior high students one summer. As a writer, I worked with the verbally talented kids to help them create poems and stories. A musician directed the vocalists and those who played instruments, and a drama coach worked with the starstruck thespians. But perhaps most interesting to me was Maggie, the dance teacher, a ballet choreographer. At the end of the week, she and the dancers made up graceful movements and dance steps to interpret the poetry that was written and read by my students. After watching Maggie choreograph and dance, I complimented her. In reply, she said—as if we all shared this kind of talent—"Oh, I just think in movement all the time. That's how my mind works. When I hear music or poetry, I see dance steps and a whole flow of movement in my mind." To me—a person who thinks primarily in words, not in movement or pictures—this was an amazing talent.

Marsha, a ceramics and pottery artist, can look at a lump of red clay, see a porcelain angel, and then create a whimsical, colorful one in an afternoon. My sister-in-law Lou Ann has the analytical, mathematical, and administrative talent to create a financial plan for an entire city. Just as God has done with each of these women, he has designed *you* with gifts and talents, and he has wonderful, and sometimes surprising, plans for how he wants you to use them. My heartfelt hope is that you'll discover those gifts within you and utilize them not only as a way of expressing who you are and what you think and dream but also as a way of blessing others and glorifying God.   —CHERI

> To be honest, Lord, sometimes I've wondered why you made me the way you did. But you knew me before I was born and know just how I was sculpted, from nothing to something. I want to trust your heart even when I can't see your hand. I give myself with all my uniqueness and quirks to you for your purposes.

God, our wise and creative Maker, has been pleased to make everyone different and no one perfect. The sooner we appreciate and accept that fact, the deeper we will appreciate and accept ourselves and one another, just as our Designer planned us.   —CHARLES SWINDOLL, PASTOR, AUTHOR, EDUCATOR, AND RADIO PREACHER

APRIL 25
The Creative Spark

In his grace, God has given us different gifts for doing certain things well. So if God has given you the ability to prophesy, speak out with as much faith as God has given you. If your gift is serving others, serve them well. If you are a teacher, teach well. If your gift is to encourage others, be encouraging. If it is giving, give generously. If God has given you leadership ability, take the responsibility seriously. And if you have a gift for showing kindness to others, do it gladly.   ROMANS 12:6-8

Because the creative spark within you is a reflection of God's creative Spirit, when you exercise it by using your gifts, you will experience an irrepressible joy. This is the same kind of joy Eric Liddell, an Olympic runner, spoke of in the movie *Chariots of Fire* when he said, "God made me fast; and when I run, I feel his pleasure." When you are using the gifts God gave you, you find yourself operating at maximum effectiveness with a minimum of weariness because you are doing what you were made for. It is the same Spirit that inspired the gift of leadership, the ability to motivate people; artistic talent, the ability to write poetry or fiction; the ability to make money; creativity in any field; organizational and administrative talents; people skills; gifts of mercy, teaching, and encouragement; musical talent, and all the others I could name.

How can you discover and develop these gifts and experience this kind of joy? The first thing to do is to take your ordinary, daily life and place it before God as an offering. Make it your aim to live in intimacy with Christ and to follow him in the unique plan he has for your life. Let him change you from the inside by the power of his Word and his Spirit. The better you know Christ, the more you'll be at home with how he made you and the more you'll be able find your true self. Christ will bring out the best in you, and you'll discover your unique gifts—even gifts you didn't know you had. As Christ lives through you, it will bring you great joy and God great pleasure.   —CHERI

Father, I'm thankful that the creative spark within me is a reflection of your eternal, creative Spirit. Thank you for being an extraordinary God who takes ordinary people, like me, and makes something beautiful and purposeful out of their lives.

Thank God for the way he made you. You are special, distinct and unique. You were not made from a common mold.   —ERWIN W. LUTZER, PASTOR AND AUTHOR

APRIL 26
A Bright Future Filled with Hope

> "I know the plans I have for you," says the LORD. "They are plans for good and not for disaster, to give you a future and a hope." JEREMIAH 29:11

I once saw a cartoon in which two children are peering inside a grand piano. The little girl instructs the small boy, "There are millions of songs in there, but you've gotta punch the right keys to get them out."

God gives us inspiration, great ideas, gifts and talents, projects to do, words to write, and songs to play, but we have to apply the perspiration necessary to "punch the right keys" and not let rejection or failure hold us back. When dreams or plans fall through and you wake up to a reality very different from the one you had planned on, it's important to remember today's verse, for it is God speaking, telling you that although this is the way things are now, he has a purpose, a bright future filled with hope for you. Look at the words that come after today's verse: "In those days when you pray, I will listen. If you look for me wholeheartedly, you will find me" (Jeremiah 29:12-13). Seek God with your whole heart and embrace his plan, and then watch as he guides you in purposes greater than you could design for yourself.

Sometimes it helps to list some of the personal strengths, creative or inner abilities, acquired skills, innate intelligence for certain tasks, and spiritual gifts God has given you. Prayerfully pick one of the personal gifts or goals that you really want to pursue and develop. Share your dream with a trusted friend to bring the idea out of fantasy and into reality. Brainstorm together how you're going to begin pursuing your passion. If you encounter rejection along the way, consult with God for course correction if needed, and keep going. The Lord will direct your steps.
—CHERI

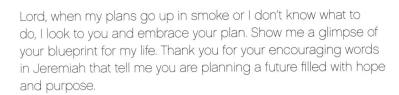

Lord, when my plans go up in smoke or I don't know what to do, I look to you and embrace your plan. Show me a glimpse of your blueprint for my life. Thank you for your encouraging words in Jeremiah that tell me you are planning a future filled with hope and purpose.

That we are alive today is proof positive that God has something for us to do today.
—VACHEL LINDSAY (1879–1931), AMERICAN POET

APRIL 27
For His Glory

> Whatever you do or say, do it as a representative of the Lord
> Jesus, giving thanks through him to God the Father.
> COLOSSIANS 3:17

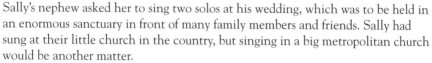

Sally's nephew asked her to sing two solos at his wedding, which was to be held in an enormous sanctuary in front of many family members and friends. Sally had sung at their little church in the country, but singing in a big metropolitan church would be another matter.

"Lord, help me to get my breath, to sound good, to not get emotional," Sally prayed. She so wanted to shine. But when the time came for her solos, nerves and the formality of the occasion got the best of her, and she lost all voice control, had an attack of coughing, and lost her breath during the last song. To her it seemed like a disaster. Afterward, humiliated and angry at God, she vowed she'd never sing in public again. It seemed he hadn't helped her do the very thing she'd so wanted to do well.

After a time, though, Sally was asked to sing at a worship service in her small country church, and she accepted. Since she didn't have time to prepare anything new, she chose to sing the same song she'd sung for the wedding. That Sunday morning, as she struggled again with fears about her "performance," God whispered to her heart, *Who created you, Sally? Who made your voice?*

"You made me, Lord," she answered, "and you made my voice."

Yes, your voice is mine, and I will use it. It's not for your glory but for mine.

That Sunday morning Sally's singing was totally different. Instead of focusing on herself and her voice, she focused on the One who had given her that voice. With a new freedom, she sang beautifully without a hitch and gave God her heartfelt thanks and praise. The fear that had caused her to lose voice control was gone, replaced by a new joy and confidence, not in herself but in God.   —CHERI

> Lord, so often I have my eyes on myself and my abilities or
> disabilities. Forgive me, and help me to do everything for your
> glory and by your grace. May my focus be you, wonderful Savior,
> and not myself.

God can do great things with our lives, if we but give them to him in sincerity.
—ANNA ROBERTSON BROWN LINDSAY (1864–1948), WRITER AND POET

APRIL 28
Are You Willing?

[Daniel prayed,] "O LORD, you are a great and awesome God! You
always fulfill your covenant and keep your promises of unfailing
love to those who love you and obey your commands. But we have
sinned and done wrong. We have rebelled against you and scorned
your commands and regulations. . . . As you see, our faces are
covered with shame. This is true of all of us, including the people
of Judah and Jerusalem and all Israel, scattered near and far,
wherever you have driven us because of our disloyalty to you."
DANIEL 9:4-7

Because of a severe stutter, Hannah Hurnard was a withdrawn, fearful girl who
dreaded being around people. But when she surrendered her heart to Christ at age
twenty, he began to transform her life. While attending an open-air Christian
meeting, Hannah felt a call to be a missionary but had no idea where she'd go.
After spending four years with an evangelistic group, she went to Ireland. While
reading her Bible one day on a hillside, she saw how Daniel identified himself
completely with the sins of the Israelites when he fasted and prayed.

She sensed God asking her, *Hannah, would you be willing to identify yourself
with the Jewish people the same way Daniel identified with the Israelites?*

Because she had no particular fondness for the Jews, she was upset by the
question. "Lord, I have no desire to be with them at all. How could I be a missionary to people I don't even like?"

*If you are willing to go, I will help you love the Jews and identify with them. It all
depends on your will,* God replied to her heart.

Hannah knelt and told God she would obey. Her friends doubted the decision, and her doctor said she could never withstand the rigors of working in such a
climate. She applied to the only mission she knew of in Palestine and was rejected.
But Hannah persevered, and eventually, paying her own expenses, she did go to
Israel to minister to the Jewish people. Because of her unique gifts and her willingness to go wherever God sent her, she was launched into a lifelong ministry of
evangelism, speaking, and writing books that touched millions of people around
the world for Christ.

She lived a life vastly different from that of anyone else in her British family
or circle of friends, but it had a fruitfulness and joy that was both supernatural and
satisfying. —CHERI

Lord, I want to be willing to do your will. Please show me the way.
Take my fears, and give me courage to follow you.

God's will is easy to find if we want it. Really, the only people who miss his will are
those who have no use for it. The months and years may show us that we've taken
a strange, roundabout way, but if our hearts are right, our feet will never go astray.
—DAVID ROPER, PASTOR AND WRITER

APRIL 29
What about My Mistakes?

[The Lord] will give a crown of beauty for ashes, a joyous blessing instead of mourning, festive praise instead of despair.
ISAIAH 61:3

"There's no such thing as a mistake in drawing," Melissa's elementary art teacher told the class. "So don't try to erase all your blunders. Every squiggly line, every misplaced circle or splotch of color can be made into something creative and new." Then with a few skillful strokes of her paintbrush, she showed the children how to change what looked like a messed-up painting into a work of art.

Since then, there have been lots of splotched and squiggled canvases in Melissa's life: mistakes and messes of her own making or pain because of the mistakes of others. Sometimes she's tempted to sink into regret and think, *If only I could erase that. . . . If only it hadn't happened, my life would be so much better.* But in those times, she hears God remind her that although he doesn't erase history, he can use even our individual mistakes to create something beautiful if we bring all the squiggled lines and broken pieces of our lives to him, admit our failures, and ask for his help.

Can God really change something ugly or broken into something beautiful? There's no sin, mistake, or heartache he can't redeem if we'll give it to him. We may see only the sorrow or crisis in our lives or feel the ache of defeat, but as today's verse tells us, he can bring amazing beauty out of a heap of ashes. If an earthly artist can save a botched drawing and turn it into a lovely piece of art, how much more can God's love redeem every mistake in our lives! Hurts and losses in our own lives become bridges that enable us to reach out and comfort others. Dreams that have died are brought to new life. And weaknesses become blessings because they draw us closer to our Creator.

Can God create something beautiful out of our mistakes? He specializes in that kind of art.   —CHERI

Father, how grateful I am that you can bring beauty out of ashes, something good out of the mistakes I have made. I bring them to you, trusting you to be the glue in my life, to mend and heal my heart and soul, and to produce by your love and grace something beautiful.

The goodness of God knows how to use our disordered wishes and actions, often lovingly turning them to our advantage while always preserving the beauty of his order.   —BERNARD OF CLAIRVAUX (1090–1153), FRENCH CLERGYMAN

To Ponder with a Friend

1. What gifts, qualities, and even unique "quirks" about yourself could you thank God for making a part of your wiring? Make a list and thank him one by one for these specific parts of your design.

2. Have any of these gifts lain dormant? Which one would you most like to develop? Do you perhaps even sense God nudging you to pursue one of these?

3. Has there been a time when you had an opportunity to share your talents with others and, like Sally in the April 27 devotional, learned to move through your fears to sing, play an instrument, write, paint, serve, etc., by relying on God's strength and grace? If so, what did you feel and experience?

4. Reread Isaiah 61:3. From what broken pieces, mistakes, or "ashes" would you like God to bring beauty? Write them down, or if you feel comfortable doing so, share with a trusted friend and pray about them, releasing them to the Lord for his process of restoration.

APRIL 30
Wrong Standards

Teach me your decrees, O LORD; I will keep them to the end. Give me understanding and I will obey your instructions; I will put them into practice with all my heart.   PSALM 119:33-34

Diane was thrilled when the well-known author and speaker, whom I'll call Mrs. Perfect, hired her as an assistant. Her job description included arranging events and travel details, pressing Mrs. Perfect's clothes, packing and handling her bags, fetching ice, tracking details, and taking on any other responsibilities Perfect tossed her way.

Before each platform appearance, Diane would slice a fresh lemon into thirty-two precise slices for munching or dropping into ice water. Then during the presentation, she would sit to the side, armed with a yellow pad for the to-do list Perfect would fire at her on their way back to the hotel. Diane had learned to take notes quickly; an irritated Perfect would snap instructions if she had to repeat anything.

About two months into the assignment, Perfect had screamed at Diane for not packing the backup cell phone, even though it hadn't been needed on the trip they were finishing. Diane had apologized and even cried, promising to check her list more carefully the next time. For several days afterward, the thought *I'm so stupid* kept running through her head as she scurried to finish each item on her daily to-do list. Clearly, something needed to change.   —SANDRA

Lord, often I have shaken my head at people who follow media celebrities. I've even accused them of being shallow and needing to "get a life." But if I'm honest, I know I've placed ministry leaders on pedestals. I tend to think if they've appeared on a certain TV or radio program, spoken to thousands, or written a Christian best seller, then they must be more righteous than the rest of us. Help me to stop adoring human personalities and remember we are all sinners, saved by grace—your grace.

Nearly all men can stand adversity, but if you want to test a man's character, give him power.
—ABRAHAM LINCOLN (1809–1865), SIXTEENTH PRESIDENT OF THE UNITED STATES

MAY 1
Sad Truth

May the Lord make your love for one another and for all people grow and overflow, just as our love for you overflows.

1 THESSALONIANS 3:12

While Diane struggled with feelings of inadequacy, she witnessed something the following weekend that let her know she wasn't the one with the problem.

At a Florida conference, a timid-looking woman approached Mrs. Perfect in the ballroom lobby.

"I must tell you how much I admire you," she managed. "In fact, I have every one of your books."

Perfect smiled. "Every one? There are five books in the first series alone."

The woman nodded. "And seven in the second."

Perfect glanced at her watch. "Yes, and my latest book is available at my booth. Do buy it, and I'll autograph it for you. Well, I must run."

The timid woman took a deep breath to gather courage and said, "May I hug you before I go?"

Perfect looked appalled. "Oh, I'd rather you didn't," she said. "My makeup and hair are just so, and I don't want to be mussed up."

The timid woman's face flushed as she nodded and quickly turned away. Diane felt embarrassed and heartsick. Her long-admired mentor, the one she had held up as an example of "The Perfect Christian Woman," had proven herself to be just another stage performer.

Diane noticed the woman did not stop to buy a book after the presentation. The next morning, Diane saw her checking out of the hotel even though the conference would continue for another two days. She wondered what the woman would do with all of Perfect's books once she arrived home. Probably nothing. She would just make sure she never again asked for something as "intimate" as a public hug. —SANDRA

Lord, it's easy for me to criticize people like Mrs. Perfect. After all, would it have killed her to give the woman a quick hug? But have I ever been thoughtless like that? Have I ever reacted hastily, not realizing the pain or embarrassment my quick words caused? Help me to think before I respond. And help me to respond out of a heart attuned to you.

Going to church doesn't make you a Christian any more than going to a garage makes you an automobile. —BILLY SUNDAY (1862–1935), AMERICAN EVANGELIST

MAY 2
New Insight

Because of the privilege and authority God has given me, I give each of you this warning: Don't think you are better than you really are. Be honest in your evaluation of yourselves, measuring yourselves by the faith God has given us.   ROMANS 12:3

That evening after the day's sessions when Diane tried to talk to Perfect about the scene, she was met with bewilderment. Perfect didn't understand why "fans," as she called the women in her audiences, were always wanting to hug her. With a dismissive wave of her hand, she let her young assistant know the discussion was over.

As Diane continued to ponder the insensitivity her boss had displayed, she wished two things: (1) that Mrs. Perfect hadn't worried about an adoring "fan" mussing her hair or smudging her makeup, and (2) that the admiring woman hadn't expected so much from just another human being.

Diane was learning the hard way that people, no matter what their position, are just people. And in her close work with Perfect, Diane had also learned that whenever she set her expectations of another person too high, sooner or later, she was bound to be disappointed. And judging from the way she had let her own devotional life slide lately, she knew she was heading toward discouragement, which could quickly propel her into disheartenment. She suddenly understood the accounts she had heard of other workers in Christian ministry who left not only their public ministry but even the church.

Now she had a decision to make: She could resign her position as assistant to Mrs. Perfect. Or she could take a deep breath and continue in her role but without the gushy adoration.   —SANDRA

Lord, Diane did the right thing by trying to talk to her employer about this situation. I probably either would have ignored it or developed an "attitude." Help me to tackle the issues that need tackling, but always in your right time and only after I've prayed.

The trouble with most of us is that we would rather be ruined by praise than saved by criticism.
—NORMAN VINCENT PEALE (1898–1993), AMERICAN PREACHER AND AUTHOR

MAY 3
Facing the Consequences

> We who are strong must be considerate of those who are sensitive
> about things like this. We must not just please ourselves. We
> should help others do what is right and build them up in the Lord.
> ROMANS 15:1-2

After much prayer and a return to her own study of the Word, Diane decided to resign her position. She offered to stay until a replacement was found, but Perfect was furious at what she called Diane's lack of gratitude and insisted Diane leave immediately. She drove home in tears.

The next morning, though, she called several friends to ask if they knew of other job opportunities. Soon she cautiously accepted a position with another author, whom I'll call Mrs. Peace. Diane was delighted and relieved to find that Peace lived out her faith each day and quietly taught the young woman what it means to listen to the Lord even in the midst of an intense schedule.

One of the lessons Diane learned from her new boss was the truth of Romans 15:1-2: "We who are strong must be considerate of those who are sensitive about things like this. We must not just please ourselves. We should help others do what is right and build them up in the Lord."

As she watched her employer encourage the other members of the speaking team, she saw the truth of the Lord's words in John 13:34-35 lived out: "I am giving you a new commandment: Love each other. Just as I have loved you, you should love each other. Your love for one another will prove to the world that you are my disciples."

This woman had a gentle way of encouraging her teammates and her staff as she publicly pointed out their strengths. If she had a suggestion about something one of her staff members should consider, that suggestion was offered in private. And always, Diane watched in quiet amazement.   —SANDRA

Lord, that old English proverb about catching more flies with honey than with vinegar is true. And as I remember that flies and bees and butterflies are attracted to sweetness and repelled by tartness, help me to remember that people are drawn to kindness and repelled by criticism. Help me to sweetly and lovingly speak your truth to this hurting world.

Kindness has converted more sinners than zeal, eloquence, or learning.
—FREDERICK WILLIAM FABER (1814–1863), BRITISH HYMN WRITER AND THEOLOGIAN

MAY 4

Gentle Words

Make every effort to respond to God's promises. Supplement your faith with a generous provision of moral excellence, and moral excellence with knowledge, and knowledge with self-control, and self-control with patient endurance, and patient endurance with godliness, and godliness with brotherly affection, and brotherly affection with love for everyone. 2 PETER 1:5-7

One serene afternoon, as Diane and Peace checked the travel itinerary for the next week, Diane timidly thanked her boss for never yelling at her. Then she asked how she managed to bring out so much good in others.

Peace smiled. "Oh, I do plenty of yelling," she said. "I just reserve that for the neighborhood dogs digging in my flower garden, not for fellow travelers in this thing we loosely call 'life.' The Lord taught me something a long time ago: If he could love and use Peter, even though he knew the salty old fisherman was going to deny him publicly three times, then who am I to judge how folks are going to turn out?"

Peace put on her glasses, reached for her ever-present Bible, and turned to John 13:38. "This is just one of the Gospel accounts in which Jesus predicted that the very man who had just said he would lay down his life for the Lord would, in fact, deny him three times before daybreak. And by the time we get to John 18:27, that's exactly what happened."

She flipped through several more pages. "Now look in Acts 2. Here, Peter is preaching at Pentecost. And in verse 41, it says about three thousand people became believers that day. Even more followed that number, all through the preaching of the very one who had denied the Lord three times."

Peace smiled at Diane. "To see the best in others without being blind to their weaknesses is an example our Lord set numerous times. And as long as we keep our eyes on him and off ourselves, miracles will continue to happen, first in us and then in the folks around us."

As Diane's employer took off her glasses, Diane made a mental note to read those Scripture passages for herself that evening. *So this was what it meant to be a follower of the Lord and not of oneself.* —SANDRA

Lord, thank you for reminding me you never are finished with any of us, not even me. Help me not to sit in judgment of others. Help me to see them as you do. And help me to see myself through your tender eyes as well.

Life is short and we have not too much time for gladdening the hearts of those who are traveling the dark way with us. Oh, be swift to love! Make haste to be kind.
—HENRI FREDERIC AMIEL (1821–1881), SWISS PHILOSOPHER, POET, AND CRITIC

MAY 5
Watching Closely

The LORD is close to all who call on him, yes, to all who call on him in truth. PSALM 145:18

The young singer, whom I'll call Paula, was nervous as she approached the tour bus. She had been invited to sing backup for a well-known Christian couple for the entire summer. While she was thrilled at the opportunity, she also was nervous. On stage, they were a loving pair. But what if that was just for appearances? What if they were rude to each other privately? What if they were rude to her? Her short career already had exposed her to singers who proclaimed joyous faith on the church platform but who were short tempered and sarcastic once they were away from the adoring crowds.

As Paula climbed the bus steps, she breathed a silent prayer: *Lord, please let this couple be all I think they are. I don't need another disappointment.*

Just as she settled into a seat in the fifth row and placed a travel pillow in the small of her back, the famous couple stepped onto the bus. The wife, Beatrice, smiled.

"Paula, honey, you're already here. Are you ready for an exciting, exhausting summer?"

"I hope so."

Beatrice's smile widened. "Oh, I *know* you are! The folks will love you. Let's see; it's my turn to pray before we start." Her sincere prayer for travel mercies, protection for all whom they were leaving behind, and sensitivity to the Spirit's leading at each concert gave Paula much to ponder as the bus pulled out of the parking lot.

She took a deep breath. *Well, Lord, here we go.* Then after a long moment, she added, *And help me to look to you and not to them.*

The bus shifted gears and merged into highway traffic. The long summer tour had begun. —SANDRA

Lord, I confess I'm like Paula, looking to others and hoping not to be disappointed as they live out their faith. Help me not to be so quick with my judgments. Help me to concentrate less on them and more on you.

What is Christian perfection? Loving God with all our heart, mind, soul, and strength.
—JOHN WESLEY (1703–1791), ENGLISH EVANGELIST AND FOUNDER OF METHODISM

MAY 6

A Godly Example

Every time I think of you, I give thanks to my God. Whenever I pray, I make my requests for all of you with joy, for you have been my partners in spreading the Good News about Christ from the time you first heard it until now. And I am certain that God, who began the good work within you, will continue his work until it is finally finished on the day when Christ Jesus returns.

PHILIPPIANS 1:3-6

In the weeks that followed, Paula was astonished at the couple's patience with each other, with their staff, and with her. If bad weather or detours caused them to arrive at the next event too late for a proper practice session, they talked over the program on the bus. If their driver missed an exit in rush-hour traffic, they made an effort to calm his frustration. If they were tired or grouchy, they chose to sit apart quietly for a time instead of throwing barbed comments at each other.

One of the biggest surprises for Paula, though, was learning that Beatrice was a homebody who dreaded travel. But because she shared her struggle between her longing for the comforts of home and her desire to serve the Lord alongside her husband, she quietly passed on her personal strength to Paula. And along the way, she set a godly example for others facing their own challenges in ministry.

Today, Paula credits her experience on that tour with starting her own singing ministry: "I started that summer afraid I'd be disappointed. But as I became less preoccupied with pedestals and more concerned with spiritual growth, I learned the lessons the Lord had for me."

And that made all the difference.   —SANDRA

> Lord, help me to be less interested in so-called heroes and more interested in your personal calling for my life. Give me strength for my personal journey. Help me to discard my tendency to envy others. And along the way, may I encourage my fellow travelers.

What happens when God grants the gift of genuine Christian fellowship? Deep, joyful sharing replaces the polite prattle typically exchanged by Christians on Sunday morning. Sisters and brothers begin to discuss the things that really matter to them. They disclose their inner fears, their areas of particular temptation, their deepest joys.   —RONALD J. SIDER, THEOLOGIAN AND CHRISTIAN ACTIVIST

To Ponder with a Friend

1. Have you ever adored someone in a public ministry? If so, whom?

2. If you could work for anyone in the public eye, what would you like your job to be?

3. Do you ever envy those with far-reaching public ministries? Why or why not?

4. What challenges do you think you would face if your sphere of influence were extended?

MAY 7
The Voice of the Lord

> The voice of the LORD echoes above the sea. . . . The voice of the LORD is powerful; the voice of the LORD is majestic. The voice of the LORD splits the mighty cedars.   PSALM 29:3-5

God spoke, and there was light. He spoke, and there was sky, land, and sea. God spoke, and the land burst forth with every kind of grass and seed-bearing fruit. God spoke, and animals were created, humanity was made in his image, and all creation was established. When God spoke, life came forth.

But God didn't stop speaking when Creation was complete. Psalm 50:3 states that our God approaches and he does not keep silent. He spoke to people in the Bible—patriarchs such as Abraham and Jacob, prophets, and disciples—and he is still speaking today. God has always been so creative in his communication. Sometimes he spoke through angels, other times through dreams, visions, or a burning bush. He spoke audibly to Saul on the road to Damascus (see Acts 9:3-6). When Balaam wasn't paying attention, God spoke through Balaam's donkey (see Numbers 22:28). God makes the earth shake, as Psalm 29:7-9 describes: His majestic voice can strip forests bare or strike like lightning. But God also communicates through a still, small voice, as Elijah experienced (see 1 Kings 19:12). The marvelous news is that hearing God isn't a special privilege reserved only for priests and prophets, seminary graduates, or ministers. It's not just for those who are smart or especially gifted. God has many things to say to *you*, and he wants to bless your life with direction and purpose as you listen and follow. All it takes is a listening heart.
—CHERI

> Lord, thank you for your constant nearness and for never ceasing to speak to me. Give me a heart that is listening and attentive to what your Spirit might be impressing on my spirit today.

We begin by first quieting our fleshly activity and listening to the silent thunder of the Lord of hosts. Attuning ourselves to divine breathings is spiritual work. . . . We must hear, know, and obey the will of God before we pray it into the lives of others.   —RICHARD FOSTER, QUAKER THEOLOGIAN AND AUTHOR

MAY 8
A Listening Heart

> The LORD says, "I will guide you along the best pathway for your life." PSALM 32:8

Sometimes we approach prayer like the woman who made an appointment with a physician because she was having health problems. When it was her turn, she went in to the examining room and told him her symptoms. But before the doctor could give her a diagnosis or treatment plan, she ran out of the room and went on to the next appointment in her schedule book. In doing so, she missed the very solution and help she needed.

Prayer, the dialogue between us and God, isn't just about what we say to him. If it were, it would be a one-way conversation. There's also the *listening* part of dialogue. When I'm having a conversation with a friend at Starbucks, each of us wants to hear what the other person has to say. So we talk, and we also listen to each other.

I don't know about you, but I can be so caught up in the petition part of prayer that I don't allow God to get a word in edgewise. The Lord has much to say to us if we will just listen. Sometimes God speaks through his written Word. Other times, he speaks to us through a glorious sunset or a night sky spangled with stars: "The heavens proclaim the glory of God. The skies display his craftsmanship" (Psalm 19:1). We may hear him through a sermon, or we may recognize his whisper during the silence of our devotional time or as we walk on a snow-covered road. God speaks in times of joy, but it seems we most often pay attention and hear him most clearly in times of anxiety or pain. C. S. Lewis observed that pain "is God's megaphone to rouse a deaf world."

One thing is sure: When God speaks from his heart to yours, when you hear him and obey, something changes. Healing begins, or an attitude is transformed. A relationship is restored, or we receive needed direction. And sometimes his whispers are meant simply to reassure us of his love. Will you listen to what God has to say to you today?   —CHERI

> Lord, I confess I'm not the best listener, either to other people or to you. Forgive me for sharing my petitions and then not tuning in to what you have to say. Give me the faith to believe you will speak to me. I surrender to you anew today.

God is whispering to us well nigh incessantly. Whenever the sounds of the world die out in the soul, or sink low, then we hear these whisperings of God. [He] is always whispering to us, only we do not always hear because of the noise, hurry, and distraction which life causes as it rushes on.
—FREDERICK WILLIAM FABER (1814–1863), BRITISH HYMN WRITER AND THEOLOGIAN

MAY 9
Mighty, Remarkable Secrets

This is what the LORD says—the LORD who made the earth, who formed and established it, whose name is the LORD: Ask me and I will tell you remarkable secrets you do not know about things to come.   JEREMIAH 33:2-3

These verses, which Corrie ten Boom, the marvelous missionary from Holland, called "God's Private Telephone Number," are really quite amazing. They mean that God invites us not only to come to him in prayer but to do so believing that he promises to answer us and tell us *remarkable secrets*, things that only God knows. These are more than likely things we *need* to know that we'd never discover unless we asked and listened.

I once heard one of the leading eye surgeons in the country say that when he was on a difficult case in the operating room and had no idea what to do next, he relied on today's passage. He called on God, resting on his promise in Jeremiah 33:3, and asked him what he should do next and how to operate to restore the patient's sight or to correct the problem. The surgeon said that God had never failed to answer him, even showing him surgical procedures never done before and giving him supernatural wisdom.

Let me encourage you to ask God to show you "remarkable secrets," and then pay attention when he taps you on the shoulder in the middle of your commute or while you're at the computer. Take a "listening walk," not to list prayer requests or talk to God but to *listen* for what the Lord's Spirit will impress on you. Read his love letter to you, the Bible, with a listening heart, and stay tuned in to his Spirit through the day. As you listen and respond to the One who loves you the most, he will guide you as the apple of his eye, and your life will be blessed beyond your dreams or imagination.   —CHERI

Lord of love, I am calling upon you with this problem or dilemma: _____. I want to hear your voice and know you more. Quiet my heart, and help me to be still and know that you are God, as you show me wonderful and unsearchable things I do not know.

If you keep watch over your hearts, and listen for the voice of God and learn of him, in one short hour you can learn more from him than you could learn from man in a thousand years.
—JOHANN TAULER (CA. 1300–1361), GERMAN MYSTIC AND THEOLOGIAN

Getting God's Viewpoint

[Jesus said,] "My sheep listen to my voice; I know them, and they follow me." JOHN 10:27

When Connie's children were very young, she began to realize that she and her husband were not taking the same approach to rearing their children. He had a different temperament and a distinctly different parenting style. She had a master's degree in child development and years of professional experience with children, and she was sure her way was *the right way* to handle their kids. If only her husband would change and do things *her way.* One day in frustration she sat on her bed and began to pray about the conflicts they were having: *God, when are you going to show Stan that I'm doing this right and that he should come on board and parent the way I do?* she asked.

Quietly, yet as clearly as she'd ever heard anything from God, her heart heard him whisper, *If both of you were exactly the same, one of you wouldn't be necessary!* She knew *she* didn't want to be the parent who wasn't needed, nor did she want her husband to be expendable. When Connie heard God's viewpoint, a dramatic change took place in her attitude. She began to value her husband's parenting style instead of criticizing it. She started to appreciate his gifts and his unique way of relating to their kids, to celebrate their differences instead of being irritated by them. As a result, they had more harmony as parents, and a happy peace descended on their home.

On what situations in our lives do we need God's perspective? Let us ask him for his viewpoint, for what he wants us to see or understand. Today's verse assures us that the infinite God of the universe is also the Shepherd of our lives who says his sheep *do* hear his voice.   —CHERI

Thank you, Jesus, for your promise that your sheep hear your voice. I lay down my agenda and the ways I see things and ask you to speak to me. Open my spiritual ears so I can hear your voice and follow you more clearly day by day.

Clearly, we are creatures built for listening, not just for talking. If God tells us to listen, surely he will not leave us hanging.
—TIMOTHY JONES, PASTOR, CAMPUS-MINISTRY LEADER, AND AUTHOR

MAY 11

Waiting Quietly

> Let all that I am wait quietly before God, for my hope is in him.
> He alone is my rock and my salvation, my fortress where I will
> not be shaken. My victory and honor come from God alone. He is
> my refuge, a rock where no enemy can reach me.   PSALM 62:5-7

Waiting seems to be a lost art today. Most of us don't want to wait for anything. We want fast food, short lines at the grocery store, and instant answers to prayer. Most of all, we don't want to wait for help if we are in the midst of trouble or pain.

In Psalm 62, David poured out his heart to God, describing his difficulties, the enemies who were trying to kill him, and the lies and curses spoken against him. But on the battlefield of life, in the midst of every trouble, David looked up and waited quietly before God. That was one of the distinctives of David's life: He valued listening to God and waiting on him. David was honest about his complaints and problems, but he purposed to direct his gaze to the God of all faithfulness, putting his trust in the One who alone was his rock, his salvation, his fortress, and his refuge. He then could wait quietly before God and receive his guidance because he had put his hope and his very life in the Lord's hands.

David didn't trust in human nature, because it was no more secure than a breath. He didn't put his hope in riches because he knew that wealth wouldn't save him. His hope, confidence, and trust were in the Lord Almighty.

If, like David, we are looking for God to act while we're in the midst of trouble, we need to take time to wait. Finding a quiet place helps. Writing down the thoughts and verses that the Spirit brings to mind can provide guidance. Checking what we hear with godly counsel can help us to gain clarity. But waiting *quietly in hope* takes a deep confidence in the One before whom we are waiting. And God will never disappoint us.   —CHERI

> Lord, I lift my eyes up to you, my rock, my salvation, my fortress, and my refuge. Help me to wait for you in the storms, in the light, and in the dark. Let my confidence not be shaken by what my heart may feel, my circumstances may say, or my mind may think. I thank you that my confidence rests on the One who is my rock and that *you* will never be shaken.

We must wait for God, long, meekly, in the wind and wet, in the thunder and lightning, in the cold and the dark. Wait, and he will come.
—FREDERICK WILLIAM FABER (1814–1863), BRITISH HYMN WRITER AND THEOLOGIAN

MAY 12

Hearing God through His Word

Let the message about Christ, in all its richness, fill your lives.
Teach and counsel each other with all the wisdom he gives.
COLOSSIANS 3:16

Six-year-old Hannah accompanied her parents to their weekly small-group meeting and drew pictures while the adults discussed their current struggles. One young woman talked about how she had been in a "desert" and hadn't heard God speak to her in a long time. Several other adults chimed in that they, too, wished God would speak to them more often. As they spoke, Hannah took all this in. On the way home, she said to her parents, "Don't the grown-ups read their Bibles? God speaks to us every time we pick up our Bible and read it, because he wrote it! If they would just open their Bibles, I know they'd hear God talk to them."

Hannah is right. The Bible is the major source of the Lord's wisdom, counsel, and communication with us because Jesus is the Living Word and the Bible is his love letter to us. When we read the Bible day by day and seek God through the Scriptures, we hear his voice more clearly and grow to know him more and more. Countless times when I have been reading the Bible, it was as if heaven focused the beam of a flashlight on a special verse or passage just so I would notice it, write it on a card to ponder, and pray it back to God. Sometimes I have memorized a passage and then later the Spirit has brought it to my mind for a certain need or moment. How grateful I am that early in my Christian life a wiser, older woman told me that about 75 percent of God's guidance comes through his Word and if I didn't stay in his Word, I would miss the very direction, instruction, and help he has provided.

Open your Bible and read today, searching for what the Living Word has to teach you.   —CHERI

As I read your Word today, show me, Holy Spirit, how it addresses the situations in my life. Grant me a spirit of wisdom and revelation in the knowledge of Jesus, the Living Word, as I study your holy written Word.

Our private training takes place in the presence of God, through the Word of God. It is here that we learn to hear the voice of God as we keep our eyes on His Person. With our focus on Him, our minds willing and our ears open to hear His loving voice even if it directs us to painful change, we will be taught by God's Spirit.
—MARTHA THATCHER, AUTHOR AND NAVIGATOR STAFF MEMBER

Read and Listen

> The LORD says, "I will guide you along the best pathway for your life. I will advise you and watch over you." PSALM 32:8

Author and speaker Evelyn Christenson helped me to learn a wonderful way to listen to God during my times in the Bible. When she set out to earnestly seek the Lord, he taught her to begin reading a passage of Scripture and *keep reading until his Spirit stopped her*. Then she would stop right there (not rushing to get a certain number of chapters finished) to pray about what that passage said. She asked God to be her Teacher and depended on the Holy Spirit to operate in her and to give her understanding. Then she listened for what God said to her about the verses and analyzed what his reason might be for stopping her at that particular place. That would help her discover the need and determine what her part was, what step of obedience she was to take.

Sometimes the passage was a word of correction for a wrong attitude. Sometimes it brought her comfort or reminded her of God's love. Often there was specific direction for a certain situation or for a retreat she was going to do. The night before Evelyn was to have major surgery, she was reading in Romans, and God stopped her at Romans 12:1. As she pondered that verse, she realized that she had given God her soul, her mind, and her emotions but never her body! As a result, she surrendered her whole physical body so that God might be in charge of everything that concerned her in that surgery and throughout her life.

Because Evelyn has paid close attention to the Bible in this way, day by day, year by year, and precept on precept, God in his grace has never left her wandering in the dark. He has always provided just the right amount of light for the next step. He has given her wisdom that she has passed on in her books and messages. And as she has obeyed the Lord's instructions, he has changed her into the woman he wanted her to be—a woman who has inspired millions of women in the United States and around the world and has imparted a powerful vision for what happens when women pray. —CHERI

> Thank you for the Bible, which gives me light and strength. Be my Teacher, Spirit of Christ, as I give attention to your Word. May it transform me day by day.

God did not write a book and send it by messenger to be read at a distance by unaided minds. He spoke a book and lives in his spoken words, constantly speaking his words and causing the power of them to persist across the years.
—A. W. TOZER (1897–1963), AMERICAN PASTOR, PREACHER, AND AUTHOR

To Ponder with a Friend

1. Think about an experience you've had in which God's gentle whisper directed you to do something and you obeyed. What was the message, and what was the outcome of your obedience?

2. Sometimes God speaks through his Word as written in the Bible, sometimes he speaks through a sermon, and sometimes he speaks through our pain. Often he speaks in a way that is *contrary to our natural inclinations.* If you can recall a time when what he spoke to you was contrary to your natural inclinations and, in fact, *not what you wanted to hear,* share about it or write what happened.

3. What helps you to hear God and experience his presence: Being alone in a quiet place? Walking in nature? Meditating on the Scriptures? Something that is unique to the way God designed you?

4. Reread Jeremiah 33:3. Is there an area, relationship, or decision about which "you do not know" and for which you need guidance from God and to hear what he has to say?

MAY 14

Misguided Zeal

> This is what you must do: Tell the truth to each other. Render
> verdicts in your courts that are just and that lead to peace.
> ZECHARIAH 8:16

Michelle plopped the lamb chops into the skillet to brown, then halved the fresh
apricots and chopped the onions, all the while glancing at the clock. Charles
would arrive in an hour. Sighing, she wished she hadn't promised to make this
complicated dish tonight, but he always raved when she served curried lamb and
apricots. His job kept him on the road and in restaurants much of the time, so
when he was in town, she didn't want to disappoint him.

She smiled, remembering how she had studied her cookbooks before that first
dinner and then settled on the exotic-sounding dish. That night, she had watched
Charles closely as he took the first bite. How relieved she had been when he said,
"This is really good. Really. In fact, these are the best chops I've ever had."

Even though she had had a long meeting at work, she wanted Charles to
understand that he was important to her—important enough to fuss over. Besides,
she was convinced that he was working up to the Big Question, and she wanted
nothing to stand in the way.

She sautéed the onions in butter, then added the flour, salt, milk, and curry,
stirring all the while. As the sauce began to bubble, she added the mushrooms,
then poured the mixture over the chops and apricot halves she had arranged in a
baking dish. There! Now to toss the salad while the chops baked.

It was a good thing she had set the table last night after Charles called to
confirm tonight's date. But, of course, that was so much like him. *He truly is the
nicest guy in the world,* she thought. *And worth every minute I have to spend preparing
this dish.*

Just as the oven timer went off, the doorbell rang.   —SANDRA

> Lord, so often in my attempts to please others, I hear only what I
> want to hear. Help me to ask for your wisdom and discernment
> so I can hear beyond mere words.

A half-truth is a dangerous thing, especially if you have hold of the wrong half.
—MYRON F. BOYD (1932–1978), RADIO PASTOR AND FREE METHODIST BISHOP

MAY 15
Speak with Love

> We will speak the truth in love, growing in every way more and
> more like Christ, who is the head of his body, the church.
> EPHESIANS 4:15

The evening went just as Michelle had envisioned—even to the after-dinner stroll onto her patio to look at the city lights. After a long moment, Charles took a deep breath, then dropped to one knee.

Looking up, he said, "Michelle, you know I love you. When I'm on the road, I can't wait to come home because of you. Will you marry me?"

Tears welled in her eyes at his words and the old-fashioned gesture of kneeling to propose. "Oh, Charles, yes," she said. "Of course, I'll marry you."

He stood up to put his arms around her as he murmured, "Oh, thank you!"

She expected him to kiss her, but instead he stammered, "Since we're gonna be married, please don't fix curried chops again. I can't stand curry."

Michelle pulled back, stunned. Why had he let her continue to prepare a dish he hated? Then her mind raced. How would he face the challenges of marriage if he had let her believe a lie all these months?

Poor Michelle. Poor Charles. Was he really being dishonest? Or had he thought it kinder to spare her feelings only to get caught in a complication?

Charles's misguided determination not to hurt Michelle's feelings had created this tangled situation. Now, instead of delight at Charles's marriage proposal, Michelle felt only dismay.

All of this could have been avoided if Charles had followed Ephesians 4:15, which says to speak the truth in love. The first time Michelle had prepared curried chops, Charles could have said, "This dish is well prepared and tasty, but curry isn't my favorite spice."

His honest response might have hurt her feelings momentarily but would have spared her deeper hurts.

One caution: The truth is to be spoken "in love." Too often, meanness is cloaked as "truthfulness," as when a woman named Margaret criticized her new daughter-in-law's dinner and then added, "I'm telling you this for your own good."

To Michelle's credit, she didn't hold Charles's misjudgment against him. Instead, she let him know gently that she would rather hear the truth right away.

That's a great way to start a great marriage.   —SANDRA

Lord, help me to gently tell the truth and not go out of my way to
correct the world around me. Remind me that not everyone needs
to do things my way. Help me to remember that you sent the true
Messiah more than two thousand years ago and I'm not a second one.

Truth has no special time of its own. Its hour is now—always.
—ALBERT SCHWEITZER (1875–1965), FRENCH THEOLOGIAN, PHILOSOPHER, MEDICAL MISSIONARY, AND MUSIC SCHOLAR

MAY 16
Speak with Respect

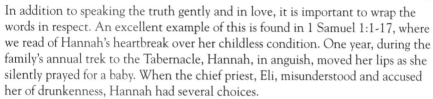

I have chosen to be faithful; I have determined to live by your regulations. Psalm 119:30

In addition to speaking the truth gently and in love, it is important to wrap the words in respect. An excellent example of this is found in 1 Samuel 1:1-17, where we read of Hannah's heartbreak over her childless condition. One year, during the family's annual trek to the Tabernacle, Hannah, in anguish, moved her lips as she silently prayed for a baby. When the chief priest, Eli, misunderstood and accused her of drunkenness, Hannah had several choices.

She could have lashed out at him, saying, "I was praying! Boy, you aren't a very good priest if you can't tell the difference between someone who is drunk and someone who is praying. Just see if I ever come here again!"

She could have tearfully slipped away, wringing her hands and whining to the Lord about being wrongly accused.

Instead, she chose a third and correct response: She communicated directly and respectfully with her accuser. In verse 15, Hannah gently answered Eli's accusation: "'Oh no, sir!' she replied. 'I haven't been drinking wine or anything stronger. But I am very discouraged, and I was pouring out my heart to the LORD.'"

After hearing her respectful statement, Eli said, "In that case . . . go in peace! May the God of Israel grant the request you have asked of him" (1:17).

By the next year, Hannah was the mother of Samuel, a future godly priest. Undoubtedly, that blessing was the result of her respectful response.
—SANDRA

Lord, I'm often quick to defend myself, convinced my words will open another's eyes. But the reality is, I'm prone to "shoot from the lip." Help me to remember that you are my defense. Help me to guard my mouth against quick retorts and to think before I speak.

Raised voices lower esteem. . . . Sharp words dull respect.
—WILLIAM ARTHUR WARD (1812–1882)

MAY 17
Pulling Weeds

'For everything there is a season, a time for every activity under heaven. . . . A time to tear and a time to mend. A time to be quiet and a time to speak. ECCLESIASTES 3:1, 7

While we are to speak the truth in love, that does not mean we ignore situations. Decades ago, I was the youngest member in a four-generation Kentucky farm household. Our little community was filled with hard workers who took pride in their well-fed livestock, neat yards, and productive gardens. But one farmer, whom I'll call Abe, preferred sitting on his porch to working his field.

In the morning, he'd sit on his front porch and watch the sun rise over the gently rolling hills. In the evening, from his narrow back porch, he had a wonderful view of the sun setting behind the hickory trees lining his property. Each spring, in a burst of energy, he'd plant a big garden but then neglect it, which resulted in a low yield. It wasn't uncommon for his family to run short of food and have to ask for canned vegetables from neighbors to get through the winter.

Our family's matriarch was my "waste not, want not" grandmother, Mama Farley, who grew increasingly frustrated by Abe's wastefulness. Finally, the day came when she finished the morning dishes early, replaced her work apron with her pretty "visiting" apron, and marched down the road to Abe's house. As usual, he was sitting in a tipped-back chair on the front porch.

"Well, good mornin', Miz Farley. What brings you here so early?" he asked.

Mama got right to the point. "Abe, you've planted another fine garden, but it's going to weed, just like other years. You've got a family to take care of."

He smiled. "Now, Miz Farley, the Lord always provides. All I have to do is pray."

Mama Farley's eyes undoubtedly narrowed as she remembered how often her canned goods had made their way to his table, but she stayed calm.

"Well, Abe," she said, "why don't you try praying while you're out there pulling weeds?"

We noticed his garden had a better yield that summer. —SANDRA

Lord, what a fine line there is between knowing when to be silent and when to speak. I confess I get those times tangled in my mind. Give me your wisdom. Shield me from prideful determination to save the world, but empower me to speak your truth gently, in love, and with respect.

Life is short, but truth works far and lives long; let us speak the truth.
—ARTHUR SCHOPENHAUER (1788–1860), GERMAN PHILOSOPHER

MAY 18
Pray First

I urge you, first of all, to pray for all people. Ask God to help them; intercede on their behalf, and give thanks for them.
1 TIMOTHY 2:1

Mama Farley's direct confrontation of Abe's laziness was needed in that situation. But sometimes it is wiser to bite our tongues and pray.

That's a lesson my mother taught me years ago. It was a rainy Saturday morning when I finally looked at the cluttered bedroom I had shared with my husband. It had been more than a year since his death from brain cancer, but I was only now realizing how crowded the room was with my little bed next to the one he had slept in during his long illness. For months I had found it less traumatic to ignore the larger bed we had shared for more than sixteen years.

But that morning, with the help of our eleven-year-old son, Jay, I tackled the clutter with determination. Soon the phone rang. It was my mother.

"You sound out of breath, honey," she said. "Did you have to run up the stairs to answer?"

"No. Jay and I were just shoving furniture around," I said. "I'm rearranging my bedroom and taking down the little bed."

My mother started to cry.

"Please don't do that," I pleaded. "You know I can't stand it when you cry long-distance."

Finally she was able to talk. "It's just that I'm happy the Lord answered my prayer," she said. "When I was over there last week and helped you fold clothes, I looked at that crowded room and asked the Lord to help you rearrange the room and go back to your old bed. And every morning since then, that's been my prayer."

The news startled me, of course, but it also got me to thinking. What if my mother had marched in and said, "You've ignored this room long enough. It's time to get on with your life"?

I'm convinced that approach wouldn't have worked because my "letting go" would have been the result of her insistence rather than my own readiness. No, a wise woman chose to ask the Lord to move a hurting daughter forward, and he did. May we remember her example when we're tempted to tell folks what their next step should be. —SANDRA

Lord, you know I pride myself on being straightforward. I like getting to the point. But even as I say that, I'm remembering times when my words were too blunt and I found myself backpedaling to explain my good intentions to the other person or rationalizing to myself my hasty words. Help me to rely more on prayer and less on verbiage.

Anything large enough for a wish to light upon is large enough to have a prayer on. —GEORGE MACDONALD (1924–1905), SCOTTISH NOVELIST AND POET

MAY 19
Kindness Spoken Here

> Better a dry crust eaten in peace than a house filled with feasting—and conflict. PROVERBS 17:1

In the entryway of Martha's home is a flowered wall hanging that reads "Kindness Spoken Here." Many of the stitches are crooked and oversized, but the words are still prominently displayed.

At my query, Martha explained, "A couple of years ago, I was under a lot of stress in my job. That spilled into my relationship with my husband and my children and then in turn adversely affected their relationships with each other. Soon our home boiled with squabbles caused by the tension."

She frowned, remembering. "Finally, my husband and I had a long talk. The result was that I got out my needlework basket and came up with this. Every time someone was unkind to another person—and I included myself in the rule—he or she had to retreat to a quiet room to pray and embroider one letter or part of a flower." Martha smiled as she pointed to the design. "By the time all of us had worked on this for a while, the stitches got smaller, and so did our stress, as we finally understood what we were allowing tension to do to us."

In today's world, stress is a reality—job stress, school stress, schedule stress, emotional stress—and unfortunately, it finds its way into many homes. By itself, stress won't destroy our families, but the way we handle it can. Maybe it's time for all of us to work on our own "Kindness Spoken Here" project. —SANDRA

Lord, too often I have allowed stress to rule my actions, my words, and even my thoughts. Help me to seek your face. Help me to absorb your thoughts so my actions and my words will be ruled by you. Teach me truly to imitate you and to make a difference not only within my own life but in the lives of those around me.

In God's economy nothing is wasted. He will redeem this time and use it for good.
—SUSAN HUNT, WOMEN'S MINISTRY CONSULTANT AND AUTHOR

MAY 20
Hearing the Truth

Consider the joy of those corrected by God! Do not despise the discipline of the Almighty when you sin. For though he wounds, he also bandages. He strikes, but his hands also heal.

JOB 5:17-18

While it is important to lovingly tell the truth, it is equally important to hear the truth. Here are a few suggestions to help us deal with criticism and help us choose which comments to accept and which to discard:

Listen to the criticism all the way through. Don't try to argue in the middle of it since doing so puts us into a defensive position and won't allow us to hear anything that may be helpful.

Understand that not all criticism is accurate. Yes, criticism often (usually!) is offered in a mean spirit. But as we listen for any comments that ring true within our own spirits, we may find a helpful suggestion.

Take notes while another is offering criticism. Jotting down both the bothersome and the helpful phrases allows us to ask questions later about specific points. Besides, it wonderfully disarms the critic.

Take the criticism at face value. Try not to bring old childhood issues such as abandonment or fear into the situation.

Apply what is useful. Listen to good suggestions, but discard wrong perceptions and get on with your life. Wallowing in feelings of self-pity created by the criticism is defeating.

Bring a sense of humor to every criticism. Years ago, I taught high school English in the Detroit area. When I presented the classical myth of Helen of Troy, whose face supposedly launched a thousand ships, one student asked, "Does it bum you out to talk about her, since your face wouldn't launch a rowboat?"

I chose to laugh rather than scold him. A grumpy response would have invited further challenges. By laughing at his barbed wit, I eliminated future verbal battles and won a new friend in that student. He, along with the others in the class, remembered my reaction long after they had forgotten his jab.   —SANDRA

Lord, I don't like hearing the truth when it's painful. Help me to sort through critical comments, change what I need to, and let the rest go. You know the thinnest part about me is my skin, so help me not to carry resentment toward the one who offered the criticism.

Unused truth becomes as useless as an unused muscle.
—A. W. TOZER (1897–1963), AMERICAN PASTOR, PREACHER, AND AUTHOR

To Ponder with a Friend

1. Have you ever been less than truthful in an attempt to spare someone's feelings? What happened?

2. What's the best response you've ever given another person in a tough situation?

3. Do you have any "Abes" in your life? If so, how do you deal with them?

4. How do you handle it when someone tosses criticism your way? How would you like to handle it?

MAY 21
Present Yourself

Sisters, I plead with you to give your bodies to God because of all he has done for you. Let them be a living and holy sacrifice—the kind he will find acceptable. This is truly the way to worship him.
Romans 12:1

The sun rose brilliantly in the East Texas sky on that September day in 1982. I was exhausted from many nights beside Mama's hospital bed in her last weeks of life, and today was her funeral.

"Cheri, would you write down the songs for my service—'Special Delivery' and 'Great Is Thy Faithfulness' . . . and that little chorus 'Beauty for Ashes' you've been singing to me? If no one in our choir will sing it, promise you will," Mama had said two weeks earlier when she was dictating plans for her "Glorious Home-coming" service. I figured surely *someone* in that big choir could sing the song, so I said yes. But after Mama died, when the pastor looked at her requests and checked with the music minister, he said no one in the choir knew it or was willing to learn it on short notice.

"You'll have to sing it yourself, or it won't be in the service," he said.

Now I was wrestling with God. I wanted to keep the promise I had made Mama. *But this is too hard, Lord. I can't do it. I'm sad and tired, and I don't sing at funerals.* Then I opened my Bible to that day's reading in Romans 12, beginning with the first verse: "Give your bodies." As I read those words, God spoke to my heart: *Give yourself to me as a living sacrifice, and I will do it through you.* And he did.

Six years later, when my first book came out and I was invited to speak at a school, I was petrified. *I didn't sign up to speak, Lord, just to write this book and articles to encourage parents. It's too hard!*

Remember Romans 12:1? Give yourself to me; go do this, and I will be with you, the Spirit directed. The same joy that filled my heart when I got up to share with those eager parents I still experience when I speak at retreats and conferences. Jesus wants to live through us. He's just looking for willing vessels.   —Cheri

Lord, once again I give myself to you as a living sacrifice. Not because that's something special but because you gave all for me.

When we are abandoned to God, He works through us all the time.
—Oswald Chambers (1874–1917), Scottish Bible teacher, YMCA chaplain in Egypt

MAY 22
The Bread of Life

> Jesus took the loaves, gave thanks to God, and distributed them
> to the people. Afterward he did the same with the fish. And they
> all ate as much as they wanted.   JOHN 6:11

In two weeks I was to fly to Chiang Mai, Thailand, to speak at my first overseas women's retreat. Women would be gathering from twenty-five different mission organizations and thirty countries. Many of them had served on the mission field and knew far more than I did about the Bible. The more I labored on the talks, the more my sense of inadequacy grew. *O Lord, help!* I cried.

My thoughts were directed to the passage I'd read that morning, where Jesus looked out at the massive crowd of hungry people who'd arrived, and the disciples wanted to send them away (see Matthew 14:15). Philip said it would take a small fortune to feed that multitude. But Jesus took five barley loaves and two fish a boy offered and had the people—the men alone numbered five thousand—sit down. After he took the bread and gave thanks, he gave bread to the people; they all ate as much as they wanted, and there were still twelve large baskets filled with leftovers (see John 6:2-11). As I read those verses, I sensed God saying, *Offer the bread you have, the messages and words I've given you, just like the little boy did. Give it to me, and I will bless it and multiply it to feed all those you speak to in Thailand.*

Suddenly my focus began to shift from *my inadequacy* to *Christ's ability.* As I spoke seventeen times in the next two weeks—to missionaries; teachers; children; and Chinese, Thai, and Buddhist people—each time I offered to the Lord my "bread." And he was faithful to distribute it in the marvelous way only he can do. Over and over I see that whether I'm in South Africa, Zambia, Arkansas, or California, I bring the bread, and Jesus shows up to hand it out to meet the needs of people's hearts. Be encouraged that he will do the same through you as you give your all to him.   —CHERI

Jesus, you can do great things with our little when we give it to you. I offer you all that I am and have for the purposes only you know. When you bring people with needs across my path, use me to touch them with your love and grace. And may it all bring you glory.

I am the vase of God,
    He fills me to the brim.
He is the ocean deep,
    Contained I am in Him.
—ANGELUS SILESIUS (PSEUDONYM FOR JOHANN SCHEFFLER, 1624–1677),
GERMAN MYSTIC-POET

MAY 23
Jesus, Our Sufficiency

> The disciples replied, "Where would we get enough food here
> in the wilderness for such a huge crowd?" Jesus asked, "How
> much bread do you have?" They replied, "Seven loaves."
> MATTHEW 15:33-34

Similar to the miracle in yesterday's devotional, Jesus enlisted his disciples to help him feed a multitude of people gathered to hear the Good News. They had no idea how the masses could be satisfied because they had little to offer them. Seven loaves of bread wasn't much when they faced hundreds of desperate, hungry people. But when they gave Jesus the resources they had, a miracle occurred. That's because it wasn't about *Jesus' disciples and their abilities or resources*. It was about *the Lord and his ability* to provide.

Jesus asks us the same question today: "How many loaves of bread do you have? What is in your 'lunch' or your store of resources that could meet another's need?" Perhaps it is hope or comfort, our testimonies of how God has changed our lives, prayers on another's behalf, a physical meal or other practical help. We may be in a wilderness in our lives and thus not feel we have much to give, but there are always needy people to feed. And when we give our "bread"—whether it's our time, our voice, our home, our money, or our special talent or skills—to Jesus, he is well able to take it and make it life and refreshment for many. He specializes in taking what we give to him and multiplying it in his way to meet the needs of others. Christ is our sufficiency when our personal resources are insufficient. And when we yield all that we have and are into his hands, we can stand back and watch as the miracles begin.   —CHERI

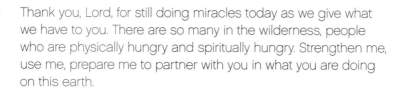

Thank you, Lord, for still doing miracles today as we give what
we have to you. There are so many in the wilderness, people
who are physically hungry and spiritually hungry. Strengthen me,
use me, prepare me to partner with you in what you are doing
on this earth.

Christ is the bread for men's souls. In him the church has enough to feed
the whole world.
—IAN MACLAREN (PSEUDONYM FOR JOHN WATSON, 1850–1907), SCOTTISH AUTHOR
AND THEOLOGIAN

MAY 24
Lord, Could You Send Someone Else?

{The Lord said to Moses,] "Now go! I will be with you as you speak, and I will instruct you in what to say." But Moses again pleaded, "Lord, please! Send anyone else." EXODUS 4:12-13

I remember approaching the noisy classroom of an inner-city school my first year out of college. Facing thirty rowdy high school boys, most of them taller than I was, and seeing a desk fly out the window just as I walked in, I thought, *Lord, could you send someone else to deal with these students?* They were a formidable group of teens for a young, inexperienced teacher like me to handle.

Just as Moses experienced a wrestling match of emotions when God said to "Go!" so might we when we are asked to do something we don't feel ready or able to perform. We look in the mirror and see only our faults and shortcomings. But we can be grateful that God views us in a much different light. He sees us through the kaleidoscope of promises placed inside us at conception. He sees us through Jesus.

As our creator, God knows the full range of the talents he gave us, and yet he is also aware of our disabilities. Moses focused on one aspect of the task—speaking—while God saw a much bigger picture. He understood the hardships and challenges ahead for this leader. He knew that Moses was not a skilled speaker, but he also knew that it was not Moses' speaking ability that would lead God's people through the wilderness. It was his faith and obedience that God would use to guide a multitude out of Egypt.

God can enable *you* as well when you obey him. Remember, just as a silver urn can be used to hold fine wine, so can a common crock. It's what is on the *inside* that matters. God knows what you are capable of, and when he uses the ordinary to perform the extraordinary, he is the One who gets the praise and honor.

God gave me strength and even a love for my challenging students. I learned things during that difficult year that I've used throughout my ministry of speaking, writing, and instructing teachers and parents. —CHERI

Father, I'm an ordinary person, but I am so thankful to serve an extraordinary God! You made me, and you see things inside of me that I may not recognize yet. You also understand what is needed to complete the task. Help me to trust you to use me in extraordinary ways.

Do you have an impossible job to do? Has the Lord told you to do it? Go ahead! When we pray, we enter God's domain from the domain of our inability.
—CORRIE TEN BOOM (1892–1983), HOLOCAUST SURVIVOR, AUTHOR

The Fruit of the Spirit

> The Holy Spirit produces this kind of fruit in our lives: love, joy, peace, patience, kindness, goodness, faithfulness, gentleness, and self-control. GALATIANS 5:22-23

A woman who had just moved to the country wanted to grow an orchard full of apple trees. She didn't know much about cultivating trees, so in early spring she took several dozen twigs from an apple tree and stuck them in the ground twenty feet apart. She carefully watered and sprinkled fertilizer all around those sticks. She watched and waited. But in the fall, she was disappointed because she had no apples to pick. Why were there no apples? Those twigs couldn't mature because they were not rooted in the tree they came from. There was no living sap to nourish them.

The same is true with our spiritual lives. It is only as we abide in Christ, which means that we live in close union with him and are yielded to his Spirit, that the virtues or "fruit" listed in Galatians will be produced. Self-effort won't bring true goodness, faithfulness, and self-control. Good intentions won't produce love, joy, peace, patience, or kindness. This fruit is produced only when Jesus lives and moves freely through us. It is *his* love touching others through our lives. *His* gentleness responding to children, *his* patience forbearing with difficult people we encounter. *His* faithfulness expressed as we keep our commitments in marriage and in our everyday lives, *his* goodness and kindness blessing others.   —CHERI

> Holy Spirit, realizing that none of the fruit or virtues named in your Word reside within my flesh, I humble myself and ask you to help me to rely wholly on you.

I have a glove here in my hand. The glove cannot do anything by itself, but when my hand is in it, it can do many things. True, it is not the glove, but my hand in the glove that acts. We are gloves. It is the Holy Spirit in us who is the hand, who does the job. We have to make room for the hand so that every finger is filled.
—CORRIE TEN BOOM (1892–1983), HOLOCAUST SURVIVOR, AUTHOR

The Exchanged Life

> You died to this life, and your real life is hidden with Christ in God. And when Christ, who is your life, is revealed to the whole world, you will share in all his glory. COLOSSIANS 3:3-4

The *exchanged life* was a term used by early Christian writers to explain the truth that when Christ died on the cross, the believers' old selves died with Christ and their new selves found meaning in living for him. As they remained in him, they experienced a spontaneous outflowing of a life rooted in and devoted to Christ. They also believed the exchanged life to mean having the same orientation that Jesus demonstrated, that he could do nothing of himself unless it was something he saw the Father doing. Throughout his earthly ministry, Jesus didn't attempt anything on his own initiative. Instead, he said the Father who lived within him *did his work through his Son.* That's the exchanged life: believers surrendering and exchanging *their lives and desires* for God's purposes.

When we live in this kind of yieldedness on a daily basis, the Lord is free to be in our hearts and in our thinking, to love even the difficult, hard-to-love folks, and to pray through us in harmony with his will. We lay down our plans, and God shows us his plans, which are far greater than we could imagine. He promises to fully support those who have exchanged their lives for his.

As the early Christians found, we, too, will discover this is an awesome way to live, a great investment of our hours, days, and years on earth.   —CHERI

> Father, forgive me for hanging on to my way of living life. I want to lay down my life and agenda so that your life can be manifested. I ask for your help, Holy Spirit.

The world has yet to see what God can do with and for and through and in a person who is fully and wholly consecrated to Christ.
—HENRY VARLEY (1835–1912), BRITISH EVANGELIST

MAY 27
A Broken Vessel

We now have this light shining in our hearts, but we ourselves
are like fragile clay jars containing this great treasure. This makes
it clear that our great power is from God, not from ourselves.

2 CORINTHIANS 4:7

As Christians, we have a tendency to be perfectionists in how we live, work, parent, and generally "do" life. We want to be the perfect family, have the ideal marriage, achieve much, and have our kids please us, which sometimes brings on
undue pressure. One husband said his wife was so busy trying to turn him into the
father and husband of the year, she rarely gave him a chance to *be himself.*

The truth is, there are no perfect families or people. No perfect husbands,
wives, mothers, or fathers. The only perfect parent is God, and look at the trouble
he had with his first kids, Adam and Eve! God is working on each of us to cause us
to want his will and to do what pleases him, but as long as we are on this earth,
we'll be under construction, works in progress, *not* finished. For God has put his
treasure in "fragile clay jars," and thus we are prone to break or crack. Why would
God do this? So the world around us will see that *the power we live by is not ours but
God's.* The Lord doesn't need perfect vessels to do his work anyway. If he waited
for his people to be perfect, who would he have to carry on his work in the world?

Throughout history God has worked and lived through very imperfect vessels: Peter, impetuous and disloyal in Christ's final hours; Jonah, who ran from
God's call; Elijah, who got so discouraged that he wanted to die; and David, who
said in Psalm 31:12, "I am ignored . . . as if I were a broken pot," and certainly
made his share of mistakes. Are there flaws or cracks in your life? That is the very
place God's grace and forgiveness can shine through to the world as God brings
healing and restoration. He offers the mercy of a fresh start when we turn from our
sinful and hurtful ways to live our lives his way. Can the world see the light of
Christ shining through our brokenness?   —CHERI

> Lord, my God, here are the pieces of my broken life. Search my
> heart and show me the sin I need to confess and turn away
> from. Bring beauty out of my brokenness, for I give myself to you.

To be spiritually useful to God we must periodically travel the wasteland of brokenness. In this desert God tenderly picks up our shattered pieces and remolds them
into the image of his Son. . . . No matter how broken we feel, God won't allow the
pain to destroy us.   —JUDITH COUCHMAN, AMERICAN WRITER, SPEAKER, AND EDITOR

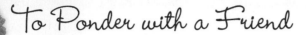
To Ponder with a Friend

1. What is in your "lunch" or your store of resources that God could use? Probably more than you think! However abundant or meager, offer it with thanksgiving to Jesus, who will multiply and divide it in his miraculous way to meet the needs of others.

2. What's the most stretching and difficult task you've ever been assigned? Perhaps it was a class of challenging students, as I described in the devotional for May 24, a flock of active toddlers around your ankles, a group of contentious coworkers, or perhaps an impossible load of responsibilities.

3. What did you learn in this week's devotionals, especially May 22, 23, and 24, that you can apply to your challenging task? Then ponder again Corrie ten Boom's quote at the end of the devotional on May 24.

4. Consider the theme of the fruit of the Spirit (May 25). On a day-to-day basis, how do you stay connected to the vine-life of Jesus so your life will exhibit this kind of fruitfulness?

5. Do you know a person who lives the "exchanged life" in a meaningful way? What might the "exchanged life" look like for you? What changes might it bring?

MAY 28
Choosing Well

God has not given us a spirit of fear and timidity, but of power, love, and self-discipline.   2 TIMOTHY 1:7

Years ago, I invited a perfectly healthy relative for dinner two weeks later. Her reply? "Oh, I don't plan that far in advance. I might be sick."

We may shake our heads at such a pessimistic attitude, but how many times do we give up when facing our own opportunities? How many times do we expect the worst? I'm convinced Detroit industrialist Henry Ford was right when he said, "Whether you think you can or you think you can't, you'll be right."

True, we don't have control over everything that happens to us, but choosing to live with a "victim mentality" can undermine how we respond to common challenges. Displaying such an attitude can even include thinking God is out to get us. Karen understands that mind-set. For years, she thought God was sitting up in heaven with a celestial baseball bat, just waiting for her to get out of line. Obviously, she was projecting a perception of her stern father onto the person of God. It took a monumental leap of faith for her to trust the 2 Timothy 1:7 promise of God's provision of a spirit of power and of love, but she chose to believe what he said. She now says that decision gave her a new attitude and a new life. That's one leap of faith we all need to make.   —SANDRA

Lord, I understand Karen's previous view of you. Too often I worry about everything and emotionally wait for the "other shoe" to drop. Help me to release my fears into your hands and to accept your spirit of love and power and self-discipline.

Confidence in the natural world is self-reliance; in the spiritual world it is God-reliance.
—OSWALD CHAMBERS (1874–1917), SCOTTISH BIBLE TEACHER, YMCA CHAPLAIN IN EGYPT

MAY 29
Learning the Truth

I lie awake thinking of you, meditating on you through the night.
Because you are my helper, I sing for joy in the shadow of your
wings.   PSALM 63:6-7

At the end of a women's retreat at which I had told stories about my Kentucky grand-mother, Mama Farley, several women stayed behind to talk to me. One young woman kept letting others go ahead, so I inwardly began to pray for her, wondering what terrible sin she wanted to confess without witnesses. Finally she and I were alone.

As I turned to her, she blurted out, "I'm not as close to the Lord as I used to be."

I often hear that statement, and it's usually followed by an admission of sin. So, bracing myself, I asked why she felt that way.

She twisted the tissue in her hands. "I used to spend at least an hour studying the Bible every morning, but now I don't."

This wasn't what I expected. "Tell me about your life," I invited.

"Well, I got married four years ago," she said. "And now we have three chil-dren, three, two, and one."

Astonished, I interrupted her. "Honey, you don't have *time* to spend an hour in the Word each morning." Then remembering retreat speakers aren't supposed to say such things, I tried again. "Perhaps you could post Scriptures throughout the house to ponder as you go through your busy days."

She shook her head, so I scrambled for another idea. "What if you saw the care of your children as part of your daily worship of the Lord? As your little ones look to you in trust, it will be a reminder you are trusting your heavenly Father."

I knew that was stretching the point, but she was desperate.

Tears were forming in her eyes. "But I want to be a godly woman like your grandmother," she said. "And there's no way she could have been that godly with-out spending *at least* an hour in the Word each morning."

I smiled as I opened my arms to her. "Honey, I *know* she didn't spend an hour in the Word each day. Mama Farley couldn't read."

At that, the tired, young mother threw herself against my shoulder and sobbed in relief. The truth about my godly grandmother had freed her from a stan-dard impossible for her to achieve at this stage of her life. And I like to think that truth also made her a more relaxed, fun-loving mother.   —SANDRA

Lord, I'm prone to accept someone else's standards of Christian discipline. And often I fail to reach my own goals because I've set them too high. Help me to ask you how to schedule my day. And remind me that as I invite you into my activities, I gain direction and peace.

God wants us to be victors, not victims; to grow, not grovel; to soar, not sink; to overcome, not to be overwhelmed.
—WILLIAM ARTHUR WARD (1921–1994), INSPIRATIONAL WRITER

MAY 30
Listen to the Right Voices

Anyone who belongs to God listens gladly to the words of God.
JOHN 8:47

If we attempt to live up to others' definitions of how our lives should go, we carry their accusing voices in our heads and mentally replay them when facing a new challenge. If I had paid attention to those voices in my own life, I wouldn't have accepted the offer to become an editor, made a cross-country move, or written books. But occasionally, especially when I'm tired or discouraged, I do remember the old taunts. On those days, I try to remember the account Kim Crabill tells about her son Trey, who pitched the deciding game in a Little League championship. On their way to the stadium that day, Kim sensed his anxiety and asked what was wrong.

"I hate it when the other team's fans yell at me," he confided.

"Do they come onto the field and yell in your face?" Kim asked, feigning naiveté.

"No."

"Can they take away your ability?"

"No," he conceded. "But they make me feel bad, and I can't concentrate."

"Don't listen to the voices," Kim said. "Look at your catcher. Think about that next pitch. The voices can't stop you. But they *can* cause you to stop yourself."

Two hours later, the game had come down to one final pitch. The batter had two strikes against him, the tying run was on third base, the winning run on second. On the mound, Trey leaned toward home plate, studying the catcher's signals for this last pitch. Then the fans for the opposing team began jeering, "Loser! You'll never get it over the plate!"

But Trey narrowed his eyes, nodded at his catcher, went into his windup, and delivered strike three to win the game.

Like that young pitcher, most of us face challenges from time to time. And often we, too, hear the jeers. Sometimes those voices come from the past, sometimes they come from the present. But they can thwart our most determined efforts if we let them.

So when we're facing a tough time, we need to remember to pray, read the Word, and seek godly counsel. But let's *also* make sure we're not listening to the voices that can drag us toward defeat.   —SANDRA

Lord, I'm grateful those old mental tapes don't have the power they once held, but I can still hear them when I'm discouraged: *You'll never amount to anything.* Or *You're out of your league.* Or *Women aren't supposed to do that.* Help me to concentrate on your strengthening, loving words and, thus, drown out those old lies.

We can overcome disillusionment and disappointments in our lives. God has given us everything we need to knock down barriers and overcome obstacles.
—THELMA WELLS, AUTHOR, SPEAKER, AND BUSINESSWOMAN

MAY 31
Don't Quit Now

Since we are surrounded by such a huge crowd of witnesses to the life of faith, let us strip off every weight that slows us down, especially the sin that so easily trips us up. And let us run with endurance the race God has set before us.   HEBREWS 12:1

Have you ever wanted to give up on a worthwhile project? I have.

I remember a long-ago morning when my latest assignment was not going well. Then my daughter, Holly, arrived home from college and insisted we go horseback riding.

"Might as well," I muttered. "I'm not getting anything accomplished here."

Within the hour, we were at our favorite stable, but the docile horse I usually rode was already on the trail for the entire day. I had no choice but to request the *second* most docile. Soon a large black horse was brought out, and I took the reins and led him to the mounting block. There, I placed my left foot in the stirrup and had just started to swing my right leg over the saddle when the horse, having decided he didn't want me on his back, cleverly and quickly began to sidestep away from the block. There I was, one foot in the stirrup and the other poised in midair.

Even back then I had neither the agility nor the dainty figure to shift my weight quickly and throw myself into the saddle. Instead, I was suspended in midair for a long moment. The stable owner stood below me, arms in the air as if to catch me when I fell. There was only one convenient part of my anatomy to push, but he knew me well enough to know he'd better not touch that. So with arms waving, he hopped from foot to foot and yelled, "Don't quit *now*, ma'am! Don't quit now!"

Holly was bent forward on her own horse, howling with laughter, so I started chuckling, which put me in greater peril. But at last, with a surge of adrenaline, I threw myself into the saddle and shoved my right foot into the stirrup. The horse gave a defeated snort, and I turned his head toward the trail.

That ride, even with its perilous start, was exactly what I needed to gain clarity and finish my project. "Don't quit now!" It's a good phrase to remember when times get tough.   —SANDRA

Lord, some days it seems as if everything is a hassle. Please help me to remember that the sweetest victories often come after the greatest challenges. Help me to listen when you gently whisper, *Don't quit now, Child. Don't quit now.*

If your determination is fixed, I do not counsel you to despair. Great works are performed not by strength but perseverance.
—SAMUEL JOHNSON (1709–1784), ENGLISH ESSAYIST, BIOGRAPHER, AND CRITIC

JUNE 1
Creative Offerings

> All glory to God, who is able, through his mighty power at work within us, to accomplish infinitely more than we might ask or think.   EPHESIANS 3:20

When Mindy was a child, unexpected company often arrived at her family's modest home right at suppertime. Her job was to stir up another batch of corn bread to stretch the meal as her mother greeted the guests. At the table, Mindy's mother would give her a wink that said, "Thanks for your help."

I think of that little girl whenever I read the John 6 account of a problem the disciples had that couldn't be solved with an extra batch of corn bread: Five thousand men and their families had shown up unexpectedly for dinner! As Jesus watched the crowd approach, he tested Philip by asking where they could buy bread. The disciple had no clue how to deal with the problem and exclaimed that working for months wouldn't provide enough money to feed such a crowd.

In the midst of their discussion, the disciple Andrew stepped forward with a little boy who apparently had offered his own lunch. But even as Andrew reported the amount of five loaves and two fish, he doubted its usefulness.

Jesus didn't argue but gave Andrew instructions: "Tell everyone to sit down" (6:10). Then he took the bread and the fish, offered thanks, and began handing out the food.

Did the little boy's eyes widen as he watched his food multiply? Was he astonished the Teacher had created a miracle out of his little lunch? Perhaps he just stood there grinning. And maybe Jesus winked his thanks.

Too often, my response to many of life's crises is like Philip's—bewilderment—because I see the problem rather than God's solution. But gradually I'm learning to offer what I can, just like Mindy's corn bread and the little boy's lunch, and watch what the Lord does.   —SANDRA

Lord, too many times I withhold what I have because I'm convinced my little won't make a dent in so great a problem. Help me to look to you rather than at the situation. Help me to trust you to multiply even the simplest gift.

Give what you have. To someone it may be better than you dare to think.
—HENRY WADSWORTH LONGFELLOW (1807–1882), AMERICAN POET

JUNE 2
The Gift of Rest

> Why am I discouraged? Why is my heart so sad? I will put my
> hope in God! I will praise him again—my Savior and my God!
> PSALM 42:5-6

Every challenge seems greater when we are sleep deprived. Just ask Jill. She had
looked forward to motherhood. But after the birth of her son, she found herself
depressed. When I dropped off a gift for her baby at lunchtime, she burst into tears,
apologized for still being in her robe, and then added she didn't understand why
she felt so "bummed."

I hadn't planned to stay for a visit, but I did exactly that. After admiring her
sleeping little boy, I made myself right at home and prepared a sandwich and cup
of tea for her. I urged her to tell her doctor about her sadness at her next checkup,
and then we talked, woman to woman, about the changes her body was going
through. I also encouraged her to eat nourishing foods, get as much rest as possible, and stop worrying about the condition of the house.

Then I quoted Psalm 42:5 to let her know her feelings were part of the
human experience. Even though this portion of Scripture was written by King
David and not by a woman who had just given birth, it still speaks to our hurts
today. This is the prayer of a believer who struggled with doubt and depression but
finally came through the shadows to hope in God.

I told Jill that in my beloved Kentucky, we explain a person's temporary
withdrawal from life with the nonjudgmental expression that she or he "took to
bed" to allow the body and spirit to heal.

She suddenly looked hopeful. "You mean sometimes the most spiritual thing
I can do is sleep?"

I smiled. "Yes, especially when your body is recovering from a major event."
Then I added, "I'm going to pray with you before I go, and then you're going to
nap while your baby is asleep. Better days *are* ahead."

Today Jill passes along the advice about "taking to bed" to other exhausted
folks. After all, when we are discouraged and weary (some Bible versions use the
words "cast down"), it takes time before we can jump back into life's fray. Yes, the
Lord is with us in all of our circumstances, but sometimes the best "weapon" we
can carry into our daily challenges is the clear head that comes from a well-rested
body and spirit. —SANDRA

Lord, my to-do list looks as if it is two miles long. So, help me to
be realistic about my responsibilities. And help me to give myself
permission to rest.

Tired nature's sweet restorer, balmy sleep!
—EDWARD YOUNG (1683–1765), ENGLISH POET

JUNE 3
God's Daily Touch

> As for me, I look to the LORD for help. I wait confidently for
> God to save me, and my God will certainly hear me.
> MICAH 7:7

I have a favorite activity to help me discourage the victim mentality: I watch for
God's extraordinary touch in my ordinary activities. It started a few years ago
whenever I bought a new calendar for the coming year. I would list all the birth-
days and anniversaries on the appropriate days, then turn to each month, plop my
finger on a random date, and write the command "Watch for God's touch" in the
space.

Then, as those particular days arrived throughout the year, I watched for
ways in which God reminded me of his presence. Sometimes his special touch
came through a new insight into a Scripture verse, an encouraging phone call
or letter, an unexpected and much-needed rebate check, or a Rocky Mountain
double rainbow. Sometimes nothing dramatic at all occurred, but I still had a
fresh awareness of God's presence because I was watching for it. Gradually, the
most amazing thing happened: Because I was looking for God's touch on specific
days, I found myself aware of it on other days as well. Today, I no longer write
"Watch for God's touch" on occasional calendar dates. Instead, I enjoy looking
for it every day.   —SANDRA

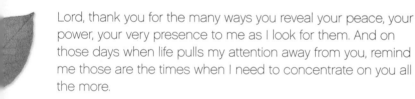

Lord, thank you for the many ways you reveal your peace, your
power, your very presence to me as I look for them. And on
those days when life pulls my attention away from you, remind
me those are the times when I need to concentrate on you all
the more.

I always told the Lord, "I trust you. I don't know where to go or what to do, but
I expect you to lead me." And He always did.
—HARRIET TUBMAN (CA. 1820–1913), FORMER SLAVE, AMERICAN ABOLITIONIST

To Ponder with a Friend

1. Do you agree attitude is important as we face a crisis?
   Why or why not?

2. What additional suggestions do you have for those trying to
   develop a good attitude?

3. Have you ever felt as if your soul were "cast down" (weary and
   discouraged)? If so, what happened?

4. When do you have the most difficulty sensing God's touch on
   your day?

JUNE 4
Filling the Void

> I lift my hands to you in prayer. I thirst for you as parched land thirsts for rain. PSALM 143:6

Within each of us is a God-shaped void that nothing, absolutely nothing, can fill except the Lord himself. Someone described this inner void as a curious, wild pain, a searching for something beyond what the world contains. As parched, dry land thirsts desperately for rain, so our souls thirst to fill this aching void in our hearts, searching and trying everything except God. Fame can't fill the vacuum, even if we appear on the cover of *People* magazine as the world's most beautiful woman, win an Academy Award for best actress, or become the newest American Idol. Wealth can't fill the void or quench our thirst, even if we make millions and end up on the *Forbes* list of the richest people in America. We can use our wealth to buy a mansion, a fancy vehicle, or an entire fleet of luxury cars. But those material things will not fill the inner void.

We can try to quench our thirst for God with human love relationships, professional achievement, or academic prowess. But this doesn't fill the vacuum either, even if we hold three earned PhDs and teach at Harvard. Power won't do it; no matter how influential we are, even as the president of a corporation or of the nation, the void remains. No matter where we search, we'll find that the fountains of wealth, fame, beauty, achievement, or relationships don't bring lasting fulfillment. Nothing truly satisfies until our hearts are connected with the God who created us and his Spirit comes to live within us.

What a wonderful thing that God has made us for himself and given his own Son so that we can enjoy a relationship with him that will fill the yearning of our souls, quench our inborn spiritual thirst, and bring endless joy, both now and for eternity. Will you thank him today for his indescribable gift? —CHERI

> Father of lights, how I thank you for making us for yourself and for sending your Son to open the way for us to know and love you. Thank you for the God-shaped void you created in me that nothing and no one but you can fill.

Naught but God can satisfy the soul.
—PHILIP JAMES BAILEY (1816–1902), ENGLISH POET

JUNE 5
Connecting with God

The LORD your God is living among you. He is a mighty savior. He will take delight in you with gladness. With his love, he will calm all your fears. He will rejoice over you with joyful songs.
ZEPHANIAH 3:17

I have been a music lover ever since I arrived on planet Earth. Among other things, my mother wrote in the baby book, "Cheri sings before she talks," and indeed I did. I even joined my big sisters in a musical group when I was six. And praising God with the whole congregation at the beginning of a church service isn't the only time I sing because I've found it's a way God has given me to connect my heart with his heart even on the busiest of days. That's just how he's wired me. Music is in my DNA.

Knowing that music is one of my best spiritual pathways, if I'm distracted during a quiet time in the morning or my mind is wandering to all the tasks I'm facing, I get out the words from a song I learned at a retreat where I spoke, and I sing, "Draw me close to you; never let me go. . . ." before reading a chapter from the Bible. In those moments of worship, I am drawn closer to God. And amazingly, as today's verse says, God rejoices over his people with joyful songs. God sings over *me*!

On another day I sing, "I cast all my cares on you," and the dusty concerns of life start to blow away with each note I sing. Music helps me turn down the world's volume and tune into God's symphony and what he's purposing for me at a certain time. It quiets my busy mind and racing heart and can even bring me into meaningful intercession for a loved one or friend.

I believe God has hardwired every person with specific and individual ways to connect with him. And if we make the most of our God-given spiritual pathways, it will help us experience the Lord's presence in marvelous ways.
—CHERI

Father, thank you for creating me for relationship with you and for giving me the gift of music, not only to praise you, for you are certainly worthy of praise, but also to help me connect with your melody and be a part of your great symphony.

Music washes away from the soul the dust of everyday life.
—BERTHOLD AUERBACH (1812–1882), GERMAN NOVELIST

JUNE 6
Room in the Forest

Just as our bodies have many parts and each part has a special function, so it is with Christ's body. We are many parts of one body, and we all belong to each other.   ROMANS 12:4-5

I love what Chuck Swindoll said once: "If God made you a duck saint, you're a duck, friend. Swim like mad, but don't get bent out of shape because you wobble when you run or flap instead of fly. If you're an eagle saint, stop expecting squirrel saints to soar, or rabbit saints to build the same kind of nests you do." There's plenty of room in the forest, he said, for each individual one of us.

Just as God has different work for each of his children to do based on how he's designed them, he provides many different ways to meet him in the forest of life. Some believers feel more connected to God when they kneel to pray. Others like to put their hands up in adoration. Some feel closer to God in a formal sanctuary with stained-glass windows. Others connect better with him in a small house church. Still others are like the woman I met who meets God on the hiking trail. Hearing the sounds of the birds, feeling God's wind rushing over her, smelling the honeysuckle along the path, all of these things contribute to her ability to connect more intimately with the Lord.

While one person experiences God's presence best while praying in a group, another's pathway is through quiet study, spiritual retreat, and solitude. Since the Lord is the One who created our individuality, he has a purpose for each of these individual styles and spiritual pathways. He made us the way we are. As long as our focus is God, he gives us much freedom in our methods of connecting with him. Our part can be to find out how we are wired, how we most easefully relate to and experience God, and then work in harmony with those bents to draw close to him.

What unique spiritual pathways bring you closer to God?   —CHERI

Lover of my soul, I am so grateful that you invite me to come out of the patterns I've boxed myself into. Thank you for freeing me from the tendency to compare my own spiritual pathways to others' spiritual methods. Show me how to best connect with you in the midst of the unique circumstances of my life and in terms of the way you've designed me.

The finger of God never leaves the same fingerprint.
—STANISLAW J. LEC (1909–1966), POLISH POET

JUNE 7
The Gift of Spiritual Vision

I look up to the mountains—does my help come from there?
My help comes from the LORD, who made heaven and earth!
PSALM 121:1-2

Perhaps music isn't how you best connect with God. Maybe you are visually sensitive and observant, so you see God in moments all throughout your days. If so, God has blessed you with spiritual vision. In devotional times, you can quite naturally (without a lot of effort) visualize that the Lord is your shepherd, willing to carry you on his shoulders like a lamb when you're weary. This mental picture helps you connect with God. You may also clearly perceive his love in the raindrops and in the first rays of morning sun—in the small, quiet moments—not just in spectacular events.

Visualizing God's truth in nature or picturing him in our mind's eye is one of the ways he's given us to connect with him. And it's biblical. Psalm 139:8-12 tells us that if we go to the heights of heaven, God is there; and even in the darkest places, God's light shines. If we "ride the wings of the morning" or go to the farthest oceans, he is there as well.

As we read in today's verses, when the psalmist looks up to the mountains, he has the spiritual vision to see that his help comes not from the mountains but from the One who made them. In every season there is a visual panorama of beauty that God created to reveal himself to us and to draw us closer: the delicate blue wings of a dragonfly, majestic pines standing in the snow, tiny green shoots of grass in the spring, millions of stars lighting the night sky, a field of vivid orange and yellow tulips. When we feel disconnected from the Lord or our eyes have been clouded by the dust of the problems swirling about us, we can ask him to open our eyes to really see his awe-inspiring creation. It offers us glimpses of God's grace in a new way.   —CHERI

Creator of all, please touch my eyes so that I can see you
in the myriad colors, sights, and wonders of your creation all
around me.

Beauty is God's handwriting—a wayside sacrament. Welcome it in every fair face, in every fair sky, in every fair flower, and thank God for it as a cup of blessing.
—RALPH WALDO EMERSON (1803–1882), AMERICAN ESSAYIST AND POET

JUNE 8

Our Gracious, Creative God

[God's] purpose was for the nations to seek after [him] and perhaps feel their way toward him and find him—though he is not far from any one of us. For in him we live and move and exist. As some of your own poets have said, "We are his offspring." ACTS 17:27-28

The longer I know God and read his Word, the more amazed I am at how creative he is at pursuing and relating to us human beings. The Lord drew me to him in graduate school (even when I wasn't attending Bible studies) through the study of seventeenth-century British poets who loved Jesus and wrote for God's glory. He revealed his irresistible love through acts of kindness strangers did for my young son when he was in the hospital. He turned on an inner light when I was reading the book of John and answered questions I'd had since my teen years that only he could have known.

Throughout the Bible God specialized in meeting his people in a variety of ways. He spoke through a burning bush, led people by a pillar of fire, sent angels with important messages, and was present on battlefields and in a lions' den. He is still so gracious in all the different ways he allows us to hear and experience him: through dreams, poetry, music, nature, and his servants. And he allows us freedom in the ways we worship him: with clapping, singing, shouting, marching, and even wordless prayer. In all of this, today's verse says, God's purpose is that we would begin to seek him and find him, though he isn't far from anyone. In fact, he is closer than our very breath, "for in him we live and move and exist."

How encouraging that there is no limit to God's ability to reach us and minister to us. We don't have to be in a church building to find God, although there are some wonderful congregations that can help us find our way to him. He isn't limited to temples and pews. If we turn to God and earnestly seek him, we will find him because he is always seeking to manifest himself to us. —CHERI

All-wise God, I want to know you more every day. Thank you for all the ways you have drawn me, met me right where I was, and revealed yourself to me. Thank you for the truth that I live and move and exist in you.

If all experienced God in the same way and returned Him an identical worship, the song of the church triumphant would have no symphony, it would be like an orchestra in which all the instruments played the same note. . . . Heaven is a city, and a Body, because the blessed remain eternally different.
—C. S. LEWIS (1898–1963), IRISH WRITER AND LITERARY SCHOLAR

JUNE 9
The Pathway of Adversity

> The LORD had arranged for a great fish to swallow Jonah. And
> Jonah was inside the fish for three days and three nights. Then
> Jonah prayed to the LORD his God from inside the fish. He said,
> "I cried out to the LORD in my great trouble, and he answered me.
> I called to you from the land of the dead, and LORD, you heard me!
> You threw me into the ocean depths, and I sank down to the heart
> of the sea." JONAH 1:17–2:3

Have you ever prayed a prayer from the belly of an emergency room or cried out
from the belly of a painful relationship or a colossal business failure? If so, you've
discovered that adversity is a spiritual pathway that brings you to God's throne of
grace. Perhaps you can relate to Jonah's prayer from the belly of a great fish.

As a prophet, Jonah had prayed many times before, but when God told him
to warn the Ninevites of impending destruction, he had run from his duty and
from the Lord (see Jonah 1:3). But God was still with Jonah when the ship's crew
decided to throw him overboard (1:15). He was still with Jonah in the belly of the
fish that swallowed his servant. The Lord was with him in his trouble; in fact, it
was that very trouble that awakened Jonah to his great need of God. As the waters
closed around Jonah, his soul fainted within him.

Buried beneath wild and stormy waves, Jonah lost all hope. But when he
cried out to the Lord from that place of desperation and despair, God heard him
and rescued him. Jonah's story contains many principles, but part of its great value
is to remind us that there is no place where the Lord cannot hear and respond to
us. There is no pit too deep, no trouble too terrible, no situation so difficult that
God cannot rescue us and restore us. When we cry out to him, he won't reject us
because our prayer doesn't follow a certain format or isn't prayed before the altar of
a formal church. We need only to cry out to him wherever we are and in whatever
"belly" we find ourselves.   —CHERI

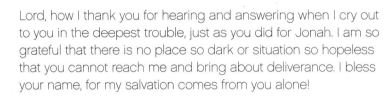

Lord, how I thank you for hearing and answering when I cry out
to you in the deepest trouble, just as you did for Jonah. I am so
grateful that there is no place so dark or situation so hopeless
that you cannot reach me and bring about deliverance. I bless
your name, for my salvation comes from you alone!

Prayer was the mighty force that brought Jonah from "The belly of hell." . . . Prayer
brought God to the rescue of unfaithful Jonah, despite his sin of fleeing from duty.
God could not deny his prayer. Nothing is beyond the reach of prayer because no
prayer is too hard for God to answer.
—E. M. BOUNDS (1835–1913), METHODIST MINISTER AND AUTHOR

JUNE 10

Getting Real

Pour out your heart to him, for God is our refuge.
PSALM 62:8

Once when I was a new Christian and attending a prayer group, I was fascinated with how differently some of the people prayed. Some prayed loudly, and a few wept as they prayed. Several prayed in a language I'd never heard, which seemed very spiritual and mysterious. So I asked an older, wiser man I knew, who'd been walking with Christ for many years, "Will God hear me better if I pray like these people? Do I need to pray in a prayer language too?"

He answered gently, "God just wants to hear from you. Be honest, be yourself, and pour out your heart to him." What good advice. Although you and I may have people in our churches or families we want to imitate because they are good role models, most of all God wants us to be honest and be ourselves, just the way he created us. That kind of honesty deepens our friendship with him. He doesn't want us to emulate other people's prayer jargon or adopt their prayer style because we think they "sound better" than we do.

The Lord has given you a distinct personality and heart, and he loves to have you express them. He made your voice, and just as I love to hear my sons', daughter's, and grandchildren's voices, God loves to hear yours—in whatever language you speak to him—because you are his child, accepted and beloved. You don't have to sound like your minister, your Bible study leader, or a more spiritually mature friend when you come to God. Come as you are. He is waiting to bless you and show you his love.   —CHERI

Forgive me, Lord, when I use clichés or expressions I've heard others use instead of just telling you what's really on my heart. I come to you today, just as I am, to pour out my thanks, my problems, and my fears.

Human personality and individuality written and signed by God on each human countenance . . . is something altogether sacred, something for the resurrection, for eternal life.
—LEON HENRI MARIE BLOY (1846–1917), FRENCH NOVELIST, ESSAYIST, AND POET

To Ponder with a Friend

1. By which of the variety of spiritual pathways described in the devotionals for June 6 and 7 is it most natural for you to meet with God, feel close to him, and really connect intimately with him?

2. Are you a duck saint, an eagle saint, a squirrel saint, a rabbit saint, or a different kind of saint? If none of these describes you and you had to pick an animal to describe what kind of saint God made you, what would it be? How does this influence or shape your spiritual pathway and bent?

3. Cheri describes in June 8 how much creativity and variety God uses when he draws an individual into relationship with him or brings someone back to his heart. In what creative or interesting ways did the Lord pursue you? It is so important that we share this part of our faith story with those we hold dear, because doing so builds trust and heart connection. Let me encourage you to take time to share your story with a good friend and to hear her faith story as well.

4. What would it be like for you to "get out of the box" you've been using to meet with God and try some different spiritual pathways we've thought about this week? After doing this, jot down or share what happened.

JUNE 11
When the Way Is Clouded

O LORD, you are my lamp. The LORD lights up my darkness. In your strength I can crush an army; with my God I can scale any wall.
2 SAMUEL 22:29-30

Sad to say, life often hands us traumatic situations. I faced one when my then thirty-eight-year-old husband was diagnosed with terminal brain cancer. While he was battling pain and the side effects of chemotherapy, I was caring for him and our two young children in addition to continuing my job as a high school teacher. Obviously, I was physically and emotionally drained.

Early one autumn morning, I left for my classroom and found myself driving through dense fog. Everything was so murky I had to drive by instinct on the back road out of our neighborhood. After proceeding at a creep for several minutes, I guessed the stop sign should be just ahead. Ah, there it was.

As I edged the car forward, I decided the fog wouldn't be as heavy on the overpass. At least I'd be able to see from there. I inched to the top and was stunned by an incredible sight. The little valleys surrounding the expressway brimmed with pink mist rather than gravylike gloom. Above the mysterious mist the sun's rays streamed through gorgeous purple and orange clouds. I gasped at the majestic scene.

Below, cars crawled through the murk I had just escaped. *If only they could have this view*, I thought.

When I had to leave the overpass and descend into the fog again, the memory of the beautiful scene went with me. I continued on to school, strangely refreshed. I knew that even as our family struggled through our own darkness, God had granted me a glimpse of his beauty and his presence in the scary murk of our family's medical crisis. And I knew, in time, he would lead me to an emotional place where I could see above my personal fog.   —SANDRA

Lord, life's fogs are scary. Sometimes they last for a mere day or two; other times they seem to go on forever. During those times, I wonder where you are, why you don't sweep away the pain. Give me more glimpses of your beauty and your presence. Help me to realize in a new way that you *are* with me.

It is not our trust that keeps us, but the God in whom we trust who keeps us.
—OSWALD CHAMBERS (1874–1917), SCOTTISH BIBLE TEACHER, YMCA CHAPLAIN IN EGYPT

JUNE 12
Increasing Courage

I fully expect and hope that I will never be ashamed, but that
I will continue to be bold for Christ, as I have been in the past.
And I trust that my life will bring honor to Christ, whether I
live or die.   PHILIPPIANS 1:20

As my family and I continued to battle our medical fog, I realized my definition
of courage had changed. In my senior year of college, I had worked as a civilian
secretary for an ROTC unit during the Vietnam War. In addition to my usual
clerical duties, I had the opportunity to view several aspects of the future soldiers' jungle survival training, including one ranger's demonstration of skinning
a snake using only his hands and teeth!

Since I was surrounded with military examples, I decided courage was best
demonstrated by fresh-faced young men rushing into battle. Then after the war
had ended, a local nursing home burned, and several firemen risked their lives
to save the elderly patients. I added them to my list of those I saw as models of
courage.

Next, I heard stories of martyred South American pastors who refused to
deny their faith even when challenged by rebel soldiers. My list continued to grow.
But always it consisted of folks whose courage was public.

Then my young husband was diagnosed with metastatic brain cancer, and
the doctors said he had as little as two weeks or as "long" as three months to live.
Suddenly I had a new example of courage: Don, who was determined not to let the
doctors bury him yet. I watched as he grabbed each day's joy, and I marveled at
how he could face death with such quiet courage.   —SANDRA

Lord, too often I look for courage in others, not realizing you offer
it to me as well. Help me to receive it from your hand. Help me
to face whatever comes my way, strengthened by your power
and your presence.

Courage is resistance to fear, mastery of fear, not absence of fear.
—MARK TWAIN (PSEUDONYM OF SAMUEL CLEMENS, 1835–1910), AMERICAN WRITER

JUNE 13
Carried by Our Father

Give all your worries and cares to God, for he cares about you.
1 PETER 5:7

I remember a long-ago night in our Kentucky farm community. I was five years old, and my parents had taken me with them to visit neighbors. By the time we left for home, the stars were already out, and our lane looked long and dark in the moonlight, especially where the thorny blackberry bushes hung over the ditches. Quickly my dad swooped me up and carried me on his strong shoulders. The night was still dark, and the bushes still had thorns, but I felt so safe I fell asleep.

There have been many times in my adult life when I've been carried by my heavenly Father. And I've noticed that though I long to be carried *away* from the darkness, I'm actually carried *through* it, just as Daniel was saved *in* the lion's den rather than *from* it (see Daniel 6:16-23). I confess, I don't like the challenges and trials that often accompany daily human existence. In fact, I've often thought I'd like God to say, "Good morning, Sandra. This is what I plan to do today for you and your family. Is that all right?" But, of course, he doesn't, and I'm left to choose once again whether I will trust him during the scary times.

A while back, I was intrigued by the word *care* in 1 Peter 5:7, so I researched it. I discovered that the word can have two meanings: our worry and God's comfort. The worrying type comes from a Greek word meaning "to divide the mind." How perfect. My mind is divided when I allow worries, distractions, and anxieties to interfere with my trust that my heavenly Father will carry me past life's dark ditches and thorny bushes. So what's my goal? To concentrate less on the situation and more on him. —SANDRA

Lord, even though I'm an adult, many times I feel like that little girl facing thorny bushes and deep, scary ditches. Help me to feel your strong arms carrying me to safety. Help me to rest in you.

God is in His heaven; God is on the throne; God is fully in charge of His world.
—J. I. PACKER, THEOLOGIAN AND AUTHOR

JUNE 14
Ordinary People, Extraordinary Courage

> Be strong and courageous! Do not be afraid and do not panic
> before them. For the LORD your God will personally go ahead
> of you. He will neither fail you nor abandon you.
> DEUTERONOMY 31:6

All of us face difficult times sooner or later. I remember being in a Southern
museum and seeing an 1863 letter from a Confederate soldier. His message, in part,
said, "Some of us are poor, some of us are rich. Some of us are old, some of us are
young. But we all bleed the same."

While I've never been in a physical war, my plunge into widowhood taught
me the truth of universal pain. And I've had many opportunities to study Scripture
passages containing the command "Be strong and courageous." From my time spent
with those numerous verses, I'm convinced displaying strength and courage is an
act of our will rather than an automatic response.

When I think of courageous decisions, I ponder my husband's quick smile
despite his cancer or my Aunt Adah's gentle acceptance of her debilitating brain
disease. Sometimes I think of people like my parents, who left the familiar to
start new lives and became part of a great migration from the South to the industrial North in the early 1950s; or missionary friends, who moved to a foreign
country; or my dear Canadian daughter-in-law, who moved to the United States
to marry my son. Sometimes the courageous face before me belongs to a stroke or
accident victim who chooses to adjust to his or her disability. Sometimes I see
single parents who climb over great obstacles to care for their children. Sometimes courage comes in the form of parents who carry to term the baby others
suggested they abort.

Through the years, I have learned courage doesn't always mean rushing into
battle. Often it calls for *staying in* the battle by trusting the Lord and putting one
foot in front of the other.   —SANDRA

Lord, choosing to be strong and courageous is not what I want
to do. When tough times come, I want to sit under a shade tree
and cheer as you fight the battle for me. But since life doesn't
allow me to do that, I ask for your strength and your victory.

There are only two or three human stories, and they go on repeating themselves
as fiercely as if they had never happened before.
—WILLA CATHER (1873–1947), AMERICAN NOVELIST

JUNE 15
"Do You Trust Me?"

I trust in your unfailing love. I will rejoice because you have rescued me. I will sing to the LORD because he is good to me.
PSALM 13:5-6

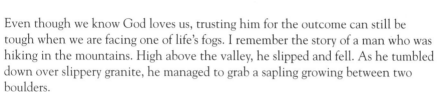

Even though we know God loves us, trusting him for the outcome can still be tough when we are facing one of life's fogs. I remember the story of a man who was hiking in the mountains. High above the valley, he slipped and fell. As he tumbled down over slippery granite, he managed to grab a sapling growing between two boulders.

"God, help me!" he called.

In answer, a voice from heaven said, "Do you trust me?"

"Yes, I trust you," the frantic man said. "Help me!"

The voice came again. "Do you *really* trust me?"

This time, dangling in midair, the man pondered the question. Finally, he answered slowly, "Yes, I do trust you."

Then he added the very human comment, "And if you'll notice, I don't have much of a choice in the matter."

The heavenly voice spoke a third time. "Then if you trust me, let go."

Let go? About this time, I'd want to have a little discussion with God. Was there a ledge just two inches below the man's toes, but hidden from view? Would he drop onto the new path and have a wonderful story to tell about God's faithfulness? Or was his heavenly Father lovingly saying, "It's time. Come home to me"?

But that's what trust means—letting go without the assurance of the ledge.
—SANDRA

Lord, trust is a tough issue. We love saying, "Isn't God good!" when wonderful things happen: healing occurs, the promotion comes through. But Lord, you are good all the time. Even when tears are running down our cheeks.

We can take the risk of throwing ourselves at the feet of Jesus. Knowing Him, we are sure He will not take advantage of us, humiliate us, or reject us. We can safely place our lives at His disposal.   —MARGARET HESS, AUTHOR AND BIBLE TEACHER

JUNE 16
Pikes Peak and God

> In peace I will lie down and sleep, for you alone, O LORD, will keep me safe.   PSALM 4:8

Life's fogs don't always come in the form of great tragedies. Sometimes they show up as disappointments: not getting the promotion for which we worked, not having our offer accepted on that dream house. Sometimes fogs come as irritants through a gum-cracking coworker or the dog who charges us as we bike in our own neighborhood. But whatever the situation, God still is there.

I live in beautiful Colorado Springs, Colorado, which faces the Front Range of the Rocky Mountains. Prominent above the city is Pikes Peak, also called "America's Mountain." The view from the top of the 14,110-foot peak inspired Katharine Lee Bates to write the lyrics to "America the Beautiful."

My tiny town house offers me a view of that majestic peak, as long as I don't mind looking across the pavement and past a couple of rooftops. So every morning, I meander down the hallway into the loft area and look out the window. If I'm looking at the peak within a couple of minutes of the sunrise, the mountain shimmers as the sun's rays hit the pink granite. On winter mornings, the rays hit the snowcap, making the snow glow even whiter. And occasionally, storm clouds obscure the view.

Yes, I'm disappointed when that happens. But I don't throw my hands up and grumble, "I knew it was too good to be true. I bought this place because of that mountain, and now it's gone! Why did I ever believe the real estate agent when she commented on the lovely view! It was all just a lie."

Of course, I don't say that. I know the Peak is still there, even though clouds have temporarily obscured the view. But how many times have we had similar thoughts about God? The wonderful truth is that he is still with us even when life's clouds obscure our view. Even when we can't see him, he hasn't lost sight of us. And what a difference that makes.   —SANDRA

Lord, it's so easy to focus on the fog, whether it's a storm covering Pikes Peak or a personal trauma hiding your face. Remind me of your presence when I can't see you. Speak to me in ways I will recognize as coming only from you.

At the root of the Christian life lies belief in the invisible. The object of the Christian faith is unseen reality.
—A. W. TOZER (1897–1963), AMERICAN PASTOR, PREACHER, AND AUTHOR

JUNE 17
Taking Refuge

The LORD is my rock, my fortress, and my savior; my God is my rock, in whom I find protection. He is my shield, the power that saves me, and my place of safety. PSALM 18:2

I'd love to be able to report I've exhausted my allotted share of fog-filled days and now can live out my remaining days trouble free. But I know life doesn't work that way, and new hurdles may be ahead. Here are some of the "rules" I've had to put into practice when things didn't go the way I thought, hoped, prayed they would:

- *Pray a lot!* The Lord helps us, but we have to ask him for help. The most profound prayer is one word: *Help!*
- *Draw strength and inspiration from Scripture.* Many folks in the Bible faced tough situations and took refuge in God. As I read the psalms, I identify with David as he pours out his anguish to the Lord. I love his honesty, especially when he calls down heavenly wrath on his enemies' heads, and I'm encouraged as I see his faith in God's presence.
- *Don't expect others to meet every need.* Even the most loving family member or dearest friend can't be all we need. Our heavenly Father never sleeps and is available to strengthen and guide us twenty-four hours a day. He's just a whisper away, even at two in the morning.
- *Help others.* As I help others during their tough times, I am reminded of God's ever-present help in my own trials.
- *Choose the right attitude.* I do have choices in life, even if they are nothing more than choosing how I respond to my circumstances. Life is often difficult and stressful, but I can choose to trust the Lord to bring good from it.

—SANDRA

Lord, as long as I draw breath here on earth, I will have to deal with personal "fogs." So help. Please help. May I feel your peace, your power, your very presence.

Your joy in the Lord is to be a far deeper thing than a mere emotion.
—HANNAH WHITALL SMITH (1832–1911), QUAKER LAY SPEAKER AND AUTHOR

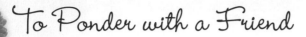

To Ponder with a Friend

1. What's your personal definition of courage? How did you arrive at it?

2. In what areas have you had to trust your heavenly Father? What happened?

3. Has anyone you know provided an example of being "strong and courageous"?

4. How have your personal fogs provided opportunities to help others?

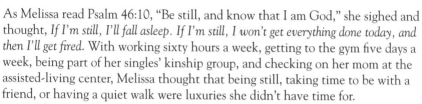

JUNE 18
An Invitation from God

Be still, and know that I am God!   PSALM 46:10

As Melissa read Psalm 46:10, "Be still, and know that I am God," she sighed and thought, *If I'm still, I'll fall asleep. If I'm still, I won't get everything done today, and then I'll get fired.* With working sixty hours a week, getting to the gym five days a week, being part of her singles' kinship group, and checking on her mom at the assisted-living center, Melissa thought that being still, taking time to be with a friend, or having a quiet walk were luxuries she didn't have time for.

Like Melissa, many women today lead lives of "scheduled hyperactivity." The old status symbols used to be a new house or car. But now people say, "You're busy? You should see how busy I am!" With our full schedules, we feel as if we're on a merry-go-round and we don't know how to get off. We talk on cell phones, juggle multiple tasks, drive while listening to talk radio, make lists of what we'll do the next hour or the next day. We live in a lightning-speed-e-mail-text-message-Blackberry-information-superhighway-YouTube-URL world that makes it difficult to have a conversation with a human being we can see—much less with our heavenly Father, whom we can't see—without being distracted.

Yet even in the maddening rush of this crazy-busy world, God tells us to be still and rest in him. The world will not stop turning if we take time for stillness. In fact, it may feel as if it has "slowed down" a bit. Would you ask God to open your heart to his gift of stillness today?   —CHERI

Lord, I admit I am rarely still or silent. Yet I long to experience rest in you and peace in my heart. Draw me near to you, and quiet me with your Spirit and your love.

Silence means rest, rest of body and mind, in which we become available for God. —HENRI NOUWEN (1932–1996), DUTCH PRIEST AND WRITER

JUNE 19
Come to Me

> Jesus said, "Come to me, all of you who are weary and carry heavy burdens, and I will give you rest." MATTHEW 11:28

Have you ever found that even when you're at a scenic place, it can be difficult to slow your pace? Georgia discovered that as she dashed upstairs to her room and grabbed some notes for the seminar she was presenting that afternoon. It was only the first day of the retreat, but already she felt caught up in the whirlwind of activities, workshops, and other time pressures. She'd hoped to have some moments to just slow down since she was away from the demands of her counseling office for two days. But it wasn't working out that way. She was tense and hurried.

On her way out the door with her notebook, Georgia glanced out the window across Chesapeake Bay and noticed a blue heron standing on the shore. Elegant and beautiful, the bird moved slowly and deliberately, jutting out its long neck. The heron paused briefly after each step, like a bride walking down the aisle. The light on the water shimmered like diamonds in the stillness. As Georgia took in the scene, she sensed God saying to her, *You were going so fast you almost missed the beauty of the heron. Stop and watch. Notice how it doesn't exert itself or hurry.*

It was the Father's gentle admonition. As Georgia stood and watched, mesmerized, she felt the tension in her shoulders melt away. Her spirit settled as she breathed deeply, realizing what a distinct contrast the heron's deliberate movement was to the fast-paced whirlwind of her life. Caught up in busyness, she had almost missed the beauty around her. But in a matter of moments, God had adjusted her priorities.

For weeks afterward, the image of the lovely blue heron came to Georgia's mind, reminding her to brush aside the clamor and hurry of the world and come near to the Lord for his promised rest.   —CHERI

> Lord, open my eyes to the reminders you graciously put in my path to call me to rest, not frantic activity. I thank you for caring for me in so many personal, loving ways.

Jesus knows we must come apart and rest awhile or we may just plain come apart.
—VANCE HAVNER (1901–1986), PREACHER, EVANGELIST, AND CONFERENCE SPEAKER

JUNE 20
Refresh My Heart

> The heavens proclaim the glory of God. The skies display his craftsmanship. PSALM 19:1

Today as I write, I'm in a big city, with traffic and noise everywhere. Perhaps like you, I'm not at a physical place away from the crush of daily demands. But I've found that no matter where we are, allowing ourselves one little window of time can do good things for us physically, help us reflect on what really matters, and most important, connect with the God who knows we're busy but waits patiently for us. He calls us near so he can shine his love into our hearts, speak to us, and heal us.

For me, that time might come as I look out the window of an airplane at the billows of clouds below. Some days, when I'm back home in Oklahoma, I sit in the sunroom that looks out on a clump of tall trees. One morning I was gazing at our collection of bird feeders hanging from the tree. Yellow, purple, black and white, and red miniature finches flitted from branch to branch. Blazing red cardinals, persistent woodpeckers, and chattering blue jays competed for a place at the feeders. The variety of winged creatures astounded me, each one different and beautiful in its own vibrant way. Looking at this microcosm, I was struck by the incredible variety of beauty God has created in the world around us. I've discovered if we pause a few minutes and look around, whether at the skies, which display his marvelous craftsmanship, or at a simple bird feeder in the backyard, we'll realize again that the same God who made these feathered friends and hung the stars in the heavens shapes and forms each of us and cares affectionately and watchfully for us. Time to be still? We hardly can live without it. The everyday blessings God gives in those sacred moments will do wonders for our whole being and quiet our racing hearts once again. —CHERI

Father, thank you for graciously giving me pauses in my day and sacred moments to refresh my heart and mind.

Lord, make me see Thy glory in every place.
—MICHELANGELO (1475–1564), ITALIAN SCULPTOR, PAINTER, ARCHITECT, AND POET

JUNE 21
An Antidote for Hurry-Up Sickness

Jesus explained, "I tell you the truth, the Son can do nothing by himself. He does only what he sees the Father doing. Whatever the Father does, the Son also does."   JOHN 5:19

Do you ever eat your lunch so fast you can't remember what you ate? get upset if you have to wait for anything and feel pressed for time even at the end of the day? Experts describe the extreme busyness that characterizes women's lives as "Hurry-Up Sickness," and their research shows it afflicts millions of women. The result of constantly living under the weight of time pressure and overload is a negative impact on our health: It doubles our chances of developing high blood pressure and suffering a heart attack or a stroke. It makes us impatient and saps the joy from our hearts.

While the experts have pinpointed the problem, they haven't found a proven fix. But God knew way ahead of time the challenges we'd face in our twenty-first-century lives, and he has an antidote for Hurry-Up Sickness. He wants to free us from the pressured, driven life and guide us back to living for what really matters. We can start by looking at what the Bible tells us about how Jesus lived and then follow his lead. Though he had an important mission to accomplish, he didn't work nineteen-hour days and burn out. The Savior didn't rush from task to task. He went for walks and rested at night. He spent time in conversation with his Father. He taught and healed multitudes, but he drew away from the crowds and took time for fellowship and meals with his friends. Jesus didn't need a Blackberry or a Day-Timer to tell him what to do every hour of the day. He did what the Father was doing and told him to do. What a good pattern for us to follow.

Before the crush of each day's tasks, spend some time with the Lover of your soul, and ask him what he wants you to do in the hours ahead. Your Good Shepherd will never fail to guide and direct you into still waters, even in a day full of service, family, and work responsibilities.   —CHERI

Thank you, Jesus, for being our perfect role model; you didn't hurry or dash about but always did what your Father told you to do, at the right time. Help me to follow your example instead of succumbing to the Hurry-Up Sickness of our society.

Work without a love relationship spells burnout.
—LLOYD JOHN OGILVIE, MINISTER, INSPIRATIONAL SPEAKER, FORMER CHAPLAIN OF THE UNITED STATES SENATE

JUNE 22
Slow Down

> We are merely moving shadows, and all our busy rushing ends in nothing. Psalm 39:6

Slow down, you move too fast. The words to the old song were drifting through my mind as the flashing lights of a police car appeared in my rearview mirror. Too late! I was racing down the highway, late to a meeting across town because two last-minute calls had kept me from leaving on time. When I saw the tall policeman head toward my car with his ticket book, I got a sinking feeling in the pit of my stomach.

"You were speeding, Ms. Fuller," he said, looking at my driver's license.

"I'm sorry, sir. You're right. I was going too fast."

"You're a lucky woman. Today I'm not giving tickets, just warnings, and here's yours: *Slow down!*"

Does the pace of life make you feel as if you're on a racetrack? I know the feeling. On a purely practical note, research shows that those who take short breaks actually achieve more each day, make fewer mistakes, and experience less stress than those who push through and never take a breather.

But more important, today's verse tells us that "all our busy rushing ends in nothing." When we really grasp this truth, we can take a deep breath, give our time to God, and dedicate at least a portion of every day to seeking him and reading his words. When we feel rushed, we can take a few moments to close our eyes and breathe slowly while thanking God for his goodness. We can move our eyes away from the laptop screen or the pile of laundry to the sky beyond the window and remind ourselves of the truth that the Author of our lives, who himself is eternal, has given us all the time we need to do everything he has truly called us to do on this day. When we operate from that mind-set, we accomplish more, not less, and we do so with an eternal perspective. —Cheri

Holy Spirit, help me to pace myself, to press the "pause" button and remember your goodness and mercy. Remind me that you are all I need and that you'll provide the time necessary to do everything that really matters today.

God gives me the gift of twenty-four hours a day; yet he is kind enough to accept in return the little time I give back to him.
—Paul Tournier (1898–1986), Swiss physician and author

JUNE 23
On the Edge of Burnout

"This is not good!" Moses' father-in-law exclaimed. "You're going to wear yourself out—and the people, too. This job is too heavy a burden for you to handle all by yourself." EXODUS 18:17-18

Not only did Moses lead thousands of people out of Egypt and through a very hostile environment, but he also served as the judge for every argument, small or large; as the intercessor for the people; and as their counsel. When Moses' father-in-law saw how Moses stood all day listening to the minor complaints of scores of people, he counseled him to slow down before he burned out.

Moses wisely heeded the advice of his father-in-law and delegated many tasks to other capable leaders. This allowed him not only to rest physically but also to refresh himself spiritually so that he could accomplish God's calling and purpose for him.

Sometimes we get caught in the same trap Moses did. It is easy to convince ourselves that no one can do the job quite as well as we can, that we are indispensable and can't ask for help. Yet delegation is the most effective form of leadership. It fosters maturity in potential leaders, and whether in our ministries or our careers, it provides a wider foundation of talents for meeting diverse needs. It fosters our trust in God and in people around us.

Have you allowed others to share the joys and burdens of what you do, or are you wearing yourself out with a burden too heavy for you to handle all by yourself? Working as part of a team helps you to retain the pleasure of service or ministry rather than find yourself exhausted and on the brink of burnout.
—CHERI

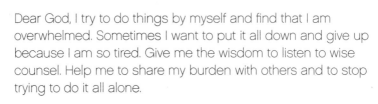

Dear God, I try to do things by myself and find that I am overwhelmed. Sometimes I want to put it all down and give up because I am so tired. Give me the wisdom to listen to wise counsel. Help me to share my burden with others and to stop trying to do it all alone.

A burden shared is a lighter load. —ANONYMOUS

JUNE 24
Wings like a Dove

> Please listen and answer me, for I am overwhelmed by my troubles. . . . Oh, that I had wings like a dove; then I would fly away and rest! PSALM 55:2, 6

At some point each of us has troubles so overwhelming, so burdensome and heavy, that we, like the psalmist, wish we had wings and could fly away and rest. The burden that drags us down may be an impossible schedule or strain and turmoil in our marriage. Maybe a dear, prickly teenager is acting out and driving us crazy instead of cooperating. Perhaps our job keeps us up late at night with extra paperwork, or we worry about losing our job entirely through downsizing. We may imagine a getaway place far from stress and problems. Perhaps we dream of a dramatic turnaround in pressing situations so we won't have to be anxious anymore. We long to escape from the difficulty so we can rest and recover. But God offers a kind of rest different from what our minds would conceive—a rest *in the midst of our distress.* It is the only true rest—an inner rest that comes from abandoning ourselves to the Lord and entrusting to him whatever troubles or problems overwhelm us.

Instead of trying to fly away from your situation, I encourage you to run straight into the arms of God, where you can rest in his care and love for you today. Know that he keeps whatever you entrust to him and that he will faithfully weave all the pieces into a pattern that is good and thus reveal his power to the watching world.   —CHERI

> O Lord, I want my problems solved and my troubles removed, but from beneath the crushing weight of this burden, I lift my eyes to you. I entrust this perplexity to you. Enable me to find my rest in you, to discover a place of deeper abandonment and peaceful security in your everlasting love. You are my only rock. You are my only rest.

How shall we rest in God? By giving ourselves wholly to him.
—JEAN NICOLAS GROU (1731–1803), JESUIT WRITER

To Ponder with a Friend

1. What tasks, activities, and demands on your time—including access to so much communication technology—keep you living in the "high-speed lane"?

2. Can you think of a recent experience you've had where your heart and soul were quieted by something in nature? Describe this experience or write about it in your journal. Thank God for this "everyday blessing" and for giving you sacred moments to experience rest and refreshment in his creation.

3. When I am stressed and overloaded, I would love to go to the beach and rest, but it's too far for me to drive there and too expensive to fly. To what place have you wished you could "fly away" when you've been overwhelmed? We may not be able to escape to those places, but we *can* experience the inner rest God offers.

4. What do you sense the Holy Spirit is saying to you this week and in this season of your life about burnout and overload versus entering into God's promised inner rest?

JUNE 25
Needed: Determination

Those who trust in the LORD will find new strength. They will soar high on wings like eagles. They will run and not grow weary. They will walk and not faint.   ISAIAH 40:31

When I was a child, one of my favorite books, which I now read to my two young grandsons, was *The Little Engine That Could.* The simple plot tells of a circus train needing to get over a mountain, but none of the strong engines could be bothered to pull the cars. Finally, the only engine left to ask was a small, unimportant engine. She had never been over the mountain and wasn't sure she was strong enough to make the difficult journey. But she knew the waiting children would be disappointed if the circus train didn't arrive, so she agreed to try. As she pulled the heavy load, she chuffed a determined little "I think I can. I think I can" with each passing mile. At last she made it to the top of the mountain amid cheers from the train's occupants. Then as she started down toward the town, the little engine chuffed a happy "I thought I could. I thought I could."

What if we carried that same determination when we looked at the mountains in our lives? It's sad but true: We often won't attempt a project because we are afraid we will fail.

My fifth-grade teacher wouldn't allow the word *can't* to be spoken in our classroom. If one of us muttered, "I can't do this," when facing a new math concept or trying to memorize a long vocabulary list, she would say, "Can't is a coward, too lazy to work." We had no choice but to tackle the chore. Amazingly, we usually found that starting was the hardest part and that the task was easier than we had anticipated.

Even in adulthood, we occasionally need the reminder to refuse to mutter, "I can't," and like that little engine, to make the choice to *try.* That may be the very fuel we need to get us over the next mountain.   —SANDRA

Lord, too often I feel like the little engine that won't even try. Help me to ask for your help and then go forward, determined to tackle the mountains in my life. Help me to run and not grow weary. Help me to hold on to the hope you offer.

Hope is a vigorous principle; it sets the head and heart to work and animates a man to do his utmost.
—JEREMY COLLIER (1650–1726), ENGLISH THEATER CRITIC AND THEOLOGIAN

JUNE 26
Productive Hope

> I prayed to the LORD, and he answered me. He freed me from all
> my fears.   PSALM 34:4

Have you ever been treated unfairly or been disappointed in a job situation? I have
too. But time and time again, I've seen good come out of adversity when I've given
the situation to the Lord. I'm convinced he still is in the creation business and can
bring his good out of tough situations. One of my favorite stories illustrates that
thought.

The new boss at the office always left written instructions for the entire staff,
including the evening cleaning crew. A janitor who could not read or write was
fired when he failed to respond to the written messages.

But instead of giving in to discouragement, the man grabbed a fresh helping
of hope and began his own cleaning business that resulted in numerous commercial
contracts. Eventually he became very wealthy, even able to buy several buildings.

During an annual financial checkup, his banker was astounded when he
discovered his prominent customer was illiterate.

"Just imagine what you'd be if you could read and write!" he exclaimed.

The man smiled. "Yes, I'd still be the janitor in the building I now own."

This story could have had an entirely different ending, one filled with bitterness and blame. But because a fired janitor grabbed on to hope and refused to give
up, he built a new life.   —SANDRA

Lord, I'm quick to blame you when things don't go my way. Help
me to give my disappointments to you. Help me to trust you to
reconstruct them and bring your good out of my pain.

You and I must be willing to be taught and to trust God's wisdom as He deals with
us, sometimes in a chastening way, to help us learn what He wants us to know.
—J. I. PACKER, THEOLOGIAN AND AUTHOR

JUNE 27

Active Hope

> Keep on asking, and you will receive what you ask for. Keep on seeking, and you will find. Keep on knocking, and the door will be opened to you. For everyone who asks, receives. Everyone who seeks, finds. And to everyone who knocks, the door will be opened.
> MATTHEW 7:7-8

It was the summer of 1976, and I wanted to attend a writers' conference the following year. But after reviewing our finances, my husband and I found we couldn't afford the fees. Further, we had two young children, and I couldn't be away from them for a week. Yes, I was disappointed, but as I talked it over with the Lord, a funny down-home saying dropped into my mind: "There's more than one way to skin a cat."

As I pondered how to apply that to my situation, a new thought began to form. The conference grounds where we vacationed often sponsored afternoon workshops in addition to the daily missionary and Bible presentations. Okay, I couldn't go to the writers' conference. But what if I brought the writers' conference to me?

Gradually, I began to make lists: what the main presentations should contain, who the lecturers should be, what the break-out sessions should include, which magazine and book editors should be invited. With each list, I began to gain hope. And each bit of hope provided another idea.

Then I talked to my editor at the magazine for which I most often wrote to see if such an idea were feasible, and she agreed to be the main lecturer. Once the professional details were finalized, I presented the tentative program to the director of the Bible conference grounds and asked for his permission. To my delight, he liked the idea of providing yet another opportunity for the summer guests to expand their skills.

I ran that workshop each summer for nine years and rejoiced as I saw fellow writers published and my own writing credits increase. Then a couple of years after my husband died, our children and I moved to New York so I could accept an editorial position. I turned the writers' conference over to a gifted writer who expanded my vision. Now more than three decades later, that annual gathering continues to grow, resulting in numerous published articles and books.

What about you? Is there something you want to do but think it's out of your reach? Grab on to hope and talk the plan over with the Lord. And remember, "There's more than one way to skin a cat."   —SANDRA

Lord, thank you for reminding me I don't have to be locked in to doing things the way they've always been done. When I'm standing between hope and fear, help me to remember that and choose hope.

Hope is an adventure, a going forward, a confident search for a rewarding life.
—KARL MENNINGER (1893–1990), AMERICAN PSYCHIATRIST

JUNE 28
New Insight

> Always be full of joy in the Lord. I say it again—rejoice!
> PHILIPPIANS 4:4

For years as I studied the Bible, I read Philippians 4:4 with the emphasis on only one idea: rejoice. I thought the verse said, "*Always be full of joy* in the Lord. I will say it again—*rejoice*" (emphasis added).

So I pasted a smile on my face, thinking that's how good Christians faced life. But life in this world includes having bad things happen. In my case, distant relatives died, a friend's house burned, a major investment evaporated. These were not things in which I could rejoice. But even as I hurt for each situation, I tried to keep a happy countenance.

Then my young husband was diagnosed with brain cancer. Suddenly I was faced with a scary future that didn't offer anything joyful. One evening, after my husband and children had gone to bed, a concerned friend called from out of state. He and his wife had held on to their deep faith despite having faced numerous trials, so I poured out my frustration at not being a good enough Christian during my family's crisis.

"Why can't my Christian walk be a walk?" I asked. "What am I doing wrong?"

My friend stifled a chuckle. "Who told you it's supposed to be a walk?" he asked. "It's a slugfest!"

A slugfest? In a single moment, I not only received a verbalized description of the battle we were waging against cancer, but I also was given permission to mourn the loss of the bright future we had planned. That night as I read Philippians 4:4, I saw it through new eyes. The verse tells us to always be full of joy *in the Lord.* Not in people, not in circumstances, but in the *Lord.* And even with tears running down my face, I knew I could rejoice because he was with us then and would be in the days ahead. —SANDRA

Lord, what a relief to know I don't have to rejoice in bad news. All I have to do is rejoice in you—in your peace, your power, your very presence.

There is no escape from an aching soul, only denial of it. The promise of one day being with Jesus in a perfect world is the Christian's only hope for complete relief. Until then we either groan or pretend we don't.
—LARRY CRABB, PSYCHOLOGIST, SPEAKER, AND AUTHOR

JUNE 29
When Life Isn't Fair

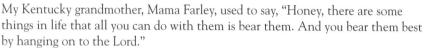

Lead me by your truth and teach me, for you are the God who saves me. All day long I put my hope in you. Psalm 25:5

My Kentucky grandmother, Mama Farley, used to say, "Honey, there are some things in life that all you can do with them is bear them. And you bear them best by hanging on to the Lord."

Of course, I didn't want to bear my problems. I wanted them fixed *now* and in *my* way. That was before life taught me the truth of Mama Farley's statement and before I met Elizabeth Smith, one of Mama's neighbors who attended the little church just down the road.

In our Kentucky community, the center of our social and religious life was that building perched on the bank of the Cumberland River. The little white clapboard structure had survived numerous floods, the Great Depression, and even the widening and paving of the road just outside its front door.

On Sunday mornings, the preacher would ring the bell shortly after nine thirty to let folks know he had arrived. Soon the community would gather, and we would exchange news from the past week. Sarah would ask about distant relatives or laugh appreciatively at the latest grandbaby story. Minnie often pulled a promised quilt pattern out of her apron pocket. And always Elizabeth Smith smiled as she leaned over her short cane. Even as a child, I towered above her. My aunt told me Elizabeth had been dropped by the "granny woman" who had attended her birth, and her little back had been twisted. No medical teams had been available to help her, and little Elizabeth, bent almost double, had leaned on a tiny cane, even in childhood.

The adult Elizabeth had every legitimate reason to complain about the tragedy that had altered her life forever, but I never heard her grumble. In fact, just before we entered the church each Sunday, she always smiled at whoever was standing nearby and said, "Isn't Jesus sweet?"

Isn't Jesus sweet? I stood dumbfounded at her words. Would I have said that if I'd been in her place? Or would I have pulled bitterness into my every sentence? Those were questions I didn't want to ponder.

Elizabeth has long been in heaven, but her words remain in my mind and heart. And I love thinking of her standing straight as she finally looked into the face of her sweet Jesus. —Sandra

Lord, I confess the words *Isn't Jesus sweet?* are not the first ones out of my mouth when life seems more than I can bear. Help me to remember Elizabeth's example. And remind me that you truly are sweet, even when life is sour.

Hope not only bears up the mind under sufferings but makes her rejoice in them.
—Joseph Addison (1672–1719), English essayist, poet, and dramatist

JUNE 30
Hope in a Student's Hand

> God has not given us a spirit of fear and timidity, but of power,
> love, and self-discipline.   2 TIMOTHY 1:7

My Northern seventh-grade English teacher didn't hold much hope for my scholastic future. After all, I had a Kentucky twang and preferred talking to my friends over listening to her. Then one day she handed out white wallet-size pamphlets listing basic grammar principles. As I sighed over yet more rules, the words written in red on the front cover grabbed my attention:

> I will study and prepare myself, and someday my chance will come.
> —ABRAHAM LINCOLN

My neighbor's niece had given me the vision of going to college someday, but I didn't know how to accomplish that goal. Now, suddenly, a practical plan was placed in my hands: All I had to do was study while I was waiting for that someday. I began to listen in class, started turning in my homework, took the writing assignments seriously, and studied for each test. The teacher may have marveled at such a drastic change in my attitude and grades. Perhaps she even congratulated herself for finally getting through to someone she saw as a difficult student. But I know what turned my attitude around: basic hope. I was given a practical and simple plan to attach to my previous dream. That gave me the confidence to achieve a college education that included earning a postgraduate degree, to teach for fifteen years in public schools, to write numerous books, and to speak throughout the world—and all because hope was placed in my hand.

I still have that little white and red pamphlet.   —SANDRA

Lord, help me to remember that even the simplest words can provide hope for someone who doesn't have a clue how to achieve a distant dream. Help me to provide that hope to those around me.

Hope, the balm and lifeblood of the soul.
—JOHN ARMSTRONG (1709–1799), SCOTTISH PHYSICIAN AND POET

JULY 1
Ignoring the Hope Stealers

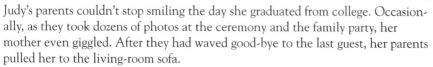

> The thief's purpose is to steal and kill and destroy. My purpose is to give [my sheep] a rich and satisfying life.   JOHN 10:10

Judy's parents couldn't stop smiling the day she graduated from college. Occasionally, as they took dozens of photos at the ceremony and the family party, her mother even giggled. After they had waved good-bye to the last guest, her parents pulled her to the living-room sofa.

"We have something important to tell you, honey," her mother said. "And when you hear it, you'll understand why we waited until now."

Judy, bewildered, looked at her parents' shining faces.

Her mother took a deep breath. "When you were in junior high, your class took some standardized tests. When the results came back, we were called in by the counselor and were told you would never graduate from high school because of your low scores. We were stunned but determined not to tell you about the meeting because we didn't want you to get it into your head you couldn't graduate."

Then Judy's mother smiled again. "And I told that counselor he'd better not tell you the scores, either, because you were going to graduate from high school *and* college!"

Judy's mind raced as she remembered the many nights her parents had taken turns tutoring her in math and quizzing her before various tests. How they had cheered her on during the four long years of college, saying she could do anything she wanted to do. And what she wanted to do was be a teacher. Today's graduation had provided that hard-won certificate.

Seeing Judy's bewildered look, her mother continued. "The only reason we decided to tell you now is because we never want you to make that counselor's mistake and tell parents their child can't do something. We want you to be optimistic about every child's potential and suggest positive, concrete ways parents can help children fulfill their potential."

Judy's eyes filled with tears as she hugged her parents and managed to whisper a hoarse "Thank you."

Today, Judy's teaching career has spanned two decades, during which she has encouraged students to reach their dreams. And when parents are discouraged about their child's progress, Judy tells them of her own parents' determined hope that changed her life.   —SANDRA

> Lord, help me to remember that people often become what we tell them they are. Help me to offer hope to others. Help me to offer that same encouragement to myself, too.

When you say a situation or a person is hopeless, you are slamming the door in the face of God.   —CHARLES L. ALLEN (1913–2005), AMERICAN PASTOR AND COLUMNIST

To Ponder with a Friend

1. Has a hopeful attitude ever made a difference for you during a tough time? How so?

2. Has a fresh insight about a particular passage of Scripture ever made a difference in your life?

3. Do you know someone who could be bitter but has chosen a better attitude?

4. Has a seemingly unimportant pamphlet or bit of writing ever offered encouragement to you?

JULY 2

Crafted by God

[The Lord said to Jeremiah,] "I knew you before I formed you in your mother's womb. Before you were born I set you apart and appointed you as my prophet to the nations." JEREMIAH 1:5

Eve woke up in the cabin at the retreat center and looked over at her roommate, who was sweeping long hair out of her eyes into a quick ponytail. Even though they'd had little sleep from talking with their small group until the wee hours, Courtney looked as if she had stepped out of a fashion magazine. *I wish I had her hair,* Eve thought. *It takes hours to get my hair to look like that.* Courtney dated the lead singer in a Christian band, was like a magnet for friends, and seemed to lead a charmed life. *If only I had her face, her body, her great singing voice and talents, then life would be perfect,* Eve thought. She knew envy was displeasing to God, but she couldn't help comparing herself to her friend. Around Courtney and cute girls like her, Eve felt unattractive and inadequate.

Much of Eve's struggle with comparison and her envy of other girls was related to health issues: open-heart surgery at age five, severe asthma, juvenile rheumatoid arthritis since age twelve—all of this kept her from having a straight, girlish walk or the figure the world calls appealing.

One day when Eve was again struggling with her tendency to compare herself with others, she was reminded of what God had said in Jeremiah 1 and realized that he had known her since before she was born. When she researched the Hebrew word for "know," she learned that it carries with it the idea of intimacy, the same word the Bible uses to describe a man and woman being physically intimate. God's love flooded Eve's heart as she realized the Lord cares so much that he formed her with all her intellectual attributes and physical characteristics. No longer did she feel like a genetic accident. God himself had shaped her body and personality.

You, too, have been known and crafted by God for a distinct purpose, and he will complete what he has started in you.   —CHERI

Father, I'm so thankful that you knew me before I was ever on planet Earth, and nothing about me is an accident. Thank you for your perfect plan and for the way you've shaped me inside and out to accomplish my part in it.

It is such a comfort to know that before we were born, God had already made his plan for us. He gave us gifts and qualities, and he will surely not waste them now that you are a Christian.
—CORRIE TEN BOOM (1892–1983), HOLOCAUST SURVIVOR, AUTHOR

JULY 3
A Masterpiece of His Grace

We are God's masterpiece. He has created us anew in Christ Jesus,
so we can do the good things he planned for us long ago.
EPHESIANS 2:10

In the days following Eve's revelation that God had known her even before she
was conceived, his Spirit continued to encourage her. *No one else can be the person
or fulfill the purpose I made you for. In fact, you're a masterpiece of my grace. Your true
identity is in Christ. When you find my purpose for your life, it will cause you to focus on
me instead of on yourself.* He repeatedly nudged her to stop comparing herself with
others and instead to fix her eyes on Jesus and to pursue the passion he had given
her for the medical field and missions.

As she studied advanced science and anatomy courses in nursing school, she
became excited about how the human heart and lungs work. *Wow,* she thought,
*even with my physical limitations, everything else that could have gone wrong works
perfectly.* God really did make me "wonderfully complex." (See Psalm 139:14.) She
learned to avoid the comparison trap by seeing herself as the Lord sees her rather
than as the world sees her and to value what he values. Finally, she realized the
enemy uses the comparison trap to turn us into ineffective, self-absorbed, depressed
people. She arrived at the place where she could see that the Lord had shaped her
for his purposes. Even the medical problems and stays in the hospital she'd once
regretted had contributed to her compassion for hurting people and her desire to
serve in the medical profession. Now, as a pediatric nurse for children with chronic
illnesses, Eve has an unusual understanding and skill that her superiors and her
patients recognize. *This is what I was made for,* she has thought time after time.

Just as Eve discovered that she is a character in a beautiful book, you are too.
God himself is writing the story of your life. And although you're in the middle of
the book, where you are to work hard to show the results of your salvation (see
Philippians 2:12), be assured, dear friend, that you can trust God for the next step.
—CHERI

> God, I struggle at times with the comparison trap, so help me to
> focus on you and to realize more and more my true identity in
> Christ Jesus. Thank you for being the author of my story and for
> making me with a grand design in mind!

Think of times in your life that made you wish for all the world that you had the
power to make time stand still. . . . Something in your heart says, Finally it has
come. This is what I was made for! —JOHN ELDREDGE, AUTHOR AND COUNSELOR

JULY 4
A Square Peg in a Round Hole

> Whatever I am now, it is all because God poured out his special
> favor on me—and not without results. . . . It was not I but God
> who was working through me by his grace.   1 CORINTHIANS 15:10

I'll never forget the summer night I sat in an auditorium on a Minnesota college
campus surrounded by 250 people I'd never met, and yet I felt entirely at home.
Joseph Bayly—author, poet, and founder of David C. Cook Publishing Company
(now Cook Communication Ministries)—was speaking to the gathering of the
Decision School of Christian Writing participants and explaining some of the
characteristics common to many writers: They are sensitive, curious, and determined. They are lovers of words. They see things differently and sometimes don't
fit the flow of what others are doing. They are expressive and verbal (even opin-
ionated) in wanting to share their ideas.

As this man went on, a quiet assurance settled into my heart. That's what
I am, a writer. By God's grace, I am what I am. Sure, I was a wife, a mother, and
a sister. But God had given me the heart of a writer. During my childhood, my
parents and siblings had often said, "You're just too sensitive!" In the high school
teaching career I'd pursued, I always felt a bit like a square peg in a round hole.
Some on the faculty had even said, "You're kind of a misfit among us. You're
always thinking outside the box or trying something different." And though I'd
been trained for classroom teaching, at times I felt as if I were in a wilderness, in
spite of the fact that I loved the students and the literature I taught.

But this writing conference was different. Although I had just met these
people from different backgrounds and states, they felt like family. Writers are still
some of my favorite people. Although there have been many obstacles, writing has
been my life's work for the twenty-five years since that evening in Minnesota, and
by God's grace, fruit has been borne. How grateful I am that God made me the way
I am, quirks and all, and sent me across the country to find out why.   —CHERI

> Lord, I trust your heart toward me even though I cannot always
> see your plan. And I trust your divine plan to bring forth fruit from
> my life.

You are the only person on earth who can use your abilities. No one else can play
your role, because they don't have the unique shape that God has given you.
—RICK WARREN, PASTOR AND AUTHOR

JULY 5

God's Mirror

> All of us who have had that veil removed can see and reflect the glory of the Lord. And the Lord—who is the Spirit—makes us more and more like him as we are changed into his glorious image.
>
> 2 CORINTHIANS 3:18

When we look at a photo of the elderly Mother Teresa, dressed in her simple white sari and her head scarf with bands of blue, tending a homeless man in the streets of Calcutta, she doesn't look beautiful by the world's standards. At age eighteen she left her home in Albania to join a group of Irish nuns and served by teaching children and being a principal for seventeen years. Then God's call came for her to pour out her life for the sick and dying, and in 1952 she opened the first Home for the Dying in India. Known as the "Saint of the Gutters," Mother Teresa had a beauty that came not from makeup or fine clothes but from her humility, integrity, and sacrificial love for the poorest of the poor in India and around the world.

Long before she became famous and drew large crowds whenever she visited a city, she lived a servant's life in hiddenness, seeking no glory for herself. However, as she gave herself to God and was transformed into his likeness, she became a mirror of the glory of the Lord, and all who were in her presence saw Christ and felt his transforming love.

Perhaps you think that only great ministers and servants like Mother Teresa are transformed into the likeness of Jesus. But today's verse is for each of us who believe in and belong to Christ. Yes, when Jesus comes again, he will transform our bodies so that they will be like his glorious body (see Philippians 3:20-21), but he desires to change us and make us "more and more like him" to reflect his character, his love, and his grace here on earth. Give yourself for the first time—or again—but give all you know of yourself to God, body, soul, and spirit, and ask him to transform you from the inside out so you will be a mirror that reflects him to those around you.   —CHERI

> Lord, thank you for the knowledge that I am to become a mirror and reflection of your love and glory. I am unable to do this for myself, but I give myself to you and ask for your glorious power to transform me into your image and likeness more and more.

If Christ lives in us, controlling our personalities, we will leave glorious marks on the lives we touch. Not because of us but because of him.
—EUGENIA PRICE (1916–1996), AMERICAN AUTHOR

JULY 6
Caring for Your Weakest Part

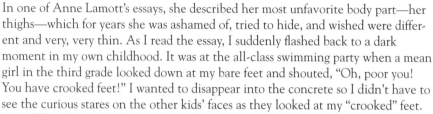

In Christ lives all the fullness of God in a human body. So you
also are complete through your union with Christ.
Colossians 2:9-10

In one of Anne Lamott's essays, she described her most unfavorite body part—her
thighs—which for years she was ashamed of, tried to hide, and wished were different and very, very thin. As I read the essay, I suddenly flashed back to a dark
moment in my own childhood. It was at the all-class swimming party when a mean
girl in the third grade looked down at my bare feet and shouted, "Oh, poor you!
You have crooked feet!" I wanted to disappear into the concrete so I didn't have to
see the curious stares on the other kids' faces as they looked at my "crooked" feet.

When I compared them to my four sisters' beautiful, perfectly shaped feet or
my friends' feet, I felt inferior. And what do we do when we are ashamed of something? You've got it—we hide it! I almost never wore sandals, and although I
wanted to wear strappy, open-toed high heels like other women, I figured, *Why
flaunt my worst feature?* Besides, a whole day in heels would land my feet in the
emergency room for treatment.

Fast-forward a bunch of years to when I was given a gift certificate for a
pedicure and discovered how much less my feet hurt when they were taken care
of. I even liked them better with my toenails painted. I have become more and
more accepting of this part of my body. The truth is, I am not complete or acceptable because of the shape of my feet, my thighs, or my nose but because I am complete and accepted in Christ Jesus. I've even begun to be thankful that God gave
me just the feet he wanted me to have; they are part of my individuality—not
beautiful by the world's standards but strong enough to hold up as I've run and
walked my way through countless miles and many years of life.   —Cheri

Father, I thank you for the way you've made my feet, my hands,
my hair, the size and shape of my body, unique parts and all.
Help me to be grateful instead of complain about your design.

Certain defects are necessary for the existence of individuality.
—Johann Wolfgang von Goethe (1749–1832), German poet and dramatist

JULY 7
Accepting Our Imperfection

Each time [God] said, "My grace is all you need. My power works best in weakness." So now I am glad to boast about my weaknesses, so that the power of Christ can work through me. . . . For when I am weak, then I am strong.   2 CORINTHIANS 12:9-10

Paul, though he was a great apostle of Jesus Christ, didn't try to appear perfect. He didn't have a problem admitting that he had weaknesses. Today in our culture, just the opposite is true: We are encouraged to hide or deny our weaknesses and instead pursue perfection. In only a few minutes at a bookstore newsstand recently, I saw these articles featured in different magazines: "Perfect Skin Tips," "Perfect Flat Abs," "The Perfect Jeans for Your Body."

Many women feel crushing pressure from the media and even from the church to strive for perfection. But from a biblical perspective, trying to be perfect is a mistake, because it's not the effort to appear perfect but the *embracing of our own imperfection* that draws us to God. The pursuit of excellence is worthwhile and valuable, but when it becomes a drive for perfection, it can become unhealthy and even be a major roadblock to a vibrant connection with God.

Saints of old tell us that from our awareness of our flaws flows the need for help with what we can't accomplish alone. In seeking God's help, we accept our own imperfection and humanness; this leads us to admit that we are not God (the first step in any human being's recovery from alcoholism or any other sin, bad habit, or problem). Out of that admission grows humility, and out of humility we can receive the grace the Lord has for us and trust in him instead of in ourselves. When we are weak, he is strong, and we are strong in him. What glorious freedom!   —CHERI

Jesus, I want to give up the relentless drive for perfection and instead accept and acknowledge my weaknesses. In doing so, I draw near to you and thank you with all my heart that when I am weak, I become strong because of my dependence on you!

God can exercise his mercy when we admit our defects. Our defects acknowledged, instead of repelling God, draw him to us, satisfying his longing to be merciful.
—RAPHAEL SIMON (1909–2006), PSYCHIATRIST, AUTHOR, AND CISTERCIAN MONK

JULY 8
Be Grateful for What You Are

Whatever is good and perfect comes down to us from God our
Father, who created all the lights in the heavens. He never changes
or casts a shifting shadow. He chose to give birth to us by giving us
his true word. And we, out of all creation, became his prized
possession. JAMES 1:17-18

*I wish I had her trim shape. I wish I had her exciting job. Why aren't my clothes as cool
and stylish as hers? I wish my house were decorated in a more updated way. . . .*

Researchers say it's part of our American mind-set to desire to have more, go
further, be happier, and look better than our parents and especially than our neighbors and friends. While a little friendly rivalry can spur on our exercise efforts if we
have a workout partner, being green with envy at what others have can send us
into a downward spiral.

One of the best antidotes to the comparison trap is gratitude for what God
has given us and for what we are. When we appreciate our own abilities and the
gifts God has given us, contentment and peace settle in our hearts. We realize that
every good gift comes from God, as today's verses tell us. We are not to pridefully
compare ourselves with others but to be grateful because out of God's whole creation, he has made those who belong to his Son his choice possession, and we are
beloved by him. That truth alone is reason for great thanksgiving and rejoicing.

Whenever you are feeling insignificant or "less than," let me encourage you
to write a list of the blessings and gifts God has given you, the attributes and characteristics he has crafted in your life. The dark clouds of regret will begin to clear,
and you'll be grateful once again for what you are and for what God has graciously
given you. —CHERI

My Lord, you are an amazingly loving and giving God. How I
thank you that in your goodness, you chose to make me your
own child by giving me your true word and making me your
choice possession. Thank you for your unchanging love!

On days when I feel insignificant, I think about the new person I am and the spe-
cialness of the relationship I now have with Christ. If I ever catch my reflection
in a mirror and see a questioning woman wondering, *Who am I?* I respond, *I am a
woman who is unique in the universe and certain of my personal worth because I am
loved by God and complete in Christ.* —SUE BURNHAM, AUTHOR

To Ponder with a Friend

1. Anne Lamott, Eve, and Cheri each had an unfavorite body part. As either a child or an adult, has there been a feature of your body you are ashamed of or wish were better, smaller, or just "prettier"? When you compared yourself with others in this area, how did it make you feel?

2. What situations most tempt you to get caught in the comparison trap? What can you take away from this week's Scripture verses and devotionals that can help keep you free of this negative pattern of comparison?

3. When have you ever discovered or experienced your weakness and imperfection as bridges to spiritual awakening or a closer walk with Christ? Describe or write about it.

4. Often we try, even subconsciously, to make ourselves more like others who we think look great or seem successful. Look at Romans 8:29 and 12:2. Whom does God intend for us to be conformed to or become more like, and what does this mean? What qualities might that involve?

JULY 9

Accepting Another Path

Long ago the LORD said to Israel: "I have loved you, my people, with an everlasting love. With unfailing love I have drawn you to myself." JEREMIAH 31:3

One of my hometown neighbors, Katherine, never married. One Saturday as we sipped green tea, she confided that as a young woman she had fallen in love with handsome Thomas, who had arrived in town to take over his uncle's business. Katherine was painfully shy and couldn't bring herself to speak to him, even though he attended her family's church and soon became the teacher for the adult Sunday school class she and her sister, Minerva, attended. The theological questions she longed to ask stuck in her throat, and she kept her eyes downcast for fear they would reveal her adoration.

Then late one Sunday afternoon Katherine answered the door and found Thomas standing there, clutching his hat. He had come to ask her father's permission to court her sister! Thomas and Minerva married a few months later.

Katherine could have chosen to become bitter or to withdraw further. Instead, she dried her tears and drew closer to the Lord through honest prayer and daily reading of his Word. And even though she maintained a close friendship with her sister, she did drop out of the class Thomas taught and began what became a forty-five-year stint as a Sunday school teacher for sixth-grade girls. The first week, she stammered through the lesson. The next week, she forced herself to look into each young girl's face as she talked. Gradually, she gained confidence with each returned smile. Within a few years, she was exchanging letters with former students who had gone on to become nurses, teachers, and wives while she continued to welcome each year's new batch of sixth graders. And always she encouraged both groups with reminders of God's peace and presence no matter the circumstances.

Because Katherine chose to help others instead of wrapping herself in self-pity and bitterness, she made a profound difference in the lives of hundreds of women, including me. —SANDRA

Lord, help me to trust you with my disappointment when it is still fresh and painful. Help me to give you my hurt and then watch with confidence for the good you will bring from it. My head longs to trust you, but often my heart is afraid.

Our body is the most gracious gift God has given us, and if we hand over the mainspring of our life to God, we can work out in our bodily life all that he works in. —OSWALD CHAMBERS (1874–1917), SCOTTISH BIBLE TEACHER, YMCA CHAPLAIN IN EGYPT

JULY 10
When the Dream Is Broken

The LORD is close to the brokenhearted; he rescues those whose spirits are crushed. PSALM 34:18

For years, Mildred had saved a portion from her school cafeteria paycheck with the dream of owning a fabric store. She had made her own clothes since her teens, learned to quilt from her grandmother, and spent Saturday afternoons studying sewing magazines. When she married, she continued making her own clothing and delighted in sewing tiny outfits for the three babies who arrived within four years. And always she envisioned smiling at future customers and helping them select the right fabric for a new project.

When the building that had housed a long-ago general store became available, she was thrilled. With her proud husband looking on, she signed the sale papers and handed over the down-payment check. She wrote another check for the insurance company and gave that to her husband to mail. Then, every spare minute, she painted walls and hung bright curtains at each crooked window. By the time school was out for the summer, her first customers were signing up for sewing lessons.

Then, the night before the first class, she received a frantic phone call from the woman across the road from her little shop: "Your store is on fire! I've called the fire department, but they're not gonna get here in time."

Mildred and her husband arrived as firemen jumped from their trucks, hooked up their hoses, and sprayed water through a window shattered by the heat. But it was too late. Mildred clutched her husband's arm as they watched the roof collapse. Soon only a smoldering pile of ancient wood remained.

While the rest of the firemen checked for hot spots in the rubble, the fire chief approached. "I'm sorry this happened, folks. But I'm glad nobody was hurt. Buildings can be replaced. People can't. Good thing for insurance, huh?"

He turned toward his men, who were spraying the rubble one final time.

But Mildred barely noticed his farewell. For as soon as the fire chief mentioned insurance, she had felt her husband's arm tighten. She had to know. "Honey, you did mail the insurance check, didn't you?"

Her husband bit his lip. "I meant to. I really did. But then I got busy and figured you'd need the money down the line. After all, that building stood empty all these years and nothing had happened."

His voice trailed off as Mildred's shoulders slumped. After a long moment, she raised her eyes to look once more at the ashes of her dreams and then turned toward the car. —SANDRA

Lord, I keep asking you for the life I want. Now I'm asking you to help me to live the life I have. Help me to see you even through tears. Help me to live this life in your power.

This is not the life I wanted, but it is the life I have.
—2004 INDONESIAN TSUNAMI SURVIVOR

JULY 11
Bear Meat Fried in Bear Grease

Not that I was ever in need, for I have learned how to be content
with whatever I have.   PHILIPPIANS 4:11

Have you ever committed to an assignment you later regretted? I have. I remember
the bookstore job my husband and I accepted years ago at our favorite Bible conference. I anticipated a summer of joyful ministry. Instead, I was surprised to learn
how rude and impatient even Christians can be. Although we had made a commitment for the remainder of the summer, I started counting the days until we could
go home. Still twenty-eight more to go—four more weeks of disappointment and
homesickness.

Early one August morning, I hugged my Bible and spoke aloud, "Lord, you
know how miserable I am. What do I do now?"

I steadied myself for the expected reminder about how "God causes everything to work together for the good," from Romans 8:28. Instead, the phrase *bear
meat* popped into my head.

Bear meat? Where did that come from? Then I remembered the story a long-
ago Sunday school teacher had told:

"An old trapper, snowbound in his cabin, couldn't get fresh supplies. For
days, he ate nothing but bear meat fried in bear grease. Finally, he prayed for the
Lord to give him something he could really enjoy. Know what the Lord gave him?
Bear meat fried in bear grease!"

Even though I wasn't ready to shout, "I love it here!" I did smile at the
reminder of the difference the trapper's change of attitude made. I had no choice
but to work on my attitude as well.

First, I asked the Lord to help me to be grateful for what I could and to give
me the strength to ignore the rest. I started by making a game out of smiling at rude
customers. Then I looked for something each day for which I could be thankful.

Sometimes those thankful moments came through conversations with a
speaker I admired. But most often they came through simple joys I had previously
ignored. Suddenly even watching the progress of ripening blackberries along the
path to the store brought happiness.

Gradually, the twenty-eight days passed. Yes, I was happy to go home, but
I was also wiser. I finally had realized that even when we must wade through disappointment, the Lord is with us. And he can take the tedium of "bear meat" and
turn it into a feast if we will ask him to.   —SANDRA

Lord, I confess I want what I want. Help me to rejoice in what
I have. And help me to look for the things for which I can be
thankful despite the circumstances.

The best thing one can do when it's raining is to let it rain.
—HENRY WADSWORTH LONGFELLOW (1807–1882), AMERICAN POET

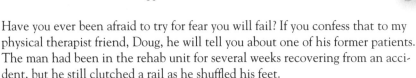

JULY 12
The Purposeful Fall

All who listen to me will live in peace, untroubled by fear of harm.   PROVERBS 1:33

Have you ever been afraid to try for fear you will fail? If you confess that to my physical therapist friend, Doug, he will tell you about one of his former patients. The man had been in the rehab unit for several weeks recovering from an accident, but he still clutched a rail as he shuffled his feet.

The doctors insisted he had no physical reason for his tiny, cautious steps, but he ignored their pronouncements. So they assigned Doug to him.

During their first session, Doug watched the patient take fear-filled steps. "Why do you walk like that?"

"I'm afraid I'll fall," the man replied.

"Did you ever fall when you were a kid?"

"Sure, lots of times," the man said.

"Where?"

"On the grass."

Doug nodded. "How about when you were older? Did you ever fall then?"

The man smiled. "Sure. I played softball. I was always falling—diving after a ball, going for a base."

Doug nodded again. "Okay, we're going for a walk on the hospital lawn, and I'm going to trip you. You're going to fall. And you're going to see it's all right."

The man wasn't sure he could do that, but Doug coaxed him outside. As they walked along, talking about their favorite sports teams, Doug suddenly tripped his patient, just as he had promised he would, and the man sprawled in the grass.

For a moment he lay still, as if he were mentally checking for broken bones. Everything was intact. He stood up and grinned at Doug. Then he bounced up and down and even gave a little jump. He was going to be just fine.

I wonder how often I've been like that man, disappointed by life and afraid to try again. What would happen if I invited the Lord to walk with me?

—SANDRA

Lord, like that man who was afraid to walk, I want safety. I want comfort. Help me to take your hand. And help me to know you are walking beside me, even if life trips me.

We must not be deterred from embracing the blessed privilege of divine guidance by a dread of the dangers that environ it.

—HANNAH WHITALL SMITH (1832–1911), QUAKER LAY SPEAKER AND AUTHOR

JULY 13
When You Must Smile

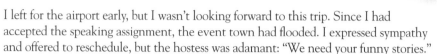

Worry weighs a person down; an encouraging word cheers
a person up. PROVERBS 12:25

I left for the airport early, but I wasn't looking forward to this trip. Since I had accepted the speaking assignment, the event town had flooded. I expressed sympathy and offered to reschedule, but the hostess was adamant: "We need your funny stories."

I didn't want to be funny. My grandparents had been flooded out when the Cumberland River jumped its banks. I knew about loss of family photos and family treasures. How could I offer anything to women who had faced that? *Oh, Lord, please help!* was my constant prayer.

As I approached the automatic check-in, an agent called for attention.

"A storm is approaching, so we're trying to get you out early. If you have a ticket for the 8:25 through Chicago, step over here for immediate departure."

Before I knew it, I was on a packed plane, in a window seat in the back. I always ask for a forward seat on the aisle, so this seat assignment assured me the trip was off to a bad start. Just as I settled in, my seatmate arrived.

"This earlier flight sure was a surprise, huh?"

"Sure was." I was in no mood for chitchat.

"You going to visit grandkids?"

Now I was irritated. What an arrogant assumption that any woman with gray in her hair and wearing slacks didn't have corporate reasons for being on a plane.

"No. Business."

"Oh. What do you do?"

I sighed. "I talk."

"Really." It crossed my mind that he wanted to add, "Could have fooled me." Instead he said, "What about?"

It was time for a showdown. "Look," I said. "I'm known for my funny stories. I tell about goofy relatives and zany experiences. But this time I'm going into a town hit by flooding, and I don't *want* to be funny."

He settled a flat pillow behind his neck. "Well, you can be grumpy after you speak. Those folks need to laugh. They won't forget their pain. They'll just be reminded good days will come again."

I murmured a surprised "Thanks" as he closed his eyes. Then I looked out the window and watched the plane head for the sky. I had almost missed God's answer to my plea for help. —SANDRA

Lord, how often do I ask for your help and then not recognize it because it comes through an experience or person I don't like. Help me to be open to your voice and your answers, no matter the source.

God's wisest saints are often people who endure pain rather than escape it.
—CHARLES SWINDOLL, PASTOR, AUTHOR, EDUCATOR, AND RADIO PREACHER

JULY 14
Wounded Prayer Warrior

> The Holy Spirit helps us in our weakness. For example, we don't know what God wants us to pray for. But the Holy Spirit prays for us with groanings that cannot be expressed in words.
> ROMANS 8:26

Amy looked out her window, wishing she had the energy to go outside. But by staying in, she didn't have to fight panic.

When the attacks started, she had made an immediate appointment with her doctor. After doing numerous tests, he suggested she see a counselor. So, she had seen counselor after counselor. They all said her agoraphobia was the result of problems rooted in her childhood. But that diagnosis didn't provide a solution, and medication was only a feeble attempt to treat her symptoms.

Amy sighed. "Lord, I feel thrown out by the world," she whispered. Settling herself on the sofa, she picked up her Bible and pulled out cards she'd saved showing Jesus with children on his lap, leaning against him. She especially liked the one of the giggling little girl with her arms clasped around his neck. *What would it have been like to be hugged like that?* she thought.

Her counselors had said her mother wasn't capable of giving unconditional love. But Amy remembered her mother showing great affection toward a younger sibling. *It was just me,* she thought. *I must have been the type even a mother couldn't love.*

Amy had married young to get away from home, but her husband left her for another woman. Now, alone and feeling useless, she longed for a friend who would call or send a note to say, "I'm praying for you. How are you?"

Well, that wasn't happening. And she couldn't do anything except ask the Lord to help others. So, with the pictures of Jesus and the children still on her lap, she opened the church bulletin, which the secretary sent each week. On the back, she read the names of homebound or hospitalized members. As she touched her fingertips to each name, she prayed.

Occasionally she wiped tears or circled names of those who had been on the list for a long time. To them, she would send a card to say they hadn't been forgotten. As she finished praying, she again picked up the picture of Jesus and the little girl. Then she closed her eyes and imagined Jesus hugging her and all the hurting people for whom she had just prayed. *Perhaps I'm of some use, after all,* she thought. And she hugged the picture again.   —SANDRA

Lord, life has a way of constantly disappointing us. Help us— help me—to give you those disappointments and then to march boldly into your sunshine. Thank you that even when we feel as if "all we can do" is pray, we are part of your great love to this hurting world.

It is by those who have suffered that the world has been advanced.
—LEO TOLSTOY (1828–1910), RUSSIAN NOVELIST AND PHILOSOPHER

JULY 15
Invest While I'm Gone

Before [the nobleman] left, he called together ten of his servants and divided among them ten pounds of silver, saying, "Invest this for me while I am gone." LUKE 19:13

In the autumn of 1970, my husband, Don, and I visited out-of-town friends and helped with their teen hour on Sunday evening. Both Don and I were high school teachers and enjoyed chatting with the students over refreshments. One senior girl especially impressed us with her vivacious and intelligent comments, so as typical teachers, we asked her where she planned to go to college. She tossed her head.

"Oh, Dad said I don't have to worry about going to college since the Lord will return before I graduate."

Well, here it is almost four decades later, and the Lord still hasn't shown up. I wish I knew where that young woman is now. Was she disappointed when graduation night arrived but the Lord hadn't? Did she dismiss everything her father said after that? Is she still complaining his failed prediction ruined her life?

I often think of her as I read Luke 19:11-27, where the Lord presents a cryptic account of his own kingship and coming reign through the parable of a nobleman who planned a long journey. Before the nobleman left, he divided ten pounds of silver among his ten servants. In their currency, one portion of the silver was worth about three months' salary, so each man was being entrusted with a substantial amount and commanded to put the money to work.

When the nobleman returned after a lengthy absence, his first two servants had invested their share and seen it grow ten and five times greater. But the third servant presented his master with the same amount of silver he had received, saying that because of his fear he had hidden the money and kept it safe. His master scolded him for doing nothing and ordered that this servant's portion be given to the servant who had multiplied his investment by ten.

I hope that senior girl from years ago was like the first wise servant. I hope she grabbed the opportunity to live a full life while she faithfully waited for the Lord to appear. —SANDRA

Lord, thank you for this reminder to continue the work you have given us even as we watch for your return. Help us to work as if we will be here forever as we wait.

Worry never robs tomorrow of its sorrow, it only saps today of its strength.
—ARCHIBALD JOSEPH CRONIN (1896–1981), SCOTTISH PHYSICIAN, DRAMATIST, AND WRITER

To Ponder with a Friend

1. Have you ever had to deal with a deep disappointment? If so, what was the situation?

2. What do you think is the greatest challenge for those who have experienced fear or disappointment?

3. What advice would you give to those who are afraid they will fail?

4. What was the best advice you've ever received about dealing with fear or disappointment?

JULY 16
In the Storm

> As they sailed across, Jesus settled down for a nap. But soon a fierce
> storm came down on the lake. The boat was filling with water, and
> they were in real danger. The disciples went and woke him up,
> shouting, "Master, Master, we're going to drown!"   LUKE 8:23-24

In spite of our position as God's beloved people and heirs, sometimes our spiritual
eyesight becomes clouded by the storms of life or difficult circumstances. Maybe
like me—and the disciples on the stormy sea—at times you find yourself so overwhelmed with the trials and tumultuous waves that threaten to capsize you that
you cannot see the Lord—who is right there with you, who promises never to leave
you or forsake you, who is ahead of you, behind you, and within you.

Panicked and terrified by strong winds of adversity, Jesus' friends thought
they might drown. And so do we. I love what Anne Graham Lotz said about this
tenuous state of mind: "When we are faced with great problems, our tendency is to
focus on the hands of God, what he has not done for us and what we want him to
do for us, instead of focusing on the face of God, simply who he is. Our depression
can deepen through this kind of self-preoccupation. Often, in the midst of great
problems, we stop short of the real blessing God has for us, which is a fresh vision
of who he is."

We can attend church regularly and miss seeing Jesus. We can have extensive theological knowledge and lose sight of the Savior. And in troubled times, we
may lose the sense of his power. But seeing and encountering Jesus isn't just something we "want," like sprinkles on a cake's icing; it's something we *need*, an ingredi-
ent vital to a sustained life of faith. This week we will discover what happens when
people have the eyes of their hearts renewed and gain a new vision of the King.
—CHERI

> Lord, you said if we look for you in earnest, we will find you. Wash
> my eyes so that I can see your glory and grace. In the midst of
> my mundane or chaotic life, I trust you to reveal yourself to me.

One glimpse of the King and you are consumed by a desire to see more of him and
say more about him.   —MAX LUCADO, AUTHOR AND MINISTER

Searching for God

Search for the LORD and for his strength; continually seek him.
PSALM 105:4

David was called a man after God's heart because, in whatever situation he found himself, he searched for God. Psalm 105 tells us we are called not only to praise God, give thanks to him, proclaim his greatness, and let the whole world know what he has done but also to *search for the Lord and his strength and to keep on searching*. To search means to look carefully and thoroughly in an effort to discover or find something important. It doesn't mean to look once and then go on to pursue other things. It means to search *always* for God, which in the original Hebrew has the sense of *seeking wholeheartedly, continually, constantly, regularly, and daily*. And as we search for the Lord, we are also seeking his strength rather than our own for all the challenges we face in living and being his followers.

It is encouraging to know that as we search for God, he comes and reveals himself to us and then manifests his strength in our lives. He promises that when we seek him, we will encounter him, because he does not hide his character from his people. Over and over throughout the Bible, through his Son, Jesus, through his Spirit, and through creation, he has revealed his heart, his glory, and his nature so that we might know him. God promises that those who devote themselves to searching for him and knowing him will find all their needs met in him (see Deuteronomy 4:29; Jeremiah 29:13; Acts 17:27-28). —CHERI

Lord, thank you for calling me again to search for you and for the many promises in your Word that you will come and strengthen me and reveal yourself so I can know you more intimately. Cause me to seek you with all my heart, to search for you daily and continually throughout my life, and to depend on your strength for today.

Our God loves to come; he wants to come forth in us, to rise up in us in all his beauty. —MARGARET THERKELSEN, AUTHOR AND SPEAKER

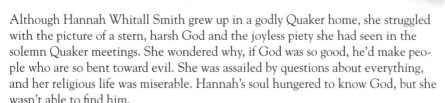

JULY 18
A Flash of Illumination

> Anyone who belongs to Christ has become a new person.
> The old life is gone; a new life has begun!   2 CORINTHIANS 5:17

Although Hannah Whitall Smith grew up in a godly Quaker home, she struggled with the picture of a stern, harsh God and the joyless piety she had seen in the solemn Quaker meetings. She wondered why, if God was so good, he'd make people who are so bent toward evil. She was assailed by questions about everything, and her religious life was miserable. Hannah's soul hungered to know God, but she wasn't able to find him.

After the death of Hannah's first child, five-year-old Nellie, she began to earnestly seek the Lord. On a beach trip with her family, she took only her Bible and a determination to find God. Sitting in the sand, she read the book of Romans, where she discovered that *"while we were still sinners,"* Christ died for us (Romans 5:8, emphasis added). As she glimpsed God revealed in the face of Jesus, her vision of the love of Christ made her radiantly happy. In a flash of illumination, she knew without a doubt that she didn't have to try to be righteous or pious. Jesus had paid the price and offered her *his righteousness*. In those moments Hannah spent in God's presence, his extravagant love not only healed her grief but brought salvation to her soul. The old passed away, and the new came (see 2 Corinthians 5:17).

From that point on, Hannah Whitall Smith served God as a faithful wife, mother, and grandmother through terrible trials, financial reversals, an unfaithful husband, and prodigal children. She preached throughout England and America and wrote the beloved classic *The Christian's Secret of a Happy Life* and other works, which have inspired millions of people with the truth that we can not only endure testings and troubles but also live abundant, overcoming, and joyful lives.   —CHERI

Lord, like Hannah Whitall Smith, I long to see you as you really are, to know you more, and to experience a joyful Christian life. Grant me a flash of illumination regarding your extravagant love so that I, too, will never be the same.

Many are partakers of God's grace who have never seen Jesus. Once you have seen Jesus, you can never be the same, other things do not appeal as they used to do. . . . If you have a vision of Jesus as He is, experience can come and go; you will endure "as seeing him who is invisible."
—OSWALD CHAMBERS (1874–1917), SCOTTISH BIBLE TEACHER, YMCA CHAPLAIN IN EGYPT

A Life-Changing Encounter

In the beginning the Word already existed. The Word was with God, and the Word was God. He existed in the beginning with God. God created everything through him, and nothing was created except through him. The Word gave life to everything that was created, and his life brought light to everyone. The light shines in the darkness, and the darkness can never extinguish it.

JOHN 1:1-5

At age twenty-nine I found myself asking, like the old Peggy Lee song, "Is that all there is?" I'd done everything I thought would bring happiness: married, had children, earned my graduate degree, lived in a cute redbrick house with white shutters on a pleasant street. I'd made a commitment to Christ when I was twelve, and we went to church weekly, but God seemed more like a distant relative than an intimate friend, and I had an empty place inside that none of the wonderful things and people in my life had filled. One day while my toddler boys napped, I combed through the bookcase, looking for something I hadn't read. Finally my hand hit upon a dusty New Testament I'd used in a college class. I hadn't read *that* book in a long time.

I sat down on the couch and began to read the first few pages of Matthew as rain splashed on the window beside me. After Matthew, I tackled Mark and Luke, page by page, chapter by chapter, day after day as I'd read so many textbooks before. Several weeks later, I started the book of John: "In the beginning the Word already existed. The Word was with God, and the Word was God." As I read those words, the eyes of my heart were renewed, and Christ's light permeated the room. As unbelief and doubt melted away, I soaked in the truth on the page: that the Word is Jesus, and he has been with God from the very beginning. He created everything, and nothing was created except through him. In him, in Jesus, is *life*, and his life is the light of all humanity. Christ came to bring light to *my darkness* as well. Because of this life-changing encounter with Jesus, I have never been the same. I began a spiritual journey and adventure that has continued to this day, thirty years later.   —CHERI

Lord Jesus, you are so creative and individual in the ways you come to us and reveal yourself. Grant me intimate encounters with you in the days and weeks ahead.

Our Savior lives, and if we let it happen, if we accept his presence, our lives will be changed forever.   —JIMMY CARTER, THIRTY-NINTH PRESIDENT OF THE UNITED STATES

JULY 20
Coming Home to the Father

See how very much our Father loves us, for he calls us his children, and that is what we are! 1 JOHN 3:1

Maybe you are one of those fortunate women whose mothers and fathers reflected the Lord's love for them. Parents have many jobs and responsibilities, but one of the most vital is to be the picture or reflection of God that he intends them to be so their children will eventually turn to their heavenly Father and receive his unfailing love.

As humans, our perception of God tends to be shaped by our earthly parents. Terri was the child of missionaries, but because her parents were cold and critical, she perceived God as being the same way. On the other hand, my friend Peggy had a gentle, loving dad, so when she came to Christ as a teenager, it was easy for her to experience God's love and comfort.

How we view our heavenly Father is directly related to our experiences with our own fathers, because we see God through the filter of our parents'—and especially our fathers'—love or lack of love. This view carries right into adulthood and can greatly influence our relationship with our heavenly Father. Although God's love is unfailing and unconditional, many of us avoid him because of the "father flaws" we saw as we grew up.

The good news is God can use the very holes in your life that resulted from imperfect fathering or from life's losses to draw you into his arms and make you the beneficiary of his perfect fathering. He can fill the gaps of the love you needed and didn't receive. Regardless of how adequate or inadequate your earthly father (or parent) was, you don't have to remain stuck in the perception of God you've carried since childhood. The eyes of your heart can be renewed as you bring those faulty views to the altar, forgive those who misrepresented God, and ask the Lord to enable you to see him accurately and to enjoy him and trust him now and forever. —CHERI

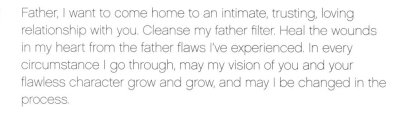

Father, I want to come home to an intimate, trusting, loving relationship with you. Cleanse my father filter. Heal the wounds in my heart from the father flaws I've experienced. In every circumstance I go through, may my vision of you and your flawless character grow and grow, and may I be changed in the process.

Jesus invites you and me, in his name, to come into his Father's presence through prayer, crawl up into his lap by faith, put our heads on his shoulder of strength, feel his loving arms of protection around us, call him "Abba" Daddy, and pour out our hearts to him. —ANNE GRAHAM LOTZ, AUTHOR AND EVANGELIST

The Face of God

> The Son radiates God's own glory and expresses the very
> character of God, and he sustains everything by the mighty
> power of his command. HEBREWS 1:3

What a marvelous thing it is that God reveals himself in the Bible and through Christ, the eternal Word. Our verse today tells us that Jesus is the face of God, the visible image of the invisible God. From Genesis to Revelation, God gives us countless snapshots of himself. We can trust in the fact that the Bible is not just a collection of nice stories, not myths that are representations of truth, but "true truth," as Edith Schaeffer said, so that through it we can know God and come to love and surrender our lives to him. However, we may have to lay down the false notions about God that we have taken from our culture, our education, or movies or art, in which he is often portrayed more as a caricature than as the infinite Creator of the universe.

The comedy *Oh, God!* portrayed him as a wisecracking old man with a cigar. The 2003 movie *Bruce Almighty* humanized God as a dignified Higher Power who posed as a janitor. Popular songs describe God as being distant and leaving us to fend for ourselves. From what movies, books, college courses, and songs have you gained ideas about God? Do these represent his loving-kindness and his invitation to people to enter into a new relationship with him through Jesus Christ? How do they line up with what the Bible says about him?

When you read the Bible, especially the Gospels, do so for the purpose of encountering the Lord, not just getting through your day's reading. Ask him to speak to you, to guide you, and most of all, to open the eyes of your heart to see him as he really is and experience his reassuring love and peace at the core of your being. As you do this, you will not only discover wonderful truths in his Word; you will also rediscover Jesus Christ, the living Word. —CHERI

Thank you, Father, for your desire to reveal yourself to me and to give me abundant grace to enjoy your presence. I praise you that you are always drawing me to yourself and that you have given me the gift of your Word that I might know you more intimately.

The Bible is a perfect picture of God. . . . One of the main reasons we have the Bible is to show us what God is like. It is a revelation of God to us. And the better we know him, the closer our relationship can be with him.
—JOSH MCDOWELL, APOLOGIST, EVANGELIST, AND WRITER

JULY 22
Renewing Our Minds with God's Promises

The LORD's promises are pure, like silver refined in a furnace, purified seven times over.   PSALM 12:6

Ruth Bell Graham was very burdened for her eldest son, who for years had been running away from God and other people's expectations of what he "should be" as Billy Graham's son. He smoked, drank, fought, and was expelled from college. One night Ruth couldn't sleep and as usual became preoccupied with worry about her son. *What will happen to him? Where is he tonight? When will he come home?*

As she battled her fears and imaginings, she heard God whisper, *Stop studying all the problems and start studying my promises.* She couldn't mistake the voice; she knew it was God's. So Ruth switched on the lights and opened her Bible. As she read, she realized what had been missing in all the prayers for her son: thanksgiving and worship. Straightaway she set down her Bible and let the Scriptures she had read renew her mind and her faith. She began to worship God, thanking him for his precious and pure promises, thanking him not only for her son but even for the heartaches and trials he had brought to her life. It was as if a light had turned on. As her fears vanished and her mind rested on God and his promises, it dawned on her that worship and worry simply couldn't live together. She could choose to worry, or she could choose to worship. It wasn't a difficult decision to make.
—CHERI

> Father, I confess that I've been studying my problems much more than dwelling on you and your precious promises. Renew my mind by your truth, and renew my heart that I may see you and worship you.

If only we would stop lamenting and look up, God is here. Christ is risen. The Spirit has been poured out from on high.
—A. W. TOZER (1897–1963), AMERICAN PASTOR, PREACHER, AND AUTHOR

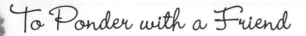

To Ponder with a Friend

1. As Oswald Chambers once said, "Once you've seen Jesus, you will never be the same." What happened when you first got a glimpse of Christ Jesus? How did this bring about change in your life?

2. Faith looks at God instead of looking inward at our inadequacies or being preoccupied with the big waves in our stormy situation. Is there an area of your life where you need to refocus and seek a deeper revelation of God's love for you? What is that area?

3. What emotions do you feel when you hear the word *father*? When you think of God, what image or words come to your mind?

4. Is there someone you need to forgive who misrepresented God in your early life? If you feel comfortable doing so, would you write down his or her name? Your heart and your perception of God can be renewed as you bring those faulty views to the altar, forgive people who didn't reflect God's love to you, and ask his Spirit to clean your spiritual vision. He will give you a new, accurate view of the heavenly Father and the Son he sent so that you could know and enjoy him now and forever.

JULY 23
Choose Wisely

> The LORD God is our sun and our shield. He gives us grace and
> glory. The LORD will withhold no good thing from those who do
> what is right.   PSALM 84:11

Tara noticed the new guy in her apartment complex right away. He was tall, good
looking, and punctual, always arriving home from work at 6:15. He was the most
interesting person in her life at the moment since a previous relationship had left
her feeling vulnerable and lonely. But from the first day he smiled at her at the
mailbox cluster, she had something to look forward to.

From her front window she could see his black truck enter the complex and
head toward the nearby mailboxes before pulling into his parking spot. Tara kept
her postal key by the door, so she often "happened" to be at the mailbox as his
vehicle pulled up.

At first, she just wanted to get a closer look at his square jaw, so she would
merely offer a quiet "Hello" or "Nice day, isn't it?" as she retrieved her stack of
junk mail. But his quick smile and compliments on her attire or her hairstyle
would cause her to linger. Her loneliness began to lift as she searched for conversation that would lead to topics of mutual interest. But soon she realized they
didn't have much in common. She could tell his Sundays didn't include church
because he and his buddies set off early to climb boulder-filled mountain trails in
their customized vehicles. He didn't like music—not country/western, classical,
or the hymns she found comforting. And to her amazement, he didn't like sports,
not even their own local championship teams. Still she plotted their mailbox
meetings.   —SANDRA

> Lord, help me not to panic and just settle for whatever is
> available, whether it is a potential spouse, a job, or some other
> new situation. Teach me to listen to you and to wait for you, who
> know best, to provide your best.

We are half-hearted creatures like an ignorant child who wants to go on making
mud pies in a slum because he cannot imagine what is meant by the offer of a
holiday at the sea. We are far too easily pleased.
—C. S. LEWIS (1898–1963), IRISH WRITER AND LITERARY SCHOLAR

No Room for Panic

> Do not be afraid or discouraged, for the LORD will personally go ahead of you. He will be with you; he will neither fail you nor abandon you.   DEUTERONOMY 31:8

Tara's neighbor would pick up his mail, offer a few sentences of conversation, flash his smile, park his vehicle, and disappear into his apartment. One Sunday afternoon, when he was boulder climbing again, Tara returned from church and munched a sandwich as she looked out the window toward his place. Soon she found that she was in an argument with herself.

Why are you longing for a guy who doesn't have one thing in common with you?

"I don't know that. We haven't really talked except by the mailbox."

That's right. And if you have to plot it, it's not a good situation. He offers a few insincere compliments, and you're ready to follow him anywhere.

"Well, anything is better than nothing."

Oh, really? Remember hiking last spring and watching vehicles climb boulders? You were horrified.

"I could learn to like it."

Oh, yeah. For the first ten seconds. And you love music. What if he grumped about that?

"Well, marriage is filled with compromise."

Marriage? You're thinking marriage already? Are you willing to accept less than you want just for the sake of being married?

Tara sighed. "Maybe I should invite him to dinner. What's that old saying about God helping those who help themselves?"

No! Don't try to manipulate a relationship, her spirit persisted. *You want to share life with someone special, not just settle for anyone who comes along.*

"But what if I don't ever get married?"

If that's what God has for you, don't you think he will give you the grace to accept and even embrace it?

Tara frowned. This self-argument had taken a turn she didn't like.

—SANDRA

Lord, I do want the good you want for me, but I'm afraid to let go of long-held dreams. Help me to remember that you are loving and kind and that you protect me even when I demand my own way.

My child, it will be better for you if you accept my decisions without complaint. Do not ask me to defend my actions or to explain why one person is favored and another seems slighted. The answers to those questions go far beyond your comprehension.

—THOMAS À KEMPIS (CA. 1380–1471), DUTCH CLERGYMAN AND WRITER

Taking Charge

A peaceful heart leads to a healthy body; jealousy is like cancer in the bones. PROVERBS 14:30

The panic of being alone *forever* welled up inside Tara.

"Lord, show me what to do!" she said, putting both hands on top of her head. Immediately the thought came: *Trust me. Don't try to help me.*

"Help you? Is that what I've been trying to do?"

She eased herself onto the sofa and picked up her Bible from the coffee table. Last month her Sunday school speaker had said something about Abram and Sarai—later renamed Abraham and Sarah—trying to "help" God when the child he had promised them hadn't been conceived as quickly as they expected. Tara turned to Genesis 16 and settled back to read. Sarai followed a common practice in that ancient culture and gave her Egyptian slave, Hagar, to her husband, Abram, saying they would get their family through her.

However, once Hagar became pregnant, she undoubtedly flaunted her condition and even began to despise Sarai for putting her in that position. Her mistress blamed Abram for the grief, mistreated Hagar, and caused her to run away. As she hid in the desert, an angel approached and spoke encouraging words of the numerous descendants she would have. Then the angel sent her back to the tent of Sarai to await the birth of her son, Ishmael. It would be another thirteen years before the promised son, Isaac, was born. His birth would rekindle the old envy and jealousies (see Genesis 21:1-10).

With her hand on her open Bible, Tara prayed, "Help me to wait for your perfect plan, God. Help me not to run ahead of you."

She read several more chapters, then crossed the room to select a music CD. As she pulled it from its case, she heard the familiar rumble of her neighbor's truck returning from the mountains. This time, she didn't even bother to glance out the window. —SANDRA

Lord, Sarai and Abram thought they had the perfect plan to fulfill their longing for a son. But because they ran ahead of you, they created two Middle Eastern races who still hate each other all these many centuries later. Help me to remember that the effects of my actions ripple out beyond my immediate situation.

Acceptance says, "True, this is my situation at the moment. I'll look unblinking at the reality of it. But I'll also open my hands to accept willingly whatever a loving Father sends." —CATHERINE MARSHALL (1914–1983), WRITER

JULY 26

Single Again

As the deer longs for streams of water, so I long for you, O God.
PSALM 42:1

Tara isn't alone in her longing to be married. A while back, a newly single-again woman, whom I'll call Phyllis, contacted the ministry where I worked, asking for encouragement. I had been widowed for several years, so her letter was forwarded to me. Her plea had been triggered by her pastor's challenge to the singles' group to think about their use of money.

"Pretend you have one million dollars," he said. "How would you spend it?"

Phyllis wrote, "I don't need a million dollars. I need to know how to live as a single in this married world. I was married a long time and thought my future was secure. I married the second man I ever dated. He was my lover, my companion, my best friend. Now that he's gone, how do I find life again? How can I enjoy coming home to an empty house?

"I need to know God has a plan for me. But in the meantime, how do I survive in a married world? Any man I'd date today wouldn't want to talk about my former husband, but I can't pretend those years didn't happen. Where do I go for the answers? Do any answers exist?"

Here's how I began my reply: "Dear Phyllis, Tonight, my two teens are away on a youth retreat. My house is silent too. It wasn't so long ago even an hour of this silence would have been oppressive and would have driven me to switch on every light and turn on the radio full blast.

"But gradually I've learned to be comfortable with the silence, and I've made friends with empty rooms. You can, too, Phyllis. But first, give yourself time to heal from the loss of a special part of your life. Think of it as an amputation. And be assured that while you can't control this cut, you *can* control how long it will bleed. After all, longing for the situation not to have happened merely wastes energy. Energy you need to face a bright future."

Then I wrote page after page of practical advice, but all of my words featured one theme: "Yes, this is a lonely time. But be gentle with yourself while you heal. Good will come if you don't settle for second best."   —SANDRA

Lord, the what-ifs and if-onlys loom in my thoughts, and I'm tired of wondering where I went wrong. Pull me onto your path of joy and hope. Let me know brighter days are ahead. And help me to keep putting one foot in front of the other.

God whispers to us in our pleasures, speaks in our conscience, but shouts in our pains; it is his megaphone to rouse a deaf world.
—C. S. LEWIS (1898–1963), IRISH WRITER AND LITERARY SCHOLAR

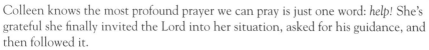

JULY 27
Start with Prayer

Fools think their own way is right, but the wise listen to others.
PROVERBS 12:15

Colleen knows the most profound prayer we can pray is just one word: *help!* She's grateful she finally invited the Lord into her situation, asked for his guidance, and then followed it.

After her divorce, she reconnected with her high school boyfriend, Phil, and felt like a teenager again as she waited for his calls and checked her e-mail often for his "thinking of you" notes. He said he couldn't take calls at work and his cell phone had been acting up, so she couldn't call him. For their dates, he preferred quiet evenings, so Colleen often prepared dinner, and then they would watch a DVD, sitting close together on the sofa. Once when they drove to a mountain park for a sunset walk, he stopped for gasoline and had to borrow money from her to pay the bill because his credit card wouldn't go through.

"The company must not have posted my payment yet," he said.

The next weekend, he borrowed two hundred dollars to tide him over since his employer's accounting office hadn't gotten around to reimbursing him for out-of-pocket expenses. Then, over dinner, he contradicted himself about when his divorce had been finalized. When Colleen questioned him, he shrugged. Warning bells were clanging in her head, but she refused to listen.

The next day, though, a nagging doubt hovered. Finally, she did what she wished she had been doing all along. She prayed: *Lord, you know how lonely I've been. And you know how Phil has brought fun and energy back into my life. But something is wrong, and I don't know what it is. What do I do?*

The question was barely formed when the idea popped into her head to call a private investigator. She grabbed the phone book and called the first one listed in the business pages. The man listened, said he'd heard her story too many times before, and asked for Phil's full name and date of birth. In a few minutes, with the help of modern computer software, Phil's financial problems, dates of his marriage and the births of his children were on the investigator's screen. There was no record of a divorce.

That simple answer to prayer gave Colleen the courage to leave a toxic relationship and avoid a future broken heart.   —SANDRA

Lord, help me to ask for your guidance rather than rush ahead into potentially harmful situations. And thank you that as I ask, you will guide.

Some of our shortest prayers are our most effectual ones.
—RAYMOND EDMAN (1900–1967), PASTOR, DEVOTIONAL WRITER, AND FOURTH PRESIDENT OF WHEATON COLLEGE.

JULY 28
Accepting Peaceful Silence

I waited patiently for the LORD to help me, and he turned to me and heard my cry. He lifted me out of the pit of despair, out of the mud and the mire. He set my feet on solid ground and steadied me as I walked along. PSALM 40:1-2

Just as Colleen's prayer led her to the truth about her boyfriend, Allison's prayer led her to face the truth about what her loneliness was causing her to do. Following her divorce, she had kept her schedule so filled, her friends rarely found her home. She went to movies, attended every special presentation at the fine arts center, and if nothing else was interesting, strolled the mall looking for the latest bargains. After several weeks of watching her frantically run from one activity to the next, a coworker teasingly asked what she was running from. The comment touched a nerve.

That night Allison forced herself to sit quietly in her living room for five minutes. In those quiet moments, she realized she indeed had been running to avoid being alone.

She leaned back against the sofa. *Lord, I'm afraid of the silence in this house. I'm afraid of being alone. So help me to make friends with this place and with myself.*

She went to bed early that night, but the next day she made a conscious effort to work on friendship with herself, beginning with a little pampering that involved more evening walks and bubble baths and fewer shopping trips.

She also realized she previously hadn't enjoyed being home because it held so many sad memories. Once she decided to face the regrets filling each room and invite the Lord's healing and forgiveness into each one, she found she could let go of those painful memories and be comfortable in her home.

We can follow Allison's example. Once we've accepted the reality of our situations, we can begin working *through* them instead of running *from* them. Taking the time to discover who we are will reveal a far more interesting person than we ever dreamed. —SANDRA

Lord, I confess my endless activities and full social calendar mask my pain. After all, if I'm busy, I don't have to listen to the silence around me. But that busyness also keeps me from hearing your voice. Help me not to be afraid of silence. Remind me that I hear you best in quiet moments.

I am not in the whirlwind of activity, but in the still, small voice of communion. Find it my child, and hold to it, and you will be energized.
—FRANCES J. ROBERTS, AUTHOR, POET, AND SONGWRITER

JULY 29
Reaching beyond Pain

[God] comforts us in all our troubles so that we can comfort
others. When they are troubled, we will be able to give them
the same comfort God has given us.   2 CORINTHIANS 1:4

Everyone hurts at one time or another. And even reading the scriptural reminder
that our experiences can be used to encourage and help others going through the
same things doesn't always encourage us. After all, at the beginning of our traumas,
few of us are interested in comforting others. We're too busy slugging through our
own challenges and wishing for days gone by. Since we all compare ourselves with
others who we think are more blessed and less lonely, the trick is to get that comparison going in the right direction.

So instead of sighing each time we see "perfect families" at church or in the
mall, we need to look for others who are alone and lonely. This is where we sometimes have to get a little tough with ourselves. After all, if we allow ourselves to
hurt every time we see an intact family, we're going to hurt a lot. We don't have to
be victims of envy. We do have the choice of whether we want to be *better* women
because of what we have experienced or *bitter* women because of the blows life has
handed us.

Lots of people need us. The problem is, we want to be needed by the people
we need. Life doesn't work that way. But we can ask the Lord to bring his good out
of our circumstances and let us make a difference in someone else's life. After all,
we may be miserable, but that doesn't mean we have to act miserably. Reaching
out to help others actually helps us.   —SANDRA

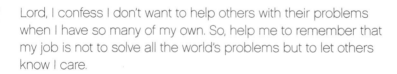

Lord, I confess I don't want to help others with their problems
when I have so many of my own. So, help me to remember that
my job is not to solve all the world's problems but to let others
know I care.

A four-letter word causes us enormous problems: self. Our self-inclination will send
us reeling unless we have settled the core issue: What is our life purpose? Once
God's glory is our purpose, then we have a center point to which we can relate
each decision and each situation.
—SUSAN HUNT, WOMEN'S MINISTRY CONSULTANT AND AUTHOR

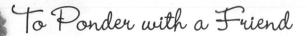

To Ponder with a Friend

1. Do you ever get impatient for God to provide good things? Why or why not?

2. Read Genesis 16.   How might the world be different if Abram and Sarai had waited for God to unfold his plan?

3. Have you ever filled your schedule to avoid the silence of being alone?

4. Do you ever long for the past? If so, what helps you to let it go?

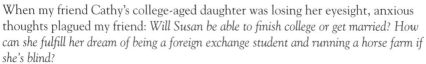

JULY 30
From Panic to Peace

You will keep in perfect peace all who trust in you, all whose thoughts are fixed on you! ISAIAH 26:3

When my friend Cathy's college-aged daughter was losing her eyesight, anxious thoughts plagued my friend: *Will Susan be able to finish college or get married? How can she fulfill her dream of being a foreign exchange student and running a horse farm if she's blind?*

Each morning as Cathy met with the Lord, God drew her attention to a different verse that comforted her and helped her to focus on *what his words said* instead of on what she felt. If she focused on negative circumstances or saw doctors' reports, she spiraled down into depression and worry. One morning when she was reading Isaiah 26:3, she had an idea: to write the verses God highlighted in her morning reading on index cards and carry them everywhere she went so she could focus her thoughts on them. As she did this, she found it not only kept her from dwelling on the worrisome whys and what-ifs but also gradually transformed her thoughts from worry and sadness to serenity and peace.

In time, Cathy typed the verses on blue cards and put them in small resealable bags to give to other women in need, and they became known as the "Peace Packet." She took them to the emergency room when a friend's husband had a heart attack, sent them to a missionary in South America, and gave them to a young mother whose husband had left her. Years later, Cathy's Scripture packet is still bringing peace to women around the world.

You can make your own packet: On colored three-by-five cards, write verses that speak to your situation and carry them with you. Repeat the promises in your own words, telling God you are depending on him. For example, "God, you said you would lift the fallen and those bent beneath their loads. Now I trust you to do this in my life" (see Psalm 145:14). Read your cards in the morning, at lunch, and at bedtime, and watch your peace grow.   —CHERI

> Father, you said that if I would trust in you and turn my thoughts
> often to you, you would keep me in perfect peace. Help me
> to focus on your Word instead of on my anxieties, and as I do,
> please fill me with your marvelous, out-of-this-world peace.

Just as saving faith comes through hearing the gospel, so also the faith to trust God in adversity comes through the Word of God alone. . . . Only from the Scriptures, applied to our hearts by the Holy Spirit, do we receive the grace to trust God when we are afraid.   —JERRY BRIDGES, AUTHOR

Giving Away Your Cares

> Give all your worries and cares to God, for he cares about you.
> 1 PETER 5:7

We women carry many things in our purses: cell phones or Blackberry devices; wallets with all manner of identification, credit cards, and stamps; breath mints, small hairbrushes, pens and notebooks. I wish I could say I travel light, but that's not the case. My purse is full of things I use daily and other items I *might* need: a small address book, lipstick and concealer, photos of my grandkids, checkbook, pain relievers and allergy pills.

Students carry heavy backpacks. And just like our weighty purses and heavy backpacks, our hearts carry burdens and cares: concerns about our troubled teenagers, financial burdens, and a load of worry if we have a deployed loved one. We carry anxiety about the future or about the possibility of being downsized out of a job. But no matter what our burdens are, in today's verse, God invites us to *give all of them* to him. The word *cares* in 1 Peter 5:7 means "all our worries, all our burdens, all our concerns." That covers everything, including whatever wakes us up in the middle of the night and all the anxious "tapes" playing in our heads when we're driving to work or carpooling kids.

Just as the Lord carried the burden of our sin on the cross, he wants to carry the people we are worried about, the emotional concerns, the relationship problems, the burdens of fear and shame that exhaust and discourage us. What a great invitation! What a matchless promise! He cares about us watchfully and affectionately. We can release *all* that concerns us to the One for whom nothing is impossible and who can handle this and every problem when we release them to him.
—CHERI

> Lover of my soul, you are so gracious to carry my burdens, to invite me to cast my heaviest cares on you. Thank you for loving me and caring for me so affectionately.

Through faith you have become a child of God, you have been saved, and through faith you also achieve victory over worry, fear, and other sins. Cast your burdens on the Lord. You do that when you pray.
—CORRIE TEN BOOM (1892–1983), HOLOCAUST SURVIVOR, AUTHOR

AUGUST 1
Acceptance: The Door to Peace

Don't love money; be satisfied with what you have. For God has
said, "I will never fail you. I will never abandon you." So we can
say with confidence, "The Lord is my helper, so I will have no fear."
HEBREWS 13:5-6

Janie sat on the floor surrounded by piles of bills. She was glad her husband was
home from rehab, but she was sick of fielding calls from bill collectors, of working
all day and coming home to concerns about how she would pay what they owed.
On top of that, she was angry at God because of the seemingly unanswered
prayers about their finances. She was angry at her husband and terrified about his
unemployment. As tears coursed down Janie's cheeks, she remembered what a
counselor had told her at their family meetings: "Acceptance is the answer to all
your problems. For in acceptance there is peace."

Janie got out her journal and began to list all the problems they faced and
the fears and anxieties she was feeling. *Lord, I've prayed, tithed, and worked, and
nothing has opened up to us. I know that if you wanted to, you could change things in a
moment or a day. But you haven't, so I accept the way things are today, the things I can't
change. I ask you to show me the things I can change, and help me to trust you in the
midst of our problems today, in the here and now.*

For the first time in a long time, Janie felt peace begin to replace her worry.
Instead of wishing things were different, she remembered the blessings God had
provided in their wilderness and how he'd never failed or abandoned them. As
acceptance and gratefulness grew, anxiety and anger dissipated.

Is there an area of your life where you need to grow in acceptance? Just as
Janie learned, acceptance isn't giving up; it's saying, "This is my situation, and I
embrace the reality of it. But I also open my hands to accept what my loving
Father sends." The peace that comes from this kind of acceptance is sufficient for
any of our earthly trials.   —CHERI

Father, grant me your grace to be content with what I have and
to accept my present circumstances, knowing that you will never
fail or abandon me. I take comfort and am encouraged to say
with confidence, you are my helper!

First, the Lord brought me here. It is by his will I am in this strait place. . . . He
will keep me in his love and give me grace in this trial to behave as his child.
Then, he will make the trial a blessing, teaching me the lessons he means me to
learn and working in me the grace he intends for me. Last, in his good time he
can bring me out again, how and when he knows.
—ANDREW MURRAY (1828–1917), SOUTH AFRICA WRITER AND PASTOR

AUGUST 2
From Control to Peace

> Shadrach, Meshach, and Abednego replied, "O Nebuchadnezzar, we do not need to defend ourselves before you. If we are thrown into the blazing furnace, the God whom we serve is able to save us. He will rescue us from your power, Your Majesty. But even if he doesn't, we want to make it clear to you, Your Majesty, that we will never serve your gods or worship the gold statue you have set up."
>
> DANIEL 3:16-18

I've found that the more things we try to control, the more anxiety we feel and the less peace we experience. How do we get out of the control trap? How can we experience quietness and peace in the midst of crisis? A look at the story of Shadrach, Meshach, and Abednego in Daniel 3 gives us a model.

The three young Israelite men were about to be thrown into a fiery furnace because they refused to bow to the Babylonian idols. They faced a crisis as severe as anything we might ever encounter in life. And if God didn't come and deliver them, they knew they would surely die. Our verses today express their response: They committed themselves to God and prayed in faith, believing that God would answer and yet trusting him completely with their situation. They were saying, in essence, "Even if you don't deliver us, Lord, we are still going to trust you!"

These young men knew something that we need to remember: *We* are not in control (and it may seem that evil forces in the world are), but *someone* is: the Lord God Almighty who created the earth we inhabit and the heavens and is still in charge of it all, regardless of how things may look. The situation you are in didn't take God by surprise, and there will be a time when he brings you through it, as he uses it to shape and mold you to be more like Christ and prepare you for what's ahead. He is the source of our peace. —CHERI

Thank you, blessed Controller of all things, that I don't have to try to control and fix everything but can entrust myself to you, who alone knows the way that I go. Bring my soul into peace and rest as I trust in you.

Trust God where you cannot trace him. Do not try to penetrate the cloud he brings over you; rather look to the bow that is on it. The mystery is God's; the promise is yours. —JOHN R. MACDUFF (1818–1895), SCOTTISH MINISTER AND DEVOTIONAL WRITER

AUGUST 3
A Promised Peace

> [Jesus said,] "I am leaving you with a gift—peace of mind and heart. And the peace I give is a gift the world cannot give. So don't be troubled or afraid." JOHN 14:27

When Jesus spoke these words to his disciples, he was on a journey to the Cross and knew his followers would face confusion, fear, and sorrow. That's why he told them these things while he was still with them (see John 14:25). He would not leave them alone or comfortless. He would send the Holy Spirit to dwell within them, teach them everything they needed to know, and remind them of what Jesus had taught. And through the Spirit, the legacy Jesus was leaving them was *peace*— a peace that is beyond all human understanding, a peace that money can't buy and that isn't like the transient peace the world offers. The disciples didn't have to be troubled or afraid no matter what hard times they would face because they had peace with God through Christ.

Maybe you wonder how you can have peace when you're facing the loss of your job, a family crisis, or the prospect of surgery. With threats of terrorism around the world and the uncertainty of the economy, where is peace to be found? This verse tells us that peace is found in Christ. Just as God gave peace to his followers—men who were flawed and afraid and would even abandon their Savior in his hour of need—he offers peace to us. Not because we have it all together or are worthy of his gifts, but because he is the Prince of Peace and all who are called by his name are recipients of his peace.   —CHERI

Lord Jesus, you promised a daily supply of peace to all those who believe in you and trust you. I ask you now for the peace I need today through your Holy Spirit, who lives in me.

In Christ we are relaxed and at peace in the midst of the confusions, bewilderments, and perplexities of this life. The storm rages, but our hearts are at rest. We have found peace at last!   —BILLY GRAHAM, AMERICAN EVANGELIST

AUGUST 4
Our Source of Safety and Security

Those who live in the shelter of the Most High will find rest in the shadow of the Almighty. This I declare about the LORD: He alone is my refuge, my place of safety; he is my God, and I trust him.   PSALM 91:1-2

When Lisa Beamer's husband, Todd, died in the crash of Flight 93, which was hijacked by terrorists on September 11, 2001, her dependence on God as her source of safety and a realization of a bigger picture enabled her to experience a peace and inner strength that mystified the media and inspired a nation. What was her secret? The foundation of Lisa's strength was that her security was in God rather than in anything or anyone in this world. She chose the Lord's thoughts instead of her own and thus was able to look at things as he did.

On the day Lisa's husband died, symbols of human power and security—the World Trade Center and the Pentagon—were shaken. Lisa faced the impending birth of their daughter and the prospect of raising three children alone in the midst of great uncertainty, grief, and loss. And not just once but day after day she had to deal with the question of where she was going to find true security as a single mother. She found that security in a loving heavenly Father, who cannot be shaken and who would always be faithful to her and her children, so she could trust him completely. In the years since that painful day, God has never failed her.

We may not face anything with the enormity of what Lisa Beamer dealt with, but we are all bound to face a tragedy, a crisis, or a storm that is uncontrollable and not of our choosing. By getting our own big-picture perspective on life, we will realize and experience that the Lord is our only source of security, and therefore, in him we find our peace.   —CHERI

> Father, I come to you as my refuge and my only source of security in this life and in eternity. I choose to rest in your shadow.

If God be our God, he will give us peace in trouble. When there is a storm without, he will make peace within.
—THOMAS WATSON (1629–1686), PURITAN THEOLOGIAN

AUGUST 5
Riding Out the Storm in Peace

You need not be afraid of sudden disaster or the destruction that comes upon the wicked, for the LORD is your security. He will keep your foot from being caught in a trap.   PROVERBS 3:25-26

The headlines of the past few years have been full of calamities and disasters. In addition to 9/11 and other terrorist attacks around the world, there have been hurricanes and widespread floods, tornadoes, war in the Middle East, a catastrophic tsunami, and dangerous wildfires here and abroad. It's enough to cause some people to avoid watching the news. We live in an increasingly violent, uncertain world, and anxiety about disasters is on the rise. Those uncontrollable, huge events crash into our lives and change things forever.

"I can handle the day-to-day struggles like sickness and financial problems, my husband not paying child support, or the possibility of losing the house," a woman told me. "But I couldn't handle a major disaster. I don't know if my faith could stand that kind of test or if I would survive the tragedy."

Larry Jones, cofounder of Feed The Children, has seen firsthand some of the worst disasters in our time: famine in Ethiopia, war in Bosnia, Hurricane Katrina, the tsunami in Indonesia. His ministry has been there to deliver planeloads of food, medical supplies, and clothes. He says that these disasters and ones like stormy marriages, financial upheavals, and physical storms like cancer can't always be avoided or prevented. But we *can* choose the way we respond to them. He has seen over and over that if we choose our reaction, we can tap into God's provision and ride out the storms in his peace. As we choose to believe God's promises, trust his provision, and put our powerlessness in God's almighty power, we will find him faithful.   —CHERI

Lord, you hold me in the palm of your hand; you surround me and dwell within me by your Spirit. Therefore, though everything around me is shaken, I can trust you.

Be assured, if you walk with him and look to him and expect help from him, God will never fail you.
—GEORGE MÜLLER (1805–1898), CHRISTIAN EVANGELIST AND COORDINATOR OF ORPHANAGES IN ENGLAND

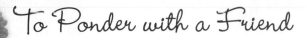

To Ponder with a Friend

1. What are you carrying in your "emotional backpack"? What have you learned in this week's devotionals about what to do with the burdens and anxieties that make your heart heavy?

2. What circumstances, dangers, people, or things push *your* panic button? How do you react?

3. After the 9/11 terrorist attacks it was said that freedom and fear were at war. The same can be said about our lives spiritually. What steps might you take to release your fears and to rest more fully in the freedom Christ gave you through his sacrifice on the cross?

4. What can we learn in Isaiah 26:3-4 about how we can know and experience peace even in the midst of turmoil? Take a few moments to reflect on and share what it would be like to live in this kind of peace.

AUGUST 6
A Poor Reaction

[Jesus said,] "I have told you all this so that you may have peace in me. Here on earth you will have many trials and sorrows. But take heart, because I have overcome the world."   JOHN 16:33

My friend Connie works at the service desk of a major retail store. Recently a customer tried to return a twenty-nine-dollar sweater she said she had purchased there a few days before. But the sweater code didn't match the supposed receipt or any of the other sweaters in the store. After Connie explained her inability to refund the money, the woman loudly demanded to see the manager. When he appeared, he looked at the mismatched codes and stood by Connie's decision. The woman glared at them, then yelled, "You've ruined my life!" and stormed out of the store.

Connie and the manager stood there, stunned. Finally the manager turned toward his office. "Life ruined over a sweater? That woman's got bigger problems than dealing with the two of us."

Those of us who have experienced some of the world's trouble Jesus mentioned in John 16:33 shake our heads at this customer's reaction. Either she had never encountered stress before, or she had never learned how to deal with it. After all, stress is part of life. Normal stress is the everyday stuff that makes us check our to-do list repeatedly. *Distress* includes those 9/11 traumas we can't control. But in both types of situations, how we react makes a big difference. Ongoing stress can adversely affect our immune systems and leave us open to colds, backaches, and even heart attacks. Thus, it's important to save our dramatic reactions for the truly important situations—not twenty-nine-dollar sweaters.
—SANDRA

> Lord, help me not to overreact to daily stress. Help me to look to you and to see each situation through your eyes. Help me to know what to let go and what to work to change.

People who fly into a rage always make a bad landing.
—WILL ROGERS (1879–1935), AMERICAN ACTOR AND HUMORIST

AUGUST 7
Say No Occasionally

Jesus said, "Come to me, all of you who are weary and carry heavy burdens, and I will give you rest." MATTHEW 11:28

Do you ever feel as if you are on a runaway train racing toward a deep chasm? I do too, sometimes. But since I've learned stress will always be part of life, I now remind myself it is *my* hand on the throttle. And because my hand is controlling the speed, I have the power to control it. For me, that means I have to say no more often.

Of course, there are times when a family, neighborhood, or national emergency takes top priority and my slower schedule is thrust into high gear again. But for normal situations, giving myself permission not to join every good organization, chair every fund-raising drive, or organize every neighborhood party gives me time to enjoy truly important activities such as spending more time with the Lord, my family, and even myself.

I learned to say no a while ago, and it was a good thing because shortly after my get-a-backbone decision, a radio listener decided I sounded hospitable and sent me a letter to say she and her daughter were going to stay with me the next month when they visited my town. I replied immediately, saying that was impossible. Then I included the phone numbers of three or four inexpensive local motels and wished her God's blessing. I did not offer any reason for my response. After all, had I said, "Oh, I'm sorry, but my place is too small," she might have replied, "Oh, we'll just sleep on the floor."

Yes, there are times when we open our homes. Yes, there are times when some of our guests sleep on the floor. But we must be the ones who decide when those times will be. And giving ourselves permission to say no eliminates unnecessary stress. We don't have to carry burdens not meant for us. —SANDRA

Lord, why do I feel as if nothing will be accomplished if I'm not in charge? Is that pride? Are my control issues that deep? Am I looking for praise? Help me to ask you which activities I should accept. And once I have done so, help me not to be afraid of the reactions of others.

I have read in Plato and Cicero sayings that are very wise and very beautiful; but I have never read in either of them: "Come unto me all ye that labour and are heavy laden." —SAINT AUGUSTINE (354–430), CHURCH FATHER

AUGUST 8
Share the Load

[Jesus said,] "Take my yoke upon you. Let me teach you, because I am humble and gentle at heart, and you will find rest for your souls. For my yoke is easy to bear, and the burden I give you is light." MATTHEW 11:29-30

When I read the Lord's invitation to accept his yoke, I'm reminded of my long-ago farm days. A yoke-like piece of harness called a collar sat like a large leather necklace across the shoulders of each mule. Connected to the rest of the harness and attached to the wagon via a metal tug, the collars distributed the load's weight more evenly, making the animal's work easier. Even now I remember our mules, Jack and John, not even breathing hard as they pulled wagons holding several times their weight. Without the collar, the mules would have strained muscles as they struggled forward.

So if a leather collar protected our mules and made their work easier, how much more protection would the Lord's yoke provide for us? As I lean into my work, guided by his direction, I accomplish much more than I would have in my own power.

And just as our mules could pull more weight together than they could alone, we can accomplish more if we team up with one another. So I share my workload with others, too. For example, I'm a great believer in "child labor" in the home. Even a toddler can pick up toys. As children get older, they can handle bigger chores and even learn to do their own laundry. After all, any child who can program a VCR and operate a computer certainly can run a modern washing machine.

I'm also convinced having a cleaning lady not only makes good sense but is biblical. If you don't believe me, take a look at Proverbs 31:15: "She gets up before dawn to prepare breakfast for her household and plan the day's work for her servant girls." This woman could accomplish all she did because she had servants! So if getting a cleaning lady will lighten your load and allow you to accomplish other things, consider doing it. Every two weeks I greet mine with a hug. After we've caught up on family news, she keeps me organized as I work ahead, filing correspondence and sorting files.

If you feel you can't afford to pay someone to clean your house, there's another option: Some of my young friends take turns helping each other clean their houses. Others have friends in for dinner when the house is getting too messy. Funny how preparing for company provides a burst of energy.

Yes, work shared goes faster. And accepting the Lord's yoke makes life easier.
—SANDRA

Lord, human nature is such that we will always be yoked to something. Thank you for offering your yoke to make my challenges lighter.

It seems amazingly difficult to put on the yoke of Christ, but immediately we do put it on and everything becomes easy.
—OSWALD CHAMBERS (1874–1917), SCOTTISH BIBLE TEACHER, YMCA CHAPLAIN IN EGYPT

AUGUST 9
Procrastination Creates More Stress

> Don't brag about tomorrow, since you don't know what the day
> will bring.   PROVERBS 27:1

During an especially stressful season, our editorial office displayed a silly poster
with drawings of various-sized frogs. The caption said, "If you have to eat a lot of
frogs, eat the biggest one first." The point was, of course, we were to tackle the big
assignments right away. Once those were completed, the smaller ones would seem
effortless.

What if we applied that philosophy to our daily tasks and to our ever-present
to-do lists? After all, usually the worst thing about a chore is dreading it. So, how
long will it take to complete? Thirty minutes? Four hours? A week? If I add that
amount of time to all of the hours I worry about a project, dread it, and wonder
why I ever agreed to do it, I will have doubled if not tripled the time it originally
would have taken.

Not only does procrastination create stress, but it can also cause us to engage
in unhealthy activities instead of jumping into the work. Sometimes we eat too
much. Sometimes we go shopping. Some folks decide to have another glass of
wine. Sometimes we get busy with other worthwhile projects—just not the one we
should be spending our time on. If I am sweeping the garage or making fudge when
my adult children stop over, they'll say, "Writing not going well today, huh?" And
they're usually right.

So let's stop dreading tasks and start doing them. Sure beats eating frogs!
—SANDRA

> Lord, I do waste time worrying about a project, a household
> chore, an unwritten note. Help me to ask for your help and then
> jump into the task. I'm tired of wasting energy on dread.

Nothing is so fatiguing as the eternal hanging on of an uncompleted task.
—WILLIAM JAMES (1842–1910), AMERICAN PSYCHOLOGIST AND PHILOSOPHER

AUGUST 10
Don't Worry about What Others Think

We [run with endurance] by keeping our eyes on Jesus, the champion who initiates and perfects our faith. Because of the joy awaiting him, he endured the cross, disregarding its shame. Now he is seated in the place of honor beside God's throne.   HEBREWS 12:2

I used to create mountains of stress for myself just by worrying about what others were thinking about me: my weight, my Kentucky accent, my feisty attitude, my child rearing, even my cooking. Actually, I was giving others far too much credit because they weren't really thinking about me all that much. They had plenty of their own problems to ponder. But it took me a long while to realize that truth as I continued to put myself into even more stressful situations.

For instance, years ago we attended our first Memorial Day potluck at a Michigan Bible conference. Our little community was filled with good Dutch cooks, so instead of anticipating the great time we were going to have, I worried about what dish I would take. I pored over my cookbooks, discarding recipe after recipe. Finally, I settled on Hot Chicken Salad: chunks of white meat, onions, and celery baked in a cream sauce and topped with Italian bread crumbs and cheddar cheese. The morning of the event, I pulled the steaming casserole dish from the oven and showed it to my husband, Don.

"This is what we're supplying," I said. "Make sure you take a lot of it."

Whenever the four of us attended potlucks, Don always escorted five-year-old Jay through the line, and I took four-year-old Holly. This time, I was distracted as friends commented on Holly's cute hairstyle, and the two of us were separated from Don and Jay. Finally, as we approached my casserole, I saw one large scoop had been taken out—that would be Don's—and one small scoop, undoubtedly Jay's. My worst potluck nightmare was coming true: I was going to lug home an almost full dish. So, trying to disguise my embarrassment, I said to my little daughter, "This looks good, doesn't it, Holly?"

She nodded, then chirped in her four-year-old voice, "Uh-huh. That's ours, huh, Mama?"

The women nearby smiled. I was caught, a victim of my own self-imposed stress.   —SANDRA

Lord, help me to fix my eyes on you and not on my notions of what others have achieved. Help me to remember that you died to give me not only future eternal life but present joy and strength.

Tell me to what you pay attention, and I will tell you who you are.
—JOSÉ ORTEGA Y GASSET (1883–1955), SPANISH PHILOSOPHER, WRITER, AND STATESMAN

AUGUST 11
Take Five-Minute Vacations

> Despite Jesus' instructions, the report of his power spread even faster, and vast crowds came to hear him preach and to be healed of their diseases. But Jesus often withdrew to the wilderness for prayer. LUKE 5:15-16

When you saw today's title, "Take Five-Minute Vacations," did you roll your eyes and think, *Yeah, right. Like I've got time for that.*

Well, yes, we do. If Jesus could withdraw from all the pressing needs around him, we can too. In fact, those times of withdrawal allowed him to hear from his heavenly Father and to be refreshed before confronting the next challenge. In taking those times, he provided a perfect example for us to follow to recharge our spiritual batteries. And, in addition to strengthening prayers, we can toss relaxing moments into our schedules.

When my corporate job thrust me into a windowless cubicle, I pinned a poster of Pikes Peak on the wall so I could periodically stretch my eyes. I've also made attending local farmers' markets a relaxing habit. I need the vegetables anyway, so why not add the fun of seeing the bright colors displayed in booths set up under shade trees in a nearby park?

Heidi loves early-morning walks, but her work schedule as a nurse made that difficult. She seldom found the time until the day she realized almost three-fourths of the clinic's patients made appointments because of stress-related illnesses, including high blood pressure, frequent colds, and irregular heartbeats. Realizing the human body has limited ability to deal with continuous stress, Heidi knew she had a choice: She could spend time enjoying a walk in the fresh air, or she could spend time sitting in the doctor's office as a patient. Suddenly she had found the motivation she needed for those energizing walks. —SANDRA

> Lord, often I take better care of my car than I do of myself. Help me to follow your example of withdrawing from the crowds to pray. And help me to take better care of the body you have given me.

Jesus knows we must come apart and rest awhile, or else we may just plain come apart.
—VANCE HAVNER (1901–1986), PREACHER, EVANGELIST, AND CONFERENCE SPEAKER

AUGUST 12
Discard Stuff; Gain Peace

Don't store up treasures here on earth, where moths eat them and rust destroys them, and where thieves break in and steal. Store your treasures in heaven, where moths and rust cannot destroy, and thieves do not break in and steal. Wherever your treasure is, there the desires of your heart will also be.   MATTHEW 6:19-21

For years I owned a yellow dress. I look ghastly in that color, but it had been a gift from a relative. I wore it only when I visited her, but when we moved to New York, the dress went too. When we moved to Colorado, I had gained too much weight for the dress, but it still made the journey. I thought I would lose the pounds before I next saw the relative. That didn't happen, but the dress stayed in the closet, taking up space and adding stress each time I saw the yellow glow.

Then a friend mentioned her company was collecting professional clothing for young women who graduated from their professional-development program.

The following Saturday I lined up four boxes and inspected everything in my closet, including accessories. The items I wore often, I piled on my bed. The rest went into the boxes. In the first, I placed clothing I wasn't ready to make a decision about. I put gently used business clothing into the second box and gave a victory yell when I added the yellow dress. The third box held casual outfits for The Salvation Army resale shop. Into the fourth box I tossed items to be thrown away, including a stained T-shirt.

As I placed my favorite items back in the closet, I decided to take another look at the clothes I hadn't been sure I could part with. Nothing there had been worn during the previous six months. With no regrets, I tossed everything in that pile into the resale-shop box.

I felt such satisfaction from clearing the closet clutter, I analyzed the knick-knacks near the TV. Did I really need eleven ceramic owls? All but one went into the giveaway box. Next I sorted my books and kept only my favorites. Several boxfuls of Christian classics went to my church library. More would be sold to my local used-book store. I still had enough books left to start a small-town library, but the stressful clutter was out of my home and mind. Not a bad project for a Saturday!   —SANDRA

Lord, I'm still surrounded by possessions. Help me to keep eliminating the stuff in my life and in my heart. Letting go of clutter allows me more time to enjoy your creation and the loved ones around me. I love the space I've created in my home. Help me not to fill it again.

Many people cling to their possessions instead of sharing them because they are worried about the future. But is not such an attitude finally unbelief?
—RONALD J. SIDER, THEOLOGIAN AND CHRISTIAN ACTIVIST

AUGUST 13
Does It Really Matter?

Turn away from evil and do good. Search for peace, and work to maintain it. PSALM 34:14

As I've grown older, I've learned to shrug off many things that once would have upset me. Thus, when a waitress dumped a glass of water into my lap recently, I accepted her apologies with, "Oh, I've had worse things happen," as I helped her sop it up.

I can mutter, "Let it go. Let it go," when another driver cuts me off on Interstate 25. And if I run into a rude clerk, I tell myself she's worried about her four-year-old grandson who is seriously ill. Am I being dramatic? Of course. But isn't that more fun than taking rudeness personally?

Perhaps I don't get as upset over the little stuff now because I've finally learned the futility of useless tension. Or maybe it's because I had to face my young husband's death from brain cancer when our children were just ten and eight. Believe me, that puts life and daily stress into proper perspective. I had two small children who needed me, so I had no choice but to cling to the Lord, discuss everything with him, and trust him to take us through each day.

But his voice and his direction weren't always clear, so when I faced a cross-country move that would provide a wonderful ministry opportunity but would take us away from extended family, I took a long walk through an old cemetery. As I studied the names and dates on the crumbling stones, I reminded myself nothing really matters if it doesn't matter for eternity. My children and I made the move in record time. We still encountered occasional stress. But whatever came along, the Lord helped us handle it. After all, relying on him is the best solution to stress.
—SANDRA

Lord, thank you for the times I haven't given in to stressful situations. But I know other ones are waiting. Help me to remember that I don't have to react poorly.

Be about your Father's business. There will always be plenty of other people occupied with the affairs of the world.
—FRANCES J. ROBERTS, AUTHOR, POET, AND SONGWRITER

To Ponder with a Friend

1. What is the most stressful part of your life?

2. Have you ever overreacted because of stress? If so, would you care to describe the situation?

3. What helps you deal with everyday stress?

4. What advice do you have for others struggling with stress?

AUGUST 14
Put On Your Oxygen Mask

Don't you realize that your body is the temple of the Holy Spirit,
who lives in you and was given to you by God?
1 Corinthians 6:19

As women, in addition to handling multiple responsibilities in the workplace—
whether it's our home or an office—we serve many people: perhaps aging parents;
our own children, adolescents, or grandchildren; students, if we are teachers; or
young people at church. With all these people to care for, it's easy to forget to take
care of ourselves and our own bodies, the physical homes God gave us to live in.
The results can be damaging.

We may think, *I can't take time out for me. That's too selfish, and I've got too
much to do.* If that thought has ever crossed your mind, let me share an analogy
with you. On a plane to Brazil recently, our flight attendant pulled down a yellow
oxygen mask and demonstrated an important principle (even though many passengers ignored her): *Secure your own mask before helping the child or another person who
needs assistance.* That's not only helpful information for flying. It is also practical for
everyday living. We need to take care of ourselves so we can take care of others,
whoever those "others" are.

Is this really a spiritual topic? Yes! Taking care of our bodies, where the
Holy Spirit dwells, is essential to a life of fruitfulness, and thus it is a very spiritual issue. If we fail to care for our own bodies, we get depleted, depressed,
exhausted (and perhaps irritable, impatient, and joyless) and can't take care of
anyone else, much less handle our other challenges, jobs, or areas of ministry.
This week we will look at this important topic so that we can better care for the
temples God made, through which to manifest the love and work of Christ on
the earth.   —Cheri

Father, thank you for the body you gave me, and thank you that
it is your dwelling place. Help me to take care of it so that I might
serve you, and those you've given me to serve, more fully and
joyfully.

Our body is the most gracious gift God has given us, and if we hand over the mainspring of our life to God we can work out in our bodily life all that he works in. It
is through our bodily lives that Satan works and, thank God, it is through our
bodily lives that God's Spirit works. God gives us his grace and his Spirit; he puts
right all that was wrong, he does not suppress it nor counteract it, but readjusts the
whole thing; then begins our work.
—Oswald Chambers (1874–1917), Scottish Bible teacher, YMCA chaplain in Egypt

AUGUST 15
Honor God with Your Body

You do not belong to yourself, for God bought you with a high price. So you must honor God with your body.

1 CORINTHIANS 6:19-20

So many women start out in a bad place and feel that they're stuck, that nothing is ever going to change. Sheri Rose Shepherd did, and as a teenager she made a lot of poor choices, from the friends she hung out with to the junk food she consumed. By the time Sheri was sixteen, she was sixty-five pounds overweight, and her physical condition was getting worse. She was already at risk for health problems that don't usually occur until adulthood. Sheri's stepmother encouraged her to turn to God for help, but for a time Sheri ignored that advice and continued in her downward spiral until she finally turned to the Lord.

With God's help and guidance, she made some positive changes and began exercising and eating the right foods for the right reasons: not to have a perfect, skinny body or to attract attention but *to honor God with her body*. The improvements both physically and emotionally were so transforming that Sheri eventually began to share what she had learned with other women. She produced a fitness video and has written books that have inspired hundreds of women to make better choices about their health.

The Lord made you spirit, soul, *and body*. He took special care in creating every part of your physical body and breathed his life into you. He designed you from your head and hair color right down to your toes. Now, just as he does with all the other gifts he's given to you, God wants you to take care of your body—to value, accept, and be grateful for the way he made you, not to hate your hair, thighs, or shape. Most of all, he wants you to honor him with your body.
—CHERI

Thank you, my Creator, for making me spirit, soul, and body and for breathing life into me. From the top of my head to the bottom of my feet, I want to honor you with my body.

We do not stop exercising because we grow old—we grow old because we stop exercising.
—DR. KENNETH COOPER, MEDICAL DOCTOR, AUTHOR, AND "FATHER OF AEROBICS"

AUGUST 16
Born to Move

[The Lord] fills my life with good things. My youth is renewed
like the eagle's!   Psalm 103:5

If you were like most toddlers, you may have been like the Energizer Bunny,
spontaneously moving, playing, jumping, pounding, dancing, running. At that
age, you didn't have to worry about getting enough exercise. But every year,
children become a little more sedentary until, by the time they become teenagers,
many are inactive and are well on their way to becoming overweight couch
potatoes.

Let's take a look ahead to what happens if you proceed on the path of inactiv-
ity through your twenties, thirties, and beyond. Depending on your age, that may
seem like a long way in the future, but that time will be here before you know it.
If you're like most women, your metabolism will start to slow down in midlife,
and by that time, keeping fit can be as difficult as swimming upstream, especially
if you haven't already been in the habit of making time to exercise. But it's not
impossible!

If the only exercise you get is heading to the kitchen for morning coffee and
to the car that takes you to the office or on errands, you'll likely join the millions
of adults who are overweight and don't have the energy needed for all the tasks
and challenges ahead. You may feel overwhelmed when God has another responsibility or "mountain" of difficulty for you to climb, because you're *just too tired*. But
the truth is, instead of using up all your energy when you exercise, you actually get
more energy. It's kind of like having a bank account into which you make deposits:
The more you invest in moving your body, the more energy you'll have to draw
out. And because daily exercise speeds up your metabolism, your body can better
burn the calories you consume, so a wonderful side benefit of exercise is weight
control. And to a lesser or greater extent, we all need that!

You were born to move, not just during childhood but throughout your life
on earth. Your body is the only one you have, so let me encourage you to be good
to it. And may the Lord renew your youth and strength like the eagle's.
—Cheri

Thank you, Lord, for designing my body to move and not to be
sedentary. Renew my youth like the eagle's, that I might better
rejoice in you and serve you.

Be good to yourself. If you don't take care of your body, where will you live?
—Kobi Yamada, author

AUGUST 17
How Can I Find the Time?

Run to win! All athletes are disciplined in their training. They do it to win a prize that will fade away, but we do it for an eternal prize. So I run with purpose in every step.   1 CORINTHIANS 9:24-26

Running was the *last* thing on my mind. I'd been so busy trying to keep up with two active preschoolers, nurse a baby, and take care of household chores that many mornings I found myself saying, *I'm so tired, Lord. Please give me enough energy to get everything done and get through the day.* This was especially true if I had been up with a sick child during the night. Gradually I had grown less active and had begun resorting to a daily dose of caffeine to pull me out of the "afternoon slump."

One afternoon I felt that God was responding to my prayer for more energy, but not in the way I expected: *If you want more energy, move your body,* he seemed to say. So my husband, Holmes, and I came up with a plan. When he strolled in the door from work amid the welcoming whoops of the boys, I showed him the snacks on the kitchen counter, handed him baby Alison, and jogged out the door to the track behind our house.

I huffed and puffed around the track the first time. Passed by every runner out there, I trudged my way around the second and third time. But as I persevered, I found the stresses of a broken washing machine and a stack of medical bills awaiting payment melting away with the miles. Before long, I began to discover some surprising benefits besides increased strength: Without dieting, I lost weight, and my PMS symptoms decreased. My mood got happier, and I could handle everyday stresses better. With more energy, I hopped out of bed before the kids woke up and could enjoy time with God (there is a strong correlation between physical and spiritual health).

Since that first day, many years ago, I've always made time to exercise. It's one of my "nonnegotiables," just like prayer and time in God's Word, which energize my spirit. If I want to keep running the race God has marked out for me, I've got to keep moving. And year after year I continue to experience the life-giving blessings of making time to move my body.

See you later—I'm going for a walk!   —CHERI

Thank you, Lord, for the body you've given me—legs that can move, arms that can swing. Grant me the strength and determination to run the race of life with endurance and to take care of the body you've given me.

Finding the time and making your workout a priority in taking care of yourself will determine whether you win for the long run. It's a lifegiving process.
—OPRAH WINFREY, TALK-SHOW HOST

AUGUST 18
Starting Small

Do not despise these small beginnings, for the LORD rejoices to see the work begin, to see the plumb line in Zerubbabel's hand. ZECHARIAH 4:10

In the Old Testament book of Zechariah, the phrase "small beginnings" refers to laying the foundation of the Temple in the rebuilding of Jerusalem. We often apply it to enterprises we undertake in jobs or ministry, but we can also apply the principle to small beginnings in taking better care of our bodies. One thing I love about walking is that we can start small: We don't have to change into special clothes, pay to join a gym, and work out for an hour to get fit. Instead, we can aim for twenty minutes (even two ten-minute intervals) a day of brisk walking and build from there.

Doctors used to think that we had to do aerobic exercise for more than an hour to receive any benefits. But now research has proven that just thirty minutes a day of brisk walking (as if you are hurrying to get somewhere) will produce a good level of fitness.

How can you manage that? If you have children, trade babysitting time with a neighbor. Walking with a partner is a great motivator. Walk your dog. Our canine friends need to move to stay healthy as well. On a Saturday, you might put your small children in a stroller and with your husband or friend, walk to a park or a nearby coffee shop. If you're one of those people who best connect with God in the outdoors, try prayer walking. Most of all, make exercise fun. If walking isn't your cup of tea, find something you do enjoy. It could be strength training, Pilates, hiking, tennis, or step aerobics. What matters is that you get moving and keep it up for a lifetime. Your body will thank you! —CHERI

Creator of all life, I want to be a good steward of the body you have entrusted to me. Help me to respect my body, to treat it kindly, to move it, and to do what I can to keep it strong and help it thrive for your glory.

Exercise is essential to get oxygen to your cells. God created us to be physically active. Oxygen brings life to our body, detoxifies our blood, strengthens our immune system, heightens concentration and alertness, rejuvenates and revitalizes unhealthy cells, slows down the aging process, and helps depression.
—SHARI ROSE SHEPHERD, INSPIRATIONAL SPEAKER AND WRITER

AUGUST 19
Eating for Life

Whether you eat or drink, or whatever you do, do it all for the glory of God.   1 CORINTHIANS 10:31

There is a great deal of worry today about what we eat and how we look. Recent headlines warn of the dangers of tainted food from overseas. We try to eat plenty of vegetables and fruits but then hear a report that pesticides or E coli bacteria have made spinach or apples unsafe. Many of us worry about whether eating carbs will make us fat, and some of us long to look like the skinny models we see in magazines.

Although today's verse was penned centuries ago, it has much application for us today. It tells us to eat and drink *for the glory of God*. We're not to be overly preoccupied with our bodies or with what we should eat. There is so much more to life than the food we put in our stomachs. As we've seen this week, we're accountable for the gift of life we've been given, and God wants us to be good stewards of our bodies. Part of that stewardship is choosing to eat a variety of good foods, not obsessing about food but making wise choices about what we eat, and then eating in moderation. We all know the toll that eating high-fat, high-sugar foods takes on our health and that eating nutritious food (fruits, veggies, and whole grains) plays a role in preventing many illnesses. Eating healthy food for the purpose of sustaining life and renewing our strength is a great goal. If we continually commit our bodies and food issues to God, ask him for wisdom, and turn to him (not a late-night pint of ice cream) for comfort, he will guide us.

As you endeavor to eat right and exercise, avoid doing it to have a perfect body you can flaunt or to glorify yourself. Instead, do it to glorify God and to have the physical and mental energy to do all he's called you to do.   —CHERI

Holy Spirit, take control of my eating and grocery shopping. Let me not worry about food or be preoccupied with my body. Instead, let me be filled with your wisdom and make life-giving choices about what I eat and drink. Apart from you I can do nothing, not even change my eating habits. I ask you to help me and to be my comfort so that I won't turn to food for what only you can supply.

Those who think they have no time for bodily exercise [or healthy eating] will sooner or later have to find the time for illness.
—EDWARD STANLEY (1826–1893), EARL OF DERBY

AUGUST 20
Sweet Dreams

> You can go to bed without fear; you will lie down and sleep soundly.   PROVERBS 3:24

Many in our nation are becoming caffeinated insomniacs, and research shows that the people who have the hardest time sleeping are *women*. Our lives are so busy, our days so packed, that we often sacrifice sleep in an attempt to get everything done, and thus deprive our bodies and brains of needed rest. New research shows that women who sleep less than five hours a night are more likely to become obese. What's the connection? As we sleep, a hormone called leptin, a major factor in controlling appetite, rises in our system. So when we don't get enough sleep, the lower leptin level causes us to be hungrier and eat more.

Besides making us cranky and tired, lack of sleep also causes increased fatigue, hostility, and less attentiveness on the job, and our appearance suffers too. Our moms were right when they said, "Get your beauty sleep."

One of the benefits of being God's child is peaceful sleep: "I lay down and slept, yet I woke up in safety, for the LORD was watching over me" (Psalm 3:5). Our bodies and souls can rest and confidently dwell in God because we know that the One who never slumbers cares for us and restores us while we rest.

If you are having trouble getting enough sleep to function at your best, let me encourage you to take some practical steps to help yourself: Give yourself time to "parachute down" at night. Take a warm bath. Avoid caffeine at night, and relax during the last half hour of your day instead of working until you turn out the light. Give God your cares and worries, because it's hard to enjoy pleasant sleep when you're worrying about your problems. Meditate on today's verse, and ask God to give you the gift of sleep that he promised his loved ones (see Psalm 127:2) so that you'll wake up with a new lightness in your step. Sweet dreams!
—CHERI

> Father, I thank you for peaceful sleep, for you promised that those who love and trust you will rest confidently in you. I ask you, Jesus, to keep Satan from interfering with my sleep or harming my dreams, and I entrust myself to your loving care.

When you have accomplished your daily task, go to sleep in peace; God is awake.
—VICTOR HUGO (1802–1885), FRENCH POET, NOVELIST, AND DRAMATIST

To Ponder with a Friend

1. Are you a social exerciser or would you rather exercise in a more solitary way? Since many of us can be more consistent if we exercise with a partner, who would be a potential exercise partner for you?

2. What are the top ways you enjoy (that is, like or look forward to rather than dread) "moving your body"? What sport, exercise, or activity would you like to be involved in but never seem to have time for?

3. Most women tend to be "caretakers": for children, men, parents, friends. What are the benefits of caring for our own bodies, listening to their clues and signals, and responding to those signals instead of neglecting our bodies?

4. What is your biggest hindrance or obstacle to a healthy, fit, and active lifestyle? How could you overcome this? Brainstorm with a friend and list the ideas you come up with.

Theme: The Power of Words

AUGUST 21
Plant Words Wisely

> Sometimes [the tongue] praises our Lord and Father, and sometimes
> it curses those who have been made in the image of God. And so
> blessing and cursing come pouring out of the same mouth. Surely,
> my brothers and sisters, this is not right! JAMES 3:9-10

Recently I passed a local church displaying this on their announcement board:
"Thoughts, words, and prayers are like seeds."

As I continued on my errand, I pondered the truth of how even small
thoughts, words, and prayers can grow to produce a mighty harvest for good or for
evil. Memories of some of those seeds tumbled through my mind before I settled on
one from my days in the corporate world. I had made a bad mistake on an order I
submitted for my department in a major organization. But in the midst of my
panic, I asked myself, *Wait, what's the worst that could happen because of this?*

Well, I could get fired, was my immediate thought. I was confident no one was
going to ship me to Siberia (even though the thought may have crossed a few
minds), but I knew I needed to fix the situation. So instead of continuing to wring
my hands, I breathed a prayer and went to the department head to confess.
Inwardly trembling, I fully expected him to yell at me. Instead, he understood the
lack of communication I'd gotten caught in and told me which unit supervisor
could help me. Then, rather than tell me how stupid I was (I already knew that),
he smiled and said, "This is not the worst thing we've had happen here, you
know."

Well, I hadn't known that, and he was kind to point it out. Later, I was still
so astonished by his quiet, professional response, I began to analyze my own reactions to others. How many times had my panic increased another's trauma? How
often had I ignored an opportunity to bring peace to an emotional storm? Those
reflections gave me something to think about and work on.

Indeed, our thoughts, words, and prayers do produce a harvest. So, let's consider their power and sow carefully. —SANDRA

Lord, help me to be aware of the power of my words. May I open
my mouth to speak kindness, comfort, and encouragement
when needed, and strength and loving correction when
required.

Cold words freeze people, and hot words scorch them, and bitter words make them
bitter, and wrathful words make them wrathful. Kind words . . . soothe, and quiet,
and comfort the hearer.
—BLAISE PASCAL (1623–1662), FRENCH MATHEMATICIAN AND PHILOSOPHER

AUGUST 22
Offer a New Perspective

The Sovereign LORD has given me his words of wisdom, so that I know how to comfort the weary. Morning by morning he wakens me and opens my understanding to his will.   ISAIAH 50:4

Emily had trouble making decisions. Even selecting a birthday card could throw her into a panic. More than once she bought two cards, one serious and one humorous, and sent both of them to the same individual. Most of her friends thought the action excessive and a little strange, but they shrugged it off. One friend, though, decided to ask her about it at lunch.

Emily hesitated but finally answered, "When I can't decide which card someone would like, I send both so they'll be happy with at least one."

Her friend nodded. "Okay," she said. "But one card is enough."

Emily frowned. "But what if you don't like the card I picked out?"

"I just think it's great when someone remembers my birthday," her friend answered. "You could send your greetings in green crayon written on a brown paper bag, and I'd still be thrilled."

Emily shook her head. "Boy, I wish my grandma had had that attitude. She found something wrong with every card I ever sent her."

Her friend leaned forward. "Emily," she said, "that was then. This is now. You're an adult. You don't have to keep trying to please a dead grandmother."

Emily exhaled as if she had been holding her breath for a long time. And all because a supportive friend took the time to help her see a situation differently.
—SANDRA

Lord, help me to remember that what I see as small encouragement can make a world of difference to someone who is hurting.

Kind words can be short and easy to speak but their echoes are truly endless.
—MOTHER TERESA (1910–1997), FOUNDER OF MISSIONARIES OF CHARITY IN CALCUTTA, INDIA

AUGUST 23
Overdue Restoration

Fathers, do not provoke your children to anger by the way you
treat them. Rather, bring them up with the discipline and instruction that comes from the Lord.   EPHESIANS 6:4

My friend Marian went antique browsing one afternoon with her seventy-two-
year-old neighbor, Ruth. In one shop, Ruth gently picked up a doll with soft curls.

"I used to have a doll just like this when I was a little girl," she said, her eyes
glistening. "I named my doll Hannah. And I loved her as though she were the little
sister I'd always wanted. I was learning to sew and was excited about the wardrobe
I would make for her.

"My father was a pastor of a small church, so we had very little. But it didn't
matter; I had Hannah. Then one afternoon, my parents came into my room while
I examined a scrap of velvet from the box of material a neighbor had given my
mother. The piece was just large enough to make a jacket for Hannah.

"I looked up at my parents. Both had a this-will-be-good-for-you look on their
faces, as though they were about to give me some awful-tasting medicine. Then my
father told me he had just visited a poor family who had a daughter my age.

"'She's never had a doll,' he said.

"My heart froze as my father continued, 'So we'd like you to give her your
doll as unto the Lord.'

"Even before he finished the sentence, I was shaking my head. But my
mother leaned forward and took Hannah out of my hands.

"'Shame on you for being so selfish,' she said. 'You have so much.'

"I didn't see I had so much. I only had Hannah."

By the time Ruth finished telling the story, tears were running down her
cheeks.

Marian hugged her. "Buy this doll for yourself," she insisted.

"What?" Ruth stammered. "Buy myself a doll? I'm too old for that nonsense."

Marian shook her head. "No, you aren't. Buy the doll. Sew the clothes now
you wish you could have sewn then."

Ruth smiled and bought the doll. Sometimes she looks at it in the rocking
chair in her bedroom and thinks maybe, just maybe, it's the real Hannah.

—SANDRA

Lord, help me not to be harsh in dealing with the children
around me. Help me to understand their world. Help me to
provide loving lessons that will enlarge their hearts without
crushing their tender spirits. And help me not to expect them
to be the solution to the world's problems.

The most successful parents are those who have the skill to get behind the eyes
of the child, seeing what he sees, thinking what he thinks, feeling what he feels.
—JAMES C. DOBSON, PSYCHOLOGIST AND AUTHOR

AUGUST 24
Family Stories

[Jesus said,] "Where two or three gather together as my followers, I am there among them." MATTHEW 18:20

One of my recent happy memories is of a trip my dad and I took to his grandfather's homestead deep in our beloved Kentucky hills. In the evenings, as we sat on the porch and listened to the whip-poor-wills, Dad told stories of how the members of the strong community of his childhood had stood together against floods, failed crops, and epidemics.

Sunday morning, we attended the "Preaching and Dinner on the Grounds" at the family cemetery. Wooden folding chairs were set up under the pines on top of the hill. Gradually, the people gathered, greeting one another and asking about absent kin. The service began with "Amazing Grace," sung in a slow, twangy way, followed by the more peppy "Now Let Us Have a Little Talk with Jesus," complete with resounding bass. The next song, "When the Roll Is Called Up Yonder," was the signal for the worshipers to leave their chairs and greet one another. By the second stanza, the women were hugging and crying, and everyone was ready for the sermon.

Tall, rugged Preacher Howard then strode to the lectern and announced, "We meet in the cemetery as a reminder we're all gonna die and meet the Man who hung between two thieves to save us."

Then he started "preaching hard," his words punctuated by the women's *Amens* as they glanced toward their men swapping stories at the side of the cemetery. The children played tag near the old stones that marked the graves of our ancestors and chased each other toward the plywood tables soon to be spread with the finest in country cooking. The rule of most Kentucky cooks seems to be "Honey, I'd rather have a bushel too much than a teaspoon not enough," so at the closing hymn, the overflowing picnic baskets were opened, and we filled our plates with the abundance from hillside gardens and country henhouses. Clusters of relatives balanced plates on the tops of gravestones and traded gossip. I breathed deeply of the mountain air, refreshed by the family stories and no-nonsense presentation of the gospel.

Okay, so the country cooking helped too. —SANDRA

Lord, help me to remember to look for you in ordinary activities. Help me to sense you in the loving acts of those around me. And may others sense you through my actions and words.

Life is made up, not of great sacrifices or duties, but of little things, in which smiles and kindness and small obligations win and preserve the heart.
—SIR HUMPHRY DAVY (1778–1829), ENGLISH CHEMIST

AUGUST 25
We Become What We Are Told

Let us think of ways to motivate one another to acts of love and good works.   HEBREWS 10:24

I'm convinced we become what we are told. Tell a child he will never amount to anything, and watch him wither. Tell a child she can accomplish whatever she puts her mind to, and watch her try.

During one of my Kentucky trips, I stopped at a gift shop, where I discovered several cloth dolls designed by Wanda Chapman. I recognized the material from which their dresses were made—feed sacks! During the Depression, thrifty farm-wives had made undergarments, nightgowns, and aprons from the muslin sacks, so some enterprising marketing genius came up with the idea to make the cloth sacks out of brightly colored material and charge a few extra cents. In our own farm days, my mother could make a dress for me from one sack.

Those memories came in a rush as I reached for the doll dressed in a white and purple feed sack covered by an old tea-towel apron embroidered with purple and blue flowers. Attached to the cloth hand was a wicker basket filled with little pieces of homemade lye soap. I read the accompanying handwritten card:

> Cameron Leah Irvin is No. 122 in this series. When Daniel Boone cut a pass through the Cumberland Gap, Cammie's grandfather Irvin was with him. She comes from a long line of proud, resourceful mountain women. She learned early to make soap from lye and hog fat, and quilts from any tiny bit of fabric left over from sewing.
>
> She knows how to make beans and corn bread take the place of meat when there is no meat to be had.
>
> She grew up hearing from her mama that mountain women are smart, loving, strong, and beautiful and so she became just that.

The rest of the card described the doll's attire, but I concentrated on the sentence emphasizing how she became what she had been told she was. As I wiped tears from my eyes, the clerks mouthed to each other, "We just sold another doll." And they had. "Cammie" now has a prominent place in my office to remind me of the power of words.   —SANDRA

Lord, thank you for the kind words others have spoken into my life over the years. Help me to speak those same loving and strengthening words into the lives of others.

Wise sayings often fall on barren ground; but a kind word is never thrown away.
—SIR ARTHUR HELPS (1813–1875), ENGLISH WRITER

AUGUST 26
One Story's Power

[God] saved us, not because of the righteous things we had done, but because of his mercy. He washed away our sins, giving us a new birth and new life through the Holy Spirit. TITUS 3:5

Just before we left for Wednesday-night service, I received word my cousin, whom I'll call Eddie, had committed suicide. I drove to church in an emotional fog, pondering details of the shotgun blast, the collapse into his mother's arms.

At church, I dropped my children at their classes, then slipped into a back pew. I tried to listen as Dr. Hess taught, but I was too worried about Eddie's soul.

Then Dr. Hess interrupted himself. "That reminds me of a story," he said, and he launched into an account of the crew of a nineteenth-century whaling ship: Two of the sailors were Christians who shared their faith with the crew members. Most of their fellow crew members either ignored them or attended their Bible studies. But one sailor cussed them repeatedly.

One afternoon the angry sailor was coiling ropes on the deck just as the ship pitched dangerously, tossing him and the ropes overboard. The crewmen scurried to pull the ropes up, wondering if he would still be in one piece. They'd seen this happen to crew members before.

As they hauled his body back on board they were amazed to see he was intact. They rolled him over a barrel to force the water out of his lungs. Suddenly, he spewed seawater, then coughed, fighting for breath. Finally he spluttered, "I'm saved! I'm saved like those two!" And he pointed toward the Christians.

"When I hit the water and felt the ropes tighten, I knew I was a goner," he said. "And I knew if those guys were right, I was going to have to face God alone. Just before I blacked out, I thought, *Jesus, I'm sorry. Please stand with me.* Now I'm saved."

Dr. Hess concluded, "He went on to live a godly life. But if he had died in the ropes, the Christians would have thought he had gone to a Christless eternity. We are not to judge the destination of another's soul."

As he turned back to the lesson, he said offhandedly, "I don't know why I told that."

But I knew. Maybe in Eddie's final moments, he had remembered our grandmother's pleas to turn to Jesus. Maybe the Lord was wiping tears of regret and repentance from Eddie's eyes at that very moment.

Later, I told Dr. Hess how much I had needed his story—and the Lord's comfort. —SANDRA

Lord, thank you for speaking through others when we need encouragement and hope. Help us to be sensitive to the prodding of your Spirit when you are asking us to offer that same strength to others.

It is not your hold of Christ that saves you, but his hold of you!
—CHARLES HADDON SPURGEON (1834–1892), BRITISH PREACHER

AUGUST 27
Unexpected Kind Words

[The Lord said,] "Forget all that [has happened in the past]—
it is nothing compared to what I am going to do. For I am about
to do something new. See, I have already begun!"   ISAIAH 43:18-19

One Saturday in Michigan wasn't going well. I was having trouble balancing the checkbook yet again, and my car mechanic said the rocker arm (whatever that is) had to be replaced. I wanted to run away but settled for taking my children for hamburgers. When we entered the restaurant, I saw one of my former students, I'll call her Donna, working there as a waitress.

Oh, good, I thought sarcastically. *I'm tired and discouraged, and now I run into one of the most troublesome students I've had in fifteen years of teaching.*

I could still see her in the front row of fifth-hour classics class, arms folded and eyes daring me to make the lesson interesting. Well, I wasn't going to disappoint my children by going to another restaurant. I would just pretend I hadn't seen her.

Lord, just keep us from being seated in her section, please, I prayed inwardly. So where did the hostess lead us? Right to Donna's section, of course. But as I started to ask for a booth near the window, Donna spotted us and came rushing over.

"Mrs. Aldrich! This is so neat!"

Sure, it'll be easier to poison me, I thought. But I managed a feeble smile.

"Guess what!" she said. "I'm a Christian now!"

My mouth dropped open, but Donna bubbled on. "My sister got saved at college," she said. "And it bugged me she was always witnessing to me. Then I'd go to your class, and while we were studying the Greeks and Romans, you'd bring in something interesting from the Bible, and I'd get angry all over again. But I couldn't get what you both said out of my mind. And last year, I got saved!"

I was too choked up to talk, so I gave her a hug. God had encouraged me by placing me exactly where I didn't want to be. And he showed me that words—her sister's and mine—had pointed Donna toward heaven.   —SANDRA

Lord, I'm quick to order you around, telling you to keep me away
from all situations and people who make me uncomfortable.
Help me to get my instructions *from* you instead of trying to give
them *to* you.

Jesus did not come to explain away suffering or remove it. He came to fill it with his presence.   —PAUL CLAUDEL (1868–1955), FRENCH POET, DRAMATIST, AND DIPLOMAT

To Ponder with a Friend

1. Do you agree words have power? Why or why not?

2. Do you agree children become what they are told? Why or why not?

3. Does your spirit still hold on to words from long ago? If so, would you care to share them?

4. With what words do you encourage those around you?

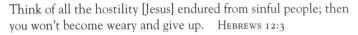

AUGUST 28
Press On

> Think of all the hostility [Jesus] endured from sinful people; then
> you won't become weary and give up.   HEBREWS 12:3

Perhaps you've heard the encouragement that you can be anything you want to
be if you're willing to work for it: teacher, physician, writer, engineer, mother,
missionary, or any number of other equally worthy pursuits. However, being
successful in life and career takes dogged perseverance because the path to attain-
ing most goals worth reaching is strewn with obstacles and setbacks. It's very easy
to quit in discouragement before you reach the end.

Florence Chadwick's experience has something to say to us about this. Many
years ago this world-champion, long-distance swimmer, who had already swum the
English Channel, was set to swim from the California coast to Catalina Island. But
on the morning Florence dove into the water for the forty-six-mile swim, it was so
foggy she couldn't see her trainers' boats around her, and the water chilled her to
the bone. Her trainers had to use rifles to drive away the sharks who were circling.
After fifteen grueling hours in the water, Florence grew more and more discouraged. Finally, she could go no farther and asked the trainers to take her out of the
water.

When she got into the boat, she saw she was only a *half mile* from Catalina's
shore. She had stopped within sight of her destination! Sometimes we, too,
become shrouded in a fog of discouragement or weariness, and it looks as if we're
making no progress at all. But Florence's experience reminds us not to give up too
soon. We need to keep praying and keep going and gather others around us to help
us persevere. The breakthrough may be just around the corner.   —CHERI

Lord Jesus, when I am tempted to give up, strengthen me and
give me the perseverance to continue.

As you go along your road in life, you will, if you aim high enough, also meet resistance . . . but no matter how tough the opposition may seem, have courage still
and persevere.   —MADELEINE ALBRIGHT, FORMER U.S. SECRETARY OF STATE

Fight the Good Fight

Fight the good fight for the true faith. Hold tightly to the eternal life to which God has called you, which you have confessed so well before many witnesses.   1 TIMOTHY 6:12

In Paul's final instructions to Timothy, expressed in these verses, he impresses on his young disciple the need to hold fast, stay the course, fight the good fight. Paul knows that the road ahead of Timothy will not be easy. Wherever the gospel of Christ is preached, there will be opposition, at times persecution, and Paul had experienced more than his share of those.

But Paul knew the greatest battle is not with flesh and blood. It's against the "evil rulers and authorities of the unseen world" (Ephesians 6:12). The battle is over what we believe—that Jesus Christ, God's only Son, died for our sins and conquered death through his resurrection. It is a "good fight" because those who persevere will win the prize of eternal life promised to those who confess Jesus as Lord.

Does the battle around you continue to rage no matter how hard you fight? Have your enemies, seen and unseen, gained the upper hand? Have you grown weary of doing well or lost sight of the prize? God alone is our refuge and our strength. We were never called to fight our battles alone. When we seek God in prayer and acknowledge our weakness and weariness, he will fight the battle for us. Someday, we will stand at the gates of heaven and gaze in wonder at the prize in front of us. As the battles behind us become a fading memory, we will declare, "Yes, indeed, it was a good fight!"   —CHERI

Heavenly Father, help me not to grow weary in the battles I face but to continually ask you to fight the good fight on my behalf. Give me faithfulness and perseverance. Thank you for your promise of eternal life and victory.

Jesus invited us, not to a picnic, but to a pilgrimage; not to a frolic, but to a fight. He offered us, not an excursion, but an execution. Our Savior said that we would have to be ready to die to self, sin, and the world.
—BILLY GRAHAM, AMERICAN EVANGELIST

After You Have Done All, Stand!

Joshua told the commanders of his army, "Come and put your feet on the kings' necks." And they did as they were told. "Don't ever be afraid or discouraged," Joshua told his men. "Be strong and courageous, for the LORD is going to do this to all of your enemies." JOSHUA 10:24-25

When I think of perseverance and the presence of enemies in our lives, I'm reminded of a missionary to India named Miss Mitchell. When she left for India, it was the high point of her life, a dream come true that she'd prayed for and felt God had called her to. However, after arriving, the young woman was overwhelmed by culture shock, not only by the Indian culture but also by loneliness and homesickness. She had difficulty learning the language and began to dislike the very Indian people with whom she'd come to share Christ. She longed for a husband, children, and a home of her own. The final blow came when she fell very ill with amebic dysentery and the doctor told her that her very survival depended on leaving India.

It seemed her ministry was coming to a disappointing and rapid end. Although she hated the thought of letting God down, she started packing to go home. The morning she was scheduled to leave, she read from Joshua 10. In the passage, five enemy kings fled in the heat of battle to the cave at Makkedah to hide from Joshua's men (see Joshua 10:16). When the kings were discovered, Joshua ordered stones to seal the mouth of the cave and told his captains later to put their feet on the necks of the five doomed kings before putting them to death.

When Miss Mitchell read the words "Fear not," she realized that *she, too, had five enemies* that threatened to end her service: illness, problems with the language, lack of love for the Indian people, homesickness, and her desire for a husband. She wrote each "enemy" on a piece of paper. Then, to symbolize her decision to take authority over them, she put her foot on one after another, proclaiming her trust in the all-powerful, resurrected Lord to defeat them. She unpacked and began to spend time praising God instead of complaining about problems. And as she stood firm in her faith, not only did her perspective change, but her circumstances began to turn around. —CHERI

Sovereign Lord, we all have enemies. Help us not to be afraid or shrink back, but after we have done all we can, help us to continue to stand.

All that is necessary to break the spell of inertia and frustration is this: act as if it were impossible to fail. That is the . . . command of the right-about-face that turns us from failure toward success.
—DOROTHEA BRANDE (1893–1948), AMERICAN WRITER AND EDITOR

AUGUST 31
When Tempted to Quit

> We are not fighting against flesh-and-blood enemies, but against evil rulers and authorities of the unseen world, against mighty powers in this dark world, and against evil spirits in the heavenly places. . . . Stand your ground.   EPHESIANS 6:12-14

Just like Miss Mitchell, you will face things that may tempt you to quit as well. But whether it's a job that gives you trouble, a difficult teenager, or an accounting course you're struggling with, today's verses encourage you *not to give up*. When you face even the toughest problems of life and are tempted to throw in the towel, tie a knot and hang on. Stand your ground. As the missionary did, after you have done all you can, stand!

Do you want to know the rest of the story? When Miss Mitchell took authority in the name of Christ over the five "enemies" of God's calling for her in India and put her trust in the mighty, all-powerful God to defeat them just as he did the five enemy kings in Joshua's day, a breakthrough came. She quickly recovered from dysentery. She found a language tutor and eventually became fluent in the language so she could communicate the gospel to the Indian people. Her homesickness fled, and God gave her love for the Indian people. A young man in the region eventually proposed, and she and her family spent many years in a fruitful, fulfilling ministry in the country God had called her to.

That doesn't mean she didn't encounter problems or sickness again, but she knew the One who is always present and stands ready to help in times of trouble. The circumstances of our lives may change; we may encounter spiritual attack, or the world may be in an uproar, but our position within the safety of God's love and protection remains constant.

Do times of trouble come in the lives of saints? Most definitely. Will God be there to strengthen us and help us persevere? Yes! He has promised to do just that, and he always keeps his promises.   —CHERI

Victorious Lord, in the battles of life, grant me perseverance to stand, stand firm, and never give up.

Most of the important things in the world have been accomplished by people who have kept on trying when there seemed to be no hope at all.
—DALE CARNEGIE (1888–1955), AMERICAN WRITER AND LECTURER

SEPTEMBER 1
Persevering in Prayer

One day Jesus told his disciples a story to show that they should always pray and never give up. "There was a judge in a certain city," he said, "who neither feared God nor cared about people. A widow of that city came to him repeatedly, saying, 'Give me justice in this dispute with my enemy.' The judge ignored her for a while, but finally he said to himself, 'I don't fear God or care about people, but this woman is driving me crazy. I'm going to see that she gets justice, because she is wearing me out with her constant requests!'" LUKE 18:1-5

Maybe you can relate to a young woman who told me at a retreat that she wished answers to prayer came as easily as a can of pop could rush down a vending-machine chute into her hand. She could pray earnestly about an issue for a few days. But when God didn't answer her prayers according to her timetable, she found herself frustrated and inclined to quit.

Jesus knew that we humans would struggle with this aspect of prayer, so he told this story, recorded in the book of Luke: A widow came repeatedly to a godless judge who was evil and uncaring, and the judge ignored her. But she kept showing up and asking, day after day. This was a determined woman, and she wouldn't give up! Finally, because of her persistence, the judge granted the widow a favorable decision. Here's the lesson: If a corrupt judge will render a just decision to a woman he cares nothing about, how much more will God, who is rich in love and compassion toward his people, answer when we "cry out to him day and night"? (18:7).

Jesus encourages us to be like that persistent widow, and that means we've got to develop a *marathon mentality* of prayer rather than a *sprint mentality*. We're in this for the long haul and must P-U-S-H: Pray Until Something Happens! No matter what obstacles we face or how big the mountains are, God's arm is not too short to save, and he calls us to persevering prayer. —CHERI

Lord, I confess that perseverance in prayer is not my strong suit. Grant me the persistence of this widow, who never gave up. Help me to keep on praying and to gather others who will help me to stand in prayer until the answer comes.

Every single believing prayer has its influence. It is stored up toward an answer which comes in due time to whomever perseveres to the end.
—ANDREW MURRAY (1828–1917), SOUTH AFRICA WRITER AND PASTOR

SEPTEMBER 2
Dressed for Battle

Put on every piece of God's armor so you will be able to resist the
enemy. . . . Then after the battle you will still be standing firm.
Stand your ground, putting on the belt of truth and the body armor
of God's righteousness. For shoes, put on the peace that comes from
the Good News so that you will be fully prepared. . . . Hold up the
shield of faith to stop the fiery arrows of the devil. Put on salvation
as your helmet, and take the sword of the Spirit, which is the word
of God.   EPHESIANS 6:13-17

Paul tells us that if we are going to persevere and be able to stand in the midst of
the troubles and battles of life, we must be dressed in God's armor. This is not ran-
domly selected attire. Every piece listed in this passage is essential if we are to resist
the enemy and be victorious: We need *faith* as our shield to stop the fiery arrows
the enemy aims at us. *Salvation* in Christ protects us from Satan's lies. We must also
wear the sturdy *belt of truth* and take up the *sword of the Spirit*, which is the Word of
God, so that we are prepared to recite Scripture to the enemy of our souls, just as
Jesus did in the wilderness (see Matthew 4:1-10).

The pieces of armor described in this familiar passage represent our "equip-
ment" for fighting spiritual battles. But they also describe Jesus Christ. He is the
security of our salvation, the champion and perfecter of our faith (see Hebrews
12:2). He is the Living Word, so keeping our minds set on him unravels Satan's
deceptions. He is our peace (see Ephesians 2:14), and as we focus on him, we don't
need to fear the enemy or the situation. We can pray (because prayer is part of our
spiritual arsenal) and live in peace.

Although the armor of God is very important, putting it on or saying it as a
mantra isn't a lucky rabbit's foot or a ritual we complete before God will hear us.
On the contrary, the armor is a word picture to help us understand how God has
prepared us for spiritual warfare through Jesus Christ. When we clothe ourselves in
him and trust him, we are prepared for battle.   —CHERI

> I thank you, Lord, for the privilege of partnering with you in
> your purpose to advance your Kingdom, set captives free, and
> stand against the forces of darkness. As I put on your armor
> and clothe myself in your righteousness, may the enemy be
> defeated and you be glorified in my life.

When you get into a tight place and everything goes against you 'til it seems as
though you could not hold on a minute longer, never give up then, for that is just
the place and time that the tide will turn.
—HARRIET BEECHER STOWE (1811–1896), AMERICAN AUTHOR

SEPTEMBER 3

Pressing toward the Goal

I press on to possess that perfection for which Christ Jesus first possessed me. No, dear brothers and sisters, I have not achieved it, but I focus on this one thing: Forgetting the past and looking forward to what lies ahead, I press on to reach the end of the race and receive the heavenly prize for which God, through Christ Jesus, is calling us.   PHILIPPIANS 3:12-14

A study was done on what separated sports stars such as Venus Williams and Tiger Woods from others who had just as much talent but didn't win the championship, the prize. It wasn't that the stars had more innate strength or ability. According to the researchers, what set them apart was their ability to stay focused and persevere under stress.

This is a key for us in our spiritual lives as well. But our focus isn't on a sports championship, as sought after as that goal might be. It's on the Lord himself! The prize Paul is describing is much greater than winning an Olympic gold medal or the U.S. Open. Our goal is to center our lives on Jesus Christ and become all God created us to be so that we can fulfill our purpose on earth.

In today's passage, Paul prefaces the message by admitting that he doesn't have it all together; he hasn't attained perfection and doesn't have it made. And neither do any of us! But Paul was in the race, reaching out for Christ, who had so wondrously reached out and saved him. He's saying, "Look, I'm not an expert; I haven't got it made. No one has." But he's got his eye on the goal, where God is beckoning him onward to Jesus. Paul is not turning back, and we are not to turn back either.

These marvelous verses encourage those of us who want everything God has for us to keep focused on that same goal. How can we persevere? How can we keep from turning back when the going gets tough? By "keeping our eyes on Jesus" (Hebrews 12:2), by drawing near to him day by day, and by discovering him and loving him more and more through his Word.   —CHERI

Jesus, I want to run with active persistence and patient endurance the path you've appointed for me. Thank you for the cloud of witnesses, like Paul, that surrounds us and encourages us with words of hope to fix our eyes on you.

Don't measure the size of the mountain; talk to the One who can move it. Instead of carrying the world on your shoulders, talk to the One who holds the universe on his. Hope is a look away.   —MAX LUCADO, AUTHOR AND MINISTER

To Ponder with a Friend

1. What tends to "dismay" or discourage you into quitting something you have started, whether it's a spiritual discipline, an exercise program, a new relationship, or a work project? What makes you at times want to give up praying for a specific need or person?

2. Think about the most helpful thing someone has done for you when you were under pressure or having a bad day that spurred you to not grow weary but to *persevere in doing what God called you to do*. Write about this or share it with a friend.

3. What can we learn from athletic stars described on September 3 about what builds the endurance and perseverance to stay the course until the prize is won? How can you apply this to your life?

4. The Christian life is a marathon, not a sprint, and so is our prayer life. About what need or request have *you persevered in* and seen the rewards of your faith and persistence?

SEPTEMBER 4

Welcoming God's Provision

This same God who takes care of me will supply all your needs
from his glorious riches, which have been given to us in Christ
Jesus.   PHILIPPIANS 4:19

Jay, our ten-year-old son, was memorizing Philippians 4:19 for Awana and had written it on yellow paper. That verse was on the kitchen counter when I came home from the hospital to tell him and his eight-year-old sister, Holly, their dad had died. I studied the verse for a long moment, breathing a prayer for strength, and then called the children in from the other room, where they had been watching TV with their aunt. Our new, sad life had just begun.

Many times in the days ahead I quoted Philippians 4:19 aloud as a prayer and usually added a silent *Even this need, Lord?* as I faced a new challenge. But whenever I took the time to ask the Lord for his help, he gave it, whether I was balancing the checkbook, making decisions about my children's school, or pondering a cross-country move. Day by day I was learning more about his presence and more about the strength he had placed within me.

I also was learning the truth of what my husband, Don, had said the morning before he died: "Just remember, San, the Lord never promised us an easy road. But he did promise to always be with us on that road." Truly, inviting the Lord into my grief made all the difference in the journey.   —SANDRA

> Lord, this business of grieving is hard work. Help me to lean on
> you and to draw strength from your abiding presence. Help me
> not to question why awful things happen but to be grateful that
> you not only understand my tears but also sometimes cry with me.

There is only one being who can satisfy the last aching abyss of the human heart, and that is the Lord Jesus Christ.
—OSWALD CHAMBERS (1874–1917), SCOTTISH BIBLE TEACHER, YMCA CHAPLAIN IN EGYPT

SEPTEMBER 5

Helping Others

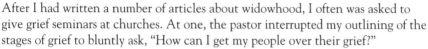

> We want you to know what will happen to the believers who
> have died so you will not grieve like people who have no hope.
> 1 THESSALONIANS 4:13

After I had written a number of articles about widowhood, I often was asked to
give grief seminars at churches. At one, the pastor interrupted my outlining of the
stages of grief to bluntly ask, "How can I get my people over their grief?"

The poor man was carrying an unrealistic burden and, undoubtedly, trying
to rush those in his congregation toward his concept of proper grief.

"Your job isn't to get them over it," I answered. "Your job is to help them
through it."

He visibly relaxed and settled in for the rest of my presentation, in which I
explained the four basic stages of grief: numbness, searching, disorientation, and
resolution, and the effects of each. I explained I wasn't using the stages to pigeon-
hole folks but to help them through a confusing, frightening time. Then I read
1 Thessalonians 4:13 and emphasized how the verse doesn't say we aren't to grieve
but rather we aren't to grieve like those who have no hope. I noticed the pastor
was taking notes.

I later wished I had asked him if he had ever experienced the death of someone close, but I already was convinced he hadn't. After all, we can intellectualize
death all we want, but until we have walked grief's road, we do not understand its
full impact. Yes, we can rejoice in heaven's reality, but we also miss the presence of
someone special.

By the way, the folks who helped me the most were not the ones who told
me not to cry, as if good Christians can't weep, but those who understood my hurt,
wrapped me in a hug, and cried with me.   —SANDRA

> Lord, guard my mouth from spewing pious words. May my
> presence be a comfort to those who are hurting. And help me
> to remember that you, too, wept.

How shall we comfort those who weep? By weeping with them.
—FATHER ALEXANDER YELCHANINOV (1881–1934), RUSSIAN ORTHODOX PRIEST AND
EDUCATOR

SEPTEMBER 6
The Breathin' Part

[God] will wipe every tear from their eyes, and there will be no more death or sorrow or crying or pain. All these things are gone forever. REVELATION 21:4

When my beloved grandmother Mama Farley died at age ninety, Don and I decided five-year-old Holly and six-year-old Jay would attend the Kentucky funeral with us. During the long drive, we talked about heaven and told our children that Mama—the part we couldn't see—was already with the Lord. Then I, a veteran of Southern funerals, told them about the part they would see. She'd be lying in a big box, called a casket, and would be surrounded by flowers. A lot of peole would be in the room, I said, and many would be crying because Mama Farley couldn't talk to them anymore. I talked about the sad hymns the people would sing, what the minister would say, and even about the procession to the cemetery after her adult grandsons carried the casket to the big car called a hearse. Then, most important of all, I asked if they had any questions. Jay wondered about practical matters, such as how they put the casket in the ground, but Holly just stared at me, her eyes round with silent wonderings.

When we arrived at the funeral home, we held the children's hands and walked into the flowered area. I studied Mama Farley's dear, ancient face and thought of the godly example she'd been. Lost in my memories, I was startled by Holly's whispered question: "Is Mama breathing?"

We hadn't anticipated that, and it required more than just a quick "No, of course not." Suddenly this business of explaining death to *myself* had become difficult. How could I help a child grasp what I couldn't?

"Well, Holly . . ." I stalled, searching for something both simple and theologically sound. Jay turned from flipping the casket handles to face his little sister.

"No, Holly, she's not breathing. Remember? The breathin' part's in heaven."

Since that long-ago April day, I've stood before all too many caskets. But even with tears running down my cheeks, I find comfort in the memory of a little voice confidently announcing, "The breathin' part's in heaven." And that makes all the difference in being able to bear the grief.   —SANDRA

Lord, help me not to be quick to provide "proper" answers. Help me to hear your wisdom through the children around me. And help me to find peace in the knowledge that those who trusted you in life are safe with you in heaven.

There is a land of pure delight,
    Where saints immortal reign;
Infinite day excludes the night,
    And pleasures banish pain.
—ISAAC WATTS (1674–1748), ENGLISH THEOLOGIAN AND HYMN WRITER

SEPTEMBER 7
Be Honest

> The Holy Spirit helps us in our weakness. For example, we don't know what God wants us to pray for. But the Holy Spirit prays for us with groanings that cannot be expressed in words.   ROMANS 8:26

Debi had the life she had long dreamed about: She was married to a pastor and was the mother of a five-year-old son. Then one day her husband came home, slammed the door behind him, and said he was tired of being a minister. Debi stood stunned, waiting for an explanation. Instead, her husband added, "And I'm tired of being married," and stormed upstairs to pack a suitcase.

For a while, Debi thought he would cool off, apologize, and come back home. Instead, she found herself in divorce court. Then her husband signed away all parental rights, to avoid paying child support, and disappeared. Of course, Debi had questions, wondered what had happened and what she could have done differently. But there were no answers, so Debi determined to get through this as she thought a good Christian woman should. Her I-can-do-this attitude rolled on for four years.

One Saturday afternoon, her then nine-year-old son ran in screaming from his baseball game. Debi turned to see him clutching his left hand as blood ran down his arm and dripped off his elbow. She lunged at him.

"What happened? Let me see your hand."

But her son backed up. "No! You'll hurt me."

"Honey, I can't help you if you won't let me see it."

Finally she was able to pull him into a chair and pry open his fingers. She expected to see bone and severed tendons. Instead, it was just a surface cut that bled a lot. She washed and bandaged the child's hand, gave him a hug, and smiled as he ran back to his game.

As she put away the first-aid kit, she spoke aloud. "Wasn't that something, Lord? There he was saying, 'Help me,' but he wouldn't show me the hurt!"

In that quiet moment, it was just as if the Lord said, "I know, Debi. I know." As she realized she had never shown anyone, not even the Lord, her hurting heart, she sank to the floor and sobbed out four years of pain.

Her healing had begun.   —SANDRA

Lord, often the worst lies are the ones we tell ourselves. Help me to be honest with myself and with you. Help me to trust you with my broken heart.

Honesty is looking painful truths in the face.
—AUBREY THOMAS DE VERE (1814–1902), IRISH POET AND CRITIC

SEPTEMBER 8
Concentrate on What Is Left

> Have mercy on me, O God, have mercy! I look to you for protection. I will hide beneath the shadow of your wings until the danger passes by. PSALM 57:1

Jamie's mother had managed to prepare the traditional Thanksgiving dinner despite her grief over the death from cancer of her twenty-eight-year-old son, Nicholas. When Jamie and her family arrived, she and her husband seated their three young children at the table and glanced at the empty chair where Nicholas usually sat. As she fastened a bib around the neck of her two-year-old, Jamie remembered the stories her brother had told last year about his high school pranks. Although she had laughed at his description of the chemistry teacher's reaction that sent Nicholas to the principal's office, she had been concerned that Nicholas was giving her ten-year-old son ideas. She had started to scold him in her usual big-sister way, but Nicholas winked at her as he grinned and asked everyone to hold hands as he thanked the Lord for "The turkeys gathered for another year to eat turkey."

As Jamie sighed at the memory of that last dinner before the cancer reappeared, her eight-year-old daughter turned to her grandmother. "My friend Sarah says her family always says three things they are thankful for before they eat Thanksgiving dinner. Let's do that too."

But Jamie's mother snapped at the child, "I have nothing to be thankful for! Just hush and eat."

Jamie patted her disappointed daughter on the shoulder and exchanged a sorrowful glance with her husband. Yes, she understood her mother was grieving for Nicholas; she was too. But didn't her mother see she still had a loving daughter, a concerned son-in-law, and three healthy, beautiful grandchildren? Couldn't she have been thankful for them?

Good question. Yes, what if we concentrated on what we still have instead of on what we have lost? —SANDRA

> Lord, when I can't thank you for the situation, help me to thank you for your presence, your peace, your abiding love. Help me not to question *why* but to accept your comforting arms.

One act of thanksgiving when things go wrong with us is worth a thousand thanks when things are agreeable to our inclination.
—SAINT JOHN OF AVILA (1500–1569), SPANISH PREACHER, AUTHOR, AND MYSTIC

SEPTEMBER 9
It's Okay to Cry

[God] comforts us in all our troubles so that we can comfort others. When they are troubled, we will be able to give them the same comfort God has given us.   2 CORINTHIANS 1:4

A few months after my husband died, Rachel approached me one Sunday morning after worship. As she hugged me, she said, "I must tell you what an inspiration you've been to me as I've watched you adjust to widowhood. I'm so impressed you never cried after Don died. What faith!"

I stared at her, astounded. To let her continue to think I hadn't cried would be a lie. But would the truth make her think less of me? Finally I said, "I'm sorry to disillusion you, but I did cry after Don died. In fact, I even screamed a few times. It's just that you never saw me cry."

She looked startled, but I continued. "I wish life's grief would stop with me. It won't, though. And when your turn comes, it will be okay for you to cry. The Lord understands tears."

I knew Rachel was disappointed, but I couldn't let her continue to think good Christians are always dry eyed. That would have been dishonest on my part and would have set her up for unhealthy future grief.

We can look to Jesus as our perfect example of how to handle sorrow. He lamented over Jerusalem (see Matthew 23:37; Luke 13:34), wept at the tomb of Lazarus (see John 11:35), and fell anguished to the ground in the garden of Gethsemane (see Matthew 26:39; Mark 14:35). If he could cry, we can too.

Soon after our talk at church, Rachel had an opportunity to give her own honest tears to the Lord. Her daughter and son-in-law had been trying for years to have a baby, and they were thrilled when their pregnancy went full term. But in the final week, the baby suddenly went into fetal distress and died. If Rachel still had been caught in the misunderstanding that faith keeps us from tears, she would not have been able to hug her daughter and cry with her.   —SANDRA

Lord, thank you for your example of tears. Thank you for allowing us the healing that can come when we cry, and thank you for holding us as we sob.

Let tears flow of their own accord; their flowing is not inconsistent with inward peace and harmony.
—LUCIUS SENECA (CA. 4 B.C.–A.D. 65), ROMAN STATESMAN, DRAMATIST, AND PHILOSOPHER

SEPTEMBER 10
The Warmest Gift

Give, and you will receive. LUKE 6:38

As the first Christmas after my husband's death loomed, I called The Salvation Army and offered myself and my children to deliver food baskets. The staff welcomed our help, but the morning of our assignment was so bitterly cold I couldn't get warm, even with my new coat tightly buttoned.

Still, I had promised, so the three of us made deliveries up rickety steps to above-the-store apartments and weather-beaten houses near the railroad tracks. We carried in the bags of food and offered a hearty "Merry Christmas!" along with each good-bye, but the cold continued to penetrate my coat and my heart. I was cold, the weather was miserable, and I couldn't see I was making a great difference in anyone's life. After all, if we hadn't been delivering the groceries, someone else would have been.

Then we arrived at the last tired little house, where we were invited in. Everything was clean, but the floor tiles were worn down to the wooden boards beneath. The curtains had been mended so many times the stitches made a pattern in the thin material. As I set down the bag containing a small turkey, potatoes, green beans, cranberry sauce, and rolls, the elderly couple thanked me repeatedly. All I had to do was smile and walk out the door, but there was a wistfulness in the couple's voices as they invited us to "stay awhile." So we remained for a brief visit, and upon discovering the woman's need for a coat, I gave her mine.

She hugged me and whispered, "God bless you, honey," as tears rolled down her cheeks. All I could do was whisper back, "Thank you for letting me do this."

When my children and I left, we waved good-bye from the driveway. Then my daughter turned to me. "Mom! It's freezing out here! And you gave away your coat!"

I gave her shoulders a little squeeze. "I know. But this is the warmest I've been all day. In fact, it's the warmest I've been in a very long time."

And truly it was. —SANDRA

Lord, this world is filled with lonely, hurting people. I can't solve all their problems, but I can make a difference. Help me to first see the needs of others and then do what I can. And may I take my instructions about whom I help only from you.

All we have done for ourselves alone dies with us; what we have done for others and the world remains and is eternal.
—ALBERT PIKE (1809–1891), AMERICAN ATTORNEY, SOLDIER, AND WRITER

To Ponder with a Friend

1. What is your earliest memory of the death of someone special?

2. What comforts you in times of grief?

3. Has a child ever given you a different perspective about death? How so?

4. If you could tell someone only one thing about God's comfort, what would it be?

SEPTEMBER 11
Lord, Change Me

> Don't copy the behavior and customs of this world, but let God transform you into a new person by changing the way you think. Then you will learn to know God's will for you, which is good and pleasing and perfect. ROMANS 12:2

I remember one of the times I prayed the life-changing prayer "Lord, change me!" To say it was a stressful time is an understatement. My husband, Holmes, was in a dead-end job and depressed (and I was angry and frustrated with him underneath my veneer of politeness). Our twenty-year-old daughter was living with us, and she was struggling with some personal problems of her own.

My tendency was to think, *If Holmes were just happier and less depressed; if only he could get a better job so we'd have more income and I wouldn't have to work double to try to make ends meet; if only Ali could get in a better place and not be so down. Then everything would be okay, right?* Wrong. I encouraged my husband, gave our daughter unwelcome advice, tried to cheer both of them up, and prayed harder that they would change. Then one day it hit me: I couldn't change them at all. I could only be willing to work on *my issues* and ask God to change *me.*

Today's verse shed much light: Be transformed (that is, changed) by "changing the way you think." The prayer I prayed that day and many other days following led to my going to counseling, joining a support group of women dealing with family-of-origin issues, and asking over and over again, "Lord, change me—not my husband, not my daughter, not our situation, but *me, from the inside out.*"

The results of that prayer and the long journey that followed have been painful at certain points, but they have definitely been worth it. And as I got my focus off my dear ones' problems and asked God to change my heart, God worked faithfully and steadily in their lives as well, for he works within each of us who belong to him, to cause us to desire to do what pleases him.

Would you, too, pray this powerful, life-changing prayer and mean it?
—CHERI

> Lord, change me—not my husband or my friend who's being difficult, not my children, my grumpy neighbor, or my boss. Please change me from the inside out.

Change, indeed, is painful, yet ever needful; and if memory have its force and worth, so also has hope.
—THOMAS CARLYLE (1795–1881), SCOTTISH ESSAYIST AND HISTORIAN

The Prayer of Relinquishment

[Hannah said to Eli,] "I asked the LORD to give me this boy, and he has granted my request. Now I am giving him to the LORD, and he will belong to the LORD his whole life." 1 SAMUEL 1:27-28

The prayer of relinquishment, giving back to God what is dearest, is the first recorded prayer by a woman in the Bible. Hannah had told God that if he fulfilled her deepest desire for a child, she would relinquish that child to God for his service, and she kept her promise. She gave God her beloved, firstborn son, Samuel. Her prayer of release wasn't only for the day, as her child hopped on the school bus for kindergarten, to return in the afternoon. Her little guy was going to live at the Tabernacle *for the rest of his life.*

Who or what is most important to you? Can you picture yourself placing that person or other desire in God's loving hands, along with your self-will, your plans, and your desires for outcomes? Although it's one of the toughest prayers to pray, the prayer of relinquishment, or letting go, releases the most power and grace. And though it doesn't guarantee that things turn out the way we want, the prayer of relinquishment does invite the power and grace of God into the situation.

What were the results of Hannah's releasing Samuel to God? Her sorrow turned to joy. Freedom and blessing abounded. As she dedicated Samuel to the Lord, her heart sang a song of praise that has rung down the ages: "My heart rejoices in the LORD!" (1 Samuel 2:1). Later, God blessed her with three more sons and two daughters (see 1 Samuel 2:21).

As Samuel grew, God protected him and used him in a great way as his chosen spokesperson in a crucial time in Israel's history. —CHERI

Help me to be willing to give whatever I hold most dear to you, Lord, to entrust it into your care, your goodness, and your love.

The weakest saint can experience the power of the deity of the Son of God if he is willing to let go.
—OSWALD CHAMBERS (1874–1917), SCOTTISH BIBLE TEACHER, YMCA CHAPLAIN IN EGYPT

SEPTEMBER 13
The Jesus Prayer

The faithful love of the LORD never ends! His mercies never cease.
Great is his faithfulness; his mercies begin afresh each morning. I
say to myself, "The LORD is my inheritance; therefore, I will hope
in him!" LAMENTATIONS 3:22-24

The story is told of an elderly priest who had to undergo very serious, delicate
surgery. Many friends didn't expect him to survive the surgery and recover. In the
last moments of consciousness before the anesthetic took effect, the priest heard
his surgeon repeating in a whisper, "*Gospodi pomiluy, Gospodi pomiluy, Gospodi
pomiluy,*" which in Russian means, "Lord, have mercy on us." How comforted he
was to hear that prayer from the lips of the man who would be cutting into his
body. The priest did survive the surgery and served God for several more years.

Ancient Christians called this short, powerful prayer the Jesus Prayer, and
they often prayed it in the rhythm of breathing: *Lord Jesus Christ, Son of God, have
mercy on us.* This prayer covers a lot of bases. It can cover the mercies we need for
our marriages, our own physical problems, our mistakes. We can pray it for others:
"Lord Jesus Christ, Son of God, have mercy on my friend who is in her last weeks
of life." "Lord Jesus Christ, Son of God, have mercy on my nephew who is in a
destructive lifestyle." And we can pray it for ourselves: "Lord Jesus Christ, Son of
God, have mercy on me in my point of need today."

When we pray for God's mercy, we can do so in confidence, for we are asking
the Lord to manifest the very essence of his being. He is the God of mercy and
compassion who, Scripture tells us, dispenses *new* mercies every morning and at
every point in our lives.   —CHERI

Thank you, Father, that your mercies begin afresh every day. You
have a portion of mercy to grant me each day if I will but ask.
Lord Jesus Christ, Son of God, have mercy on me.

God's mercy is boundless, free and, through Jesus Christ our Lord, available to us
now in our present situation.
—A. W. TOZER (1897–1963), AMERICAN PASTOR, PREACHER, AND AUTHOR

SEPTEMBER 14
The Clean-Heart Prayer

Create in me a clean heart, O God.   PSALM 51:10

When a woman I met at a retreat in New England asked me for a good way to start her busy day with God, I suggested she let the shower be her cue to ask for a clean heart. She prayed the very next morning, "Lord, create in me a clean heart and renew a right spirit within me. Cleanse me of sin." As she prayed, a number of sins came to her mind, and one by one she confessed those to God. The woman began to weep, and as the tears flowed, she gave God her shame for past misdeeds and failures. She named the people she'd been angry at and asked his forgiveness for harboring resentment. It may have been a longer-than-usual shower, but when she stepped out of the bathroom that day, she didn't have just a clean body. She was a new person in Christ Jesus. The old had passed away and the new had come (see 2 Corinthians 5:17).

Although one of her friends had been dragging her to church every Sunday, this woman hadn't experienced any connection with God whatsoever. Yet when she used this simple but powerful prayer, everything changed, for this is a prayer God loves to answer!

Of course, we don't have to be in the shower to pray the clean-heart prayer. Repentance and confession are vital parts of our spiritual journey, not only at the point of salvation but throughout our lives. And although having a clean heart is a requirement for effective prayer and close fellowship with God, we can't clean up our own hearts. We can, however, regularly ask the Spirit to remind us of recent sins, and we can confess them and receive God's forgiveness.   —CHERI

> Father, are there any secret sins that are hindering me? Is there anyone I need to forgive or a word or deed that has displeased you? Please show me now, and give me the humility to confess those things and accept your forgiveness. Create in me a clean heart, and renew a right spirit within me!

In confession . . . we open our lives to healing, reconciling, restoring, uplifting grace of him who loves us in spite of what we are.
—LOUIS CASSELS (1922–1974), UNITED PRESS INTERNATIONAL SENIOR RELIGION EDITOR

SEPTEMBER 15
A Prayer for Affection

Love each other with genuine affection.   ROMANS 12:10

Today's verse is the basis of the most powerful prayer I've prayed for our marriage of thirty-eight years: "Lord, help us to love each other with a genuine affection." Paul meant this verse as an admonition to the Roman church, but it applies to all of *our* relationships as well.

C. S. Lewis once said, "Affection is responsible for nine-tenths of whatever solid and durable happiness there is in our lives." Yet how lacking so many marriages are in real, genuine affection, which one dictionary defines as fondness, tender attachment, or warmhearted love.

Affection busters such as stress, busyness, anger, and unforgiveness drain the life out of many relationships. I first noticed today's verse when our marriage was in a dry wilderness and some of those affection busters had done damage. Although my husband and I were committed to each other, our marriage was anything but affectionate. I wrote Romans 12:10 on an index card and tucked it in my Bible. Day after day, it resounded in my heart and in my prayers. As I confessed my own lack of love, I realized that although our human love may wax and wane, God's *never* changes or runs out. He is a God of great affection who exults over us with joy and loves us (and our spouses and other loved ones) with tenderness, generosity, and an intimacy beyond our wildest dreams. We can tap into his inexhaustible supply of love for anyone in our lives or families. We don't have to pretend; we can be real: "God, my well of love has run dry. Would you love my husband (or sister or child) through me and give me your affection for him?" As I prayed this over the months (it was not a quick work!), the Holy Spirit placed his love for my husband in my heart and gave us a fresh affection for each other that continues to this day.   —CHERI

> Lord, help me to love _____ with a genuine affection. Help me to experience your love and then to love others with that same unconditional love.

There is nothing you can do to make God love you more! There is nothing you can do to make God love you less! His love is unconditional, impartial, everlasting, infinite, perfect! God is love!
—RICHARD C. HALVERSON (1916–1995), PRESBYTERIAN MINISTER AND FORMER U.S. SENATE CHAPLAIN

SEPTEMBER 16
The Prayer of Agreement

[Jesus said,] "If two of you agree here on earth concerning anything you ask, my Father in heaven will do it for you. For where two or three gather together as my followers, I am there among them." MATTHEW 18:19-20

Five women showed up for the first Moms In Touch meeting in Carrollton, Texas, and quickly discovered that four of them had a child with special needs. None of the women had ever had someone to pray with about their child's disabilities. My, how the mascara ran that day! Anxieties melted away as they experienced the incredible feeling of bearing one another's burdens, and they went away feeling that God had given them something they really needed: a sense that they weren't alone. In the next few years of weekly prayer together, they saw God answer many prayers for their kids.

I love how today's verses underscore the importance of praying together in agreement with other believers. It's as if the Lord is saying to us women, *I have a secret for you! If you'll take time to come together and get in agreement with my will, joining your prayers like a symphony, I'll be right there with you, and I will ramp up the power!* Just as those Texas women experienced, God offers us a great gift in the prayer of agreement. As this verse tells us, while there is power in an individual's prayer, united prayer has even greater power. In addition, group praying gives us the opportunity to put into practice Paul's admonition to "share each other's burdens" (Galatians 6:2). When our hearts beat in united prayer, our love for one another and Christ increases, our faith grows, and most important, God's will and purpose are accomplished. May each of us, in every season of life, have and *be* faithful prayer partners and experience God's power as we pray in agreement with others.   —CHERI

Father, you know the problems that stress us and press in when we are alone, until our spirits are almost crushed. Thank you for giving us one another and the prayer of agreement, which has such power. Please provide a prayer partner for me and for all those I hold dear.

Praying with other people gives us new sisters . . . in Christ. The more we pray with other people the more we begin to trust them, and the more honest we all can be about our real problems, not just surface ones. Genuine togetherness is a God-given state, and hearts are joined in his presence. We can depend upon that presence because he has said, "I am right there with them."
—ROSALIND RINKER (1907–2002), MISSIONARY, AUTHOR, AND CONFERENCE SPEAKER

SEPTEMBER 17
A Prayer for Humility

When a certain immoral woman from that city heard [Jesus] was
eating there, she brought a beautiful alabaster jar filled with expensive perfume. Then she knelt behind him at his feet, weeping.
Her tears fell on his feet, and she wiped them off with her hair.
LUKE 7:37-38

When Kathy came to Christ and began to read the Bible, it was as if God took a
big yellow marker and highlighted verses that revealed how little humility she and
her husband had. She was struck by 1 Peter 5:5, which says, "God opposes the
proud but favors the humble." But the story in Luke 7 was the clincher. Jesus had
been invited to a Pharisee's home for a meal. While he was there, a woman came
in and wept as she anointed Jesus with expensive perfume.

That's what I want to be like, Lord, Kathy prayed. *Humble enough not to care
what others think, to simply be obedient and respond to you.* She had no idea that this
is a prayer God loves to answer, but as she continued to ask for humility, God
began to work. Then months later, through a painful situation at their church in
which her husband was not voted onto the Search Committee and negative,
humiliating things were said about them in front of the entire congregation, her
heart was broken. Through her tears, she remembered those prayers for humility
and told her husband about them. The impact of the power of his wife's prayers
was so great that he gave his life totally and completely to Christ.

Their home and marriage changed; his business became Christ centered.
More than ten years later, they are still humbly and faithfully serving at their
church. And God paved the way for Kathy to launch the Worldwide Moms'
Day of Prayer. When women criticized her vision, saying that she hadn't been
involved with the prayer concerts or groups as they had, it rolled off her back like
water because all she wanted was to be like the woman who had poured the perfume on Jesus' feet. She wasn't trying to impress anyone. More than anything, she
wanted to be obedient and humble.   —CHERI

Lord Jesus, humility must be very important to you because you
came to the world clothed in humility and we're to become like
you. Since your Word says you are drawn to humble people but
resist the proud, work within me a heart of humility.

The more humble one is at God's feet, the more useful he is in God's hand.
—WATCHMAN NEE (1903–1972), CHINESE CHRISTIAN AUTHOR AND CHURCH LEADER

To Ponder with a Friend

1. Is there a person, problem, or situation about which you need to "let go and let God," in other words, stop trying to manage by yourself and give to Jesus? If so, share that with a trusted friend and together do the work of relinquishment, which invites the Lord to work in his way and timing and brings freedom to us in the process.

2. In what area of your life do you most need God's mercy right now? Let me encourage you to pray the Jesus Prayer specifically for that point of need.

3. A. W. Tozer once said that because Jesus Christ came to the world clothed in humility, he is always found among those who are lothed with humility. Scripture affirms that God is drawn to humble people, not to the proud (see James 4:6). After reading the September 17 devotional entry, how do you feel about praying for humility?

4. When you think about Jesus' telling us to forgive our enemies and pray for them, how do you feel: indifferent, curious, encouraged, angry, or some other emotion? Read Matthew 6:12-15; Mark 11:25; and Ephesians 4:32. What do you sense God wants you to do with your response?

5. Reread Rosalind Rinker's insightful quote (September 16) about praying in agreement with other women. What has been your experience of praying with your sisters in Christ?

SEPTEMBER 18
Keeping the Past out of Sight

> I focus on this one thing: Forgetting the past and looking forward
> to what lies ahead, I press on to reach the end of the race and
> receive the heavenly prize for which God, through Christ Jesus,
> is calling us.   PHILIPPIANS 3:13-14

On my refrigerator door is a yellowed *Peanuts* cartoon. Charlie Brown is on the pitcher's mound, and Lucy is handing him the ball.

"Sorry I missed that easy fly ball, Manager," she says. "I thought I had it, but suddenly I remembered all the others I've missed."

As she turns away in the final panel, she says, "The past got in my eyes."

Can you identify with that situation? I sure can. One morning while playing tennis, I missed a perfect forehand, then grumbled at myself, embarrassed to have performed poorly in front of my new partner, Iris. I missed the next shot as well. Again, I apologized.

Iris said softly, "Play the next ball, Sandra."

The next ball? Of course. Just like Lucy, I had been so intent on replaying the missed shot in my mind that I was missing the balls after that one too.

Unfortunately, I can identify with the past getting in my eyes in more areas than just sports. But in life's journey, I've learned it is possible to let go of experiences that keep us from being open to the good future God wants to give. I also know letting go is a process: We first look at the events honestly, then learn to understand their power, and finally, use that new understanding to move confidently into brighter days.   —SANDRA

Lord, it is easy to let the past get in my eyes. But when I let that happen, I miss seeing the joy waiting ahead. Help me to look to you. Help me to leave the past in your hands in exchange for a brighter future.

The family you come from isn't as important as the family you're going to have.
—RING LARDNER (1885–1933), AMERICAN WRITER

SEPTEMBER 19
Choose to Let Go

> Anyone who belongs to Christ has become a new person. The old life is gone; a new life has begun! 2 CORINTHIANS 5:17

Too many people blame parents or childhood events for the way their lives have turned out. Sure, our childhood sets the precedent for who we are as adults, but our fates aren't set in stone. At some point in the journey, we can decide the unhealthy familial patterns will stop with us. Whether we get the needed encouragement to rebuild our lives through counseling or personal spiritual awareness, we do not have to cling to past trauma or pass it on to our children.

A few years ago, Karen called her parents to thank them for early Christmas gifts. After the usual chitchat, her dad said, "I wish you could be home for Christmas."

Scenes of earlier holidays darted through Karen's mind: her father's grumpiness if he was awakened too early, her having to beg him to open the pitiful little gifts she gave, his complaints about relatives who stopped in. . . . Karen had long ago given up hope of having a tension-free holiday with her family of origin, so she concentrated on her own children and tried to create peaceful memories they would carry into adulthood.

Thus, instead of arguing with her father over the phone that morning, she gently replied, "I know." Then as she watched her children playing quietly near the Christmas tree, she thought, *I am home.*

Much of Karen's inner peace came from having accepted, years earlier, the fact that although her dad had not been what she had needed as a child, he had done the best he knew how. She found emotional freedom by giving up her desire to open her father's eyes to the hurtful things he had done. Then, determined not to pass the family pain along to her own children, she concentrated on each day's joy instead of yesterday's pain. —SANDRA

Lord, it is so easy to blame a toxic childhood for all of my challenges today. Help me to let go of those sad memories so I can embrace the good future you have waiting. And help me to offer quiet forgiveness to those who couldn't offer what I needed.

The greatest benefits God has conferred on human life, fatherhood, motherhood, childhood, home, become the greatest curse if Jesus Christ is not the head.
—OSWALD CHAMBERS (1874–1917), SCOTTISH BIBLE TEACHER, YMCA CHAPLAIN IN EGYPT

SEPTEMBER 20
Release Old Patterns

> Imitate God, therefore, in everything you do, because you are his dear children. Live a life filled with love, following the example of Christ. He loved us and offered himself as a sacrifice for us, a pleasing aroma to God. EPHESIANS 5:1-2

For many people, the holidays are filled with memories far from a cozy gathering around the fireplace. And when extended families do gather, tension, disappointment, and increased stress abound, with everyone trying to pretend nothing is wrong.

Melinda knows that scenario all too well. When her family of origin gets together, the results are disastrous since her adult siblings revert to their childhood patterns in the way they react to one another and to their parents. Her brother, even at forty-two, believes his status as only son entitles him to special privileges, such as insisting his elderly mother prepare his favorite dishes for each meal, and his sisters follow his whims for each day's activities. Melinda's younger sister, the one her father called "Beauty," is a buyer for a major department store chain, but under the old roof, she assumes the whining personality of the eight-year-old she used to be. Melinda's older sister, a talented professional, can't relax and becomes the controller once again as she cleans out cabinets and rearranges their mother's kitchen. Even Melinda, an award-winning teacher, again finds herself belittled by her siblings.

Why does Melinda find these actions so painful? Because she realizes she and her siblings are adults acting like children. And when she is performing the old role, she experiences the same feelings she felt years ago. Emotionally, she has moved back into that early situation where others were pounding her self-esteem and she was convinced she was not lovable.

When old childhood roles are being played out in the lives of adults, no one appreciates the accomplishments each one has made in the passing years. Wisely, though, early in their marriage, Melinda encouraged her husband to join her in shaping their own holiday traditions. Then, throughout the year, they invite her siblings to visit separately to get to know them as adult individuals. By refusing to stay in the old role, Melinda has found a way to keep the past from getting in her eyes. —SANDRA

> Lord, help me not to slip back into the patterns of my family of origin. Help me to be an example of strength and peace. May family members see you through me.

There is never much trouble in any family where the children hope someday to resemble their parents.
—WILLIAM LYON PHELPS (1865–1943), AMERICAN AUTHOR AND SCHOLAR

SEPTEMBER 21
Similar Characteristics

You have turned my mourning into joyful dancing. You have taken
away my clothes of mourning and clothed me with joy.   PSALM 30:11

When I worked in a New York editorial office, the staff planned an article on adult
children of alcoholics, and I was chosen to attend an Adult Children of Alcoholics
(ACA) convention. Though I don't like placing folks into pigeonholes, I was
amazed at some of the similarities among those raised in dysfunctional homes:

- On the inside, an adult child from a dysfunctional family, whom I'll call
  a CDF, is a needy person trying not to be needy. She has grown up in a
  house filled with fear of abandonment, fear of confrontation, fear of being
  left out, fear of anger.
- For the CDF, control is a big issue. Since his childhood home was usually
  out of control, he will attempt to control any area open to him, often with
  endless rules and lists.
- A CDF doesn't know what "normal" is, including how relationships
  between family members are supposed to work.
- A CDF often makes a wonderful employee because she trusts outer direction rather than inner direction. She's always looking to someone who
  will show her how the system is supposed to work.
- A CDF would rather deal with the pain he knows than with the pain he
  doesn't know. This is often seen through a CDF's being addicted to
  "empty wells," that is, partners who are emotionally unavailable.
- The CDF continues to internalize what her parents said. She doesn't
  process "You're stupid; get out of my sight" as the mumblings of a drunk or
  an emotionally unstable adult but as a true statement about her own lack
  of value.

Emotional freedom comes as CDFs realize their parents could not do any better.
But coming to that realization and accepting that conclusion may take years.
—SANDRA

> Lord, I don't like fitting a pattern. I like to think of myself as a
> strong individual who is molded in your unique way, not as a
> "cookie-cutter creature." But help me to know patterns can serve
> a useful purpose. After all, if I can see how I got into a situation, I
> will also see the way out.

Those who wear the shoe know best where it pinches.
—CHARLES HADDON SPURGEON (1834–1892), BRITISH PREACHER

SEPTEMBER 22
Letting Go of Bad Memories

> In my distress I prayed to the LORD, and the LORD answered me and set me free. PSALM 118:5

Those still bound by sad memories of a toxic childhood can't give themselves encouragement and often can't accept it from others. Dwelling on past injustices, believing negative things people said, or rejecting the idea they deserve anything good, in fact, creates a barrier to good things. For example, self-talk such as *Well, of course I failed—why did I even try!* doesn't help with the challenge at hand; it only focuses attention on the problem instead of on a possible solution.

Think of the difference even this simple change could make: *Well, that didn't work. What are other possibilities?*

Letting go of the past means just that: letting go. After all, that's what forgiveness means. I've lost count of the times I've reminded an angry woman that holding a grudge hurts only her, not the other person. I've even said, "He's not losing sleep over this; you are. You have to let this go." I've never insisted either for myself or for others on an immediate and flippant "Hey, it's okay you were rotten to me. No problem. Really." I stress forgiveness is a process we must work through. And it doesn't mean being best friends with that other person. It just means not dwelling on his or her miserable past actions.

One of my Denver friends, Dr. Linda Williams, offers great forgiveness advice: "Forgiveness is the willingness to live with the consequences of another's sin." I like that. Many times we can do nothing but choose to live with the memories of another's wrong actions and get on with life. Our emotional freedom comes as we make the decision to stop giving that past situation power over the present.
—SANDRA

Lord, I confess I don't want to forgive those who have hurt me. That sounds too much like letting them off the hook. But the truth is, they aren't the ones suffering—I am. I want freedom. Help me to let go of the past and accept your bright future.

As we practice the work of forgiveness we discover more and more that forgiveness and healing are one. —AGNES SANFORD (1897–1982), WRITER

SEPTEMBER 23
Be Patient with Yourself

The LORD will guide you continually, giving you water when you are dry and restoring your strength. You will be like a well-watered garden, like an ever-flowing spring. ISAIAH 58:11

When Freda was young, her father had taken his own frustration about life out on her and would tell her not to expect to achieve anything worthwhile. As an adult, Freda's way of overcoming that trauma was to keep in her purse a list of positive thoughts she had either read or heard. She would pull out the list every time the memory of one of her father's sarcastic comments threatened her plans.

Some time ago, she struggled with wanting to take an interior design class at the local college. Finally, she decided to go for it, but when she arrived at the campus to register and saw the young, happy students choosing classes and buying books, she seemed to hear her father saying, "You're out of your league."

But this time, instead of agreeing with that mental tape and going home, Freda pulled out her list and read, "The past can't hold you prisoner unless you give it permission."

Taking a deep breath, she prayed for strength, signed up for her class, and headed for the bookstore. She was determined to replace her fear of failure with the excitement of achieving her dream. Soon that accomplishment opened the way for her to dare to reach more of her goals. —SANDRA

Lord, why do I listen to those old negative words when I have your words of encouragement and strength? You, Creator of the universe, Maker of heaven and earth, love me and want so much for me, yet I refuse to accept your blessings because I'm too busy remembering the mean things said to me in the past. You offer freedom. Help me to accept it.

The larger the God we know, the larger will be our faith. The secret of power in our lives is to know God and expect great things from him.
—ALBERT BENJAMIN SIMPSON (1843–1919), CANADIAN PREACHER, THEOLOGIAN, AND AUTHOR

SEPTEMBER 24
Standing Ready

[Lord,] you go before me and follow me. You place your hand of blessing on my head.   Psalm 139:5

Those whose childhoods caused them to try to be doers and fixers carry a gotta-fix-this mentality into adulthood. I remember a single-parent friend who was heading toward financial trouble. I was in a position to help, but I didn't want her to look to me first. In the past I had gotten caught in situations where folks expected me to rescue them from minor frustrations as well as major challenges. Sometimes I wondered if they ever prayed before they picked up the phone, or if their first thought was, *Call Sandra. She'll take care of this.*

So I wanted my friend to look to God as her Source, not to me. But I also didn't want to deny help to someone in legitimate need. As I thought of my friend's pattern of getting herself into deep financial waters, I prayed for her and read and reread the Scriptures, wondering if I should offer my help. Did my faith mandate rescuing her? I understood the single-parent plight all too well, but I wanted her to learn more about the Lord and more about the strength he had given her. And deep down, I knew she needed financial counseling more than she needed my check.

One Sunday morning, those thoughts were heavy on my mind as I entered my usual row at church. In the quiet moments before the service began, I glanced around, taking mental roll call. The usual folks were in place, including my friends Larry and Mary Ellen. They were sitting behind the dear, elderly gentleman I'll call Mr. Smith, who was growing more feeble each week. But he had insisted he would continue to be in church as long as the Lord allowed. So each Sunday, we marveled at his determination to be independent and held our collective breath each time he pulled himself to his feet.

On this particular morning, Mr. Smith seemed even more frail as he stood for a hymn. Then he wobbled as he backed toward his chair. Immediately, Larry's arms were at his shoulders, not touching him, but ready. Mr. Smith made it safely and hadn't known Larry was ready to catch him if need be.

I let out the breath I was holding and realized I had just witnessed exactly how I needed to respond to my friend. I wasn't to rush in and carry her, but I was to be ready to help if needed. That settled, I sang the next hymn with even greater enthusiasm.   —Sandra

Lord, what a relief to know I don't have to solve everyone's problems. Help me to remember that only you can do that. Help me to do those things I am supposed to do but to leave the major rescues to you.

Charity is helping a man to help himself.
—Moses Maimonides (1135–1204), Jewish philosopher, jurist, and physician

To Ponder with a Friend

1. What was your childhood like? What situations do you wish had been different?

2. What do you think about behavioral patterns? Is it helpful for us to know about them, or do they then merely become emotional crutches?

3. Have you ever needed to forgive someone? How did you handle the situation?

4. What balance between help and independence have you needed in your own life?

SEPTEMBER 25
Living in Freedom

> I prayed to the LORD, and he answered me. He freed me from all
> my fears. Those who look to him for help will be radiant with joy;
> no shadow of shame will darken their faces.   PSALM 34:4-5

These verses tell us that although fear is a normal, human reaction to danger or
crisis, God has an answer for our fear. We may fear death, failure, or people. We
may be frightened about taking a new step, fearful of suffering, or afraid of what
might happen tomorrow. Whatever it is, we don't have to be ashamed of being
afraid or stuff our fears and try to look brave. Instead, the very fear that plagues us
can be a handle that presses us into the Lord's presence. He invites us to pray to
him and to lay down our fears instead of being paralyzed by them.

The psalm from which today's verses are taken reminds us to fear and take
refuge in God and go to him instead of turning to others (see Psalm 34). But often
we tend to take our fears everywhere *except* to God. We might tell our best friend,
the person on the other end of the crisis hotline, or our sister across the country
via e-mail. It's great to have friends when we're stressed or afraid, but God is the
One who can do something about our concerns and problems.

An amazing thing happens when we are willing to open up to the Lord about
our fears. A great exchange takes place, and in return for our giving our fears to
him, he infuses us with faith, hope, and love. As F. B. Meyer said, "God incarnate
is the end of fear; and the heart that realizes that he is in the midst . . . will be
quiet in the midst of alarm."   —CHERI

> Lord, I look to you to deliver me from all my fears. Thank you for
> your promise that you answer me, free me from fear and shame,
> and cause me to be radiant with joy.

Fear imprisons, faith liberates; fear paralyzes, faith encourages; fear sickens, faith
heals; fear makes useless, faith makes serviceable and, most of all, fear puts hope-
lessness at the heart of life, while faith rejoices in its God.
—HARRY EMERSON FOSDICK (1878–1969), AMERICAN CLERGYMAN

SEPTEMBER 26
From Fear to Faith

> God has not given us a spirit of fear and timidity, but of power, love, and self-discipline.   2 Timothy 1:7

"I was afraid that was going to happen!" said the mother of a teenage driver who had just been involved in his first wreck. Have you ever said something similar? It's natural to be anxious at times about things over which you have no control. But being chronically fearful drains your energy, diminishes your physical strength, and can even keep you from living up to your potential.

Scientists believe that we have a certain supply of emotional energy for every day and year we live. They call that supply "calendar energy." If we use it up "too soon" by being worried and anxious, we can literally run out of the energy needed for daily life and face burnout.

That is why Jesus told us not to waste our time worrying about what might happen tomorrow, because today has enough challenges of its own (see Matthew 6:34). He gave us gifts and abilities to use in serving him, but he knew that fear—of failure or of what others might think—can cause us to keep those talents in the closet. It causes us to miss taking advantage of opportunities as they arise.

If you've ever struggled with fear or anxiety, you're not alone. A major survey showed that fear is the number one emotional issue for women today. But you do not have to be imprisoned, paralyzed, or disheartened by fear. God loves you and can help you to live not in fear but in faith—faith that will liberate you and empower you to be all God created you to be.   —Cheri

> Lord, when I am afraid or my heart is disturbed within me, turn me from fear to faith, and empower me to trust you with all my heart.

All of us have reservoirs of full potential, but the road that leads to those reservoirs is guarded by the dragon of fear.
—Paul Tournier (1898–1986), Swiss physician and author

SEPTEMBER 27
When I Am Afraid

When I am afraid, I will put my trust in you.   Psalm 56:3

Once when I was a child, our family was on a road trip to New Mexico when my sister Georgia, who had fallen asleep leaning against the car door, went flying out of the car onto the highway. Papa raced her to the emergency room at a local hospital, and Georgia survived with only abrasions from head to foot.

But "car phobia" was a long-term effect for the rest of us. So when I got married, I figured "backseat driving" was my job, and it drove my husband crazy. Once, we were on our way to Colorado with our three kids. The children were asleep in the backseat as we drove through western Oklahoma late at night. Then, out of nowhere, a blinding white mass of snow streamed horizontally toward our windshield. In moments we couldn't see the stripes on the two-lane road or even the side of the road for the blizzard that surrounded us. That old fear began rising within me. "Slow down, honey," I said to my husband. "Pull over or stop or something."

My hand gripped the armrest, and my foot was on the invisible brake. At first Holmes was annoyed, then he grew more irritated at my anxiety. Knowing that my husband was driving the best he could, I went to God and silently cried out, *Lord, please help me! I know your perfect love casts out all fear, so would you fill me with your love so I can relax and not bug my husband?*

As I continued praying, a song began to bubble up in my consciousness. "When I am afraid, I will trust in you, in God whose Word I praise, in God I have put my trust. I will not be afraid, no, I will not be afraid!" As I began to sing this tune, which I'd never heard before, first in my head and then aloud, my fear diminished. The anxiety literally shrank before me, and I grew more calm and relaxed. My hand relaxed its grip on the armrest, and we eventually drove out of the blizzard. I've never forgotten the song God gave me in the midst of that blinding, swirling snow. When we got to our destination, I found the source of those words in Psalm 56:3-4.

The words are just as true today: When we put our trust in God, we don't have to be afraid.   —Cheri

Lord, when I am afraid I will put my trust in you. God whose Word I praise, in you I have put my trust.

God incarnate is the end of fear; and the heart that realizes that he is in the midst . . . will be quiet in the midst of alarm.
—F. B. Meyer (1847–1929), Baptist pastor and evangelist

SEPTEMBER 28

Displacing Fearful Thoughts with Truth

> Come, let us tell of the LORD's greatness; let us exalt his name together. I prayed to the LORD, and he answered me. He freed me from all my fears. PSALM 34:3-4

Living free from fear is easier when things are going smoothly. But if you're suddenly diagnosed with a serious illness, a wave of fear may flood your mind. The uncertainty and what-ifs can be overwhelming as thoughts flood in: *I'll never be able to work again and support myself with the limitations I'll face. I may become so weak that I don't know how I'll cope. How did this illness slip by God's watchful care?*

The fear of illness or the reality of a serious diagnosis can be anxiety-producing for anyone. How can you respond in a way that neutralizes those fears and keeps you in the ongoing process of wholeness? The first step is to replace the lies and fearful thoughts with biblical truth. Rehearse these truths to yourself: God will supply all you need (see Philippians 4:19). Regardless of your health problems, you are strong in him (see Joel 3:10). He has given you all you need for living a godly life (see 2 Peter 1:3). He is your Great Physician, the God who is well able to care for your physical needs (see Exodus 15). You belong to him, and he will fill you with his dynamic power so you can cope with any situation (see Philippians 4:13).

When you believe and proclaim God's indestructible promises, you are enabled to trust him in the most vulnerable places and difficulties. You'll find that as you replace your fears with what the Lord says in Scripture, dread and anxiety will gradually dissipate. It's like a seesaw: The more faith grows, the more fear subsides. —CHERI

> Thank you, dear Jesus, for bearing our griefs, weaknesses, and distresses. We trust you as the Great Physician that we can bring all the things we suffer and endure to you. Thank you for calming our fearful hearts with your words of life.

Whatever illness you're facing right now, your own or that of a loved one, keep in mind that God, not your doctor, has the last word. Through God we have unlimited resources to continue to live abundantly and generously all our remaining days, be they many or few. —BRUCE LARSON, AUTHOR, SPEAKER, AND FORMER PASTOR

SEPTEMBER 29
Flying with Faith

> You saw me before I was born. Every day of my life was recorded in your book. Every moment was laid out before a single day had passed. PSALM 139:16

When my mother was diagnosed with cancer and was in Nevada for treatment, the malignancy spread to the brain, and her condition worsened. At the same time, her only son's first baby was born. The doctors told her she couldn't fly because of brain swelling, but neither could she survive the drive to Texas. My mother had had an intense fear of flying, but she wanted more than anything to get back to see that precious grandson, all of her six children, and her twenty-two grandchildren and to worship at her church one more time.

When an elderly minister came to her hospital room that night, he read Psalm 139 aloud. When Mom heard him read verse 16, "Every day of my life was recorded in your book. Every moment was laid out before a single day had passed," she knew she didn't have to fear how many days she had left because even though she was in serious condition, her days were already written in God's book. Those few words set her free to check herself out of the hospital, enjoy the most glorious flight of her life, hold that new grandbaby, and celebrate every day she had left on this earth as a gift from the God who had ordained each moment.

Through this experience I came to a renewed sense of God's sovereignty, whether I'm on the ground, on a jumbo jet flying to Africa in a storm, or on a little prop plane flying over the snow-covered mountains of Wyoming. —CHERI

Lord, I praise you for your amazing sovereignty. I am awed to realize that you not only saw me before I was born but you had already recorded every day of my life. You charted the path ahead of me and laid out every moment of my life before a single day had passed. I don't have to fear because you are with me, before me, behind me, surrounding me. Such knowledge is too wonderful for me!

I was once on a mission plane. That is always such a wonderful experience! In a large plane you forget that you are up high in the air but in a small plane you see the ground beneath you, the sky around you, and you feel really dependent on the Lord's protection. —BRUCE LARSON, AUTHOR, SPEAKER, AND FORMER PASTOR

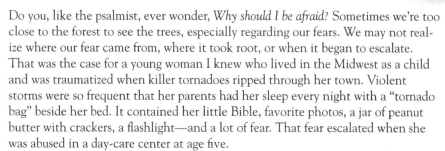

SEPTEMBER 30
Releasing Our Fears to God

I praise God for what he has promised. I trust in God, so why
should I be afraid? Psalm 56:4

Do you, like the psalmist, ever wonder, *Why should I be afraid?* Sometimes we're too
close to the forest to see the trees, especially regarding our fears. We may not realize where our fear came from, where it took root, or when it began to escalate.
That was the case for a young woman I knew who lived in the Midwest as a child
and was traumatized when killer tornadoes ripped through her town. Violent
storms were so frequent that her parents had her sleep every night with a "tornado
bag" beside her bed. It contained her little Bible, favorite photos, a jar of peanut
butter with crackers, a flashlight—and a lot of fear. That fear escalated when she
was abused in a day-care center at age five.

Fear spread to every area of her life: She was afraid of being rejected, of
failing, and much more. For many years she didn't realize why she couldn't trust
her husband or why she worked so hard trying to be perfect or why she couldn't
get emotionally attached to anyone. She kept constantly busy and tried to "buck
up" the way her dad had told her to do when she was scared. But it wasn't until
adulthood that a godly older woman encouraged her to give the Lord her heavy
"tornado bag" full of all those stormy, fear-filled nights and her fear of abuse, failure, and intimacy. As she did, her trust in God began to increase, and gradually,
faith rather than anxiety became the basis for her decisions and the foundation
of her life.

Often we, too, hide our fears behind denial, workaholism, perfectionism,
addictions, or other self-protective strategies. If you suspect fear may be at the root
of some of your problems, write down a list of fears you've struggled with. (You
may need some professional help to sort through your fears.) Ask yourself, *When
did these fears take root?* Ask God to show you what you are afraid of and what's
really behind your fear. As the Holy Spirit helps you to identify those things, give
each fear to God. He will provide all you need to move beyond your fears to a
place of trust where you acknowledge them honestly to God and seek his help.
Is there a specific fear you need to let go of?   —Cheri

Lord, I open my heart to you. Show me the fears I need to
let go of, and please replace them with a deep, abiding trust
in you.

Fear is worry's big brother. If worry is a burlap bag, fear is a trunk of concrete.
—Max Lucado, author and minister

OCTOBER 1

Power in Weakness

> Three different times I begged the Lord to take [the thorn in my flesh] away. Each time he said, "My grace is all you need. My power works best in weakness." So now I am glad to boast about my weaknesses, so that the power of Christ can work through me.
>
> 2 CORINTHIANS 12:8-9

Hannah Hurnard, an English girl who was born in the early 1900s, had such a profound stuttering problem that she didn't shop or ride on a bus without her sister or mother. She was so afraid of being ridiculed that she didn't talk with other children, and consequently, she had no friends. Her whole childhood was spent in loneliness.

With every year, Hannah fell deeper into despair. She became so depressed that she longed to commit suicide. Finally, at the urging of her father, she attended a Keswick evangelistic meeting. There, at age nineteen, she came to Christ and put herself on the altar, stuttering, fears, and all. Her fears didn't evaporate, however. Although she loved God and was growing in Christ, she still struggled with a fear of heights, crowds, the dark, death, and especially speaking in front of a group. And although she asked God to, he didn't take away her stammer; it still hindered ordinary communication with others.

One day Hannah was invited to address a Bible school audience and was overwhelmed by physical panic. But this time, instead of letting her fears paralyze her as they had before, she ignored them, and in obedience to God, she began to speak. She later said that she felt as if Jesus were standing next to her, speaking through and for her. She communicated her message without a stammer or a mistake. Those who heard her that day, and over the years when she served as an evangelist in the United Kingdom and the Middle East, felt that God had given her a gift of speaking. In regular conversation, the stammer remained. But when she spoke in factories, missions, church meetings, or hospitals, it was never apparent. Hannah learned to walk by faith and always go forward as if she could see the Lord next to her, reminding her that his grace was sufficient for her and his strength was made perfect in weakness.   —CHERI

Lord, instead of a platform for fear, may my every weakness be an opportunity to experience your strength, grace, and power.

Take my will, and make it Thine,
It shall be no longer mine.
Take my heart, it is Thine own;
It shall be Thy royal Throne.
—FRANCES RIDLEY HAVERGAL (1836–1879), ENGLISH POET AND HYMN WRITER

To Ponder with a Friend

1. What are the negative or harmful effects of fear in our lives? Have you ever felt the toll of fear in these or other ways? If so, how?

2. Sometimes the origin of our fears is a childhood trauma or event. I shared in the devotional for September 27 how something that happened in my early childhood produced a fear that followed me into adulthood. (See September 30 for another example of this.) Are you aware of a fear from childhood that still affects you today?

3. What fear or fears have you faced and overcome?

4. What truths from this week's devotions can help you to dispel fears related to illness, finances, etc.? Is there a scriptural truth that you sense God nudging you to embrace and apply in this season of your life?

OCTOBER 2

An Extraordinary Ability

> Whatever you do or say, do it as a representative of the Lord Jesus, giving thanks through him to God the Father.   COLOSSIANS 3:17

The church nursery was uncharacteristically quiet this Sunday. Normally, four or five of the infants would be crying as Elise and Marilee wound musical swings, gave bottles, and changed diapers.

But now they had a moment to catch up as they rocked babies. Marilee, a likable, talkative woman, told Elise, "I was at the women's prison again Thursday. That's such a big place, almost eight hundred inmates. It breaks your heart to go there. A new woman who calls herself 'Cat' just sits and stares at me. She doesn't follow along in the text or join the discussions. I asked the chaplain about her, but he didn't have much to say other than she's had a rough life, like most of the others. So I'm asking the Lord to use me to make a difference in her life."

What a wonderful ministry, Elise thought as she snuggled the baby. *But I could never go to a prison and teach the Bible. I don't have special gifts like Marilee.*

Elise doesn't realize that she already is doing something special by lovingly caring for the babies in the nursery. The young mothers can enjoy the worship service, knowing their children are safe. Several even find themselves calmed by Elise's gentleness and try to incorporate the same attitude into their responses at home. But if they tried to express that to Elise, she would brush aside their comments.

To make a difference is our heart's basic cry. But it may take effort on our part to see we do have extraordinary worth not only to God but to those around us. We are prone to think only a dramatic public act of service is important. However, it is more often than not the quiet kindnesses that leave a mark on hearts and lives.   —SANDRA

> Lord, I'm prone to think I can be used by you only in the big moments of life. Help me to recognize small moments as opportunities to make a big difference.

God has always used ordinary people to carry out His extraordinary mission.
—CAROL KENT, SPEAKER AND AUTHOR

OCTOBER 3

One Small Gesture, One Healed Heart

The King will say, "I tell you the truth, when you did it to one of
the least of these my brothers and sisters, you were doing it to me!"
MATTHEW 25:40

Often left alone during childhood, Trisha gleaned her concept of femininity from
the after-school "soaps." When a suicide attempt in college sent her to counseling,
she had to face her longing for motherly direction.

"When my counselor suggested I find someone to take my mother's place
emotionally," she says, "my first thought was, *How do I do that?! Go up to someone in
the grocery store and say, 'Will you be my mother?'* My counselor finally suggested I
move in with his family for a week, so I could see firsthand how his wife mothered
their children.

"That first night, I listened to her going to the children's rooms at bedtime to
pray with them and tuck them in. When she came into my room to say good night,
she actually sat on the bed and offered to pray with me, too. My prayer was pretty
short because I was so choked up; nobody had ever done that with me before, but
when she tucked the blanket around me and bent down to kiss my forehead, I
absolutely lost it. She did more for me in one evening than all of her husband's
counseling ever could."

Just one woman simply kissing a forehead helped to heal a broken heart.

But if we were to ask a number of average women what each of them could
do to influence others, most would be astounded by the question. Often, these are
the women who sit in church week after week and feel because they don't have a
public ministry, they couldn't possibly make a difference. They tend to think along
these lines: *I can't get up in front of people. I don't know enough Scripture. God could
never use me; I'm not a missionary.*

But these same women, just like the rest of us, already are being used by God
every day! As we absorb the Word and spend time with God in prayer, we are
empowered to be a friend, to care, to open our hearts and homes, to put an arm
around weary shoulders in this hurting world.   —SANDRA

Lord, help me to see the difference I make through simple
acts of sharing your love. Remind me to trust that those simple
acts will have great influence and may even reach into future
generations.

Be kind; everyone you meet is fighting a hard battle.
—IAN MACLAREN (PSEUDONYM FOR JOHN WATSON, 1850–1907), SCOTTISH AUTHOR AND
THEOLOGIAN

OCTOBER 4
The Power of a Hug

The wisdom from above is first of all pure. It is also peace loving, gentle at all times, and willing to yield to others. It is full of mercy and good deeds. It shows no favoritism and is always sincere.
JAMES 3:17

Dawn kept blinking as she sorted the files on her desk. *Concentrate*, she demanded. *This is your first day here, and you need this job, remember?*

As if she could forget! She was still reeling from the news her husband had given her several weeks earlier when he confessed he was in love with someone else and wanted a divorce.

Dawn looked up a tracking number, wishing she could find answers to her own challenges as easily. How was she going to stay sane with all she had to juggle? Tears threatened to spill onto her cheeks. *Get with it, Dawn*, she thought. *Nobody cares, anyway.*

As she turned toward her computer, a cheery voice called from the doorway, "Hi! May I bother you? I need some information."

Dawn looked up to see a woman whose smile faded as she saw Dawn's face.

"It looks like you could use a hug!" she said as she held out her arms.

Without hesitation Dawn stood up to lean against the woman's ample shoulders.

Suddenly the woman was praying in Dawn's ear: "Lord, you know all the details causing these tears, so I ask you to wipe them away by letting her know you haven't forgotten her. Help her with her challenges, Lord, and throughout this day and the days ahead, give her a squeeze just as tangible as this one. Let her feel your presence. May she know you are with her."

Only at her "Amen" did the woman release Dawn from the embrace. Then she pulled a folded tissue from her jacket pocket and handed it to the young mother.

Dawn nodded her thanks, then managed to say, "You don't know how much I needed your encouragement just now."

The older woman smiled. "Well, the Lord knew. And he hasn't forgotten you."

Oh, Dawn's unwanted divorce still went through, and she's still juggling all the responsibilities of being a single mother of three active children. But she knows she has enormous value in the eyes of God, all because of a caring woman's hug.
—SANDRA

Lord, I'm often reluctant to offer hugs even though they may be exactly what someone needs. Guide my responses, please. And help me not to be afraid of stepping into another's personal space.

He who receives a good turn should never forget it; he who does one should never remember it. —PIERRE CHARRON (1541–1603), FRENCH PHILOSOPHER

OCTOBER 5
Spring of Faith

[Jesus said,] "Those who drink the water I give will never be thirsty again. It becomes a fresh, bubbling spring within them, giving them eternal life." JOHN 4:14

During the summer of 1944, drought caused wells in Harlan County, Kentucky, to dry up. Nancy Farley, like others, boiled water from the brown Cumberland River.

She also carried water for the flowers her mother-in-law, Mintie, grew. One evening, as a grumbling Mintie poured scant dipperfuls of dirty water over the flowers, Nancy remarked the Lord would send water in his time. Mintie gave an exasperated snort. "You think he's interested in getting us water? I wouldn't count on that."

Nancy nodded. "I don't know how, but he will."

Mintie frowned and turned toward the house.

Their brick home had revealed one flaw when heavy rains fell shortly after its construction: A leak had appeared in the basement's corner. Nancy's husband had dug a three-foot basin to contain the water, but the leak disappeared, and the basin had remained dry for ten years.

One afternoon, Nancy stretched out on the sofa, again praying for rain. Immediately, she jumped up and ran to the basement.

"Come downstairs," she called to her daughter.

Nancy grabbed a chisel and chopped at the bottom of the basin.

"The sofa is over this spot," she told her daughter. "The water's here."

Suddenly the clay grew dark around the chisel, and soon springwater bubbled up. Nancy's shout of joy caused Mintie to come grumbling down the steps. When she saw the basin filling, she gasped.

"The Lord gave us water!" Nancy said. "And you'll never have to pour muddy river water over your flowers again!"

Mintie found her voice. "That will seep out by morning."

"Oh no, it won't! The Lord gave it, and he won't let it run out as long as this family needs it."

Mintie never had to use river water again on her flowers. Not only did the spring supply water for Nancy's family, but there was enough for the neighbors, too. In fact, the spring never went dry as long as a member of the Farley family owned the house.

I know because Nancy was my grandmother. —SANDRA

Lord, when I am discouraged, help me to remember times when you provided for my needs. And help me to share those stories to encourage others.

A man leaves all kinds of footprints as he walks through life. Some you see, like his children or his house. Others are invisible, like the prints he leaves across other people's lives. —MARGARET LEE RUNBECK (1905–1956), WRITER AND AUTHOR

OCTOBER 6
Silent Offerings

Share each other's burdens, and in this way obey the law of Christ.
GALATIANS 6:2

Bobbie stared at the dishcloth in her hand. *How can cotton material be so heavy?* she thought. She dropped it back into the sink. Wiping the countertop wasn't important. Nothing was important now except her children, ten-year-old Marc and five-year-old Lisa.

The house was filled with out-of-town relatives, new friends from church, and coworkers from the university. Someone had finished decorating the Christmas tree in the living room. Bobbie was having trouble sorting through the chaos. How could her husband, her beloved Bill, have died? She still needed him. Their children needed him.

Lisa came into the kitchen just then to tug at Bobbie's hand and pull her into the living room. All Bobbie wanted to do—in fact, had the energy to do—was sit on the sofa with her somber children. But there were phone calls to answer, decisions to make, and visitors to greet.

The only visitor either child was comfortable with was Christine, a young friend whose bright blue eyes sparkled with enthusiasm. Even though she lived across town, she drove over each morning to take Lisa and Marc to the park. On their return, she would bring order to the kitchen. If paper plates were sitting around, she'd gather them and take out the garbage. If dirty dishes were in the sink, she'd wash them.

Some mornings she emptied the clothes hamper, picked up any clothing on the bedroom floors, and took the laundry home. A few hours later, she'd bring the clothing back, clean and folded, and put it where she thought it belonged.

One afternoon, Bobbie noticed their unmailed Christmas cards were still on the corner table. Bill had signed and addressed each one but left them unsealed. He had planned to do that the next day when he added the stamps. Bobbie glanced at them and murmured, "I've got to add a note to those cards." Christine immediately said, "I'll take care of those." She took the stack home, typed a message saying Bill had died December 12, added stamps, and mailed the cards.

That entire week, Christine quietly moved through the house, taking care of practical needs. She was God's messenger, bringing not only order to the household but also peace to a new widow's spirit.   —SANDRA

> Lord, help me to see what needs to be done and jump in and
> do it instead of mouthing a feeble "Call me if you need anything."
> Please love others through me.

Great works do not always lie in our way, but every moment we may do little ones excellently, that is, with great love.
—SAINT FRANCIS OF SALES (1567–1622), BISHOP OF GENEVA

OCTOBER 7
A Powerless Body, Powerful Prayers

The LORD will work out his plans for my life—for your faithful
love, O LORD, endures forever. Don't abandon me, for you made
me.   PSALM 138:8

Wilma's arthritis was especially bad one morning as she limped across the living
room floor to the hospital bed where her paralyzed sister, Adah, lay. For two years,
Wilma had cared for Adah—bathing her, turning her, feeding her, and trying to
rub the achy pain out of a tired body that only vaguely resembled the woman her
sister had once been. The neurological disease had begun as a slowing down that
forced Adah first to a cane, then a walker, a wheelchair, and finally to this bed.

As Adah watched her sister limp toward her, she whispered apologetically,
"I can't do a thing."

Wilma patted her sister's arm, fighting back tears as she said a silent prayer:
Lord, give me something encouraging to say.

The answer came immediately: "You can still pray," Wilma said. "And this
family certainly needs plenty of prayer. Will you do that?"

Adah's eyes glistened as she answered, "I will."

Each morning, Wilma told her sister of particular needs and then would
hear her whispered prayers throughout the day. When a neighbor mentioned his
brother was facing a series of complicated medical tests, Wilma assured him of her
prayers. Then she added, "And I'll tell Adah. She'll pray until we get word about
his condition."

A few days later, the elated neighbor called. The doctors had decided his
brother's problem could be controlled with medication rather than surgery. But he
asked for Adah's continued prayers for the entire family. Later at work, he told
about the woman who prayed all day. Soon even strangers were calling with
requests. And, always, a woman who thought she couldn't do a thing presented
countless needs to the Creator of the Universe.   —SANDRA

> Lord, help me to remember Adah when I'm tempted to feel
> sorry for myself because I think I can't do anything. Help me to
> remember your great power instead of my great lack.

When I think of those who have influenced my life the most, I think not of the
great but of the good.   —JOHN KNOX (1514–1572), SCOTTISH RELIGIOUS REFORMER

OCTOBER 8
Ongoing Prayers

I pray that from his glorious, unlimited resources [God] will
empower you with inner strength through his Spirit.
EPHESIANS 3:16

Daily the phone rang with more pleas for prayers. And Adah, the paralyzed woman
in the Victorian house on Main Street, whispered prayers all day long. Sometimes
a worried mother tried to hold back tears as she asked for prayer for an ill child;
sometimes a child called about an ailing pet. Laid-off workers called about their
need for jobs. Once a gruff husband called, clearing his throat several times before
finally saying well, yes, he, uh, had heard Wilma's sister was a praying woman.
Would she, uh, pray for his marriage?

And as Adah prayed, healing poured into those situations.

The time came, though, when the disease captured her vocal chords. When
Adah didn't whisper her usual morning greeting, Wilma pulled the bed rail down
to hug her.

Then she said, "If you pray only in your mind, the Lord still hears you. When
I give you a request, just blink your eyes to answer. One blink will mean yes, two
blinks will mean no. Do you understand?"

Adah solemnly blinked once. Yes, she understood.

The prayer requests continued for almost another year until God welcomed
Adah into heaven. Sometimes as the relatives talk about those years, they wonder how those prayers affected Adah herself. Even in her pain, she possessed a
graciousness and peace not expected from one suffering so. Perhaps her constant
prayerfulness wrapped her in God's grace. Or maybe just being in God's presence
allowed her to transcend her circumstances. Whatever the reason, God chose to
answer mightily the prayers of someone who could do nothing but pray.
—SANDRA

Lord, help me to remember that your power is waiting to be
released as I pray. I don't understand that, but I thank you.

Certain thoughts are prayers. There are moments when, whatever be the attitude
of the body, the soul is on its knees.
—VICTOR HUGO (1802–1885), FRENCH POET, NOVELIST, AND DRAMATIST

To Ponder with a Friend

1. Do you ever think you can't do anything special? Why or why not?

2. Have you been affected by the faith of another woman? If so, when?

3. Do you ever wonder what "springs" within your own life are waiting to be released?

4. Have you witnessed God's power through prayer? If so, when?

OCTOBER 9
Small Seeds of Compassion

Remember, O Lord, your compassion and unfailing love, which
you have shown from long ages past.   PSALM 25:6

Catherine, a young English girl, came to Christ at age sixteen. Eventually she
married a young minister named William, and together they laid the foundations
for their work among the poor, first in London's East End and later throughout
England. In all Catherine did, her ear was turned to the God of unfailing love and
compassion for whom and how he wanted her to help.

One day Catherine came upon a woman with despair written all over her
face. Many had passed the needy woman, and with all of Catherine's responsibilities that day, it would have been easy for her to rush by.

Speak to that woman, the Lord whispered to her.

She may be intoxicated; don't get involved, Satan said, trying to derail her.

Resisting her fears, Catherine offered the stranger help and quickly discovered the woman lived with an abusive, alcoholic husband. Expressing her empathy
and sorrow, Catherine asked if she could come inside.

"You can't do anything with my husband," the woman said, yet Catherine
followed her into the dark room. The man was draped in a chair, jug in hand.
Catherine went to him and read him the story of the Prodigal Son. Then she earnestly prayed with him. In those moments, the man turned to God, and his family's
life began to be transformed.

As Catherine Booth and her husband, William, continued in their simple
faith, obedience to God, and compassion for people, their example inspired many
others to give themselves to the Lord's service, and The Salvation Army was
founded. Small seeds of compassion grew into a ministry that goes on around the
world, restoring the lives of the poor to this very day.   —CHERI

> Lord of unfailing love and compassion, give me eyes to see
> those who need help, and ears to hear your voice on how to be
> your hands and feet.

Christ has no hands on earth but yours. No feet on earth but yours, no eyes
of compassion on earth but yours. He has no body on earth but yours.
—TERESA OF AVILA (1515–1582), SPANISH MYSTIC

OCTOBER 10
Love Cares

If I gave everything I have to the poor and even sacrificed my body, I could boast about it; but if I didn't love others, I would have gained nothing.   1 CORINTHIANS 13:3

In our self-centered world, we often turn a blind eye and a deaf ear to "inconvenient" needs and people who would interrupt our day. Yet just as Catherine Booth was called to be the hands of Christ to those around her, so are we. God wants each of us to find distinct ways to minister to those in our world—especially the hurting and the poor—and never be too shy to offer what God has given us and share what we know of his love. As we do so, God wants us to be led by his Spirit. We are not to do the expedient thing or offer token help but rather to listen to his voice and follow his direction, doing all that we do in love.

When we try to help others, it can be overwhelming when we see the enormity of human need in our world, and sometimes the idea of responding seems like an exercise in futility. What we're doing seems like only a small drop in a huge ocean of human misery. Mother Teresa encouraged us to see that although the needs are as huge as the ocean, that vast ocean would be diminished without each of our drops. Whether it's tutoring a child from the inner city or reaching out to one broken woman as Catherine Booth did, what matters isn't what big thing we do, but that we do whatever we do out of love.   —CHERI

Savior who gave your all for us, grant me grace to give and serve out of love. May I care more for others than myself and be an instrument of your compassion.

God pays attention to our love. We can work until we drop. We can work excessively. If what we do is not connected to love, however, our work is useless in God's eyes.
—MOTHER TERESA (1910–1997), FOUNDER OF MISSIONARIES OF CHARITY IN CALCUTTA, INDIA

OCTOBER 11
Bosom Buddies

> All praise to God, the Father of our Lord Jesus Christ. God is our
> merciful Father and the source of all comfort. He comforts us in
> all our troubles so that we can comfort others. When they are
> troubled, we will be able to give them the same comfort God has
> given us.   2 CORINTHIANS 1:3-4

When my friend Lisbeth went through a double mastectomy and then chemotherapy, she took to heart this truth that God comforts us in our troubles so that
we can comfort others. She understood it to mean that what she went through
would be wasted if she didn't use her experience to reach out and help others who
suffered what she did. Remembering all the kindness and comfort that helped
her—the Bible verses friends wrote on cards, flowers that cheered her hospital
room, the small pillow with an inspirational quote, the special hat to wear when
her hair fell out—she wanted to give buckets of comfort to others. Since her recovery more than twenty years ago, Lisbeth has individually and personally reached
out to more than 250 women with cancer.

She sends cards of encouragement. She keeps blank journals on hand and
takes one when she visits someone diagnosed with cancer. She encourages them to
write in their personal "Gratefulness Journal" every day, starting with a simple list
of prompts: the phone call at just the moment you're feeling especially down, the
card from your son, the presence of a kind nurse. Even on rough days, the women
can look in the journals and see how God has worked, and that will help them to
pass on God's comfort to others.

She also started a lunchtime support group called "Bosom Buddies." In this
group, which meets monthly, Lisbeth gathers women who are battling or have
survived cancer. They chat, laugh, share what has helped them recover, and most
of all, pass on buckets of comfort. How has God comforted you in your troubles?
How can you pass that comfort on to others?   —CHERI

> Father of all comfort, as you have comforted me in my troubles,
> help me to see how I can comfort others. Open doors for me to
> give out buckets of comfort.

God does not leave us comfortless, but . . . it is in days and nights of sorrow
and trouble that the presence, the sufficiency, and the sympathy of God
grow very sure and very wonderful.
—PETER MARSHALL (1902–1949), SCOTTISH AMERICAN PREACHER AND FORMER CHAPLAIN
OF THE UNITED STATES SENATE

OCTOBER 12
The Least of These

"Lord, when did we ever see you hungry and feed you? Or thirsty and give you something to drink? Or a stranger and show you hospitality? Or naked and give you clothing? When did we ever see you sick or in prison and visit you?" And the King will say, "I tell you the truth, when you did it to one of the least of these my brothers and sisters, you were doing it to me!"   MATTHEW 25:37-40

The AIDS researcher had been working on treatments for HIV for years, yet he realized he'd never seen the human side of the disease. Wanting to help in a more personal way, Richard joined a care team to help local people with AIDS who'd been shunned by their families. Destitute and dying, they were desperate for help.

John, Richard's first care partner, was depressed and belligerent, but Richard had learned not to look for rewards for himself. His effort was all about helping John—visiting him in the hospital, delivering meals, taking him to doctor appointments. When John was about to be evicted, the team offered to help him pack his apartment and move to a friend's place. John didn't have the strength to walk to the car, so they created a makeshift gurney out of blankets for John and headed for the car. As they carried him down the steps to the icy parking lot, each person held up a corner. Richard was concentrating hard to not slip on the ice and drop John. Suddenly, as he looked down at the man they were carrying, something incredible happened. Both of John's bony arms flailed out of the blanket, but his legs were bound together like on a crucifix. John looked up at his helpers with an expression that forever was imbedded in Richard's memory: not a look of fear or pain but of total peace and love. Suddenly this wasn't the face of an AIDS patient but of another man.

When they laid John down in the new apartment across town, Richard noticed a framed picture of Christ over the bed, and that's when it hit him. *Surely I must be imagining things,* he thought. But when he told his minister, who'd also helped carry John, the minister said, "I know what you mean, Richard. I saw it too. The face of Christ."

Though Richard is a scientist and a skeptic who has been put off by church quarrels and power struggles, what he saw on that winter day grounds him, draws him back to God, and continues to renew his faith, even many years later.
—CHERI

Lord Jesus Christ, may I be a servant who feeds the hungry, shows hospitality to strangers, visits those who are sick and in prison, and so encounters you as I am a vessel of your love to them.

Jesus is who we serve in the poor, so as we get closer to them, we get closer to Christ.
—MOTHER TERESA (1910–1997), FOUNDER OF MISSIONARIES OF CHARITY IN CALCUTTA, INDIA

OCTOBER 13
Don't Waste Your Sorrows

To me, living means living for Christ, and dying is even better.
PHILIPPIANS 1:21

This was my older sister Martha's life verse, and when she died in the spring a couple of years ago, we held her memorial service at the "Show Me" Alcoholics Anonymous Club, which was her request. It wasn't a steepled church with cushioned pews and light blue carpet. It was a large, simple room with folding chairs and banners with the Twelve Steps and the Twelve Traditions of AA on the tan walls. But this was the right place to honor my sister.

This was where she had poured out her life. These were the people she loved and cared for year after year, even during the painful months of chemo and radiation when she showed up daily to lead the group or to encourage others in recovery. After the minister's eulogy and music, the microphone was open to anyone who wanted to speak. One by one people shared about the impact of Martha's life on their own. Women told how they had had no hope because of the addictions that were destroying their lives, yet Martha took them by the hand and led them, accompanied by the "Big Book," to sobriety and a restored life. Lonely and broken people told how they had found a friend and a sponsor in Martha. A man shared that the AA group had had balogna sandwiches and chips each Thanksgiving and Christmas until my sister arrived. Every holiday from then on, Martha personally cooked and coordinated a beautiful turkey dinner with all the trimmings for whoever gathered.

Martha's own life hadn't been easy. After a disastrous marriage and a divorce, she lost her children, and her life spiraled into despair and alcoholism. Fifteen years later, she joined the AA program, and it became the doorway to recovery *and* to her ministry. She gave God her broken heart and stayed sober one day at a time for more than twenty-five years. In the process, she held out a hand of compassion to hundreds of people. Martha didn't waste her sorrows; she helped others walk not only through the Twelve Steps to freedom from addiction but into eternal life as well. —CHERI

God of compassion, show me those to whom you would have me reach out. Give me eyes to see and ears to hear the cries of those around me who are crushed in spirit.

Christ can do wonders with a broken heart if given all the pieces.
—ANONYMOUS

OCTOBER 14
Scars of Suffering

Joseph hurried from the room because he was overcome with emotion for his brother. He went into his private room, where he broke down and wept.   GENESIS 43:30

It has been said that the most painful cuts of all are the ones inflicted by those closest to us. Surely Joseph's life exemplified that truth. In Genesis 43, the sight of his younger brother, Benjamin, was a painful reminder of his older brothers' cruel deception. Though God had granted Joseph favor during the dark days of slavery and his years in prison, the young man standing in front of him represented undeniable proof of what Joseph had lost: not only a brother but also his beloved father and his homeland. He had suffered for many years at the hands of wicked people, including those of his own half brothers.

Surely Joseph was tempted to repay them for their evil deeds. He held a position of great power. He could have punished his brothers a thousand times over for their actions. But instead, he blessed them by inviting them into his home for a meal. He devised a plan that would actually save their lives and provide for their families during the famine. And he chose to extend forgiveness, using the results of his suffering to give them what they didn't deserve. When others affect the course of our lives, we, too, face a moment of truth. Although we can't change the past, we have the power to affect the present and the future. We can feed the fires of bitterness, or we can hold our scars before God and ask him for the grace to forgive the past and give out of love's sacrifice.   —CHERI

Lord, I can't change the past, but I give you my hurts and scars, believing that you can bring life out of death and pain.

God will not look you over for medals, degrees, or diplomas, but for scars.
—ELBERT G. HUBBARD (1856–1915), AMERICAN WRITER AND PUBLISHER

OCTOBER 15
The Friendship House

My dear brothers and sisters, be strong and immovable. Always
work enthusiastically for the Lord, for you know that nothing you
do for the Lord is ever useless.   1 CORINTHIANS 15:58

Although her own family had lived comfortably, Louise always had compassion for
those less fortunate. At seventy, she sensed that God wanted her to open a shelter
for homeless people in Portland, Maine. She prayed long and hard about the idea.
Then, with much enthusiasm, she and her husband, Claude, took their life savings
of fifty thousand dollars and began combing Portland for a big house.

Some said, "You're too old to take on a challenge this huge."

"Impossible! You'll never find a house for that money when the market is so
high," real-estate agents told them discouragingly.

But find a house they did—a dilapidated, fourteen-room Victorian structure.
Louise talked the local jail into providing helpers, so the inmates helped restore
ceilings and floors, replace broken windows, replaster, and paint the three-story
house. Louise faced many obstacles, but God carried her and provided. Her artist
husband traded one of his paintings for appliances.

More funds were needed to open the shelter, so Louise went to churches of
all faiths and returned with contributions of blankets, furniture, food, and money.
The night before Christmas Eve in 1985, Friendship House opened its doors to
serve the homeless with a graciousness and love their "guests" had never dreamed
of (they were never called "clients"). Louise enjoyed the most fulfilling years of her
life welcoming people to Christ in their brokenness and need. God carried her as
she carried others, serving until her dying day.

Louise's work was not in vain. Many years after her death, Friendship House
(for men) and Faith House (for mothers and children) have been places of restoration for thousands of homeless people, all because of the dream and compassion
God placed in one woman's heart.   —CHERI

Thank you, God of the impossible, for carrying me as I
help others so that the work I do in your name will never
be useless.

God's care will carry you so you can carry others.
—ROBERT H. SCHULLER, AMERICAN TELEVANGELIST AND PASTOR

To Ponder with a Friend

1. Who is the most compassionate person you have known? How has that person had an impact on you, and what did you learn from him or her?

2. In what ways has God given you the desire, resources, or skills to minister to the needs of others?

3. Sometimes we think that ministries of compassion are for those in full-time service, those with a gift of mercy, or people who have a special calling on their lives. What does Christ say to *all of us believers* about this issue in Matthew 25:31-45?

4. Has the Lord used you as a vessel of compassion to another person or group? If so, what was the outcome?

OCTOBER 16
Fresh Hope

> O LORD, I am calling to you. Please hurry! Listen when I cry to you for help! PSALM 141:1

Carlos stood before the open door of his newly assigned cell. Finally the guard muttered, "Might as well go in and get used to it. You're going to be here awhile."

As Carlos took a deep breath and stepped forward, the guard pulled the barred door shut. For a long moment, Carlos stood in the dim light, looking at the place that would be his home for the next eight to ten years.

The single cot was covered with a coarse gray blanket. A stainless steel sink and commode occupied one corner. At the end of the bed was a small metal stand. Its two drawers would hold the few personal items he was allowed.

Carlos pulled open the top drawer and discovered a tattered Bible. Since he couldn't read, he picked it up merely out of curiosity and thumbed through the pages. Then he thrust the Bible back into the drawer, sank onto his cot, and buried his face in his hands, thinking of the wrong choices that had put him here.

The days that followed were filled with early rising and supervised showers. After breakfast, some of the men on his cell block took court-ordered anger management classes; others worked out in the weight room. Carlos moved slowly, thinking of his wife, Rose, and her constant prayers for him.

One night, several weeks after his arrival, Carlos realized the next day would be his tenth wedding anniversary. *Ten years*, he thought. *I had so many plans back then.*

He remembered how his wife's eyes had shone as she repeated her vows. *Rose deserves so much more*, he thought. *I know she's praying for me, but will she wait for a loser? Our boys need a daddy. They'll be teens before I get out.*

As he thought about his children growing up without their father, just as he had, pain curled around his heart. Crying was not something he wanted to do, but within his mind, he bellowed, *God, if you are real, you've got to help me!*

In the quiet moments that followed, an idea settled into his mind: *Get that old Bible and start at the beginning.* He shook off the command. *I can't read.*

The thought persisted, though. Finally, Carlos stood up, numbly thinking just holding the Bible might offer comfort. He opened the drawer. —SANDRA

Lord, life has taught me prison comes in many forms. No matter my situation, help me to seek your true freedom.

The principles of the Bible are the groundwork of human freedom.
—HORACE GREELEY (1811–1872), AMERICAN JOURNALIST AND POLITICIAN

OCTOBER 17
In the Beginning

In the beginning God created the heavens and the earth.
GENESIS 1:1

Sitting on his prison cot, Carlos opened the Bible to what he later would discover was Genesis 1:1.

In addition to simple words such as *in* and *the*, Carlos knew the word *God*. So he went through the first chapter and counted the number of words he could recognize. As he looked at the other unfamiliar words, he ran his fingers over the print as if willing their meanings to enter through his touch.

The next morning, he saw his cell-block neighbor writing a letter.

"Where'd you get the paper?" Carlos asked.

The man didn't look up. "The chaplain."

Back at his cell with newly acquired paper and pen, Carlos laboriously printed the words *beginning* and *created*, then folded the paper so it would fit in the palm of his hand. On his way to lunch, Carlos showed the paper to the man who had been writing the letter earlier.

"What are these words?" he asked quietly, afraid the man would ridicule him. But the other prisoner merely glanced at the paper and replied just as quietly, "The first word is *beginning*; the other is *created*. Why?"

"No reason," Carlos replied. "Just wondering. Thanks."

Later, in his cell, Carlos looked at the verse again and slowly mouthed, "In the beginning God created." A surge of hope ran through him, and he read the words again: "In the beginning God created."

Those five words were the start of an incredible journey for Carlos as each day he wrote two or three more words on paper and showed them to inmates he knew could read. It took him eight days to get through the thirty-one verses of chapter 1. In the weeks that followed, he not only learned to read but also discovered a hunger for what God might create in his own life.

After serving six years of his sentence, with time off for good behavior, Carlos stepped into freedom and into the welcoming arms of his praying wife. Within a few years, he had earned his GED and graduated from a local Bible school. Today, he and Rose minister in a small church filled with other folks who need the hope of those words written so long ago: "In the beginning God created."   —SANDRA

Lord, create in me a new beginning. You who created the heavens and the earth certainly can create a new being out of who I am. Help me to give you my past, my present, and my future. And help me not to get in your way.

What can be more foolish than to think that all this rare fabric of heaven and earth could come by chance, when all the skill of science is not able to make an oyster.   —JEREMY TAYLOR (1613–1667), ENGLISH CLERGYMAN AND AUTHOR

OCTOBER 18
An Important Match Point

All athletes are disciplined in their training. They do it to win a
prize that will fade away, but we do it for an eternal prize.
1 CORINTHIANS 9:25

Tiffany pushed the locker shut with her tennis racket. The team had been counting on her, and she'd lost the match. If they had won this tournament, they would
have gone on to state. But she'd missed returning that last ball, and it had cost
them the championship. And what aggravated her the most was she could have
cheated and called the ball out of bounds. It had been so close to the line her
opponent couldn't see it clearly. But, instinctively, Tiffany had called it in and had
handed the victory to the opponent.

What a dummy I am, she thought. *Who cares whether anybody lies over the call
of a ball?*

Tiffany couldn't wait to get to her car. She wanted out of this building and
away from these tormenting thoughts.

Just as she arrived at her vehicle, she heard someone call her name. She
turned and saw her coach hurrying to her. When she arrived, she put her arm
around Tiffany's shoulder.

"I was at the doubles court during your last set," she said. "So I didn't see the
final volley, but I heard about it."

Tiffany cringed, but Coach continued. "I want you to know I'm proud of you.
A lesser woman would have lied and called the ball out. The other coach was
standing behind you and saw how close it was. You've got to know, she's really
impressed with your caliber."

Tiffany muttered, "Yeah, thanks, but it cost us the tournament."

Coach nodded. "I know," she said. "But in the greater scheme of things, it's
your honesty that's going to matter, not the tournament. We have to look at ourselves every day in the mirror, and those seemingly little decisions start us on major
pathways. You did the right thing. I'm proud of you."

Coach thumped Tiffany's shoulder. "Now don't forget; everybody's meeting
at my house at six thirty. Come hungry." —SANDRA

Lord, how would I have called the ball that day in the
tournament? I want to do the right thing, but it's easy to give in
when a lot is at stake. I need your help to do the right thing.

Honesty consists of the unwillingness to lie to others; maturity, which is equally
hard to attain, consists of the unwillingness to lie to oneself.
—SYDNEY HARRIS (1917–1986), AMERICAN JOURNALIST

OCTOBER 19
The Biggest Score

Search me, O God, and know my heart; test me and know my anxious thoughts. Point out anything in me that offends you, and lead me along the path of everlasting life.   PSALM 139:23-24

It crossed Tiffany's mind not to go to the after-tournament party, but she figured if Coach had made an effort to encourage her, she ought to be there. At least Coach wouldn't let any of the other players razz her about the call. Coach was always stressing honesty.

Sometimes I wonder what makes her tick, Tiffany thought.

At six thirty, the whole team was gathered in Coach's family room, guzzling colas and trying not to drop pizza cheese on the carpet. Finally, Coach cleared her throat.

"Well, team, we had a good year," she said. "Sure, we didn't make it as far as we had hoped, but we got much further than a lot of people thought we would."

She opened the shopping bag at her feet. "You need to know I'm proud of each one of you," she said. "You've grown this year, and I'm looking forward to watching where life takes you. To close out the season, I have a gift for you."

She reached into the bag and pulled out a New Testament. "This Book contains principles that help me as I try to be a good wife and teacher as well as a good coach," she said as she handed a book to each player. "I hope you'll remember what I've written in the front: 'Love in tennis means nothing. The love in this Book means everything.' If you remember that, you'll have an easier time with all of life's matches."

Tiffany looked at the copy in her hands. *So this is what makes Coach tick,* she thought. Suddenly, she was eager to read it.   —SANDRA

Lord, in this day of so-called political correctness, I'm astonished the coach handed out New Testaments to her players. Help me to walk that fine line between appropriate action and overzealousness. Help me to stop being afraid of the few who would censure my religious freedom.

God proved his love on the cross. When Christ hung, and bled, and died, it was God saying to the world, "I love you."   —BILLY GRAHAM, AMERICAN EVANGELIST

OCTOBER 20
No More Fear

You will be secure under a government that is just and fair. Your enemies will stay far away. You will live in peace, and terror will not come near. ISAIAH 54:14

MiSook clawed the blanket away from her face and awakened with a start. Dazed, she looked around the hotel room, then realized where she was. She was a computer programmer attending a conference in Dallas. No longer was she a frightened eight-year-old back home in Korea. She drew a long breath, remembering those long-ago nights when she watched the shadows while everyone else was asleep. Nighttime had always been difficult, but after her grandmother's death, MiSook wondered what it was like to disappear from the earth. In those moments, her heart would begin to pound so intensely she could hear it beating.

Think of beautiful things, she would tell herself. *Think of Grandmother's garden.* Still, images of two-headed snakes arose each time she closed her eyes. She would hold her breath, wondering if snakes were slithering across the floor toward her sleeping mat.

Where will I be if I'm not here? she asked herself. *Will monsters eat my heart?*

She once tried to explain her terrors to her parents, but they dismissed them.

"Be strong. Control your thoughts so you can control your fate," her father had said.

But the fears had persisted throughout MiSook's childhood. And now they had followed her to Dallas.

She got out of bed and sat near the window. Her roommate was at a stage play with friends. They had invited MiSook, but she had begged off, pleading weariness. She walked to the desk to get stationery to write her parents but changed her mind.

She couldn't write to them. Her parents had always said she had to be in control of her fate. Well, she wasn't in control—not of her fate and not of her nightmares. —SANDRA

Lord, my fears are many. Help me to face them, knowing you are standing by my side. Then help me to give them to you.

Anxiety has its use, stimulating us to seek with keener longing for that security where peace is complete and unassailable.
—SAINT AUGUSTINE (354–430), CHURCH FATHER

OCTOBER 21
Peace

[Jesus said,] "I am leaving you with a gift—peace of mind and heart. And the peace I give is a gift the world cannot give. So don't be troubled or afraid." JOHN 14:27

MiSook looked at the book on her roommate's nightstand. Her roommate read it each morning, and once she had asked MiSook if she knew the Lord.

When MiSook replied, "I worship the Lord Buddha in my ancestors' temple," the roommate had gulped and changed the subject. Now MiSook wondered who her roommate's Lord was. Even back home, she had heard of the secret Great Power. Was that her roommate's Lord?

She sat for a long moment, thinking about her nightmares. Then, timidly, she slid off the chair to kneel and touched her forehead to the carpet.

"Secret Great Power, are you so great you can help me?" she asked. "If you are, I want to know you."

MiSook held her breath, hoping for an audible answer. None came, but as she raised her head, she glanced again toward her roommate's book. *Perhaps the secret Great Power is found in those pages,* she thought.

MiSook thumbed through the book's thin pages until her eyes fell on John 14:27: "I am leaving you with a gift—peace of mind and heart. And the peace I give is a gift the world cannot give. So don't be troubled or afraid."

MiSook was startled by the words. Then, wondering who was speaking, she turned to the beginning of the chapter and read,

> "Don't let your hearts be troubled. Trust in God, and trust also in me. There is more than enough room in my Father's home. If this were not so, would I have told you that I am going to prepare a place for you? When everything is ready, I will come and get you, so that you will always be with me where I am. And you know the way to where I am going. . . . I am the way, the truth, and the life. No one can come to the Father except through me."

MiSook tried to make sense of the phrases: "Trust in God" and "I am the way, the truth, and the life." *The secret Great Power has a name!* she thought.

MiSook continued reading, occasionally glancing at the door. She couldn't wait until her roommate returned; she had many questions. —SANDRA

Lord, I wonder what MiSook's roommate thought when she returned. Was she ready to answer all those questions? Would I have been? Help me to know you well enough to introduce you to others.

Christ is not one of the many ways to approach God, nor is he the best of several ways; he is the only way.
—A. W. TOZER (1897–1963), AMERICAN PASTOR, PREACHER, AND AUTHOR

OCTOBER 22
An Important Meeting

[Jesus said,] "You will stand trial before governors and kings because you are my followers. But this will be your opportunity to tell the rulers and other unbelievers about me. When you are arrested, don't worry about how to respond or what to say. God will give you the right words at the right time." MATTHEW 10:18-20

Caroline stood on the Metro North platform waiting for the 7:02 out of Mount Kisco, New York. She would have a fifty-five-minute ride to Grand Central Station. From there she would attend a meeting she was not looking forward to. The company was going to make changes, and no one at her branch seemed to know what that meant.

When the train arrived, she filed in with the rest of the passengers. Caroline stared out the window, paying no attention as those from the next stops got on and the seat next to her became occupied.

Finally, she pulled her Bible out of her briefcase and turned to Matthew 10:19: "When you are arrested, don't worry about how to respond or what to say. God will give you the right words at the right time."

She smiled. *I'm not going to be arrested,* she thought. *This is just a meeting.*

"Are you reading the Koran?" the woman next to her asked.

"No, I'm reading God's Word," Caroline replied.

"How interesting," the woman replied. "I read the Koran each morning. My day goes better if I start with it."

Caroline closed her Bible and held it out to the young Muslim. "Would you like to have this to compare to the Koran?" she asked.

The woman paused for only a moment. "Thank you. I would," she said. "Where were you reading?"

Caroline opened to Matthew 10, then turned back several pages. "You might like to start here at chapter 1 of Matthew. It begins with the genealogy from Abraham and then goes into the birth of Jesus."

The young woman nodded and began reading.

Caroline smiled. *Why am I worrying about the meeting? It's going to be a piece of cake.* And she settled against the window.   —SANDRA

Lord, I worry about business meetings, family gatherings, church retreats—anything calling for a response from me. Help me to remember that you go before me and will speak through me when I ask.

The Holy Bible is an abyss. It is impossible to explain how profound it is, impossible to explain how simple it is.
—ERNEST HELLO (1828–1885), FRENCH CRITIC AND ESSAYIST

To Ponder with a Friend

1. What Scripture passage has helped you through a tough time?

2. Have the Scriptures ever helped you overcome fear? If so, would you care to share about that with a friend?

3. Have you given a Bible to someone outside your faith circle? If so, what happened?

4. Would you give your personal Bible to a stranger? Why or why not?

OCTOBER 23

Prayer Doesn't Make Any Difference

> Dear friends, if we don't feel guilty, we can come to God with bold
> confidence. And we will receive from him whatever we ask because
> we obey him and do the things that please him.   1 JOHN 3:21-22

One Sunday night three decades ago my husband and I were gathering up our
Bibles after our time with a small group we were leading when Jane, a woman in
the group, approached us.

"You really seem to believe that prayer makes a difference. Like it's powerful
and something really happens when you pray," she said.

"Yes, we do. We've experienced the power of prayer personally, and that's
what we think makes life so exciting," I answered. Holmes and I were fairly new
at this, but we'd seen God work when we prayed.

Jane wasn't alone in wondering if prayer really makes a difference. For many
people, the biggest stumbling block and misconception about prayer is thinking it
doesn't matter if you pray because God's going to do what he's planning to do anyway. But the truth is that in God's design, he works *in cooperation with* praying believers on earth to form the bridge between earth's huge needs and heaven's unending
supply of grace. God isn't short on power! He has an irresistible, inexhaustible supply,
and when we connect our needs (or someone else's) with his might through prayer,
we actually become the conduits through which his power is released.

The results can be dynamic: In inner-city Detroit, four single women started
praying for the teenagers who were terrorizing the neighborhood with their gang
activities. One evening every week they gathered to ask God to bring the teens out
of darkness and into his light. Some time later, they heard that four teenagers had
left a gang. That night they prayed specifically for those kids. Then they felt that
God wanted them to go to the teens' apartment and share the gospel. As the women
sat on the floor with the young people, the four former gang members gave their lives
to Christ. The young women began taking them to church so that they could learn
more about the Bible. Gradually those four teens reached out to others, and through
them, God began to change the whole neighborhood. Do you want to change the
world? Then begin to pray, and watch God release his mighty power.   —CHERI

> Thank you, Father, for the privilege of cooperating with you
> through my prayers to change the world. Holy Spirit, inspire my
> prayers, and pray through me so your power will be released!

Around is a world lost in sin, above us is a God willing and able to save; it is ours
to build the bridge that links heaven and earth, and prayer is the mighty instrument that does the work. If we do our part, God will do his.
—E. M. BOUNDS (1835–1913), METHODIST MINISTER AND AUTHOR

OCTOBER 24

Short Prayers Have Little Impact

"Save me, Lord!" [Peter] shouted.   MATTHEW 14:30

One morning Deana prayed for her daughter Ruth during the few minutes they waited together for her ride to school. Ruth looked up at her and said, "Mommy, I like that! Can you do that for me every day before school and even until twelfth grade and college?" Deana had prayed only a short prayer, but it had a big impact.

One misconception about prayer I often hear is that long, eloquent, and somewhat "pastoral" prayers are the most effective and that in order for us to get any help from heaven, our prayers need to follow a specified form or be of a certain length, and they certainly need to be as well put together as the prayers of Bible study leaders.

But God doesn't look at the size or the eloquence of a prayer. He looks at the heart of the person praying. Jesus said "When you pray, don't babble on and on as people of other religions do" (Matthew 6:7). Make it short, simple, and heartfelt. Today's verse, "Save me, Lord!" which Peter prayed when he was sinking, is just one of the many short prayers in the Bible that were powerfully rewarded. The ten lepers cried out, "Jesus, Master, have mercy on us!" (Luke 17:13). Jabez prayed a short prayer, and God answered in a big way (see 1 Chronicles 4:9-10).

Your prayer might be as small as a sigh that expresses your pain, or two words—*Help, Lord!* or *Thank you!*—and God hears you. Amy Carmichael, who founded Dohnavur Fellowship in India, encouraged others to pray these short "telegraph prayers," and she did so herself. She said we all have a continual need for God's help and he's nearer than we can imagine, so near that a whisper can reach him. So she prayed, "Thy courage, Lord!" or "Thy patience, Lord," when she needed courage or patience. As she practiced this short, simple way of praying, God never disappointed her. Please don't wait until you're "good" at prayer. Pray some short, heartfelt prayers today, and watch the Lord work.   —CHERI

> Lord, I'm thankful that it's not the size of my prayer that counts but the reach of my heart to connect with you and seek your help for myself and others.

Some of our shortest prayers are our most effectual ones.
—RAYMOND EDMAN (1900–1967), PASTOR, DEVOTIONAL WRITER, AND FOURTH PRESIDENT OF WHEATON COLLEGE

God Helps Those Who Help Themselves

[Jesus said,] "Apart from me you can do nothing." JOHN 15:5

Have you ever felt helpless, powerless to do anything about a situation that you wish you could change? If so, then you are on the way to a blessing. Contrary to popular opinion and to what you may have heard countless times, "God helps those who help themselves" is not in the Bible. That phrase implies that self-effort and self-determination are key to connecting with God's grace. But the truth is actually just the opposite.

Prayer isn't for those who've got it all together and are capable, self-sufficient superwomen. Prayer is for the helpless, said Ole Hallesby, who taught that our helplessness can actually open a door to hope. When we understand just *how little we can do* coupled with our faith in *all God can do*, we are opening the door for him to work. When a baby can't say a word, she surrenders to her mom's care even before she can speak: "The little ones pray the best way they know how. All they can do is cry, but you understand very well their pleading. . . . All you need to do is to see them in all their helpless dependence on you, and a prayer touches your mother-heart, a prayer which is stronger than the loudest cry," Hallesby wrote.

It's that very dependence on God instead of your own resources that makes the difference, for when you are helpless, you open your heart and let Christ into your distress. Perhaps, like me, you breathe a sigh of relief to know that your help-lessness doesn't prevent you from coming to God but in fact, *ushers you into his arms.* He stands at the door and knocks. Let me encourage you to leave those "help yourself" efforts behind and invite him in. —CHERI

Jesus, I am weak, but you are strong. I cast off all notion of helping myself and instead come humbly to you.

Prayer and helplessness are inseparable. Only those who are helpless can truly pray.
—OLE HALLESBY (1879–1961), NORWEGIAN THEOLOGIAN AND TEACHER

OCTOBER 26
God Doesn't Want to Be Bothered

[Jesus said,] "Keep on asking, and you will receive what you ask for. Keep on seeking, and you will find. Keep on knocking, and the door will be opened to you." MATTHEW 7:7

"If I pray about a concern over and over, won't God think I'm nagging? And doesn't God just *hate* nagging? My mother taught me never to nag and that we only need to pray once about a need," a young woman told me at a conference.

"If I pray more than once for a request, doesn't it show I don't have faith, so God won't answer?" asked another.

Actually, quite the opposite is true. After Jesus gave his disciples what is known as the Lord's Prayer, he assured them that the Father welcomes prayer, and in today's verse, he encouraged them to be persistent. The verb tense used here for "asking," "seeking," and "knocking" in the original manuscript was present tense, with the sense of *continue and keep on* asking, *keep on* seeking, *keep on* knocking.

Just as an earthly father would never trick his children by giving them a stone instead of a round loaf of bread, or a snake when they wanted fish, our heavenly Father will much more abundantly reward his children spiritually for being persistent and persevering in their petitions. And there is more good guidance here: Although Jesus advised not using vain repetitions (meaning we're not to use prayer as merely a religious ritual or to attract the attention of others), he didn't say we should pray only once. In fact, many stories in the Bible tell of people who prayed multiple times: Elijah prayed seven times for rain before the drops fell from the sky (see 1 Kings 18:41-45). Jesus himself prayed three times in the garden of Gethsemane (see Matthew 26:36-44; Mark 14:32-41). Paul asked the Lord three times to remove the thorn in his flesh (see 2 Corinthians 12:7-8). Perseverance in prayer is never nagging. And just as I love to hear the voices of my own children and grandchildren when they call me, God loves to hear our voices. God wants us to ask him, and keep on asking, for the things on our hearts.   —CHERI

Gracious Father, how wonderful it is to know that you love to hear my voice! Thank you for not looking on my persistent requests as nagging. Help me not to lose heart and give up.

Whether we like it or not, asking is the rule of the kingdom.
—CHARLES HADDON SPURGEON (1834–1892), BRITISH PREACHER

OCTOBER 27

There's a Proper Way to Pray

The Holy Spirit helps us in our weakness. For example, we don't know what God wants us to pray for. But the Holy Spirit prays for us with groanings that cannot be expressed in words.   Romans 8:26

When I'm in our little Dallas apartment, I have a favorite chair to read and pray in. At home in Oklahoma, I love to sit on the sunporch and watch the birds during my morning conversations with God. I kneel when the Spirit nudges me to, pray for loved ones when on the highway, and listen for his direction when I walk the White Rock Trail. Some of the songs I sing to God are prayers, even with my eyes wide open.

Having special "prayer chairs" and formats such as ACTS (Adoration, Confession, Thanksgiving, and Supplication) are helpful, but the good thing about prayer is that the Holy Spirit helps us when we don't even know how to pray. There's no ironclad "right" way or place to pray. Just look at places people prayed in the Bible: on mountaintops, in caves, at sea, in the Temple, on a rooftop (see Exodus 19:23; 1 Kings 19:2-10; Jonah 2:1-9; Luke 1:8-10; Acts 10:9, respectively), and God heard them all. They prayed in different positions, too: with hands raised, kneeling, in bed, while singing, and even without words (see Psalm 28:2; Luke 22:41; Psalm 63:6; Acts 16:25; 1 Samuel 1:12). Wherever you are *now* is the ideal place to pray. If you're at your kitchen table reading your Bible, God would be happy if you started right there. Hands raised or folded, eyes open or closed? In a group or alone? What matters is *that you pray*, for it is the Spirit who will pray through and in you. God wants to hear from you, and he cares more about the condition and openness of your heart than about the place, time, position, or proper format of your prayer.   —Cheri

Lord, please give me a heart that pursues you and a deep desire to pray whenever and wherever I find myself!

Get out of the ruts of prayer. Pray sometimes standing up; then pray kneeling, then pray sitting down, then pray lying down on your bed at night.
—W. H. P. Faunce (1859–1930), American clergyman and educator

You've Got to Be Grown Up to Pray

Jesus called for the children and said to the disciples, "Let the children come to me. Don't stop them! For the Kingdom of God belongs to those who are like these children. I tell you the truth, anyone who doesn't receive the Kingdom of God like a child will never enter it." LUKE 18:16-17

One of the marvelous things about working with children is how their faith can rub off on us if we'll let it. When I pray with kids, I love the simple petitions they offer for friends or family. But they also have a heart for people they've never met who live thousands of miles away. When Hope Smith, a nine-year-old, was researching and writing a report on Mongolia for a homeschool project, one fact she learned about that nation moved her deeply. In a missions magazine she read that there were very few Bibles and that instead of worshiping God, the people knelt at Buddhist altars in their tents.

The fact that more than 98 percent of Mongolians were spiritually lost touched Hope's heart, and she began praying. She asked God to replace the Buddhist altars with Bibles and to send more missionaries. But she didn't stop with a onetime prayer. On her own, she remembered to pray every day for a spiritual awakening for this nation. After two years of prayer, Hope came across another, more recent, article in the missions magazine, this one titled "Hope for Mongolia." The feature story described a revival during which five hundred Mongolians came to faith in Christ as their Savior. Hope felt this was God's way of saying he had heard and answered her prayers.

During the next year those five hundred believers grew to a thousand, and the people started a church called Hope Assembly. More than two thousand Mongols gathered to worship Jesus at their first-ever Christmas service, and this church has planted others in Mongolia.

Do we have to grow up, go to seminary, or gain advanced knowledge for God to use our prayers? Hope's story shows that prayer is *all about* God and that he can use the youngest or least experienced person in our midst to have an impact on the world. —CHERI

Grant me the faith of a child, O Lord. Dispel my doubts, and inspire my prayers.

The prayer of the feeblest saint on earth who lives in the Spirit and keeps right with God is a terror to Satan.
—OSWALD CHAMBERS (1874–1917), SCOTTISH BIBLE TEACHER, YMCA CHAPLAIN IN EGYPT

If Prayers Aren't Answered, They Don't Matter Much

> The earnest prayer of a righteous person has great power and produces wonderful results.   JAMES 5:16

We love to get what we want right now, and as fast as the world and technology move, we often get it. Frozen cuisine we can microwave in moments, instant messaging, overnight mail delivery.

"Well, if my prayers aren't answered at least fairly soon, then they don't matter much, do they?" women have asked me. "Are they just bouncing off the ceiling and not reaching God at all?"

George Müller, who founded orphanages in England in the 1800s, may have wondered about that very question while he prayed *every day* for many years that his five closest friends would come to know God. After five long years of faithful, earnest prayer, George saw his first friend commit his life to Christ. But Müller went on for five more years without seeing answers. Finally, after ten years Friend Number Two surrendered his life to God. After *twenty-five more years of prayer*, two more of the men came to faith. But to Müller's great chagrin, at the end of his life, one last dear friend hadn't yet turned to God. Müller died wanting to see his lifelong friend in heaven. Did all those prayers he prayed for more than fifty years make a difference? It didn't seem so. But at George Müller's funeral, that fifth man surrendered to Christ.

The earnest prayer of a righteous man or woman (that is, one who has right standing with God the Father through Jesus Christ) *does* have great power and wonderful results, even if we have to wait for the answer or see it from heaven.
—CHERI

> I thank you, God, for your intention that no one should perish but that all would come to have eternal life. Help me to continue faithfully in prayer and to wait expectantly and with hope for your answers.

The great point is never to give up until the answer comes. The great fault of the children of God is that they do not continue in prayer; they do not go on praying; they do not persevere. If they desire anything for God's glory, they should pray until they get it. Oh, how good, kind, gracious, and generous is the One with whom we have to do!
—GEORGE MÜLLER (1805–1898), EVANGELIST AND COORDINATOR OF ORPHANAGES IN ENGLAND

To Ponder with a Friend

1. According to Ole Hallesby, what is the value of admitting our helplessness to God? How does helplessness work in the realm of spiritual life?

2. I once heard a woman say that her most powerful prayer was, "Lord, keep me on your path, and help me keep my mouth shut." What is your favorite "short prayer"? What's a short prayer God has answered in a big way, either in Bible times or in your own life?

3. If you were taught a proper or preferred way or formula for prayer, what was it? In what place or position do you most like to communicate with God?

4. What ways have you found to weave prayer into the fabric of your busy days, to pray with children, or to pray with your friends?

OCTOBER 30
The ABCs of Marriage

Submit to one another out of reverence for Christ.
EPHESIANS 5:21

Recently, I stopped by a friend's office and noticed a dozen red roses accompanied by a card that read, "Happy anniversary to my darling wife."

I offered my good wishes and asked how long she'd been married.

Cathy beamed. "Oh, twenty-eight years," she said. "*Fifteen* of the best years of my life!"

It seems for the first thirteen years of marriage, she and her husband just barely stayed together as they battled unfulfilled expectations, misunderstandings, arguments logjammed on unrelated issues, in-law problems—you name it. It wasn't until they realized they were headed for divorce court that they decided they wanted to save their marriage. Once they got serious about working at a good relationship, they transformed the turbulent seas of their marriage into an emotionally safe harbor.

My late husband and I had our share of dumb arguments in our marriage too. But in all that time, I stomped my foot only once to emphasize a point—and stepped right into the dog's dish! Not only did that destroy the spirit of the moment (it's difficult to maintain a self-righteous argument with dog food on your toes), but it also taught us the value of laughter in relieving a tense moment. Along the way, we also learned the ABCs of marriage:

- *Assumptions.* Watch them. If you assume your spouse is going to act a certain way, you're in trouble. Things are never as they first appear, either good or bad.
- *Believe* in your husband. Start with trust; don't wait to make him earn it.
- *Communicate.* We aren't mind readers, so let's not play guessing games.

Cathy and her husband chose to have a happy marriage. That option is open to others as well.   —SANDRA

> Lord, often we miss the joy you have planned because we are looking to another person to satisfy our needs. Help us remember only you can do that.

If you bring your own goals and dreams and self-awareness to a marriage, the other person can be a tremendous source of comfort and support. If you bring to the relationship nothing but your neediness, the balance is off.
—DR. LAURA SCHLESSINGER, SOCIAL AND CONSERVATIVE COMMENTATOR

OCTOBER 31
Reality Appears

Whatever is good and perfect comes down to us from God our
Father, who created all the lights in the heavens. He never changes
or casts a shifting shadow. JAMES 1:17

At the altar, most brides and grooms smile, convinced their marriage will be better
than any others they've witnessed. They repeat the vows the minister offers or
pledge their love from their own hearts, and they mean every word. They open
gifts and look forward to using them in a home filled with joy and peace. Then, full
of confidence, they're off on their honeymoon.

Bless their hearts. Often they have no idea the real work is about to begin.
And all too soon, one or both of them will have this fleeting thought: *Nobody told
me it would be like this!* If they don't know this sentiment crosses everyone's mind at
one time or another, they may be tempted to bail out.

Remember how the fairy tales of our childhood ended with "and they lived
happily ever after"? The stories featured a handsome prince and a beautiful lady
who conquered problems threatening to keep them apart, as if the main struggle
came before the marriage and not during the marriage itself. As children, we
believed once the couple had overcome all the obstacles—Snow White's poison-
apple sleep or Cinderella's wicked stepsisters, for example—the major battles were
won, and the young lovers would live out the rest of their lives in sweet harmony.

But one bright morning, even Snow White must have awakened early, stared
at the slack jaw of her snoring prince, and thought, *Who is this man?* And when
Cinderella was pregnant with Prince Charming's baby, Charming undoubtedly
stared at her swollen feet and wondered what had happened to those once-perfect
appendages that had sent him scouring the countryside for her. But once we understand swollen feet and snoring are normal parts of living "happily ever after," we
can build a solid marriage based on reality and not on a fairy-tale fantasy.
—SANDRA

Lord, help us to see those around us as people who have
the same sensitive hearts as we do. Help us to surround our
relationships with love rather than demands. May we ask for your
direction before we speak or act.

A successful marriage is an edifice that must be rebuilt every day.
—ANDRÉ MAUROIS (PSEUDONYM FOR ÉMILE-SALOMON-WILHELM HERZOG, 1885–1967),
FRENCH WRITER

NOVEMBER 1

Unfulfilled Expectations

You must be holy in everything you do, just as God who chose
you is holy. For the Scriptures say, "You must be holy because I am
holy." 1 PETER 1:15-16

As a teen, Hilda had fairy-tale fantasies about her future marriage. The hope of
meeting someone who would truly love her kept her company during lonely high
school years and carried her into college. By then, she had more sharply defined
her future with her knight in shining armor: He would stroke her hair as he asked
for the details of her day, and they'd prepare dinner together before cuddling in
front of the fireplace.

Then one morning, Jim, one of the new workers, smiled at her across a stack
of trays. At their scheduled break, he introduced himself and asked her name. She
gave it but stammered she'd never really liked it.

He looked bewildered. "That's my grandma's name. She's fun. I bet you are too."

Hilda began to look forward to going to work. As she and Jim continued to
chat on breaks, they discovered they both were business majors and enjoyed tennis.
By the time Jim asked her to attend a campus movie with him, Hilda was smitten.

They married a week after graduation. Quickly they settled into a new apartment and plunged into challenging jobs. But for Hilda, something was missing: Jim
didn't call her in the middle of his busy day, and he didn't stroke her hair when
they sat in front of the fireplace. Their Saturday-morning tennis matches had
given way to errand running and budget balancing. In fact, when she thought
about it, she wondered if they had anything in common. This certainly wasn't the
way marriage was supposed to be.

Meanwhile, Jim was bewildered when Hilda didn't laugh at his silly jokes
anymore and was becoming more and more critical of everything he did. In fact,
come to think of it, she really had changed from the sweet girl who had won him
over with her shy smile.

Had marriage changed them both that much? Of course not. Hilda had married
an image. Jim didn't fit the picture of what husbands, especially hers, were supposed to
do. And Jim had had his own preconceived notions about marriage. Without meaning
to, they had fallen short of each other's expectations. —SANDRA

Lord, when it comes to relationships, help me to look to your
Word for direction rather than to literature, movies, or my own
fantasies. Remind me of your plan: Humans were made to be in
relationship with you and with others.

And they lived happily ever after is one of the most tragic sentences in literature . . .
because it tells a falsehood about life and has led countless generations of people to
expect something from human existence that is not possible on this fragile, failing,
imperfect earth. —JOSHUA LOTH LIEBMAN (1907–1948), AMERICAN RABBI AND WRITER

NOVEMBER 2
Discarding the Fantasy

> The tongue is a small thing that makes grand speeches. But a tiny spark can set a great forest on fire. JAMES 3:5

Marriage is no place for criticism, nagging, or anger, especially if we are trying to use those methods to change our spouses.

It took a Saturday-morning blowup to open Jim's and Hilda's eyes to what they had allowed to happen. It started simply enough: Jim wandered into the kitchen with the newspaper and reached for a cup, only to discover Hilda hadn't made coffee. She was savoring herbal tea as she read the latest women's magazine, coupon-clipping scissors close at hand.

Jim could have greeted his wife, made the coffee himself, and avoided an argument. Instead, he chose to express his disappointment: "Why didn't you make the coffee? You were down here first," he snapped.

"Well, good morning to you, too," Hilda replied sarcastically, and they were off and running into a major argument that included a *Boy, have you changed* and several *You nevers*, followed by Hilda's tearful, "This isn't the way it's supposed to be!"

To Jim's credit, something clicked within him, and instead of storming out to the corner café for coffee and solitude, he chose a wiser route.

"Look, let's start over," he said and backed out of the kitchen. Then, standing in the doorway, he dramatically cleared his throat before saying, "Good morning, dear wife. My, but aren't you the picture of loveliness today as you clip coupons, sparing me from that mundane activity."

Even though Hilda knew he was kidding, she smiled. He stared, then said softly, "I've missed your smile."

They weren't cuddled up before the fireplace, and Jim wasn't stroking her hair. But as Hilda looked at her husband, she decided it was time to learn how to deal with this real man. And that realization provided a new start, one not built on a fantasy. —SANDRA

Lord, show me the little things I can do to let others know I appreciate and love them. Remind me not to be like that dear old husband who loved his wife so much he almost told her!

Let the wife make her husband glad to come home, and let him make her sorry to see him leave. —MARTIN LUTHER (1483–1546), GERMAN REFORMATION LEADER

NOVEMBER 3
Facing Tough Times Together

In his kindness God called you to share in his eternal glory by means of Christ Jesus. So after you have suffered a little while, he will restore, support, and strengthen you, and he will place you on a firm foundation. 1 PETER 5:10

Dick and Rose were grieving the stillbirth of their third child just a month earlier. Now, two friends from their Sunday school class had invited Dick for a round of Saturday golf. Rose insisted he go, saying the sunshine would be good for him.

But within an hour, Dick's friends were helping him back to the house; his mouth was bloody, and several of his teeth were broken. A golfer on another tee had blasted the ball right into the young father's face. This was the final straw for Dick. They'd lost the baby, his wife's health had been threatened, and his job at the steel mill was being phased out. They already had a stack of bills left from the baby's funeral and no insurance to cover this latest trauma.

Dick began a series of painful visits to the dentist. Then repeated infections developed. And each new setback brought fresh despair.

One evening, Dick was slumped forlornly in the living-room chair. Rose watched him for several minutes, then pulled the ottoman close to his side. She took his hand and said, "We're going to make it through this, Dick. We still have two beautiful children and each other. When we started out, we had nothing but an old Chevy with a few wedding gifts on the backseat. If we have to, we can always go back to that point and start over. But with the Lord's help, we will make it."

He looked at her for a long moment, then nodded and even managed a bit of a smile. "You're right," he said. "If it comes to that, we can start over."

They didn't end up having to start over. But the image of their old car reminded them of their commitment to marriage and to each other.   —SANDRA

Lord, sometimes commitment is the only thing that gets us through the tough days. Help us to remember, though, that as we are committed to you first, the other commitments are easier to carry out.

You'll never see perfection in your mate, nor will he or she find it in you.
—JAMES C. DOBSON, PSYCHOLOGIST AND AUTHOR

NOVEMBER 4
Childhood Lessons

When I was a child, I spoke and thought and reasoned as a child.
But when I grew up, I put away childish things.   1 CORINTHIANS 13:11

Newlyweds Kati and Ken were arguing, as usual, about who should take out the garbage. One evening, they continued the argument over coffee with an older neighbor.

"Wait a minute, you two," she said. "When you were growing up, who always took care of the garbage?"

Kati answered, "My dad," just as Ken said, "My mom."

The neighbor smiled. "So you're both assuming your home will be run by the same habits? Sounds like you two need to do a little more talking. Next thing you know, each of you will expect to be visiting your own family at Christmas and carry on exactly the same traditions you had as a child."

As Kati and Ken looked at each other with a you-mean-we've-got-more-work-to-do? look, the neighbor chuckled. "Welcome to real life, kids. Anytime you want to talk, I'm here. My hubby and I had to go through the same thing. Everybody who's trying to build a real marriage does."

Claire had to learn about building a real marriage too. She had grown up in a home where her father was often absent, preferring the company of his bar buddies to his family. Claire often wouldn't see him from Friday after work until late Sunday evening because he would be involved in long poker games.

A few months after Claire married, her husband was invited to participate in an after-work bridge game. He called to let her know he'd be late, but a furious Claire was waiting when he came through the door. She let him know she wouldn't tolerate such activity.

"I know where this stuff leads," she spouted. "You've got a reputation to uphold in our church; you can't get involved like this."

Bewildered, he took in the barrage. What was she talking about? He could have responded in kind, letting her know he'd play bridge anytime he jolly well pleased. But he chose to hear beyond the words.

Finally, as the truth dawned on him, he said gently, "It was just a few guys playing bridge for a couple of hours. No gambling went on, and nobody was drinking or fighting. I'm not your dad, honey."

Startled, she stared at him, understanding at last she had really been yelling at her dad for his long absences years earlier. With tears in her eyes, she leaned against her husband's chest, ready to begin growing up.   —SANDRA

Lord, it is easy to project my childhood hurts onto those around me today. Help me to see situations as they are rather than as I perceive them to be. And help me not to overreact.

Success in marriage is more than finding the right person: it is being the right person.   —ROBERT BROWNING (1812–1889), ENGLISH POET

NOVEMBER 5
Argumentative Kindness

Make allowance for each other's faults, and forgive anyone who offends you. Remember, the Lord forgave you, so you must forgive others.   Colossians 3:13

Francine's childhood taught her to stand toe-to-toe with anybody who thought he was going to out-tough her. But as a wife, she's learning to fight fairly. That means no yelling, slapping, or storming out of the room. She and her husband even hold hands when they're arguing! That simple gesture reminds them they do love each other and are not going to leave each other over this matter.

As one of my widow friends, Peggy, and I talked about what we wish we could do over in our marriages, she said, "I wish I'd known about the talking spoon."

At my confused look, she explained: When a husband and wife are in the midst of a disagreement, it helps if they will use a spoon as a reminder to discuss the issue rather than get sidetracked. The person holding the spoon gets to talk, and the other person must listen and can't interrupt.

When the speaker is finished, he or she asks the other, "Now what did you hear me say?"

The other responds by repeating the main points. The spoon holder may say, "Yes, thank you" or "No, that's not it. This is what I actually said." But each person is heard. What we usually do in a heated argument is try to figure out the next thing we're going to say instead of really listening.

Peggy says her husband was quick witted and gave snappy comebacks that pulled her away from the point she wanted to make. She is convinced if they had used the spoon idea, she would have felt calmer and would have expressed herself better.

So a talking spoon might be a good idea, after all.   —Sandra

Lord, so many arguments seem to be over silly things. And usually the real reason is our fear or our need for control. Help me to find a way to affirm the other person even as we disagree. And help me not to say hateful things that will damage a relationship.

Think of all the squabbles Adam and Eve must have had in the course of their nine hundred years. Eve would say, "You ate the apple," and Adam would retort, "You gave it to me."   —Martin Luther (1483–1546), German Reformation leader

To Ponder with a Friend

1. If you are or have been married, did you have a premarriage fantasy? If you're not married, are you clinging to one?

2. What do you think is the greatest challenge facing today's couples?

3. What assumptions have you noted in other couples?

4. What advice do you have for those pondering marriage?

NOVEMBER 6
The Gift of a Smile

A cheerful look brings joy to the heart.   PROVERBS 15:30

I've discovered there are many ways to give gifts that cost little in terms of time or money but can make a positive difference in another person's life. One of these is the gift of a smile. I once read that Mother Teresa advised her workers to give smiles to at least five people a day because she found it not only brought joy but was good medicine for the people they were caring for. Even when we're working to make someone else's life better, we can get so focused on the *task* at hand that we fail to acknowledge the *person*. When I put Mother Teresa's suggestion into practice and smile at five people a day (even if I get a blank stare in return now and then), I've found it often has marvelous results.

A smile dispels fear, encourages, reduces suspicion, and breaks down barriers. It connects us and brings out the best in the other person. But another great thing is that smiles have a boomerang blessing: The one smiling receives benefits too. Smiling relaxes muscles, dissolves stress, and even boosts circulation. Smiling is worth the little bit of effort it takes to notice others and respond to them kindly.

When I was a teacher, it was easy for me to think that my *instruction* was the best thing I offered my students. But the day I received the following letter, I realized that it was the little things—like the way I looked at kids—that lifted their spirits: "Dear Mrs. Fuller, I really appreciate your coming. I hope you like our classroom! You have taught me so many things about writing, but what I love is the way that you always walk into our class with a smile on your face. Your smile warms my heart and makes me happy. Thank you so much! Sara."

Why not purpose to brighten the day of five people by sharing your smile?
—CHERI

Fill me with joy, Lord, so that I'll have a cheerful look. Let my smile show your love to others, lift their spirits, and be good medicine.

It was only a sunny smile, and little it cost in the giving. But like the morning light, it scattered the night, and made the day worth living.
—F. SCOTT FITZGERALD (1896–1940), AMERICAN WRITER

NOVEMBER 7
The Gift of Believing

Don't let anyone think less of you because you are young.
1 TIMOTHY 4:12

Tommy was in the second grade the year his life intersected with his Aunt Melanie's. His parents had just divorced, and then his dad was shipped to Vietnam. Tommy's mom was battling emotional problems and couldn't care for her two sons, so Melanie, a twenty-one-year-old nurse with no kids of her own, agreed to care for Tommy and his brother while their mother went into treatment.

Melanie didn't look down on her nephews or focus on their problems. Just as Paul, the writer of today's verse, believed in Timothy when he was young and inexperienced, Melanie believed in her nephews and looked for the good in them. She noticed that Tommy had an interest in science and said one day, "Tommy, you'd make a wonderful scientist." At Christmas she bought him a microscope, and for his birthday, a science testing kit. The following year their dad came home from Vietnam and took the boys away. He worked as a long-distance trucker, so the boys were left alone a lot. When Melanie offered them a home, they said their dad needed them.

When the boys were in high school, their father left for good; Tommy's brother flew the coop, and Tommy was left on his own. He worked in a grocery store and lived without running water. But somehow, against all odds, he supported himself, graduated from high school, and managed to put himself through college. Eventually, he completed both a master's degree and a doctorate in microbiology.

After Tommy's graduation, Melanie received a letter from him: "I believed in myself because you believed in me," he wrote. "No matter how tough things got in my life, I knew I could succeed because you said I could."

Today Tommy is a prestigious scientist with a wife and three beautiful children. He didn't get a lot of things he needed when he was growing up, but during that brief year with his aunt, he got the thing he needed most—someone who believed in him.   —CHERI

> Father of love, may my actions, attitudes, and words express belief in others' potential, no matter what obstacles or struggles they face.

The deepest craving in human nature is the craving to be appreciated.
—WILLIAM JAMES (1842–1910), AMERICAN PSYCHOLOGIST, PHILOSOPHER, AND PHYSICIAN

The Gift of a Mentor

> Older women must train the younger women to love their
> husbands and their children, to live wisely and be pure, to work in
> their homes, to do good. TITUS 2:4-5

What a great gift it is when someone a little further along in life mentors you. A mentor is someone who'll teach you all she knows and welcome your questions. She may see talents you don't see in yourself and challenge you to use them. A mentor may be very different from you: ten years older, married or single or widowed. She may see motherhood as her career or be pursuing growth in the corporate world. But she has experience and wisdom that will enrich your life.

Mentors have been very important in my own journey: Kathryn, a freelance writer who taught me much about writing articles effectively and getting published. Patty, a zany, dear friend who encourages me to slow down and take care of myself when I am running on overdrive and doing too much. Through her example, I also learned how to celebrate life in each decade. Flo, forty years older than me, who opened her home for us young mothers and prayed with us for our children and husbands. She also shared stories, over banana bread and tea, of God's faithfulness.

How thankful I am for the women who came alongside me and encouraged me to be the woman God created me to be, just as Titus 2:4-5 describes. How good of God to provide spiritual moms, especially since my own mother died when she was fifty-nine. But he doesn't provide these women in the body of Christ just for me. He has them for you as well—women who can encourage, nurture, and help you learn and grow, whatever your season of life. If you don't have a mentor, ask God to bring such a woman into your life. And be willing to be used in the same way as a blessing to another woman.   —CHERI

> Father, thank you for the mentors you've put in my life. Open my
> mind to their words of wisdom. Open my heart to those I can
> mentor, which will be a double blessing as I bless their lives and
> they enrich mine.

Mentoring moments may not be prolonged, but when someone whom you respect says just the right words or gives you the attention when you need it the most, that effect can last a lifetime.

—BETTY SOUTHARD, AUTHOR, SPEAKER, AND CERTIFIED PERSONALITY TRAINER

NOVEMBER 9
The Gift of Listening

> Understand this, my dear brothers and sisters: You must all be
> quick to listen, slow to speak, and slow to get angry.
> JAMES 1:19

My husband, Holmes, is one of the best listeners I know. But for me, becoming a better listener has been a long journey. I came from a family of five talkative girls and a little brother who had to work hard to get a word in edgewise. So I've been working on the important art of listening for a long while because I've discovered that listening is 80 percent of the communication process. If we miss that part, we have difficulty connecting with those we love.

Listening is more of a challenge for women than for men: The average woman, surveys show, spends about one-fifth of her life talking. On a good day (when she goes to lunch with girlfriends, for example), she may say about thirty thousand words, and that's a lot of talking! Men, on the other hand, have only about ten thousand words they're "burning" to express on a daily basis. When a man gets home from work, most of his words for the day may already have been used up, so he wants quiet. At that point, women are just getting started, so it's no wonder that communication between husbands and wives suffers at times.

The presence of iPod media players, cell phones, and 24-7 TV doesn't help our listening skills. But when we put our hearts into listening, it can create positive connections. When we're really present in the moment, when we let our teenagers (or friends or husbands) finish their sentences instead of doing it for them, when we focus on what they have to say instead of multitasking, they feel valued and loved. Giving not just eye contact but "thought contact" as we have our minds engaged in what the person is saying makes a difference. Somebody once said the fact that God gave us two ears and one mouth should give us a clue about the importance of listening.

To whom could you give the gift of listening today?   —CHERI

Love through me, Lord, and help me to be quick to really listen
to others.

One of the best ways to demonstrate God's love is to listen to people.
—BRUCE LARSON, AUTHOR, SPEAKER, AND FORMER PASTOR

NOVEMBER 10
The Gift of Laughter

For the happy heart, life is a continual feast.   PROVERBS 15:15

With other tired travelers who'd waited at the gate, Amy boarded a packed plane to fly to her mother-in-law's house for Christmas. Her husband and three-year-old daughter were already there, but exams at the high school where she taught were late this year. She was just dozing off when the captain announced that they would be going through turbulence. *No problem*, Amy thought, cinching her belt tighter. But none of them were ready for the terrible jolt when the plane dropped suddenly, leaving most of their stomachs at the previous altitude.

The plane jumped back up, slammed down, then went up again. Anxiety grew as the lights went out and the passengers found themselves sitting in near darkness. Amy gripped her seat and closed her eyes. *Please, Lord, don't make my little girl spend this Christmas without her mother. Please let all of us reach our loved ones safely.*

In the midst of the terror, from somewhere in the front of the plane came a giggle. With the next jolt the giggle turned into a little girl's hearty laugh, and with each subsequent dip and rise, her laughter grew into one of those belly laughs only a child can produce. Row by row the feeling of joy seemed to creep through the plane. Soon the child's laughter infected all the passengers, and their groans turned into *oohs* and *aahs*. People laughed and talked with one another and were almost disappointed when the captain announced they were clear of the turbulence.

The passengers began to quiet down, and then without warning, someone in the dark began to sing, "Silent night, holy night . . ." As strangers joined their voices, peace and hope surrounded them all. Amy never got a glimpse of the laughing little girl, but she was sure God had placed her on that plane to ease their fears. A gift from heaven, you might say.   —CHERI

I can get so serious, Lord. Give me the gift of laughter, and let me give it away to lighten others' loads and ease their fears.

Laughter is God's medicine, the most beautiful therapy God ever gave humanity.
—ANONYMOUS

NOVEMBER 11
The Gift of a Hopeful Word

It is wonderful to say the right thing at the right time!
PROVERBS 15:23

He was a poor wretch of a little boy who didn't seem to have a chance. His father and part of his family had been put in debtors' prison. He'd been able to attend school for only four years, and he was often hungry. Though he had a bright, curious mind and loved to read, when he was only twelve years old, he was put to work in a rat-infested warehouse, putting labels on bottles. He found lodging in a drafty attic room with two other boys from the slums of London.

But he wanted to write. Ideas and imaginative stories filled the boy's mind, and he wrote them down. He mailed his first manuscript in the middle of the night so he wouldn't be laughed at, but story after story came back to him, rejected. When his first story was finally accepted, the publishers paid him nothing. But the editor wrote words praising his work and his potential as a writer. The young man was so overjoyed he wept. The hopeful words from the editor gave him a bright expectation for the future and changed his whole life.

He continued to write in his dark attic room, with even greater desire and enthusiasm. Without that editor's few words of praise, the young man might have stayed in the dark factories, and the world would have been much poorer for lack of his writing.

The boy's name was Charles Dickens, and he became the most famous writer of his era, the genius behind such timeless works as *A Tale of Two Cities*, *Great Expectations*, and *A Christmas Carol*.

With Dickens's amazing creativity, he brought to light the appalling social conditions of the Victorian era, particularly for poor children, and his books have inspired generations throughout the world. Just like the words of that editor, your words are powerful and have a big impact on people. Use them well!   —CHERI

Lord, give me just the right words to speak to people at just the right time to inspire hope. May my words fill their emotional tank and fuel their dreams instead of discourage them.

There is no medicine like hope, no incentive so great, and no tonic so powerful as expectation of something tomorrow.
—O. S. MARDEN (1850–1924), AUTHOR, FOUNDER OF THE MODERN SUCCESS MOVEMENT

NOVEMBER 12
The Gift of Forgiveness

> Forgive us our sins, as we have forgiven those who sin against us.
> MATTHEW 6:12

John's sister was brutally killed by two nineteen-year-olds looking for a car to steal. Both murderers were sent to death row, but that didn't take away John's pain, and it didn't bring his sister back.

Months later there had still been no resolution for John; he was still filled with despair and anger at the cruelties inflicted on his sister. Nothing helped until he began going to the state prison to talk about his sister, listen to the prisoners, and show them forgiveness and hope. These experiences became the seeds for the ministry John started, a ministry in Texas called "Bridges to Life," which brings inmates together with their victims and/or their family members. By meeting in face-to-face conversations with prisoners serving time for crimes like those that claimed the lives of their loved ones, the volunteers let the inmates see the impact of their crimes. They also listen to the prisoners' stories of abusive childhoods and bad choices and offer them the gift of forgiveness. One mother spoke to men who had committed crimes like the one that killed her daughter. She told them that just as she forgave her daughter's killer, in order to heal, they must *forgive themselves* and the people who have hurt them. Seeing the strength the victims found to forgive has given many inmates the strength to take responsibility, ask forgiveness, and forgive themselves. When these courageous men and women who have suffered so much because of crimes against them and their loved ones choose to forgive and foster reconciliation, they don't change the past. But they do change the future—for themselves and for those who committed crimes.

You and I may not face this kind of pain, but to make any real spiritual progress or experience inner health, we, too, need to forgive those who have hurt us. Holding on to grudges, resentment, and anger damages our own souls. But forgiving others frees us of the past and makes room in our hearts for peace and joy.   —CHERI

> Show me those I need to forgive, and flood me with your forgiveness, Jesus. Thank you for forgiving my sins when you died on the cross.

Humanity is never so beautiful as when praying for forgiveness or when forgiving another.   —JOHANN PAUL RICHTER (1763–1825), GERMAN WRITER

To Ponder with a Friend

1. *Merriam-Webster's Collegiate Dictionary*, 11th edition, defines the word *intangible* as "an asset (as goodwill) that is not corporeal." That means it doesn't relate to a physical, material body or thing. This week's theme focuses on intangible gifts we can give and receive, gifts that are quite valuable yet are not available for purchase at a store or shopping mall. By which of the seven intangible gifts discussed this week have you been blessed, and how was that meaningful to you?

2. Share or write briefly about someone who believed in you and your potential (or that you believed in and supported) as Tommy's Aunt Melanie did. What was the result of that belief? Who around you needs you to give the gifts of belief and hope to them?

3. Mentors—trusted counselors or guides—can make a huge difference in our lives. They may walk alongside us for a short season or for many years, but their impact is lasting. The relationship may be informal or work itself out in a more structured church setting, like our relationship with our Bible study teacher, for example. What mentors has God given you? What was the outcome of their mentoring in your life? Who has been a "spiritual mom" to you?

4. To what woman in your neighborhood, office, circle of friends, or church community could you give the gift of mentoring?

5. What was the best gift you ever received?

NOVEMBER 13

Galloping Years

[Jesus said,] "Anyone who becomes as humble as this little child is the greatest in the Kingdom of Heaven. And anyone who welcomes a little child like this on my behalf is welcoming me."
MATTHEW 18:4-5

I'm writing this on a beautiful Colorado morning, sitting in my organized home office. Through the open window I can hear the birds greeting the dawn. My house is clean. My house is quiet. My house is . . . empty.

My children, Jay and Holly, are grown and married, and I'm wondering how we arrived at this stage of life so soon. Wasn't it just yesterday I was in the thick of an endless round of zipping snowsuits, buckling car seats, wiping noses, and bandaging skinned knees? The next week, it seemed, I was helping collect bugs for school projects. But just as I found the calligraphy pen so the children could print the identification labels, they had turned into teenagers and were asking to borrow the car and talking college. One stage had swirled into the next, and suddenly I was an empty nester. Oh, sure, during those busy days of caring for growing children, I couldn't comprehend the chaos would actually end someday.

During one of Jay's college breaks, he helped me clean out an old cedar chest. As I refolded quilts, I heard Jay say quietly, "I remember him as so much bigger."

I turned to see my adult son holding a small blue teddy bear in the palm of his hand. Ah, Blue Bear, his childhood companion. I was looking at my tall, bearded son, but I was *seeing* a little boy clutching his buddy as together they faced a new Sunday school class, a visit to the doctor, or even a noisy car wash.

Somehow the years had spun past me, and the exhausting toddler whom I had lost and chased and scolded was now, along with his little sister, all grown up. Suddenly I wanted another chance at those years. And this time I wanted to do them right. But life doesn't work that way.

Jay put the little fabric bear back into the chest and then helped me fold another quilt. And I sighed, knowing I had realized too late what I'd had in those early years.

What special scenes are you carrying in your head? All too soon they will become special memories sewn forever into your heart.   —SANDRA

Lord, may I not lose today's joy because I am concentrating on today's chaos.

Children must be valued as our most priceless possession.
—JAMES C. DOBSON, PSYCHOLOGIST AND AUTHOR

NOVEMBER 14
Consider the Child

> Direct your children onto the right path, and when they are older,
> they will not leave it.   PROVERBS 22:6

Parents are fond of quoting Proverbs 22:6 to encourage mothers or dads concerned about a wayward teen by reminding them the story isn't over. That verse
is encouraging, indeed. But some Bible scholars interpret the first part of the verse
as "Train a child in *his* way." That is, take an individual child's personality into
account when applying instruction and discipline. After a phone call some time
ago, I decided I rather like that presentation.

During a chat with Dave, a buyer for a major circus based in Florida, our
conversation turned to my favorite animal, the elephant. Soon, Dave remarked
even the best trainer can't *make* a multi-ton elephant do anything and explained
how an animal's performance is the result of mutual respect. The trainers study the
animals before they begin training them, watching for those things the creature
enjoys doing.

Thus, if an elephant likes rolling things with its trunk, it will be the one
chosen to roll the gigantic ball around the ring. If a young lion rolls over a lot, the
trainer will have it do that on command in the act. If a horse doesn't flinch when
it's near the tiger cage, it will be trained to carry the tiger on his back.

I was fascinated with that insight. What if we applied this concept to our
children? What if we knew our offspring so well that instead of demanding they
do things our way, we allowed them to function in their own natural areas of
giftedness?   —SANDRA

> Lord, help me to trust the instincts you have given me when it
> comes to the children within my influence. Help me to know and
> understand their potential and their limitations.

Do not try to produce an ideal child; it would find no fitness in this world.
—HERBERT SPENSER (1820–1903), ENGLISH PHILOSOPHER

NOVEMBER 15
The Pretty Jungle

The Lord said to her, "My dear Martha, you are worried and upset over all these details! There is only one thing worth being concerned about." LUKE 10:41-42

My idea of fun is crossing items off my to-do list. So one long-ago morning, I wanted to get the letters to the corner mailbox before the early pickup. But hurrying two toddlers along a sidewalk teeming with wondrous things was impossible. Jay was fascinated by the ants scurrying across the concrete, so he'd get on his hands and knees to watch them. As his little sister joined him, Jay would chime, in his three-and-a-half-year-old voice, "Holly, look at that ant carrying the big crumb. That's like you or me picking up a car with our teeth."

Holly would coo, "Is that a daddy ant or a mommy ant?"

Where was I? About ten feet ahead, saying, "Come on. Hurry up."

Eventually we made it to the mailbox and then started home. I decided we'd walk through the vacant lot across which the neighborhood children rode their bikes to school. The path through the waist-high weeds would get us home sooner.

Calling, "Hurry up, you two," I rushed across the lot, ignoring the wildflowers on either side of the path. When I reached the sidewalk, I turned back to call another command, but the scene before me stifled the words. Toddler Jay was holding his little sister's hand as they gazed upward at the flowering weeds over their heads. Then, his voice filled with awe, Jay said, "Holly! Look at the pretty jungle!"

That morning I had the good sense to walk back to my toddlers and gather two bouquets of orange black-eyed Susans and blue cornflowers and place them in outstretched little arms. Then I plucked stalk after stalk of the flat Queen Anne's lace, bending forward to point out the black, buglike middle of the flower to my appreciative children. Then I said, "When we get home, I'll show you something magic that flowers do."

As soon as we scurried through the door, I had Jay and Holly sit at the kitchen table while I filled four large, clear glasses with water. As my children watched, I poured a few drops of green, red, blue, and yellow food coloring into separate glasses before adding the flower stalks. Even these years later, I can see those round little faces leaning on chubby hands as we watched the blooms pull the color up into the lacy petals.

To my credit, I didn't accomplish much more that day. Instead, I had begun my journey of slowing down to enjoy my children.   —SANDRA

Lord, show me how to enjoy the world through the eyes of a child. May I see flowers, clouds, and even rocks in new ways. And may I marvel at your most wonderful creation—the child.

A world without children is a world without newness, regeneration, color and vigor.   —JAMES C. DOBSON, PSYCHOLOGIST AND AUTHOR

NOVEMBER 16
Solid Direction

> You will show me the way of life, granting me the joy of your
> presence and the pleasures of living with you forever.
> PSALM 16:11

The visiting missionary held his little girl's hand as they waited for his wife in the foyer of our Michigan church. Various folk stopped to welcome him to the missionary conference, but one man scowled at him.

Instead of saying hello, he flipped the visitor's tie and said, "Kind of fancy for a missionary, isn't it?"

That grumpy man's young son was watching. Is it any wonder the little boy later, in Sunday school class, told the missionary's daughter she couldn't play with the *new* game?

We have heard our values are more *caught* than *taught*. While we nod our heads and pay lip service to that, we sometimes forget its truth in practice. But before we can put our values in front of our children, we have to decide what those values are.

One of my favorite literary scenes with that theme is from *Alice in Wonderland* as the lost, confused Alice asks the Cheshire cat which way she ought to go.

"'That depends a good deal on where you want to get to,' said the Cat.

"'I don't much care where. . . .' said Alice.

"'Then it doesn't matter which way you go,' said the Cat."

And that's just the way it is for us as parents and grandparents, loving aunts and uncles, and concerned neighbors. Before we can decide how to get children on the right path, we have to know where we want them to go.

Do we want children to be kind, generous, and watchful for God's touch each day? Then we have to lead the way.   —SANDRA

> Lord, help me to remember that I'm not just rearing a child; I'm
> shaping a life.

Everything that happens to me can help me along in my Christian life.
—E. STANLEY JONES (1884–1973), THEOLOGIAN AND MISSIONARY TO INDIA

NOVEMBER 17
Creative Strength

Be strong and courageous, all you who put your hope in the LORD!
PSALM 31:24

Does your family have a Plan B for those times when your first choice doesn't work out? During Jay's and Holly's teen years, we joked we had so many things go wrong we also had to have plans C, D, E, F, and sometimes triple Z. But I wanted them to understand, as the old saying goes, "There's more than one way to skin a cat."

As an illustration of that point, I kept a pair of carved, three-inch work shoes on my office shelf to remind us not to give up when our first plans didn't work out. The carver, a Kentucky mountain man named Fred, made several of those shoes perfectly. Once, though, while working on the top of one, he cut too deeply and out snapped a piece of the wood. He started to throw the damaged shoe into the fireplace, but then he looked at it again. Picking up the broken piece, he whittled a little mouse to set inside, just as if the creature had eaten away part of the shoe. Then, with a grin, he put a higher price tag on the item.

Not only did I want my children to have that kind of creative perseverance, but I also wanted them to think ahead. Thus, even in young childhood, they pondered questions such as "What would you do if a man in a car stopped and said he wanted you to help find his puppy?"

As they got older, the questions were more complicated: "What would you do if one of your friends wanted to copy your homework?"

When I was concerned about the peer pressure they would encounter as teens, the questions became "What would you do if a friend offered you some interesting-looking pills at a party?" I also told them until they had enough strength of their own to say no, they were welcome to borrow mine. I even suggested they reply, "Are you kidding? My mom would have a fit. That would not be a pretty sight. You've seen her. She's a big woman."

They'd chuckle, but a preplanned answer gave them an escape if they needed it.

Occasionally they used my strength to help them turn down invitations to places they didn't really want to go. Sometimes I would hear them say during a phone conversation, "I can't go there. My mom would have a fit."

Our children need creative strength for the challenges life will throw at them. And it's up to us as loving parents to help them develop it.   —SANDRA

Lord, help me to have the type of strength my children will want
to borrow as they are developing their own.

A good example is the best sermon.
—THOMAS FULLER (1608–1661), ENGLISH CHURCHMAN AND AUTHOR

NOVEMBER 18
Odd and Even

Don't use foul or abusive language. Let everything you say be good and helpful, so that your words will be an encouragement to those who hear them. EPHESIANS 4:29

As teens, Jay and Holly argued over whose turn it was to sit in the front seat. In fact, they'd sprint the last few yards toward the car door and, according to their self-imposed rule, yell, "Mine!"

But allowing that action merely caused more arguments, so I came up with the idea of "Odd and Even." Jay was born October 5, so on the odd-numbered days of the month, he sat up front. Holly was born February 18, so on the even-numbered days it was her turn to sit up front. We also used that schedule to determine who would be the main dinner-and-cleanup helper. Of course, Jay quickly figured out that the months with thirty-one days gave him an extra day of work. But I quickly pointed out it also gave him the opportunity to sit in the front seat two days in a row.

Somehow we got through those years, and Jay and Holly grew into fine young adults. But they remembered. In fact, once, when they were both home for a college break, we decided to go out to dinner together in my car. As we entered the garage, both suddenly lunged toward the front car door, calling, "Mine!" Jay won, but they took a moment to grin at each other as friends, remembering those long-ago days when they had raced for the front seat in earnest competition.

Now, perhaps the "Odd and Even" system won't work in your family. So come up with an idea that *will*. You might start by asking your children for their ideas. Believe me, there is a solution. —SANDRA

> Lord, help us to seek your answers to typical child-rearing challenges. Then help us to be creative and fun as we apply your solutions to each situation.

Children have never been very good at listening to their elders, but they have never failed to imitate them. —JAMES BALDWIN (1924–1987), AMERICAN WRITER

NOVEMBER 19
Pray the Psalms

> God's way is perfect. All the LORD's promises prove true. He is a
> shield for all who look to him for protection.   2 SAMUEL 22:31

At one time or another, every parent or grandparent worries about the path that
lies before a beloved child. Many of us find it helpful, even comforting, to use the
Psalms as a foundation for prayer. As an example, here's a prayer that follows Psalm
25:16-21: "Lord, turn to [insert child's name] and have mercy, for she is alone and
in deep distress. Her problems go from bad to worse. Oh, save her from them all!
Feel her pain and see her trouble. Forgive all her sins. See how many enemies she
has and how viciously they hate her! Protect her! Rescue her life from them! Do
not let her be disgraced, for in you she takes refuge. May integrity and honesty
protect her, for she puts her hope in you."

During Karen's son Clayton's tough teen years, Karen prayed for her son,
asking God to protect him and love him and gently bring him back into the fold.
She confesses that the word *gently* may have been a problem, as she wondered
whether God really would be gentle or would take him through the deepest pain
to jerk him back.

One of my friends got to the point with her son where she finally prayed,
"Whatever it takes, Lord. If it costs an arm or a leg or an eye, whatever it takes.
But bring him back to you."

Many of us *want* to pray that prayer, and yet we're afraid to and afraid not to.
I once believed I could create a perfect personal world if I worked hard enough at
it. Now I understand my goal is to work hard at turning impossible situations over
to the Lord. He alone can give us the internal peace we long for. He alone can
help us rest in him. The problem is, of course, we want our children to know the
richness of God's peace and power, but we don't want them to have to go through
the painful process. Let's remember the heavenly Father is shaping those we love,
not destroying them, and his allowing them to go through turmoil is part of his
training.   —SANDRA

> Lord, remind me to pray for children and teens in specific ways
> *before* they face the temptations that would pull them into
> wrong choices. And as I pray, remind me you are greater than
> any challenge.

Beware in your prayer, above everything, of limiting God, not only by unbelief,
but by fancying you know what he can do.
—ANDREW MURRAY (1828–1917), SOUTH AFRICAN WRITER AND PASTOR

To Ponder with a Friend

1. What images come to mind as you think of children?

2. What do you wish for the children around you?

3. Have you ever learned truth from a child?

4. What do you want children to see in you?

NOVEMBER 20
What Is Our Center?

> I passed on to you what was most important and what had also
> been passed on to me. Christ died for our sins, just as the Scriptures
> said.   1 CORINTHIANS 15:3

"I am totally centered and focused on motherhood and my two children. I waited
for years to have kids, and they are the most important things in my life," one
woman told me.

"I'm centered on my career; that's what my life revolves around," said
another.

What are you centered on? What's the most important thing in your life? Is
it your ministry? your family? your job? your weight? your finances? The world
offers no end of things that seem all-important to focus on. But Solomon, the one
who had it all, said that the eye never stops desiring and the senses are never satisfied, that undertaking great projects, amassing wealth, and enjoying every pleasure
and relationship will eventually prove meaningless (see Ecclesiastes 1:8–2:11).

The wisdom of Scripture says life isn't measured by what we own (see Luke
12:15). God has given us *life* in his Son. If we center our lives on the things of this
world, they will never satisfy our real longings. Without the salvation that Christ
purchased in his sacrifice on the cross, we will always come up empty because he
designed us for communion with him. He alone can fill our emptiness. Here is the
central truth: Christ died for our sins and in him is new life, life abundant, life
eternal. That's worth centering our lives on.   —CHERI

> Christ Jesus, I want to keep you and your Cross at the center
> of my life. May nothing, no matter how good it is, become
> more important or distract me from pursuing a close, living
> relationship with you.

Every character has an inward spring; let Christ be that spring. Every action has
a keynote; let Christ be that note to which your whole life is attuned.
—HENRY DRUMMOND (1851–1897), SCOTTISH CLERGYMAN AND WRITER

NOVEMBER 21

First Love

[God said,] "I know all the things you do. I have seen your hard work and your patient endurance. . . . You have patiently suffered for me without quitting. But I have this complaint against you. You don't love me or each other as you did at first! Look how far you have fallen! Turn back to me." REVELATION 2:2-5

A Christ-centered life in which God by his Spirit lives in us begins with returning to our First Love. Do you remember your first months after your commitment to Christ or experiencing renewal in your relationship with God? I recall sitting at the kitchen table, reading the Bible and listening for the "marching orders" God had for me that day. Oh, how I enjoyed just being in the Lord's presence. More than anything I desired to know God and do his will. First love, someone once said, is the abandonment of all for a love that has abandoned all. First love means such affection and devotion to Christ that we are willing to abandon everything for him, who laid down his life for us.

Maybe when you first surrendered to Christ, you ran to spend time with him; you read the Bible as if it were a gripping novel, and hung on God's every word. Then you got so busy working hard for the Lord that you lost the freshness of being with him, loving him, and basking in his presence. Other things—people, ministry, career, family—began to take first place instead of Jesus.

In today's passage, God wasn't ignoring the believers' good works. He commended them for their hard work and perseverance, how they patiently suffered without quitting. But he was calling them and all believers throughout history back to a close, loving, and vital relationship with Christ. How encouraging it is that although we can't force this kind of love or fabricate it, the Lord as our Bridegroom is always wooing us and calling us back to his love! —CHERI

Lord, often in my working and doing, I lose the simple devotion of loving you. Thank you for your invitation, "Turn back to me," and for your arms that are open wide to receive me.

I have one passion only: It is he! It is he!
—COUNT NIKOLAUS LUDWIG VON ZINZENDORF (1700–1760), GERMAN REFORMER

NOVEMBER 22
A Spirit-Controlled Life

> Those who are dominated by the sinful nature think about sinful things, but those who are controlled by the Holy Spirit think about things that please the Spirit. So letting your sinful nature control your mind leads to death. But letting the Spirit control your mind leads to life and peace. ROMANS 8:5-6

There are many forces in the world that aim to influence and control our minds: the media, trends, advertising, secular philosophy, and materialism. Yet not one of these brings us real meaning or peace. Through computers, television, malls, and music, the enemy comes in to capture our minds and dominate our thoughts. He strategically plans to draw us away from a single-minded devotion to God. He plants fears and distracts us from what's most important.

Then there's our own sinful nature. If we give in to our "natural" desires, these verses say, they will spiral us downward onto a path that leads to death. The good news is in the next verse: "Letting the Spirit control your mind leads to life and peace." When we turn aside from the world's agenda and yield our minds and personalities to Christ Jesus, the Holy Spirit becomes the major force in our lives. When this is accompanied by a daily, intentional renewal of our minds through God's Word, we gain a quiet confidence that the Lord is in control, no matter what is happening in the world around us. It will also mean that Christ has free rein to live through us and think through us by his Spirit so that others will experience his touch. And the by-products of living this way are life and peace. —CHERI

Lord, I want your Holy Spirit to control my mind, heart, and personality, so I abandon myself to you today. Direct my thoughts, words, and actions. Guard my mind from being controlled by anything that is contrary to your ways. Thank you for setting me free from sin and death through the power of your life-giving Spirit.

If Christ lives in us, controlling our personalities, we will leave glorious marks on the lives we touch. Not because of us but because of him.
—EUGENIA PRICE (1916–1996), AMERICAN AUTHOR

NOVEMBER 23
Christ Lives in Me

My old self has been crucified with Christ. It is no longer I who live, but Christ lives in me. So I live in this earthly body by trusting in the Son of God, who loved me and gave himself for me.
GALATIANS 2:20

In this verse Paul tells us the condition under which Christ lives in us: the death of our old nature or old self. Have you known the frustration of trying to put your selfish nature to death? It's about as easy as putting a fire out with gasoline. We can't destroy the old ways any more than we can make ourselves righteous. And therein lies the key.

Just as the living presence of the Holy Spirit *in* us through Jesus is our righteousness, only he can cause us to become less in ourselves in order that he might become greater in us. Our life in this earthly body must be captured by the revelation of God's unconditional love for us, which is manifested in the life, sacrifice, and resurrection of Jesus. This love is not merely a future hope; it's a present reality that he lives within us *now!* Just as light dispels darkness, Christ in us will displace what needs to die as we focus our attention on him in the best of times and worst of times. He will use our circumstances to bring us to the point where we truly learn to put our trust in him. And that is one of the main purposes of our time on this earth. —CHERI

O Lord, thank you for loving me and giving yourself for me. What an incredible thing that you desire to live through me! May the truth of your words give me the vision to trust you with all that *I* am, so all that *you* are may dwell in me.

God does not expect us to imitate Jesus Christ. He expects us to allow the life of Jesus to be manifested.
—OSWALD CHAMBERS (1874–1917), SCOTTISH BIBLE TEACHER, YMCA CHAPLAIN IN EGYPT

NOVEMBER 24
Living Letters

> Your lives are a letter written in our hearts; everyone can read it and recognize our good work among you. Clearly, you are a letter from Christ showing the result of our ministry among you. This "letter" is written not with pen and ink, but with the Spirit of the living God. It is carved not on tablets of stone, but on human hearts.   2 CORINTHIANS 3:2-3

When U.S. ambassadors leave to serve in a foreign country, they take letters of recommendation and authority to act on their government's behalf. Their words and actions can never be wholly theirs, for they don't act in their own capacities. When they speak, they are messengers for their government. When they act, their deeds reflect on the country they represent.

We are Christ's ambassadors and therefore his messengers. As today's verses express, we are a letter written not with pen and ink but with the Spirit of the living God. Although the words by which we communicate are important, on a much deeper level it is the message of our everyday actions and lives that is most influential. We are the letter from God that people read. When we swerve to cut in front of another driver, give a bad report about another person, or act in an unloving way, we are misrepresenting the Lord. Our words and actions are to reflect God, who lives inside us, to people who may never open a Bible or enter a church. We are living sermons even when we don't say a word, and we may be the *only* message from God people ever "read."

Never forget that you are an ambassador for Christ and a messenger of hope; depend on him, for as Paul said, you can't claim or count anything as coming from you, but *your power and ability and sufficiency are from God* (see 2 Corinthians 3:5). Ask his Spirit to empower you to deliver the Good News with your life and your words.   —CHERI

> Thank you, God, for the privilege of being your ambassador. Give me the power to live so that my life represents you well and the message conveyed to others will be one of love and hope. May my outstretched arms be yours to those I meet.

Christ has no hands but our hands
   To do his work today;
He has no feet but our feet
   To lead men in his way;
He has no tongue but our tongues
   To tell men how he died;
He has no help but our help
   to bring them to his side.
—ANNIE JOHNSON FLINT (1866–1932), AMERICAN POET AND HYMN WRITER

NOVEMBER 25
Complete in Christ

In Christ lives all the fullness of God in a human body. So you
also are complete through your union with Christ, who is the head
over every ruler and authority.   Colossians 2:9-10

How can we be complete, whole, and filled with all the fullness of God when there
are still broken places in our lives?

Have you ever used one of the new "invisible" bandage products? You apply
the liquid on the wound, and it both fills and covers the wound, sealing it so it can
heal from the inside. That's a wonderful object lesson to illustrate what it means to
be complete in Christ. Wherever I am broken, wherever you are broken, Christ is
poured into the wound to make us complete again. We don't have to strive to
make ourselves acceptable to God. We don't have to try to fix ourselves so we'll
appear more spiritual or clean to others. We are accepted in Christ the Beloved.
He has taken all your sins and mine, all our lacks, fears, and sorrows on himself at
the Cross.

So no part of our lives—whether physical issues, emotional issues, spiritual
issues, relational or financial problems—needs to go lacking for his presence, healing, and grace, if we will ask Jesus to fill us. It is by his wounds and suffering that
we are made whole. Whatever is broken or lacking in our lives can be made complete as we invite his presence and power to fill and cover those very weaknesses.

Though we are broken vessels, God loves to heal us and transform us into
something whole and beautiful for his purposes. When we mourn, he pours his
comfort into our hearts. When we are weak, his power strengthens us. God comes
to us in the extremity of our need and makes us not only adequate but complete
and *full* of the very fullness of God.   —Cheri

Thank you, Father, that you have made me complete in Christ.
I ask you to pour your presence into the wounds and broken
parts of my life and make me complete.

Christ is full and sufficient for all his people. He is bread, wine, milk, living waters,
to feed them; he is a garment of righteousness to cover and adorn them; a Physician to heal them; a Counselor to advise them . . . a Treasure to enrich; a Sun to
enlighten; and a Fountain to cleanse.   —John Spenser (1630–1693)

NOVEMBER 26
Christ in You, the Hope of Glory

This is the secret: Christ lives in you. This gives you assurance
of sharing his glory.   COLOSSIANS 1:27

This verse holds the truth that is at the heart of Christianity, the truth that distinguishes it from every other religion in the world. Our faith is not merely some universal spirit of goodness that dwells in humanity, which we must strive to attain. Nor is it a set of rules and regulations, which, if we follow them, will bring us into the union with our Creator for which we all desperately yearn.

The only hope and assurance we have of experiencing such a union or relationship with that object of the human quest is what God himself has given us in Christ. If we have accepted our Maker's gift—forgiveness of sin and new life through Jesus Christ—we can begin to live each day in intimate fellowship with him. That goal is no longer unattainable or hindered by our human weakness. It is an accomplished reality. Because of Christ, God's dwelling place is not somewhere on the other side of the cosmos. He inhabits the spirits of those who have been "born of God," and he continually calls to us, "Come to me."   —CHERI

Dear God, as I walk through this day, may I be aware of the fact that Jesus is actually living in me. Help me to realize that your presence in me is my only life and hope. And in that knowledge, grant me the freedom to enjoy this time together with you.

When Christians say the Christ-life is in them, they do not mean simply something mental or moral. When they speak of being "in Christ" or of Christ being "in them," this is not simply a way of saying that they are thinking about Christ or copying Him. They mean that Christ is actually operating through them; that the whole mass of Christians are the physical organism through which Christ acts—that we are His fingers and muscles, the cells of His body.
—C. S. LEWIS (1898–1963), IRISH WRITER AND LITERARY SCHOLAR

To Ponder with a Friend

1. Think back to the idea behind the devotional for November 20. At different times in your life—college phase, the twenties, career years, early marriage, or parenthood—what was your "center"? What is your "center" in this season, and what caused the shift or change in focus?

2. What do you find are the obstacles to living in such a way that you are truly experiencing Christ as your "First Love"?

3. What broken places in your life or character would you like to ask Jesus to fill and cover with his presence and, thus, to heal?

4. What does it mean to you to be filled and controlled by the Holy Spirit? Could you share a time or experience when you felt the direct guidance of the Spirit?

5. What insights have you gained this week that the Spirit is nudging you to take hold of and apply to your life?

NOVEMBER 27

True Holiday Joy

> While they were there, the time came for her baby to be born. She gave birth to her first child, a son. She wrapped him snugly in strips of cloth and laid him in a manger, because there was no lodging available for them.   LUKE 2:6-7

A few years ago, the arrival of Christmas store displays would signal a marathon tizzy of baking, gift buying, and decorating as I tried to match the images created in the best-holiday-issue-ever women's magazines.

Determined to recreate scenes from "Christmas in Every Room" articles, I fussed over making felt animals, clothespin angels, and gingerbread villages and wondered why my children didn't appreciate the magic I had slaved to create.

I finally had the holiday down to a science, but I met my own imperfection and inadequacies at every turn because my home never looked like the ones in the magazines. The sad truth is, in all that baking and buying, I'd lost sight of the *first* Christmas, in which the world's Savior had arrived as a helpless baby.

As I began to deal with my frustration through honest reflection and prayer, I realized I had been trying to match scenes brainstormed each July by a staff of twelve. Once I let go of the commercialism and concentrated on the reason behind the celebration, I gained freedom from the frenzy, and so did my family.

Now, I'm not suggesting we get rid of every aspect of the season—just those things that make us dread its approach every year, whether it's overspending or baking traditional cookies the adults don't need and the children don't like. Not sure where to start? Ask the youngsters for suggestions. They have wonderful imaginations and will love being invited to think of new ways to celebrate our Savior's birthday. Some families visit nursing homes and allow the children to give out hand-painted pictures to those who are alone that day.

Other friends make a birthday cake for Jesus, allowing the children to decorate it. Jan says their cake, with the lopsided writing and hodgepodge frosting colors, will never win decorating awards, but it's the hit of Christmas dinner, especially when everyone sings "Happy birthday, dear Jesus."

No matter what your family chooses to do, make sure it adds to the joy of this joyful season.   —SANDRA

> Lord, help me to look beyond the frenzy of today's celebration to the joy of your long-ago birth. Help me to embrace what it meant for you to arrive in human form to save us . . . to save me.

Christmas is based on an exchange of gifts: the gift of God to man—his Son; and the gift of man to God—when we first give ourselves to God.
—VANCE HAVNER (1901–1986), PREACHER, EVANGELIST, AND CONFERENCE SPEAKER

Start with Prayer

You haven't done this before. Ask, using my name, and you will receive, and you will have abundant joy.   JOHN 16:24

How did I finally get a handle on the Christmas frenzy, especially since I was addicted to the chaos? Prayer. And the annual gift list was a great place for me to begin.

The year Karen decided to simplify, she made a list of everyone for whom she purchased gifts. At first glance, she was convinced she couldn't cut corners there. But as she prayed with her eyes open, staring at the list, she had the idea to put the names into categories: immediate family, distant relatives, friends, and college chums. Next she circled the names of those she knew looked forward to her gifts. To her surprise, only eleven names remained: immediate family and two great-aunts. She had been buying gifts for the other two dozen merely out of habit.

The morning after Thanksgiving, she wrote twenty-four notes, gently asking to be excluded from gift exchanges and explaining she and her husband had decided to limit their own purchases. No one was hurt by her request. In fact, several expressed gratitude for her initiative.

Other friends have switched from buying for everyone on their lists to drawing names or setting per-gift spending limits.

Again, asking for suggestions from the children may lead to some wonderful ideas. I remember one family whose six-year-old watched his mother pack a box of canned goods for a needy family.

"How come we give food just at Christmas?" he asked.

The mother started to offer an explanation, then figured it would sound hollow. So instead she asked, "What would you like to do for them? Do you have any ideas?"

The first grader thought for a moment, then said, "We could surprise them during the year, too, and even take flowers for the mother's birthday."

By March, they had delivered three more large boxes of food along with the birthday flowers. Soon, the little guy's mother received permission from the deacon board to set up a year-round food pantry in an unused room at their church. Numerous families were helped because of one little boy's idea.   —SANDRA

Lord, help me to take a serious look—through your eyes—at my endless must-do list. If it's correct, give me strength to complete each item. If it's wrong, show me what to delete.

Christmas is not a date. It is a state of mind.
—MARY ELLEN CHASE (1887–1973), TEACHER, SCHOLAR, AND WRITER

NOVEMBER 29
Creative Gifts

Thank God for this gift too wonderful for words!
2 CORINTHIANS 9:15

Our first Christmas in New York, I heard from another mother that the students at the local high school exchanged expensive gifts. I worked on the staff of a national ministry, so our family funds were limited. Still, I didn't want my teens, Jay and Holly, to feel embarrassed about their inability to give gifts to their friends. Thus, one night at dinner we had a discussion about potential solutions. And I reminded them borrowing money from "good ol' Mom" was not an option.

Holly decided to increase her babysitting and watch for sales of items her friends would like. But Jay's work opportunities were limited, so he came up with the masculine version of Christmas baking: ten-inch M&M'S candy cookies wrapped in plastic and tied with a big red bow. He was surprised at what a hit the treats were with his friends, especially the girls, who were intrigued he could cook.

While we were pleased—even relieved—with our creative solutions to the annual challenge, we soon realized others resented our choices. In fact, one friend asked in early December if I was ready for Christmas.

"Oh, yes," I replied.

"I just hate people like you," she said.

I chuckled. "Grace, it's easy to be ready for Christmas when you don't bake, don't buy many gifts, and don't send cards."

Instead of sending Christmas cards, I try to send letters throughout the year. I do resort to group letters for news about a move or important family events, adding a personal note at the bottom. And contrary to what the advice columnists say, I enjoy the group letters filling my mailbox each year.

Instead of baking my former twelve different kinds of cookies these Kentucky hips don't need, I spend that time doing something special with friends. Instead of splurging on a zillion gifts, I often buy items for older folks and donate them through our local senior-citizens' organization. Recently, I wrote to some of my relatives telling them I had purchased gifts for several seniors in our area who didn't have family; I named the specific article we were giving that year, such as "Mary will receive the blue sweater she asked for." Often, I write a check to my favorite Appalachian mission. But always I smile, remembering the One who made my celebration possible. —SANDRA

Lord, I wonder what you think of our frenzy, our long lists, our weariness. Help us to hear and accept your invitation to come away and rest awhile with you.

It is Christmas every time you let God love others through you.
—MOTHER TERESA (1910–1997), FOUNDER OF MISSIONARIES OF CHARITY IN CALCUTTA, INDIA

NOVEMBER 30
Important Coupons

> If you sinful people know how to give good gifts to your children, how much more will your heavenly Father give good gifts to those who ask him. MATTHEW 7:11

The greatest Christmas gift we can give our children is a pleasant memory. So instead of spending our time on gingerbread villages that crumble or our money on expensive toys that break, what if we concentrated on offering an experience that would cause our families to smile, even years from now? My children are married, but they still remember the long-ago December night we impulsively donned snowsuits over our pajamas and ran outside to make snow angels on the front lawn.

One year, Dale, a member of our Sunday school class, realized he didn't really know what was going on with his children. He was determined to find out. His gift to them that year was an envelope of carefully thought-out coupons. His fifteen-year-old son redeemed his coupon for ice fishing within the first week. As he and his son dipped a line through a hole in the ice, they spent two hours talking about the day-to-day challenges of high school. Dale's eight-year-old daughter claimed dinner at her favorite Italian restaurant and let her pizza get cold because she was so busy telling Dad about every classmate.

Dale says he's never been so exhausted in his life, but he's convinced the hours he now spends with his children are a solid investment in their futures.

Dale's gifts reminded me of the coupon books my children made when they were in elementary school. I still have the one Holly gave me when she was seven. In large, wobbly printing, she promised to help me with grocery shopping and dust the low parts of the tables. Maybe I'll redeem those coupons when I'm ninety.
—SANDRA

Lord, guide me in the memories I build into my children. May they think of you when they think of me. And may they smile.

We make a living by what we get;
We make a life by what we give.
—SIR WINSTON CHURCHILL (1874–1965), BRITISH STATESMAN, AUTHOR, AND HISTORIAN

DECEMBER 1

A Surprise Gift

[Jesus said,] "Don't worry about these things, saying, 'What will we eat? What will we drink? What will we wear?' These things dominate the thoughts of unbelievers, but your heavenly Father already knows all your needs." MATTHEW 6:31-32

I knew our first Christmas in Colorado would be meager, but by then we were veterans at slim holiday budgets and creative fun. So, one December morning, I paid the winter taxes, caught up on the bills, bought groceries, and thanked the Lord we still had thirty-four dollars to get us through until the next month's paycheck. I was calm. Even with Christmas, we could coast for four weeks.

Then Jay came home from school. "Mom, don't forget I have to pay my chamber choir fees by this Wednesday."

I held my breath. "How much?"

"Seventy dollars." He dug into a box of cheese snacks.

The kitchen chair squeaked as I sat down. "Well, Jay, it's going to be interesting to see how the Lord works this out."

Holly strolled in then, so I had them both sit with me.

I opened the checkbook, explained the situation and said, "You know the prayer that went into our move. Now we're starting an adventure. We're going to see God work in ways that never would have been possible without this situation. And you may discover the joys of soup beans and corn bread, but God won't let us go hungry. My Kentucky days are going to pay off!"

Jay shook his head at the mention of the beans. "That's carrying a good attitude too far, Mom."

I leaned forward. "I'm telling you we're going to be all right. Remember how England's George Müller and the orphans in his care sat at an *empty* table and thanked God for the food they were about to receive? And before they finished their prayer, a baker was at the door, saying he'd baked too many loaves of bread that morning and could they use them? Or a milk wagon had broken down, and the driver didn't want to take the milk back to the dairy?

"Well, you just wait and see how the Lord takes care of our need for that seventy dollars."

Then we prayed, thanking the Lord for his future provision.

The next day's mail brought an unexpected utility bill—and a rebate check from Allied Van Lines for $254! Christmas would be no problem.   —SANDRA

Lord, thank you for your constant gifts. Help me not to take them for granted but to see your loving hand in each one.

God's gifts put man's best dreams to shame.
—ELIZABETH BARRETT BROWNING (1806–1861), ENGLISH POET

DECEMBER 2
The Thirty-Four-Dollar Christmas

The Savior—yes, the Messiah, the Lord—has been born today in Bethlehem, the city of David! LUKE 2:11

Even these many years later, we still refer to our first holiday in Colorado as the thirty-four-dollar Christmas.

But even with scant funds, it was an incredible day! Our family part of the morning started with our own early gift exchange. Jay gave Holly coupons for math help, and Holly promised to do several loads of his wash. One of Jay's gifts to me was a sheet of tickets for eight long walks, a sacrifice for my nonwalker! One of Holly's gifts was a free-verse poem called "Parenting," in which she thanked me for being "a great person and mom."

Of course I cried when I read it. After all, many parents don't have things like that said about them until they're dead! Not having money forced the kids to come up with creative solutions, a skill I hope they'll carry into their futures.

After our family time, four adults and ten children of "The Lost and Found Gang," as we called ourselves, arrived. Several weeks before, my new friends and I had agreed the only gifts we'd exchange would be acts of service or items we'd made. After a potluck Christmas dinner, we exchanged promises for help with errands, plates of cookies, and delightful homemade gifts, such as avocado candlesticks. It was an incredible day and all because we refused to let a lack of money spoil our fun.   —SANDRA

Lord, thank you for creating good memories and joy out of some of my toughest times. Help me to rejoice during situations instead of waiting until years later.

Give a little love to a child and you get a great deal back.
—JOHN RUSKIN (1819–1900), ENGLISH SOCIAL CRITIC, AUTHOR, POET, AND ARTIST

DECEMBER 3
Imperfect Christmases

Let all who take refuge in you rejoice; let them sing joyful praises forever.   PSALM 5:11

Most families seem to have at least one member who complains about the holiday, complains about gift giving, complains about the relatives. That person, of course, just adds more tension to an already tense time. I heard of one woman who was so tired of her husband's constant complaints about the meaninglessness of Christmas gifts that she took the money she normally would have spent on him and gave it to an inner-city children's group.

On Christmas morning, her husband unwrapped his first present from her, complaining in his usual way, only to discover a picture of a smiling ten-year-old bundled up in a winter coat. Beneath the picture, his wife had written, "This little girl is wearing a new coat given in your name. Merry Christmas."

Suddenly he was interested in opening his other gifts. He was especially pleased with the photo of two brothers clutching their first baseball gloves.

For other families, this is a sad time of year, not because of a relative's grumpiness or disdain for commercialism but because, for whatever reason, there's an empty chair at the table. I understand that feeling; my husband died just after Christmas when our children were ten and eight.

But even before grief softened our celebration, I had stopped trying to outdo the annual magazine holiday spreads. Now, each year I look forward to the celebration. I know I'll never create the Perfect Christmas that still exists in my head. But by remembering the One whose birthday we're celebrating, I can create the perfect Christmas in my heart. And for me, that's a welcome accomplishment.   —SANDRA

Lord, in the midst of my own celebration, help me to be sensitive to those whose hearts are heavy.

The joy that you give to others is the joy that comes back to you.
—JOHN GREENLEAF WHITTIER (1807–1892), AMERICAN POET

To Ponder with a Friend

1. What does Christmas mean to you?

2. Is there anything you'd like to change about the way your family celebrates Christmas?

3. What would your "Perfect Christmas" include?

4. Do you or any of your friends have an empty chair at this year's table?

DECEMBER 4
Christmas Is Coming

> That night there were shepherds staying in the fields nearby, guarding their flocks of sheep. Suddenly, an angel of the Lord appeared among them, and the radiance of the Lord's glory surrounded them. They were terrified, but the angel reassured them. "Don't be afraid!" he said. "I bring you good news that will bring great joy to all people." LUKE 2:8-10

The word *advent* means "arrival" or "coming." The season of Advent is the time on the calendar that begins four Sundays before Christmas and ends on Christmas Day. For centuries, churches have observed Advent as a time of meditation, prayer, and anticipation of the celebration of Christ's birth. It is a time for making room for him in our hearts and homes. To prepare our hearts for Christmas, this week we will look at what really matters in the holiday season and lift our gazes to the best Gift of all.

During the weeks of Advent we are preparing for the holiday by making lists and decorating. We look high and low for just the right sweater or toy for someone special. This gift-search reminds me of a shy student in an African village who was looking for a gift for his missionary-school teacher. He had very little, but he wanted to give something special to show his appreciation. On the day school let out for the holiday, he walked up to his teacher's desk and presented her with a beautiful seashell as his Christmas gift.

The student had walked many, many miles to a special inlet of the ocean, the only place such a shell could be found. "How wonderful that you traveled so far for this lovely present," said the teacher, touched by his generous gift.

At once the student's eyes brightened as he said, "Long walk part of gift." As we plan and get ready for the season, even driving to a special place to get a thoughtful gift or spending hours creating a unique meal to offer friends, let's remember that the preparation we make for family, friends, and those we serve is all part of our gift to them.   —CHERI

Thanks be to you, O God, for your unspeakable, indescribable, incomparable Gift! May we remember always your great gift of Jesus in our giving.

If we think of our heart, rather than our purse, as the reservoir of our giving, we shall find it full all the time.   —DAVID DUNN

DECEMBER 5
The Light of the World

> The Word gave life to everything that was created, and his life brought light to everyone. The light shines in the darkness, and the darkness can never extinguish it.   JOHN 1:4-5

History tells us that five hundred years ago Martin Luther, a leader of the Protestant Reformation, began the custom of decorating Christmas trees. While walking through the dark woods one night near Christmas Eve, Luther gazed at a large evergreen tree illuminated by starlight. He was struck by the beautiful sight, which reminded him of the night the angels appeared to the shepherds in Bethlehem and announced the birth of the Christ child. Luther cut down a small pine tree and brought it home. There he decorated the tree with lit candles, telling his wife and children they represented Christ as the Light of the World.

From that small beginning, the custom of decorating pine trees quickly spread throughout Europe and later to America. People added small candies, cookies, and paper and glass ornaments to the lights on the tree. Whether you and your family go out and cut your tree as Luther did (perhaps not in the forest but at a tree farm), buy one at a local lot in your city, or pull an artificial one down from the attic, as you trim your Christmas tree this year with lights and hang ornaments you've collected, may it be more than just a decoration in the living room. May it shine forth as a symbol of God's light and love in a world that is still desperate for salvation and hope, and may you think about Christ as the One who came into the world to bring God's light into the world's darkness.   —CHERI

Thank you, Father, for the incomparable gift of your Son and for the physical reminders you give us through a simple, decorated evergreen tree that our focus is to be Christ, the Light of the World.

And the light shone even brighter. Will you come and see it? The light is still there although the man, his wife, and the Child are gone. I think the light will shine forever.   —SIDNEY FIELDS (1898–1975), COMEDY ACTOR AND WRITER

DECEMBER 6
The Joy of Giving

You should remember the words of the Lord Jesus: "It is more blessed to give than to receive." ACTS 20:35

Just before Christmas in 1982, Dee and his wife, Margaret, heard from their church that a family in a nearby town was experiencing trouble. In fact, the family's kitchen cupboards were bare.

Dee and Margaret headed for the grocery store and found themselves getting carried away as they went up and down the aisles, putting cartons and boxes in their basket. White Christmases are unusual in Oklahoma, but that night a heavy snow covered the ground as the couple drove to the family's trailer and unloaded the groceries. As they chatted with the surprised parents, the family's four young children were busy inspecting the sacks and putting away boxes of cereal, cookies, and fruit.

Suddenly ten-year-old Charlie bounded from the kitchen with a four-pack of toilet tissue held high in his left hand. "Look, Mom, toilet paper!"

The mother and father shot sheepish glances at their guests as Charlie skipped toward the bathroom to put away the tissue. That was a memorable Christmas.

Dee and Margaret can't remember what gifts they exchanged among their own family members that year. They have no idea whether they received a new tie or necklace, books, or cologne. Nor can they recall what special Christmas concerts or inspiring services they attended. But they'll always remember that scene of the little boy skipping through the house with a pack of toilet tissue held high. The memory never fails to fill their hearts with joy. —CHERI

Father, thank you for the salvation and grace you have given us in Jesus Christ. Help me to rediscover the true meaning of Christmas by giving and serving others with an open heart and open hands.

It is Christmas every time you let God love others through you. . . . Yes, it is Christmas every time you smile at your brother and offer him your hand.
—MOTHER TERESA (1910–1997), FOUNDER OF MISSIONARIES OF CHARITY IN CALCUTTA, INDIA

DECEMBER 7

Silent Night

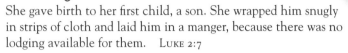

> She gave birth to her first child, a son. She wrapped him snugly in strips of cloth and laid him in a manger, because there was no lodging available for them.   LUKE 2:7

On December 24, 1818, in the small village of Oberndorf, Austria, the whole town was preparing to come to the Christmas Eve service, the highlight of the season. But the parish priest, Father Joseph Mohr, was worried. The chapel organ was broken, and because of the heavy snowfall, the repairman from the next town could not get there to fix it. The service would be devoid of the beloved Christmas music.

For months Father Mohr had attempted to write a new song to express the simplicity and holiness of Christmas, but the words eluded him. That night, as he pondered what to do about the music, he saw someone struggling through the deep snow to get to his cabin. A woman stood before him explaining that a family from over the mountain asked him to come to their home that night to bless their first child, who'd just been born. Bundling up, the priest trudged through the snow. After several hours of walking, he came to the cabin and the most beautiful scene he had ever laid eyes on.

There was the new mother in her bed smiling, as she and the father looked in the little wooden crib that held their newborn son. Father Mohr admired the baby and blessed him and his parents. Then, as he walked home through the silent snow, he thought of how much the little family was like the one in Bethlehem centuries before, on the first Christmas night. The words to a new song flowed as joy filled Mohr's heart, and as soon as he arrived home, he wrote them down. His friend, Franz Gruber, composed the tune to accompany the lyrics, and that evening "Silent Night" was heard for the first time by the congregation at Oberndorf, with Gruber playing a guitar as both men sang.

As you hear or sing this beloved carol this season, may the wonder of that first Christmas fill your heart.   —CHERI

> Lord, grant me the light of Christmas, which is faith; the warmth of Christmas, which is love; . . . the truth of Christmas, which is Christ.   —WILDA ENGLISH

Silent night, holy night,
   All is calm, all is bright
Round yon Virgin Mother and Child.
   Holy Infant so tender and mild,
Sleep in heavenly peace,
   Sleep in heavenly peace.
—JOSEPH MOHR (1792–1848), AUSTRIAN PRIEST AND COMPOSER
—FRANZ GRUBER (1787–1863), AUSTRIAN COMPOSER

DECEMBER 8
A Joyful Single Christmas

[Jesus said,] "I am not alone because the Father is with me."
JOHN 16:32

Beverly has discovered that being *alone* on Christmas Day doesn't have to be *lonely*. With so many good people willing to share the day, she usually has an invitation to go somewhere. As a guest, though, she also realizes that families enjoy being alone for at least part of the morning to open their presents, so she usually declines going until noon. That means she has the morning to herself while her friends have their "family time" together. So she has devised a plan that never fails to give her much joy and beauty on Christmas morning, even though she's spending it by herself. First she sets aside a special time for breakfast, devotions, and reading her Bible. She remembers that just as Jesus was never alone, even though he spent time in the wilderness or all night praying, she is never alone. Fellowship with the Lord fills her to the brim.

Beverly spends the rest of the time reading her Christmas cards, which she saves for the entire month just for Christmas morning. She savors every personal note, photo, and verse on the cards that come from around the country and overseas. Sometimes it takes her two hours to read all the cards, and she certainly can't be lonely with so many good wishes.

This wise woman has found there's just no sense worrying about what she doesn't have when she really has so much! By the time she finishes with the cards, she is in a cheerful mood and is hurrying to get ready to entertain and be entertained on this blessed holiday, her arms full of gifts to give, and her heart full of joy.
—CHERI

Thank you, Lord Jesus, that because of your coming to earth and giving your life, I am never alone, never forsaken, never without the fellowship of your Spirit.

I am not alone at all, I thought. I was never alone at all. And that, of course, is the message of Christmas. We are never alone. Not when the night is darkest, the wind coldest, the world seemingly most indifferent. For this is still the time God chooses.   —TAYLOR CALDWELL (1900–1985), ENGLISH NOVELIST

DECEMBER 9

Gaining Happiness

What do you benefit if you gain the whole world but lose your
own soul? Is anything worth more than your soul?   MATTHEW 16:26

A recent headline questioned, "What Makes People Happy?" The article
explained that psychologists now know it's not great riches that make for happiness but friends and forgiveness. The experts reported that materialism, the gaining of "things"—whether that's the newest cell phone, expensive clothes, or a
luxury car—is actually *toxic* for happiness. In contrast, studies with thousands of
people showed that the happiest people are those who surround themselves with
family and friends, don't care about keeping up with the Joneses, lose themselves
in daily activities and other people, and most important, forgive easily. God told
us these truths a long time ago in his Word: For a man or woman to gain the
whole world and all its riches and things and lose his or her own soul is pointless.

Putting these truths into practice, especially at Christmas, can make a difference in all our lives. When we invited a Chinese student who was attending a
local university but had never been in an American home to join us in celebrating
Christmas, we found that our traditions bloomed with new meaning as we shared
them with a new friend from across the world. We also learned that taking groceries to a needy family and participating in the Angel Tree ministry (Prison Fellowship's outreach to children of prisoners), when our kids got to help pick out the
food, toys, and gifts, brought the biggest blessing because we were involved in
making someone else happy.

Looking at things from God's perspective, in what ways could you pursue
happiness by giving yourself away during this holiday?   —CHERI

> Father God, help me to forget about myself and concentrate
> on you by loving people outside my immediate family as well as
> those at home. Show me a lonely neighbor we could invite or
> someone I can help who can't repay me.

The means to gain happiness is to throw out from oneself, like a spider, in all
directions an adhesive web of love, and to catch in it all that comes.
—LEO TOLSTOY (1828–1910), RUSSIAN NOVELIST AND PHILOSOPHER

DECEMBER 10
A Gift That Endures

I pray for you constantly, asking God, the glorious Father of our Lord Jesus Christ, to give you spiritual wisdom and insight so that you might grow in your knowledge of God. I pray that your hearts will be flooded with light so that you can understand the confident hope he has given to those he called—his holy people who are his rich and glorious inheritance.   EPHESIANS 1:16-18

Perhaps like you, I look for thoughtful gifts and stocking stuffers for family and friends. I wrap the presents to deliver later or to place under the tree. But I've found the greatest gift we can give our loved ones isn't found in a mall or online. We don't have to charge it on plastic. It won't shrink or clutter the closet after the newness wears off. Nor will it end up in next spring's garage sale. This gift is of such enduring quality, it yields the biggest dividends of anything we could give in terms of blessings, fulfillment, and real life for our loved ones long after the Christmas tree is gone and the electronic gadgets are obsolete or broken. In fact, it's even better than leaving large sums of money, a business, or a big house as an inheritance when we die.

The best trust fund of all will come through the gift of our prayers. When we pray for others, we are building them a storehouse of blessing. And when we are no longer on earth to give our loved ones gifts at Christmas, our prayers will keep giving to them. The verses for today are marvelous ones to pray for your children or spouse or other family members.

Look at what this Scripture passage asks God to impart to them: spiritual wisdom and understanding so that they'll know God and grow in him; hearts flooded with light so they will embrace the salvation Christ provided on the cross; and the wonderful future promised them, a rich and glorious inheritance that won't fade away. Let me encourage you to take some pockets of time to pray this special prayer for those you hold dear. Your prayers will make an eternal difference that lasts far beyond the holiday season.   —CHERI

Thank you, Father, that through my prayers I can be a conduit of your grace and blessing to my loved ones. I lift them to you now. . . .

Prayer moves the arm which moves the world, and brings salvation down.
—JAMES MONTGOMERY (1771–1854), ENGLISH POET, HYMN WRITER, AND EDITOR

To Ponder with a Friend

1. What did Christmas and the weeks surrounding it mean to you as a child? What are your favorite holiday memories and traditions?

2. *What really matters* or is most important to you about Christmas? Think about whether or not the things you're planning and doing actually reflect these "what really matters" values. How do your observances of the holiday actually make the season meaningful for you and your loved ones?

3. Consider what you like and dislike about how you observe Christmas:

   • What brings you and your family the most joy?
   • What stresses you out most?
   • What would you like to change?

4. How could you simplify your Christmas holiday observance? Share what has worked and not worked to bring about more simplicity and less hassle and stress.

DECEMBER 11
Searching for Perfection

> There is no one like the God of Israel. He rides across the heavens to help you, across the skies in majestic splendor. The eternal God is your refuge, and his everlasting arms are under you.   DEUTERONOMY 33:26-27

Have you ever been convinced that the *next* job will be perfect? Have you ever fantasized you could find a perfect place here on earth?

So have I. It took me awhile, but I've finally learned heaven is *not* here. Oh, I knew heaven wasn't in Kentucky, because my family had been forced to be part of the 1950s great migration to the industrial North due to the lack of jobs. And because of our northern community's dislike of Appalachians, I quickly learned heaven wasn't in Michigan, either. Then three years after my husband died, I was offered an editorial job with a ministry an hour north of New York City.

I prayed earnestly, determined not to go unless the Lord was the One inviting us. But surely a ministry would provide the perfect setting in which to serve him. So I moved my two young teens and our mellow cat to New York. Those four years in the East were interesting, challenging, and fun, and none of us would have traded the adventure; but we quickly learned heaven was not there.

Next came the invitation to Colorado Springs, the mecca of evangelical Christendom. Again the Lord was leading, so we moved. To my amazement, heaven isn't in Colorado, either. Did we miss the Lord's leading with these moves? Not at all. He had opportunities for us to minister in each location, as well as things for me to learn—including that heaven is only in heaven.

So, in case you're still looking for heaven on earth, let me spare you a great deal of wondering and wandering: Heaven is not here. Yes, keep praying, and be ready to move if God so directs, but don't move expecting everything will be perfect.

Remember, among his many promises, the Lord offers his peace (see John 16:33), his power (see Acts 1:8), his presence (see Exodus 33:14), his purpose (see Ephesians 3:11; Romans 8:28), and . . . *trouble* (see John 16:33). Perhaps we could have done without the promise of trouble, but Jesus rightly warned us. So while disappointments undoubtedly will come, we can meet them in the Lord's strength.

No, heaven is not here, but the Lord is. And what a difference that truth makes!   —SANDRA

Lord, the realization heaven is not here is a reminder my true home is with you in your celestial heaven. Thus, my search for it on earth is but an attempt to erase the homesickness I feel for my true home.

Aim at heaven and you get earth thrown in. Aim at earth and you get neither.
—C. S. LEWIS (1898–1963), IRISH WRITER AND LITERARY SCHOLAR

DECEMBER 12
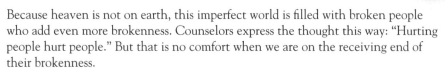

Kenneth

The LORD himself will fight for you. Just stay calm.
EXODUS 14:14

Because heaven is not on earth, this imperfect world is filled with broken people who add even more brokenness. Counselors express the thought this way: "Hurting people hurt people." But that is no comfort when we are on the receiving end of their brokenness.

I remember a student in my fifth-hour class who sat with his arms folded and his beautiful blue eyes cold and defiant. Even the newest teacher couldn't have misunderstood his silent challenge. As a veteran teacher, I knew some rough days were ahead.

Sending up a silent prayer, I introduced myself on that first day of class. I explained the material the course would cover and then called roll. Many of the students preferred a shortened version of their formal names, such as "Chris" instead of "Christopher." But when I read the name of the student with the defiant blue eyes, he insisted I call him by his full name: Kenneth. He quickly informed me only his *friends* called him Ken. Obviously, teachers did not fit that category.

Each class, Kenneth would meet even the simplest request with a penetrating stare and plain stubbornness. He would always wait until everyone else did as I asked before making his move. His smirk let me know he was complying only because he was ready to do so. Occasionally, he would nudge his textbook off the desk and onto the floor when I was trying to make an important point. The noise would disrupt the class, and his sarcastic "Oops!" would always draw a chuckle from the rest of the students.

I tried all the normally successful teaching techniques, hoping Kenneth would take an interest in some part of the course. But I couldn't penetrate the wall around him. Talking privately with him did no good; he merely shrugged, and the same critical eyes would greet me at the next class.

Finally, I concluded only the Lord could change Kenneth's attitude, so I decided to stop worrying about him and start praying. Even so, I wondered what would help dismantle that emotional wall.   —SANDRA

Lord, when I'm hurting, I want everyone around me to know it. And, I confess, I not only envy those who have never known pain but also resent them. Help me to give my pain, whatever its source, to you.

Pain can either make us better or bitter.
—TIM HANSEL, SPEAKER, SEMINAR LEADER, AND AUTHOR

DECEMBER 13
Pain Revealed

Each time [God] said, "My grace is all you need. My power works best in weakness." 2 CORINTHIANS 12:9

One evening, as I poured boiling water into a pitcher I'd used hundreds of times, the tempered glass shattered, pouring scalding water onto my thighs. Even though I received proper medical attention, the burned flesh still formed painful blisters.

The doctor suggested I take time off, but I didn't want to subject a substitute to my unruly student, Kenneth—woe to anyone who called him "Ken."

The next morning as I briefly explained what had happened, I thought I saw compassion in Kenneth's eyes. But I dismissed the unbelievable thought and began the lesson. When the bell rang, I drew a deep breath, relieved class had gone well. As I gathered my books to walk to my next class, I realized Kenneth was standing by my desk.

"I'll carry your stuff," he said. "I have study hall next."

Surely Kenneth was teasing. But as he waited, I handed him my briefcase.

Kenneth walked with me the rest of the week. On Friday, we arrived at my next class before anyone else. Kenneth placed my briefcase on the desk and stood, head lowered. Finally, he looked up.

"What degree are your burns?" he asked quietly.

"Only second degree, Kenneth. Why?" I responded.

"I just wondered," he mumbled. "Mine were third."

So my burns are the reason for his change of attitude, I thought. Aloud I said, "What happened?"

His words tumbled out about the model airplanes he'd loved working on as a seven-year-old, the almost-empty tube of glue he'd held over the candle to soften that last drop for the wing, the flash of flames, the long weeks in the hospital, the numerous cosmetic operations.

To emphasize his final point, Kenneth lifted his chin. "See? They can't get this spot right, even with skin grafts. I still have this scar. Everybody stares at it."

"Kenneth, that is a bad scar," I said. "But I never noticed it until now."

He stared at me. "Really?"

"Yes, really. Your beautiful eyes are what people notice first."

As Kenneth turned to go, he was grinning.

"Kenneth," I called, "thank you for sharing this with me."

"That's okay." He paused. "Mrs. A., you can call me Ken if you want."

I smiled. "I'd like that very much, Ken!"

Healing for both of us was well under way.   —SANDRA

Lord, help me not to spill my pain onto others. And help me to understand and be sensitive to the pain others carry.

Pain is inevitable for all of us, but misery is optional.
—BARBARA JOHNSON (1927–2007), AUTHOR AND INSPIRATIONAL SPEAKER

DECEMBER 14
Strength in a Wheelchair

We [run with endurance] by keeping our eyes on Jesus, the
champion who initiates and perfects our faith. Because of the joy
awaiting him, he endured the cross. HEBREWS 12:2

In this imperfect world, we often think we must have it all together before we can
accomplish good. But what if we didn't wait until we attained perfection before
helping others?

One of my favorite counselor friends, Lon Adams, is paralyzed from the waist
down because of a long-ago operation for a spinal tumor. Recently, after visiting a
friend at the hospital, Lon noticed a man in his early forties studying his wheelchair as they waited for the elevator. Ignoring Lon, the man walked around the
chair several times.

"May I help you?" Lon finally asked.

The man's story tumbled out. His sixteen-year-old daughter had recently
been paralyzed in an automobile accident and would spend the rest of her life in a
wheelchair. Would Lon visit her upstairs and encourage her that life wasn't over?

A few minutes later, Lon wheeled up to the bed of a beautiful young girl who
would never again race after a soccer ball or run to class. He listened as she sobbed
her fears; he answered the family's questions about paralysis and listed things he
could still do, and then he prayed with them. But later he told me he wasn't sure
how much help he'd been to her as he sat in a wheelchair himself.

"That's the whole point," I said. "If I'm ever paralyzed, I want to hear from
someone like you, not some able-bodied person telling me it's going to be all right."

While Lon saw his paralysis as a great weakness limiting his power, the newly
paralyzed teen was encouraged her life could still hold good things. And all because
an imperfect man provided perfect encouragement.   —SANDRA

Lord, help me to concentrate on your strength rather than on
my weakness. Help me to be ready to make others aware of
their abilities rather than ruminate on my own inability.

How many people stop because so few say, "Go!"
—CHARLES SWINDOLL, PASTOR, AUTHOR, EDUCATOR, AND RADIO PREACHER

DECEMBER 15
The Button Jar

Jesus Christ is the same yesterday, today, and forever.
HEBREWS 13:8

The school of hard knocks has taught me that everyone, rich or poor, intelligent or not, attractive or otherwise, carries at least one great hurt. Paige was tall and beautiful and aloof. The other girls in her dorm thought she was stuck-up because she responded to their greetings with only a nod of her head or answered their questions with monosyllables. Gradually, they stopped talking to her. If they had been patient and had attempted to draw her out more, they would have discovered she actually had a severe stuttering problem and didn't trust herself to say more than one or two words.

This is not a perfect world, and we're not perfect people, so why don't we encourage ourselves with the delicious thought it's okay for us to be different, to be who we are? To remind myself of that point, I have on my desk a pint Mason jar filled with antique buttons: tiny pearls from a baby's gown; coarse browns from a work shirt; bright blues from a Sunday dress; and my favorite, a bold red, green, and purple button that may have "fancied up" an otherwise drab winter coat.

I found the jar in an Iowa antique shop at a time when I was feeling drab, imperfect, unimportant. The jar was positioned next to another jar filled with white pearl buttons, but I ignored that first collection and purchased the one filled with contrast and color and imperfect fasteners.

Now whenever I get in one of my "I'm not good enough" moods, I need only to look at my jar of buttons to be reminded how boring life would be if we all were the same. A simple thought, certainly, but one packed with encouragement as I face the challenges of each new day.   —SANDRA

Lord, thank you for your reminders of how precious we are to you. Help us—help me—to live as if we are aware moment by moment of your great love.

Our acceptance before God is complete and secure even when we are disappointed in ourselves.   —ERWIN LUTZER, AUTHOR AND PREACHER

DECEMBER 16

Analyze and Adjust

I will keep on hoping for your help; I will praise you more and
more.   PSALM 71:14

In this imperfect world we often have to analyze a situation and adjust our attitudes and actions. That was yet another truth I had to learn as my daughter, Holly,
approached her wedding.

One evening she lamented her dad couldn't be there to walk her down the
aisle, but she planned to ask her brother, Jay, to escort her. I started praying right
then his public shyness wouldn't keep him from accepting.

The next evening, the three of us gathered in the living room, and Holly
made her request. In anticipation of this, Jay had prepared a little speech, but he
got only as far as "Holly, that's Dad's role—" before she stopped him.

"But Dad's dead!" she wailed.

"Believe me, Holly, I know," he sighed. "What I was going to say is that's
Dad's role, but *Mom* has been the one who's held this family together. *She* should
walk you down the aisle."

Now it was my turn to wail. "But Jay, I want to be the mother of the bride
and watch her come down the aisle," I protested, ignoring the enormous compliment he had just given me.

Poor Jay. He'd grown up with a mother, a sister, and a neutered cat, and now
he had two crying women to calm. Finally, Holly and I blew our noses and settled
down to discuss possible solutions. After my usual prayer of "Lord, please help," we
decided we would "tag team" the event: Jay would walk Holly down the aisle to my
pew; then I would step out and give the declaration in answer to the pastor's question "Who escorts this woman to this man?" (Notice we don't give away women in
this family.)

No, the solution wasn't our first choice, but it was a good one. In fact, as it
turned out, the three of us standing together before the altar provided a visible
symbol of the faith and hope that had carried us through tough times.   —SANDRA

> Lord, it seems as if I'm always having to "analyze and adjust."
> Help me to do that under your direction and with your help.

If God has made your cup sweet, drink it with grace. If he has made it bitter,
drink it in communion with him.
—OSWALD CHAMBERS (1874–1917), SCOTTISH BIBLE TEACHER, YMCA CHAPLAIN IN EGYPT

DECEMBER 17
Sights and Sounds of Heaven

Faith is the confidence that what we hope for will actually happen;
it gives us assurance about things we cannot see.   HEBREWS 11:1

I am convinced of the reality of a heaven beyond this world, not only through my faith, but also because of countless stories of people I've known who have stepped from this world into the next as easily as I walk from one room in my house to another.

I grew up hearing about my great-grandmother's trying to describe the music she was hearing just hours before she died. And my sweet Aunt Adah, who had not been able to speak for the last year of her life, managed to joyfully utter her mother's name as she shed her paralyzed body.

A dear friend kept his eyes closed for several days as he endured cancer's pain. Knowing the end was near, his wife stood on one side of his bed, a daughter on the other. Suddenly, he opened his eyes and turned toward the door with such a look of joy the others turned to see who had just arrived. But no one had entered. They turned back to him and realized he had died in that moment.

A friend related witnessing a similar experience with a church member. John had fallen into a coma, but a few hours later struggled to sit up, extending his arms. His wide-open eyes were focused on a corner of the ceiling. "Halfway there!" he murmured and sank back against his pillow. Several minutes later, he attempted to sit up again, hands outstretched, eyes fixed on that same corner. He lay quietly for some time, breathing roughly. Suddenly he sat fully upright and exclaimed, "Unbelievable!"

His family tried to understand. "What do you see, Dad? What is unbelievable?" But he could not tell them. Whatever he had seen, he was now experiencing.

I know medical people try to explain such experiences as an electrical charge, or some other scientific thing, that flashes through the brain as a person dies. But the night my extended family and I took turns keeping vigil beside my dying father, I pondered Hebrews 12:1, which says we are surrounded by a huge cloud of witnesses. Dad died at home in a bed set up in the living room. Normally that room is always cold in the winter, but that night it was incredibly warm from some invisible, comforting presence.

No, heaven is not here, but I'm grateful it is real and waiting for me and for all who believe in the shed blood of Jesus.   —SANDRA

Lord, thank you for earthly reminders of a heavenly home. Help me not only to be joyful about my future home there but to share that reality with others.

Cultivate a continuous habit of believing, and sooner or later all doubts will vanish in the glory of the absolute faithfulness of God.
—HANNAH WHITALL SMITH (1832–1911), QUAKER LAY SPEAKER AND AUTHOR

To Ponder with a Friend

1. Have you ever looked for heaven here on earth?

2. Have you ever been perfectly encouraged by an imperfect person?

3. Have you ever been surprised at how you encouraged someone else?

4. What is your concept of the celestial heaven?

DECEMBER 18
A Heart of Worship

God has said, "I will never fail you. I will never abandon you." So
we can say with confidence, "The LORD is my helper, so I will have
no fear. What can mere people do to me?"   HEBREWS 13:5-6

Over salad and soup one winter day, an elderly missionary named Anne shared
with me her experiences in a Japanese prison camp following nine years of service
with the China Inland Mission. She spent three and a half years as a prisoner,
during which she endured near starvation, bitter cold in winter, and scorching heat
in summer. Cruelty, rats, disease, and death were all around her, yet Anne didn't
dwell on the horrors or the suffering.

Instead, she told me, she experienced God's constant presence; led others in
the prison camp to Christ; gave the Lord every burden, worry, and fear; and saw
him work time after time. Anne seemed to possess a quiet assurance that she could
absolutely trust God because she knew his character and knew that he was worthy
of her trust.

Anne could have been overwhelmed by despair. But she didn't focus on the
what-ifs: *What if I don't survive? What if my health breaks? What if we're not rescued?*
Instead, she fixed her eyes on Jesus and his promise from today's verse that he
would never fail or abandon her. He hadn't failed her yet, and Anne knew that
she could count on him for her tomorrows. So instead of being fearful or becoming
mired in discouragement, she used her energies to serve God, to talk about Christ,
and to love those around her.

What problem or difficulty are you facing today? Whatever it is, focusing on
the Lord is vital. Just as this missionary kept her eyes on the Lord, you, too, can
develop a Godward focus. It will make all the difference in how you live your life.
—CHERI

Lord, help me to focus on you and your majesty and great
faithfulness instead of on the problems I am facing. May I be so
centered on your greatness and unfailing love that I can hope in
you no matter what.

When my eyes are on the Lord, He gives me a spirit of calmness, a strong, solid
trust and dependency that rests in Him alone. Because He is my refuge, I can live
freely and fearlessly, knowing that God is always in control.
—REBECCA BARLOW JORDAN, INSPIRATIONAL SPEAKER AND AUTHOR

DECEMBER 19
A Lifestyle of Praise

Praise the LORD! Praise God in his sanctuary; praise him in his mighty heaven! Praise him for his mighty works; praise his unequaled greatness! . . . Let everything that breathes sing praises to the LORD! Praise the LORD!   PSALM 150:1-2, 6

That day when Anne, the missionary with China Inland Mission, suggested that I focus on God instead of on the mountains of problems my husband and I were facing—an empty checkbook, the effect of a collapsed real-estate market on my husband's building projects, and the loss of our family car, hit head-on by an out-of-control motorcycle—I thought, *Praise is the last thing I feel like doing.* "Praise God even when you don't feel like it," Anne said. "Don't trust what you see, feel, or think; trust God and his Word. He's faithful even when we're not."

Why praise God in difficult times? Because praise gets our eyes off the mountains and onto the Mountain Mover, and among other benefits, it dispels fear. Research shows that fear and gratitude or praise cannot exist at the same time in our minds. Living with an attitude of praise means that we choose to focus on God's unequaled greatness in the midst of our situations. It *doesn't* mean that we deny our real feelings.

If you are experiencing fear or deep sorrow, it's possible to honestly express your feelings to God and still keep proclaiming who he is, turning to him in spite of how things look and not waiting until you feel better to do so. Drawing *near* to the Lord instead of pulling *away* from him in your distress develops faith that goes beyond your feelings.

At first you may praise God in little trickles, as I did after my conversation with Anne. But if you persist in praising him, even in the darkest of places, you will begin to see those trickles of praise becoming a fountain. You'll begin to perceive that God is still in control, even though your situation is beyond your control. Your focus will be drawn from the complexity of the problem to the sufficiency of God's infinite resources. If you're under a cloud of adversities today, tell God about your desire to praise him and ask him to give you a heart of praise. That's a prayer he loves to answer.   —CHERI

Lord, I admit I've had my eyes more on my problems than on you. I want to praise you for your mighty works and unequaled greatness no matter what's going on in my life. Your Word tells *everything alive* to give praise to you, and that includes me! So grant me the grace to focus on you, for you are worthy of praise.

Praise can heighten your awareness that distressing circumstances are God's blessings in disguise. Your trials rip away the flimsy fabric of your self-sufficiency. This makes room for God's Spirit to weave into your life a true and solid confidence.
—RUTH MYERS, AUTHOR

DECEMBER 20
Knowing His Names

> Those who know your name trust in you, for you, O LORD,
> do not abandon those who search for you. PSALM 9:10

I'm convinced that our puny or incorrect perspective of God is a big part of why we get discouraged when waves of problems hit us. When we forget how able and awesome God is, it's hard to resist negative thoughts. That's why God gives us reminders like the one in today's verse. Our faith in God develops as we *know his names*, because his names reveal his character and nature. Having lived with my husband, Holmes, for thirty-eight years, I have come to know and experience the different aspects of his nature as my companion, lover, best friend, prayer partner, generous giver, father of our children, grandfather, builder of beautiful homes, and much more.

In a similar way, we come to know more of God as we experience different aspects of his character and person—what the Bible calls his "names"—through the ways he reveals himself in its pages. Thus I've found that when I'm distressed by a situation, one of the best antidotes is to refocus on God by meditating on his names. When our homes are filled with irritation and stress, we can focus on the Prince of Peace and invite him into our midst. When we or a loved one has a broken heart or a body in need of mending, we can call on Jehovah-Rapha, the Lord Who Heals.

May we be like Moses, who "kept right on going because he kept his eyes on the one who is invisible" (Hebrews 11:27). May we believe that God is able to handle every situation and that he is sufficient for all we will face today and during the rest of our journey on earth. —CHERI

Lord, as I pray and live, remind me of your names and attributes. Reveal yourself to me right where I am. May I see you more clearly and love you more dearly day by day.

What is my dream of God's purpose? His purpose is that I depend on Him and on His power now. If I can stay in the middle of the turmoil calm and unperplexed, that is the end of the purpose of God. God is not working towards a particular finish; His end is the process that I see Him walking on the waves, no shore in sight, no success, no goal, just the absolute certainty that it is all right because I see Him walking on the sea. It is the process, not the end, which is glorying to God.
—OSWALD CHAMBERS (1874–1917), SCOTTISH BIBLE TEACHER, YMCA CHAPLAIN IN EGYPT

DECEMBER 21
Lift Up Your Voice

Sing praises to God, sing praises; sing praises to our King, sing praises! For God is the King over all the earth. Praise him with a psalm. PSALM 47:6-7

"He who sings well prays twice," St. Augustine once wrote. And that isn't limited to what takes place in a church building or a meeting. Wherever we are, music can quiet our busy minds and connect our hearts with the One who gave us the gift of music and voices to sing. Whether we sing along with a worship CD in our cars on the way to work or sing a hymn in our quiet time, God loves to hear his children sing. He cherishes and delights in praise that comes from the heart. Such a time of just singing, not as a means to an end but to merely enjoy being in his presence, is vital to a life with God. And just as parents delight in their young child's off-key songs, he hears past our broken chords of harmony, the strained efforts at melody, and the obscure rhythms and rhymes. There is no sound more pleasing to God than the voice of his child singing of his faithful love and marvelous glory. As it resounds throughout his throne room, he hears only the gratitude of the heart, which to him is irresistible. Lift your voice to God in prayer. Use a psalm that's been set to music or a classic hymn such as "Great Is Thy Faithfulness." Save the words to songs from retreats and conferences you attend. Worship God because he is the perfect, holy, almighty Creator and King of the universe and yet calls you to be intimate with him. You'll find that singing as a form of worship can become the wind beneath your wings that will carry you through everything life brings.
—CHERI

Lord, I want to be "lost in wonder, love and praise." I want to delight in you through songs that lift your name and your character high. Give me fresh revelation today, Lord, of who you are. Inspire me so that I will sing of your greatness and glory not only today but forever, for you are the King over all the earth.

When all thy mercies, O my God,
    My rising soul surveys,
Transported with the view, I'm lost
    In wonder, love and praise.
—JOSEPH ADDISON (1672–1719), ENGLISH ESSAYIST, POET, AND DRAMATIST

DECEMBER 22

Keep Looking Up

Our present troubles are small and won't last very long. Yet they produce for us a glory that vastly outweighs them and will last forever! So we don't look at the troubles we can see now; rather, we fix our gaze on things that cannot be seen. For the things we see now will soon be gone, but the things we cannot see will last forever.   2 CORINTHIANS 4:17-18

Corrie ten Boom once met a missionary who was desperate because Christians were continually being attacked and killed near her home. Corrie didn't tell the woman that the troubles would go away. Instead, she said to look down on the storms and terrible events around her from on high, from the heavenly realms, where Jesus' victory is the truest reality.

Corrie recounted how she and her sister Betsie were walking around the German concentration camp grounds praying one morning at four thirty when God performed a miracle. Betsie would say something and Corrie would reply; then the Lord would speak and they both heard him at the same time. The sisters, though surrounded by the horrors of the concentration camp, saw then that although everything around them was terrible, they could rely on the fact that God didn't have problems, *only plans.*

Corrie realized that there was never panic in heaven. And although it seemed at the time that the devil was the victor, God is faithful, and his plans never fail. He knew their future and knew the way. That vision of God's greatness empowered Corrie not to panic, even though she faced horrific loss, danger, and the death of her beloved sister Betsie soon after. It sustained her later in her life when she traveled the world to share the message of God's forgiveness and love. Just as the Lord was there for Corrie and as we keep looking up, he will be our stability in an unstable world, our unchangeable certainty when everything is changing. There is no safer place than at the center of his purpose for our lives.
—CHERI

Lord, may I have an ever-greater vision of you. Grant me a spirit of wisdom and revelation to know you and the faith to believe that you are greater than any problem or adversity. Thank you for your promise that these present troubles are small compared to the exceedingly great glory and joy that will last forever.

Keep looking in the right direction in everything you do; that is so important. Keep looking up and kneeling down.
—CORRIE TEN BOOM (1892–1983), HOLOCAUST SURVIVOR, AUTHOR

DECEMBER 23
Worth the Effort

[Moses] kept right on going because he kept his eyes on the one
who is invisible.   HEBREWS 11:27

Amy Carmichael, missionary to India and founder of the Dohnavur Fellowship, a
refuge for young girls, once asked an insightful question: "How much are our eyes
able to see of our Lord Jesus?" Some of us take a quick look and rush back into
our activities. Others have blinders of unbelief and see little of Christ. Perhaps
we see Jesus in a worshipful moment in church, but then problems and burdens
rush in and blur our vision. Or we have our eyes fixed on ourselves and can't see
him at all.

Amy Carmichael believed that the more we know of the person or thing
we're looking at, the more we see. And it's only as we look and look and look to
the Lord that we really see. Even a woman of strong faith such as Amy Carmichael, who for more than fifty-five years rescued thousands of Indian children from
destruction and abuse in the Hindu temples, experienced what it was like to get
caught in the crush of life, to be pushed down, and thus to lose her focus. She
learned, as Moses did, that it takes a conscious effort to look up to the Lord and to
turn all her attention to him. But when she kept her eyes on the One who is invisible, she could keep going no matter what happened, whether it was physical infir-
mity, lack of funds, or other problems.

It is always worth the effort to turn from self-gazing to focus on the beauty
and perfection of the Lord, to meditate on his character. Then as his Spirit
breathes life through us, joy displaces discouragement or fear.   —CHERI

> Lord, I cast aside every request and petition, every care and
> burden, to sit before you and meditate on your beauty. Grant
> that as I go through my day I would see you in your Book, in your
> creative beauty in the earth and the skies, in your people, and
> even in those who are difficult and in great need of your love.

The Lord Jesus . . . is our Peace, our Victory, and our Joy. . . . From below things
feel impossible, people seem impossible (some people at least), and we ourselves
feel the most impossible of all. From the top we see as our Lord sees: He sees not
what *is* only, but what shall be. He is not discouraged, and as we look with Him,
our discouragement vanishes, and we can sing a new song.
—AMY CARMICHAEL (1867–1951), MISSIONARY TO INDIA

DECEMBER 24

God of Wonder

Praise the LORD! How good to sing praises to our God! How delightful and how fitting! The LORD is rebuilding Jerusalem and bringing the exiles back to Israel. He heals the brokenhearted and bandages their wounds. He counts the stars and calls them all by name. How great is our Lord! His power is absolute! His understanding is beyond comprehension!   PSALM 147:1-5

I love seeing the look on my grandchildren's faces as they jump for joy over snowflakes twirling from the sky or delight in blowing a dandelion into the wind. Little children are aware and alive, full of wonder, amazement, and awe. And I find their wonder contagious. I believe that God must love it too.

Many of us adults, however, have lost our sense of wonder and awe. This is why we are given psalms such as this one, which describes God's absolute power and creative miracles. These psalms draw us out of our ho-hum, busy existence, which takes such things as rainbows, snowflakes, and sunrises for granted, back to a childlike wonder of our great God, the God who fills the sky with clouds, gives his orders to the world, sends the snow like white wool, and hurls the hail like stones. Who created everything and possesses all power and yet cares for the weak and brokenhearted. Who counts the stars and calls each one by name but supports the humble. Who reigns over every nation and galaxy and yet delights in the simple, heartfelt devotion of those who trust him. He is a God whose understanding is beyond human comprehension. Surely a God like this can inspire our wonder and awe.

Let your heart be overwhelmed today with life's little miracles and the great things the Lord has done for you. Be glad and rejoice in him.   —CHERI

God of wonder, I lift my voice to sing praise to you. Your understanding is beyond comprehension! Your power is absolute. How good it is to sing praises to my God, how delightful and how right. I praise you, Lord.

Receive every day as a resurrection from death, as a new enjoyment of life. . . . Let your joyful heart praise and magnify so good and glorious a Creator.
—WILLIAM LAW (1686–1761), ENGLISH THEOLOGIAN

To Ponder with a Friend

1. On what do you tend to focus (or turn to for comfort or peace) when you are under stress?

2. Anne, the missionary who had been imprisoned by the Japanese, inspired Cheri to keep her eyes on God. Do you know a woman who lives with a contagious and courageous spirit of worship even when going through suffering or difficult times? How has she been a role model to you personally?

3. What helps you to connect with and refocus on God best: music, nature, praying with a group of friends, a worship service, something else?

4. In what area of your life do you need to stand firm, with your mind fixed on the Lord and his promises?

5. God has revealed many of his qualities to humanity through the pages of his Word. He promises that if we seek him with all our hearts, we will find him (see Jeremiah 29:12-13). What name or attribute (something true) of God could you focus on in this present season that would help you to trust him instead of being preoccupied with your problems, as we humans often are?

DECEMBER 25
One Rude Student

> While he was still a long way off, his father saw him coming. Filled
> with love and compassion, he ran to his son, embraced him, and
> kissed him. LUKE 15:20

Kyle was tall and sullen, and his habit of staring over the head of anyone who tried
to engage him in chitchat discouraged friendship.

One morning, a gregarious classmate seated nearby nodded in greeting, then
gestured toward the philosophy text Kyle always carried.

"Which philosopher do you like best?" he asked.

Kyle merely shrugged.

When the campus Bible club invited a philosophy professor to speak, Kyle's
classmate, a regular attendee, invited him.

The day had been especially dull, and Kyle was looking for an argument, so
he went. If there had been an award for rudeness, Kyle would have won. He often
interrupted the speaker by throwing out the name of an opposing philosopher.
Later, during the coffee hour, he ridiculed the meeting. "How can one claim intelligence while believing an archaic text?" he scoffed.

One young woman dared to challenge him. "Actually, you're the one
who's showing ignorance," she said. "You ridicule a book you haven't read." She
handed him a Bible. "Here. After you've actually read some of it, you can express
an opinion."

Caught off guard, Kyle accepted the volume and grumpily thumbed through
the pages. The study notes caught his attention, but when he realized several students were watching him, he tossed the Bible onto a nearby chair and strode out.

The following Thursday evening at the campus coffee shop, Kyle ran into his
classmate, who promptly asked him to the weekend Bible conference. To the surprise of both of them, Kyle accepted.

The first session, he slumped in his seat, arms folded across his chest. The
second session, he sat straighter but seemed to be studying the other attendees.

The third session, he followed along as the speaker read the account of the
Prodigal Son in Luke 15. Suddenly, Kyle began to read ahead, excitedly flipping
through the entire book of Luke. He had discovered the Bible wasn't boring. All
because someone dared to ignore his rudeness.   —SANDRA

Lord, it is so much easier when I ignore rude people. Help me to
remember that they need you and that they need me to be kind.

Like the father of the Prodigal Son, God can see repentance coming a great way
off and is there to meet it, the repentance is the reconciliation.
—DOROTHY L. SAYERS (1893–1957), ENGLISH WRITER

DECEMBER 26
A Sad Phone Call

God is our refuge and strength, always ready to help in times of trouble. PSALM 46:1

Candace had barely arrived in the intake room at the county jail when an officer handed her a piece of paper with a phone number on it.

"You're supposed to call this number right away," he said, handing her a portable phone.

She recognized the number as her brother's.

She stared at the phone for a long moment. If she didn't call, she wouldn't hear the news. Somehow, she knew her sons were in trouble. Six and four years old, they were living with her brother while she awaited trial for burglary and possession of stolen goods. One stupid night of smoking weed had caused all this.

"Just one little job, and we've got enough to see us through the whole month, Sweets," her boyfriend had said.

Well, that one little job had created one big mess.

"Lady, make the call," the officer said. "I gotta get you settled."

She tried to keep her hands from shaking as she dialed. And she steeled herself for whatever she might hear. There was no way she was going to cry here.

For one glorious second she was encouraged when her brother picked up the phone. Maybe everything was okay after all.

"Hey, this is Candace. What's up?"

As soon as she heard "Oh, Sis," she knew.

"What happened?" she begged.

"It's Darin, honey. Some guy went through a red light on us. Darin's side of the car was hit pretty bad—" Her brother's voice broke.

"Is he . . . ? He's gonna be okay, though, right?"

"No. He didn't make it."

Screams were forming deep within her. "What about my other baby?"

"Paul's gonna be okay, but the hospital is keeping him overnight."

He cleared his throat. "I talked to the police chaplain there. He offered to tell you, but I told him I had to do this. He'll come by tomorrow morning, though."

His voice broke again. "Sis, they aren't going to let you out to attend the funeral. I'm making the arrangements. We'll bury Darin next to Mama in Oak Grove. Okay?"

"Yeah, sure," was all she could manage before hanging up the phone. She put her hand over her mouth to keep the screams from escaping. —SANDRA

Lord, why do the innocent often have to pay for the sins of others? Please bring your good out of those sad situations.

The greatest griefs are those we cause ourselves.
—SOPHOCLES (CA. 496–406 B.C.), GREEK DRAMATIST

DECEMBER 27
A Set of Keys

[Jesus said,] "The Spirit of the LORD is upon me, for he has anointed me to bring Good News to the poor. He has sent me to proclaim that captives will be released, that the blind will see, that the oppressed will be set free." LUKE 4:18

Candace didn't remember being escorted to her cell, but suddenly there she was, sitting on the edge of the cot. She glanced around only once, then buried her face in her hands. How could her precious six-year-old be dead? He was always laughing at the silliest things. And he had just started school. He already had a sweet crush on his teacher. How could that child be dead?

And then this thought settled in: *He wouldn't be dead if you had been a decent mother and had been home with him.* She clamped her hands over her mouth. Gradually, she realized someone was outside her cell. She wiped her eyes and looked up. A tall, older woman stood there.

"You go right ahead and cry, honey," she said. "Bad news travels fast, especially in here. I know what happened. I'm sorry to hear it."

Candace nodded.

"Is there anything I can do for you?" the woman asked.

"Yeah. Do you have a set of keys?" Candace asked sarcastically.

The woman stepped closer to Candace's cell. "Yes, honey, I believe I do." And she pulled a small Bible out of her prison smock, thumbed through several pages, and held the open book out to Candace.

"I thought you said you had keys," Candace snarled.

"Honey, the keys in here will open the most important door in the world, and that's the door to your heart. I had to learn that the hard way, and obviously, you will too. Here. You read right there, Matthew, chapter 7, verse 7: 'Keep on asking, and you will receive what you ask for. Keep on seeking, and you will find. Keep on knocking, and the door will be opened to you.' You're in a mess, and you need Jesus. He's the only one who's able to help you deal with this. But you got to ask for his help."

She continued to hold out the open Bible until Candace, with tears streaming down her cheeks, stood up and gently took it from her hand.   —SANDRA

Lord, I've learned there are many different types of jail cells. Help me to always look to your Word for strength and comfort and a way out of the prison I so often create.

I never knew all there was in the Bible until I spent those years in jail. I was constantly finding new treasures.
—JOHN BUNYAN (1628–1688), ENGLISH PREACHER AND AUTHOR

DECEMBER 28
Making a Difference

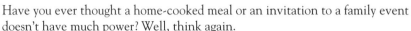

Every time I think of you, I give thanks to my God.
PHILIPPIANS 1:3

Have you ever thought a home-cooked meal or an invitation to a family event doesn't have much power? Well, think again.

On the back page of my Bible from high school is the aged autograph of Mitsuo Fuchida, a speaker I heard at a youth rally during my senior year. He told of his four long, lonely years as a student here in the States during the 1930s. After earning his degree, he returned to Japan embittered because not one American family had invited him into their home during that time. When his nation later asked him to lead the attack on Pearl Harbor, he accepted without hesitation. It was only after the war that he met a Christian who befriended him and introduced him to Jesus.

A former Ethiopian senator told me about Mangusto, a young African who had encountered only prejudice as a student in the United States during the late 1960s. When Mangusto came into power in his own country, he expelled missionaries and welcomed the Marxists, who took over Ethiopia, one of the world's oldest Christian nations.

I wonder what difference one Christian friend might have made in both those situations. Sure, kindness probably wouldn't have stopped a sneak attack or kept a government from toppling, but who can be sure? We never know how a sincere compliment, a bit of encouragement, or even an invitation to dinner will play itself out in a home or within a nation.   —SANDRA

> Lord, help me to recognize that what I see as my meager hospitality may be a rich banquet to a lonely student or a new member of my community. Show me the individuals who need my welcome.

Hospitality is a test for godliness because those who are selfish do not like strangers (especially needy ones) to intrude upon their private lives.
—ERWIN W. LUTZER, PASTOR AND AUTHOR

DECEMBER 29
The B-17 Gunner

We don't look at the troubles we can see now; rather, we fix our gaze on things that cannot be seen. For the things we see now will soon be gone, but the things we cannot see will last forever.
2 CORINTHIANS 4:18

Dr. Paul Stevens was a chaplain at a military base during World War II when a man from the control tower burst through the door. "Chaplain, we've got an emergency!"

As they ran across the tarmac, the tower worker explained a B-17 had been damaged in battle. The crew couldn't get the landing gear down, nor could they get the ball turret on the underside of the plane rotated back into the position that would allow their gunner to crawl out. Still strapped in the turret, he would be crushed when they made their emergency belly landing. The plane had been circling continuously as the crew tried to get the landing gear down manually, but the plane was too damaged.

"They've got two minutes of fuel left," the worker said. "They're coming in now. You gotta talk to the gunner. He's only nineteen."

At the tower, the chaplain grabbed the microphone. The crew had rigged the communication system to allow the gunner to talk to the tower.

The chaplain didn't waste time: "Son, do you know the trouble you're in?"

"Yes, sir!" the lad replied.

"Son, are you ready to meet God?"

Only then did the gunner's voice waver. "Yes, sir. When I was a boy, Mama took me to a little church where I heard about Jesus dying for me."

The chaplain could see the crippled plane coming in low toward the runway. He swallowed hard and then said, "Son, close your eyes. We're going to pray. And when you open your eyes, you'll see Jesus."

The man had barely started his prayer when the sickening sound of metal on asphalt came through the radio. The plane had made its deadly emergency landing.

All of us are in the drama of that plane, either as the tower manager, who knows the danger; the gunner, who is moments away from eternity; or the chaplain, who knows the only hope is faith in Jesus Christ.

With whom do you identify?   —SANDRA

Lord, help me to be ready to tell how you died, were buried, and rose again to give us eternal life.

I remember two things; that I am a great sinner and that Christ is a great Savior.
—JOHN NEWTON (1725–1807), ANGLICAN CLERGYMAN AND FORMER SLAVE-SHIP CAPTAIN

DECEMBER 30
Talking with the Relatives

For the honor of your name, O LORD, forgive my many, many sins.
PSALM 25:11

Even though I was raised in the church and heard we are to bring others to Jesus, for years I didn't know how to do that. Then one of my favorite uncles was diagnosed with lung cancer. In the midst of his medical battle, our family's beloved Mama Farley, his mother, died. He was able to attend her funeral but was hospitalized for the last time shortly after his return home. Since he was in an isolation unit, visitors had to scrub with special soap and wear head-to-toe covering to keep from passing germs to his weakened immune system. When I visited him one evening, the nurse informed me the cancer had invaded his throat, so talking would be painful for him.

Covered from head to toe, I thought he wouldn't recognize me, so I whispered, "Hi, it's me, San," as I entered his room. I patted his shoulder with my gloved hand and pulled the lone chair close to his bed.

"I hate it you're going through this," I said.

He nodded.

I paused, wondering how he would receive what I was about to tell him. In the past when any of us, including his own mother, had tried to share our faith, he would wave us away. I had to find a way to get him to listen. *Please help me, Lord.*

"I want to tell you what Jay said when we were at Mama's funeral," I said.

And I told him about my young son telling his little sister that Mama's breathing part was in heaven.

As my uncle listened, tears sprang to his eyes.

I blinked rapidly and said, "I know Mama's in heaven."

He nodded earnestly.

"And I know I'm going to see her again," I continued. "I want to know that when I get to heaven, you'll be standing right there with Papa and Mama."

Through the glass in the door I could see a nurse in the hallway.

"We don't have much time," I said, worried she would soon gesture for me to leave. But the double meaning of the words was evident too.

"May I pray for you?" I asked. "The words I say are what you can repeat in your heart to accept Jesus as your Savior."

I expected him to shake his head in his old rejecting way, but instead he gave a jerky nod and squeezed his eyes shut.   —SANDRA

Lord, I am grateful I will see this dear uncle again. But I have many other relatives and friends who need to hear the simple path to you. Give me the opportunity and the courage to share the way.

A person may go to heaven without health, without riches, without honors, without learning, without friends; but he can never go there without Christ.
—JOHN DYER (1699–1757), ENGLISH POET

DECEMBER 31
As Easy as A-B-C-C

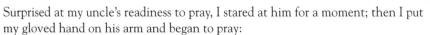

Everyone who calls on the name of the LORD will be saved.
ACTS 2:21

Surprised at my uncle's readiness to pray, I stared at him for a moment; then I put my gloved hand on his arm and began to pray:

"Lord, thank you for this dear uncle. Please be with him; let him feel your presence as he prays within his heart these words: 'Lord, thank you for loving us so much that you sent your Son to die for our sins.'"

I paused to give him time to pray that within his mind.

"'Lord, now I confess my sins and ask your forgiveness.'"

I waited for another moment, then said, "'And I receive Jesus as Savior and Lord of my life. Amen.'"

We both opened our eyes, and I patted his arm.

Then he mouthed, "Thank you."

I bent forward to kiss his forehead through my mask just as the nurse tapped on the window. My time was up.

"I love you," I said as I walked backward toward the door.

That was the last time I saw him alive. He died the next afternoon. But, oh, how much easier it was to let him go, knowing his "breathin' part" truly is in heaven.

That simple prayer was the first time I had led an adult to the Lord. Today, when I speak to audiences, I usually offer a more detailed invitation, but its message is still simple.

"Coming to the Lord is as easy as A-B-C-C," I say. "First, A: Acknowledge you are a sinner and need God.

"B: Believe Jesus died for your sins. John 3:16 says, 'God loved the world so much that he gave his one and only Son, so that everyone who believes in him will not perish but have eternal life.'

"C: Confess your sins. First John 1:9 says, 'If we confess our sins to him, he is faithful and just to forgive us our sins and to cleanse us from all wickedness.'

"C: Commit to living for him."

Of course, it's important the individual gets proper discipleship for spiritual growth, but the ABCCs are a wonderful invitation into the Kingdom.

Truly, we live in a hurting world that desperately needs a smile, a friendly touch, a kind word. Yes, our encouragement can make a difference in the daily challenges we all face, but sharing our faith can make a difference for eternity.   —SANDRA

Lord, coming to you truly is simple. So why are we compelled to make it complicated? Help me to hold out your invitation to those around me. And help me to keep it simple.

Looking at the wound of sin will never save anyone. What you must do is look at the remedy.   —DWIGHT L. MOODY (1837–1899), AMERICAN EVANGELIST

To Ponder with a Friend

1. How do you usually respond to those who are rude?

2. Should prisoners be allowed to attend the funeral of a family member? Why or why not?

3. What opportunities do you have to extend hospitality to others?

4. What sensitivities do you need to reach out to someone effectively?

Weekly Themes

About the Authors

Cheri Heath Fuller is a best-selling, award-winning author of forty books, with total sales of more than one million. With a master's degree in English literature, Cheri is a popular speaker whose messages and books provide encouragement to women both in the United States and around the world.

At women's retreats and conferences, Cheri communicates a vision of the great gift, invitation, and power of prayer and how our prayers outlive us to touch future generations. She also keynotes at national Christian-teacher conventions, parent events, and conferences for children's pastors and ministries. She has been a frequent guest on national radio and television programs such as *Focus on the Family*, *Family Life Today*, and *The 700 Club*. Cheri is a contributing writer for *Today's Christian Woman*, and hundreds of her articles have appeared in *Focus on the Family* magazine, *Family Circle*, *Better Homes and Gardens' Women's Faith & Spirit*, *Guideposts*, *Pray!* magazine, *Moody* magazine, *Marriage Partnership*, *Decision*, *ParentLife*, *Living with Teenagers*, and other publications.

Each month Cheri's e-zine, *Heart to Heart with Cheri Fuller*, reaches a growing audience of three thousand women. Her Web site, www.cherifuller.com, has a monthly column for mothers, helpful articles, Bible studies and book guides, and other resources that keep visitors returning to the site.

Cheri, a former Oklahoma Mother of the Year, and her husband, Holmes, have three married children and six grandchildren and live in Oklahoma.

Sandra Picklesimer Aldrich, president and CEO of Bold Words, Inc., in Colorado Springs, is a popular speaker and the author or coauthor of eighteen books, including *From One Single Mother to Another*, *Will I Ever Be Whole Again? Living through the Death of Someone You Love*, and *Men Read Newspapers, Not Minds*.

Sandra has a Master of Arts degree in literature and communications, but she says it is her "PhD in the School of Hard Knocks" that has made her a much-in-demand guest on hundreds of TV and radio programs, including repeated appearances on *Focus on the Family*, *The 700 Club*, *Midday Connection*, *Prime Time America*, and Family Life Radio.

In addition to radio and television appearances, she is a popular speaker throughout the United States as well as Canada, Germany, and England. Her events range from Women of Virtue conferences, women's and couples' retreats, military-base presentations, single-parent events, college conferences, hospice seminars, business meetings, and educational workshops. Always, Sandra presents the serious issues of life with insight and humor.

Her five-hundred-plus articles and stories have appeared in four Chicken

Soup for the Soul books, *Writer's Digest, Focus on the Family* magazine, *Moody* magazine, *Today's Christian Woman, Discipleship Journal,* and Crosswalk.com—among others.

She is the former senior editor of *Focus on the Family* magazine and is listed in several professional publications, including *Who's Who* and *Contemporary Authors.* Visit Sandra's Web site at www.sandraaldrich.com.

Do-able. Daily. Devotions.

START ANY DAY THE ONE YEAR WAY.

Do-able.
Every One Year book is designed for people who live busy, active lives. Just pick one up and start on today's date.

Daily.
Daily routine doesn't have to be drudgery. One Year devotionals help you form positive habits that connect you to what's most important.

Devotions.
Discover a natural rhythm for drawing near to God in an extremely personal way. One Year devotionals provide daily focus essential to your spiritual growth.

For Women

The One Year® Devotions for Women on the Go

The One Year® Devotions for Women

The One Year® Devotions for Moms

The One Year® Women of the Bible

The One Year® Daily Grind

For Men

The One Year®
Devotions for
Men on the Go

The One Year®
Devotions for
Men

For Couples

The One Year®
Devotions for
Couples

For Families

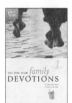

The One Year®
Family
Devotions

For Teens

The One Year®
Devos for Teens

The One Year®
Devos for Sports
Fans

For Bible Study

The One Year®
Praying through
the Bible

The One Year®
through the
Bible

For Personal Growth

The One Year®
Walk with God
Devotional

The One Year®
at His Feet
Devotional

The One Year®
Great Songs of
Faith

The One Year®
Life Verse
Devotional

It's convenient and easy to grow with
God the One Year way.